NONNUCLEAR CONFLICTS IN THE NUCLEAR AGE

edited by
Sam C. Sarkesian

PRAEGER

PRAEGER SPECIAL STUDIES • PRAEGER SCIENTIFIC

Library of Congress Cataloging in Publication Data

Main entry under title:

Nonnuclear conflicts in the nuclear age.

  Bibliography: p.
  Includes index.
  1. United States--Military policy--Addresses,
essays, lectures. 2. World politics--20th century--
Addressess, essays, lectures. 3. Military policy--
Addressess, essays, lectures. I. Sarkesian, Sam
Charles.
UA23.N68   355'033073   80-15281
ISBN 0-03-056138-8

Published in 1980 by Praeger Publishers
CBS Educational and Professional Publishing
A Division of CBS, Inc.
521 Fifth Avenue, New York, New York 10017 U.S.A.

0123456789   038   987654321

Printed in the United States of America

PREFACE

As the United States enters the decade of the 1980s, its political-
military policy remains in a state of transition, uncertain in its goals
and questionable in its military capability. To be sure, American preoccupation with Soviet nuclear capability has developed an apparent
determination to make U. S. forces in NATO more effective. In non-
European areas, however, the United States seems to have lost much
of its effectiveness. While this may be the result of a number of political-military factors, there is much validity in the argument that the
real cause is the chastening experience in Vietnam. The Vietnam War
cannot be blamed for all of the current problems of U. S. military
capability and political will. The fact remains, however, that the
present generation of American military leaders gained their combat
experience in Vietnam. The American political leadership still re-
calls, and is sensitive to, the political turmoil of the 1960s and early
1970s. The result may be a psychological retreat from power, if not
actual retrenchment, with all of its implications for Western allies
and America's ability to influence world events. Thus Soviet and
Cuban activity in many non-European areas of the world seems to have
gone unchallenged by the United States or its allies. Yet, the importance on non-European areas to the security of the West appears to
have increased both in terms of energy sources and national security
interests.

Concern with these issues has prompted a number of short-term
solutions, most of which tend to proceed from one of two opposite
assumptions. Some military men as well as civilian decisionmakers
feel that a battalion of Marines or a battalion of U. S. paratroopers
can solve many problems in these areas. Others insist that the United
States cannot intervene militarily in Third and Fourth World areas
without becoming enmeshed in an indigenous nationalistic reaction and
a people's war—shades of Vietnam. Hence, solutions must be nonmilitary in nature.

There is a middle view—one that has not been clearly formulated.
This presumes that national security policy should be pragmatically
based, not exclusively military in orientation, but not militarily
timid either. Unfortunately, such a policy is frequently perceived as
vacillating and unpredictable.

While there is no particular ideological orientation to this volume (the authors provide a variety of perspectives), what does emerge
is the call for a national security policy that is not limited to capability in the strategic sphere but is credible in the nonnuclear realm
as well: military posture that is based on the ability to deploy credible nonnuclear forces combined with a political will to employ such

forces when necessary. It is also argued that such a policy expands the utility of nonmilitary instruments of policy.

Specifically, there is a call for a balanced military force that is flexible in its organizational structure, adaptable in its military skills, with a political-social element in its professionalism, and capable of quick deployment into nonnuclear conflicts. Additionally, there is a need to articulate a purposeful international role with realistic goals directly correlated with military capability and political will. Finally, there is a need for leadership that is firm and clear in its commitment, and credible in its actions.

The dilemma is that the United States cannot seem to re-establish its political-military effectiveness without some demonstrated military capability and political resolve to employ force to achieve specific policy goals. These considerations raise a number of questions. What policy options are available to the United States to protect its interests, without violating the moral and ethical basis of its political purpose? Can a viable policy short of nuclear exchange and general war be established without resorting to a Vietnam type of involvement? What have the past three decades illustrated in terms of such a political-military policy?

The purpose of this volume is to seek answers to these questions. While some questions may remain unanswered, and some answers may raise more questions, the intent here is to temper theoretical analysis with practical policy considerations. In developing these papers, the authors were convinced that serious discussion of nonnuclear conflicts needs to be revitalized if U. S. policy is not to be rigidified by the Vietnam experience, nor motivated by militarily dominant solutions to restore American credibility.

A realistic assessment of these issues must include an understanding of the policy and posture of friends as well as potential enemies. Attention must also be given to the evolving international security environment, particularly the volatile conditions in a number of developing systems. An American "go it alone" policy in nonnuclear conflicts may be the least effective one. To develop a broad-based policy, therefore, requires some attention to the goals and capabilities of potential allies, be it in the West or among the developing nations.

This is not a volume advocating military intervention. Indeed, there are a number of occasions when nonintervention is the best policy choice. Rather, the intent is to clarify the dimensions of U. S. political-military policy, the possible contingencies, and the alternatives that may arise as a result of nonnuclear conflicts. This dimension includes the recognition that capability and resolve to commit military force in various parts of the world has a direct impact on the ability to deter. The concept of deterrence in its broadest sense rests on both nuclear and nonnuclear capabilities.

establishes a framework for further studies. We have not nor did we intend to provide a set of answers. It is our conviction, however, that the very process of seeking answers will clarify issues and stimulate serious reassessment of American political-military policy in the nonnuclear framework.

The ability to influence various areas of the world rests in no small measure on perceived military strength and political resolve. The use of force to achieve political-military goals without actually engaging in conflict is perhaps the epitome of political-military effectiveness. As suggested earlier, the effectiveness of other instruments of policy are related to the perceptions of political-military strength.

Concern over these issues was the basis for a number of papers presented at two separate conferences: the International Studies Association annual meeting in Toronto (March 1979) and the Midwest Political Science Association annual meeting in Chicago (April 1979). Two panels were organized to deal with the general topic of nonnuclear conflicts. The Toronto panel was titled "Instruments of Defense and Foreign Policy: A Comparative Analysis of Nonnuclear Conflicts." Its purpose was to develop a broad framework for evaluating the various capabilities and contingencies facing major powers in nonnuclear conflicts. The Chicago panel titled "U.S. Military Posture and Policy: Low Intensity Conflict," was focused specifically on the United States. Roman Kolkowicz considerably expanded his presentation at the Toronto meeting for the chapter in this volume. The chapter by Lawrence Grinter and the chapter by William Whitson were not presented at either meeting, but were written specifically for this volume.

The organization of the volume follows the general theme of each panel. Chapter 1 discusses the broad dimensions of nonnuclear conflicts, a framework for examining such conflicts, and the policy choices and contingencies facing various nations. Chapters 2 and 3 focus on the United States, its political-military issues and policy environment. Chapter 4 deals with international dimensions and major powers: Europe, the Soviet Union, China, and Japan. Chapter 5 draws conclusions from these earlier chapters and identifies broad areas of political-military policy. While there is attention to the policy of individual countries, the primary thrust is on the character and nature of low-intensity conflicts, military posture and capabilities, and policy implications.

The authors make no claim that the assessments here exhaust the treatment of these subjects. The nature of the subject and the variety of perspectives defy a one-time set of answers or definitive framework—at least at this time. Our claim is more modest. We feel this volume provides reference points for critically assessing nonnuclear conflicts (particularly in terms of U.S. policy) and

CONTENTS

LISTS OF TABLES AND FIGURES

1
INTRODUCTION: CHARACTERISTICS AND POLICY ISSUES OF NONNUCLEAR CONFLICTS

This chapter provides a framework for the study of political-military posture, capabilities, and policy regarding nonnuclear conflicts. Using the concepts of "Strategy" and "Method," the author identifies and discusses various categories in each concept, the political-military posture and capabilities these require, the ways in which they relate to each other, and their implications for policy, particularly for the United States and Western Europe. The Third World areas are increasingly important to Western interests and it is in such areas that nonnuclear conflicts are most likely to occur. Thus the writer concludes that liberal democracies are in a difficult position for responding to nonnuclear war. The Soviet Union, using surrogate forces, has exploited a variety of situations in Africa and Latin America, while the United States appears to lack the flexibility and adaptability to respond.

1
NONNUCLEAR CONFLICTS: CHARACTERISTICS AND POLICY ISSUES
Sam C. Sarkesian

Nuclear war and its prevention remain serious and persistent issues of international politics and military strategy. This is well recognized by serious students, and little needs to be said about the continuing need to find long-term solutions to these issues. Most people also realize that nuclear weapons have created a political-military enigma. Nations possessing the most destructive weapons fear their use because of the unacceptable levels of destruction likely to be inflicted in a nuclear exchange. As a result, nuclear military forces have lost their freedom of action and have become wedded to one strategic option—nuclear war. It is an option few would adopt except in the most critical situations. The very fear of deploying nuclear forces has provided a degree of freedom of action to those states possessing effective nonnuclear forces. One consequence is the frequency of nonnuclear conflicts, which have increasingly tested the ability of major powers to affect events in many parts of the world.[*]

During the first decade of the nuclear era, there were relatively clear ideological boundaries and adversary groupings. The issues appeared clear and the enemy identifiable. Nuclear capability

---

[*]Nonnuclear conflicts as used in this chapter refer to the entire range of policies and activities that have a high propensity for employing military forces, except for major or nuclear wars. This employment of force is not limited to combat, but includes a variety of methods and strategies in which military force (or its perceived use) can influence the environment and actions of other states without resort to battle.

was closely related to conventional war capability, so that nuclear
weaponry appeared to strengthen the efficacy of conventional military
force. The changed world order (i.e., the collapse of colonialism
and the rise of China) and with it a considerably more complex security environment, made Cold War military strategy and force postures increasingly out of tune with the nature of political-military
challenges of the new order. One consequence for the West is an increasing inability to respond to world events outside the European
context. At the same time, the West appears to lack the resolve to
employ military force in all but the most critical security challenges.[1]
Yet a high state of military preparedness and presumed capability is
meaningless without political will. Without it, the military institution cannot be an effective instrument of state policy.

These preliminary observations provide a variety of reasons
for serious examination of nonnuclear conflicts, not the least of which
is the frequency of wars throughout history. But perhaps the most
compelling reason is that military force is an important instrument
of state policy.[2] This may be self-evident, but many tend to overlook
the fact that even in the nuclear age, force is employed by many
states, large and small, to achieve political goals. During the period
1946-71 (covering a major part of the nuclear era), there were 149
nonnuclear conflicts of one kind or another, in which the proper employment of force was the major policy consideration.[3] Thus, though
we may deplore war, most states find military force and its use indispensable for survival and necessary in the conduct of international
politics.[4]

> The outlook may be disheartening to some Americans,
> but the alternative is worse. Military power continues
> to play an important part in world affairs. The nation
> can only protect itself and its interests abroad if it is
> willing to spend what is necessary to maintain a credible
> military posture.[5]

The employment of force, however, has become more complex and more difficult to implement. A variety of nationalistic attitudes regarding sovereignty and anti-imperialism has created a
political-psychological barrier against interference in internal matters. The proliferation of conventional weapons and the spread of
the doctrine of "people's war" have provided technological means
and strategic guidelines that make foreign military intervention a
risky and costly matter. The value system of a liberal democracy,
with its emphasis on justice and human rights, has created a significant moral and ethical restraint on the employment of force. Finally,

the nuclear "stand-off" between superpowers, and their intercon-
necting and overlapping linkages to a variety of other powers prompts
caution in their foreign policy goals to avoid direct superpower confrontation. Although there are a number of other reasons, those
listed here provide major clues regarding the complexity and high
risk/cost factors in employing force.

Thus in the current environment policymakers are faced with
a number of political and military problems that extend beyond nuclear
considerations. Similarly, those seriously engaged in studying national security problems and employment of military force are faced
with difficult moral issues. If one is convinced that war is evil, then
it is hard to suggest the use of military force except in times of clear
(and calamitous) national crisis—if then. A logical extension of this
position is to deny the legitimacy even of studying force employment.
If one recognizes the evil of war but qualifies this by an awareness
of the "realities" of international politics, then the employment of
force for advancing important political-military goals can be made
acceptable. It is hard to rationalize a middle position. But in
either case attention can be focused on the prevention of nuclear
war.

These observations are important for the purpose of this chapter, which is to revitalize intellectual debate on the employment of
force in nonnuclear conflict, and in this context to provide a framework for studying such conflicts. We do not intend to develop a military strategic or tactical treatise on nonnuclear conflicts. Nor do
we intend this to be a moral or legal discourse on war.[6] However,
by focusing on salient political-military issues of nonnuclear conflicts
and the general policy and military posture these may necessitate,
we hope to identify reference points from which intellectual perspectives and critical inquiry can surface.

As has been stated, the primary concern here is the examination of nonnuclear conflicts. Nevertheless, a few observations need
to be made at the outset with respect to nuclear conflict. The next
two decades will probably witness an increase in nuclear proliferation
and the decrease in the utility of "nuclear superiority." Although it
may be argued that such proliferation will increase the prospect of
nuclear war, it may also be argued that acquisition of nuclear weapons will prompt countervailing pressures against their use—barring
nuclear accidents or "irrationality" in the conduct of international
politics by nuclear states. In any case, if the immediate past is any
guide, it is likely that states will continue to employ nonnuclear force
as an instrument of state policy. Finally, the study of nonnuclear
conflict is realistic only if placed within the context of a nuclear
world.

AN OVERVIEW OF DETERRENCE

Since deterrence is a basic factor in the relationships between major powers, it is a logical starting point in this study. In simple terms, deterrence is the ability of a state to project a political credibility and military capability to discourage another state (or states) from taking a course of action deemed inimical to the interests of the deterring state. It may also be used to influence other states to adopt nonabrasive policies toward the deterring state. Deterrence, in its broadest meaning, must include capability and credibility beyond nuclear strategy.

Although deterrence is the cornerstone of major-power security relationships, there are differences in the perception of deterrence and in the capabilities of the major powers. In no small way, these differences can be attributed to the character of nonnuclear conflict. The ability of a state to engage in a variety of nonnuclear conflicts and to employ force is a major indicator of its deterrent capability. A nuclear power incapable of deploying credible forces in nonnuclear confrontations makes itself vulnerable to the most unambiguous type of nuclear blackmail: it must either engage in nuclear war or withdraw from the conflict. One might easily argue for example that, in the Middle East and parts of Africa, Israel (a nonnuclear power, at least as of this writing) has a more credible nonnuclear capability than England (a nuclear power). Similarly, with its New Look strategy of the 1950s, which threatened nuclear devastation against any adversary challenging its "national interests," the United States placed itself in a zero-sums game situation. Either nuclear weapons had to be used or credibility would be lost. The ineffectiveness of this policy soon became apparent, for the variety of nonmilitary instruments of policy become seriously weakened if they lack a credible military component.

Additionally, the inability of the deterring state to adopt policies and programs to respond to the failure of deterrence (actual nuclear exchange) while basing its military credibility solely on nuclear forces reduces the very effectiveness of those forces and of deterrence capability. Adversaries can translate such a narrow view of deterrence into a "nuclear win" situation, that is, they may be willing to engage in nuclear war, convinced that they can win over the long run. The perceived inability to respond to situations (labeled, in some instances, "broken-back" wars) beyond the failure of nuclear deterrence may also suggest to adversaries that those adopting such a limited deterrence posture lack resolve, are indecisive, militarily timid, and may well succumb to nuclear blackmail. Under these circumstances it is hard for any major power to play a decisive role in world affairs.

Finally, the success of deterrence is also a function of the state's ability to employ military force along with other nonmilitary instruments of policy. The effective synchronization of these instruments can create an environment susceptible to the influence of a particular state and project an image of resolve, coherency of policy, and purpose. Such a condition may be sufficient to affect or prevent another state from adopting abrasive policies toward the deterring state.

As one scholar notes:

> At the political level, I would argue that the erosion of the Western position has been much faster and more profound than is generally realized. So many of the gains usually cited are, in fact, superficial, diplomatic, not structural or likely to be long-lasting. The ability of an American secretary of state to shuttle through the Middle East in an attempt to arrange a peace should not be confused with the structures of real influence—steady purpose, geographic proximity, large arsenals, treaties of friendship—all the things which, taken together, elicit respect and fear.[7]

U.S.-STYLE DETERRENCE

Over the past thirty years the actions of major powers have made it clear that they do not intend to use nuclear weapons in conflicts that do not directly and immediately affect their own survival. Outside the European context, therefore, nuclear force is not enough to pursue policies that may depend upon the employment of force. The Soviet Union seems to have grasped this fact and shaped its military capability to include a nonnuclear flexibility without apparently surrendering any of its nuclear effectiveness. By the use of surrogate forces, for example, the Soviet Union is able to influence politics in Africa.[8] It has also shown its ability to exploit nonnuclear wars in various areas and support or deter insurgency wars as its policy dictates. While it is difficult to determine long-range benefits, the Soviet Union appears to have reaped a number of short-term gains by its policy. Equally important, it has demonstrated its resolve to pursue political-military policies outside the European framework, which, in itself, has provided an impetus paving the way for the use of nonmilitary instruments of policy.

Since the denouement in Vietnam, the United States, contrary to the Soviet Union, has lost both capability and credibility outside the European arena. Few would argue with the United States' focus on NATO and a strong political-military base in Europe. Yet it appears that this preoccupation has led to neglect of other areas. Much of this neglect can be traced to the U.S. experience over the past two decades.

In the aftermath of the Korean War, the U.S. New Look defense strategy was developed around nuclear weapons not only as a means of defense, but also as an instrument of coercive diplomacy. This strategy was quickly discredited because of its inflexibility. The "bigger bang for the buck" mentality was superceded by Flexible Response as the Kennedy Administration seemed to challenge the world with the U.S. commitment to protect freedom everywhere. In so doing, the Flexible Response strategy broadened the concept of deterrence. Its purpose was to provide a controlled use of force that could respond to low-level aggression as well as other forms of threat. However, the Vietnam experience showed that this strategy was not completely effective. It could operate only if the adversary were willing to accept the strategic rules of engagement. An adversary who was willing to raise the "ante" made Flexible Response militarily irrelevant.

Since the Vietnam War, U.S. strategy seems to have developed a 1980 version of the New Look—the New-New Look. This is based on a deterrence strategy incorporating nuclear and conventional capability almost exclusively focused on Europe. Obviously, America's present military posture appears fundamentally sound in many European circles—at least with respect to the concern over NATO-Warsaw Pact relationships.

It has been difficult for U.S. policymakers to realistically translate nuclear power into usable military power outside the European framework. This difficulty may be recognized by some, but few have seriously suggested the development of an effective nonnuclear capability. In the immediate context, this has resulted by and large from a moralistic view regarding the use of force, the changed international security environment, the latest attitudes regarding the U.S. experience in Vietnam, and the reassessment of national interests.

Former Secretary of State Dean Acheson expressed a more pragmatic view:

> No American purpose, it could be pointed out, depends
> upon our using force against anyone. But we must be
> prepared to deter or meet the use of or the threat of
> force against our interests. When we speak of deterring
> the use of force against us, what do we mean? A deter-
> rent is a threat under certain circumstances to do harm
> to another, which the other believes we will do and does

not want to provoke. A threat is not believed, and therefore cannot deter, unless there is a general conviction
that the threatener has both the capacity and the intention
to carry out the threat. . . . Therefore, to deter or meet
force used or threatened on a local basis, capacity in what
are called conventional forces is required, that is, forces
which can conduct limited warfare and keep it limited.
Even these will not act as a deterrent or moderating factor unless others believe that they will be used.[9]

In retrospect, it appears that U.S. nuclear capability and perceived strength in Europe have served as an effective deterrent.
However, outside the European area, with some few exceptions, U.S.
military capability and political credibility appear inadequate. At a
time when Third World states are becoming increasingly important
to U.S. and Western political-military posture, this inadequacy is
developing a dangerous pattern—one that has already seen advances
by some major powers and a developing sense of disillusionment on
the part of some allies and friends of the West.

NUCLEAR AND NONNUCLEAR CONFLICTS:
MAJOR PREMISES

There are close relationships between nuclear and high-level
nonnuclear conflicts. But in other types of conflicts the "closeness"
diminishes rapidly. Major conventional wars are generally conceived
with a European-type scenario. Conventional operations in this context are seriously affected by the threat of escalation into nuclear
war. As a result, conventional operations tend to develop a configuration allowing a rapid shift into a nuclear posture. Battlefield characteristics of nuclear war have been discussed at length in the published literature. Here it simply needs to be recalled that they include the high vulnerability of concentrations of men and equipment,
the need for great mobility, application of intense firepower, deployment in depth, extensive and rapid communications, and the high
vulnerability of the political and social system (state survivability).
In major conventional wars, such considerations are also valid, even
if in a less compelling way. Most important, it is presumed that a
state engaging in major wars will find little need to justify its policy
to a domestic constituency. The very nature of the policy process
will necessitate or generate political justification and domestic support, regardless of the nature of the ideology or political system.
Nonnuclear conflicts, while varying in intensity and in form,
do have several common factors that distinguish them from major

conventional and nuclear wars. First, intervening states and their immediate adversaries are faced with problems of disengagement. Once the confrontation has been resolved one way or another, a particular political-military structure needs to be established and maintained in the target state. This, after all, is the purpose (more or less) of nonnuclear conflict. How can a system favorable to the dominant group be maintained while allowing the military forces of the various adversaries to disengage without creating political-military fragility in the target state? In other words, the very process and procedure of disengagement will have an impact on the evolution of the political-military system of the target state.

Second, rules of engagement are explicitly or implicitly adopted by adversaries. These rules may apply to objectives, geographic scope of the conflict, and even to identification of legitimate targets. The wars in the Middle East, Korea, and Vietnam are examples of these rules of engagement, which, for example, recognize the sanctity of capitals of states involved in the Middle East wars and permitted sanctuaries across the Yalu during the Korean War. Adherence to rules of engagement tend to be tenuous. As long as adversaries feel that such rules are mutually advantageous, they are likely to adhere to them. But actions on the field of battle may precipitate counteractions contrary to the rules. There is always the possibility of escalation or unilateral revision of the rules of engagement. The fact remains, however, that such rules constraining various aspects of the conflict are characteristic of nonnuclear confrontations.

Third, political and social factors are more pronounced and constraining. Admittedly, all wars are political. But in major wars and nuclear conflicts—where there is usually little question as to the purpose of the war in terms of national security—political, social, and economic factors are secondary to the survival of the state. In nonnuclear conflicts, the purpose of military actions is, in the main, a function of political considerations and limited goals.

Finally, involvement in nonnuclear conflicts requires distinctive military training and education—quite apart from a conventional competence. In this respect, policy-making processes and the military institutional focus and structure cannot easily transfer from a major war posture, either nuclear or nonnuclear, to the highly constrained and politically demanding nature of nonnuclear conflicts of a lesser order.

These characteristics will, of course, have different effects, depending on the type of conflict. They also develop distinct political and military dimensions. The adversary who understands this and applies it accordingly is more likely to achieve his political-military goals. However, these same characteristics make it difficult for a democratic system to engage successfully in nonnuclear conflicts.

They create a basic dilemma between the necessity of nonnuclear conflict and a system where military men are attuned to a society based on popular liberties and a conviction that "good guys never attack first." Such conflicts generally require a close integration of political, social, and military policy for success, thus requiring military operations deep within the political and social fabric of the adversary's system. They invariably involve civilian populations, stimulate nationalist sentiments, and, in many instances, establish the basis for revolutionary resistance.

BEYOND NUCLEAR DETERRENCE: SOME UNANSWERED QUESTIONS

In retrospect, one may ask whether the United States and the West can militarily intervene in areas outside Europe with any hope of achieving their political objectives. Landing troops, for example, in Angola or Mozambique to insure pro-Western control is politically simplistic and could be militarily disastrous. As a matter of fact, most Western policymakers would find it difficult to justify military intervention outside Western Europe, except in the most clearly perceived crises when national security was threatened. It is hard to conceive of a scenario in which this occurred, since it requires the most extreme assumptions, e. g., a Soviet invasion of the Philippines. If this is the case, why should the United States and the West, or indeed other major powers, seriously consider military intervention or the employment of military force, except in cases of survival?

The logic of an answer lies not in military maxims but in political purposes. By virtue of their very existence, major powers influence the environment and policy directions of other states. Regardless of the nature of their policies, major powers (like all other states) try to create a favorable climate for advancing their goals. Few states seek to intervene militarily when there are acceptable nonmilitary options for achieving political-military objectives. Even in those cases where military intervention or the use of force is the only alternative, major powers (as well as lesser states) may defer such actions because of the political and military risks and the high costs in cases of failure. Nevertheless, military power and credibility regarding its use create influence and improve the effectiveness of other instruments of policy.

Military power is an instrument of the state and a reflection of the state's ability to affect the policy of other states directly. The military institution is an organization "in being" capable of performing a variety of tasks supplementing and complementing nonmilitary instruments of policy. Thus, for example, the military instrument can serve as a conduit for the effective use of economic aid. Simply stated, military action is in some contexts a useful and even necessary political instrument.

Furthermore, most states perceive that they are confronted by hostile powers and that they exist in a hostile environment. Consequently, military force is considered a necessity for the survival of the state and a manifestation of state sovereignty. While international structures may provide an alternative for surviving in a hostile world, few states are willing to place complete trust in such associations, particularly when their national security is at issue.

Finally, the very existence of military institutions tends to generate policies for their use. In brief, the nuclear capabilities and economic interdependence of states have not produced a world order in which the threat of war or the use of force have been eliminated. Views on the use of force continue to differ, but the fact remains that force has often been used—and will continue to be used even within the context of a nuclear balance of terror.

EXAMINING NONNUCLEAR CONFLICTS

To examine nonnuclear conflicts and the employment of force in a systematic way, we need to construct a framework allowing comparison, identifying risk levels, and assessing policy consequences. There are a number of ways to do this: empirically, descriptively, or by combining both perspectives. What is presented here is primarily descriptive, focusing on political-military ends/means combinations. It also lays the groundwork for empirical examination.

Two analytical components, strategy and method, are the basis for our framework. Strategy establishes the objectives and operational guidelines. Method determines the type of operation to be conducted to achieve strategic purposes. In both components, political and military planning and their consequences are intermixed. This is reflected in the assessments of the various combinations discussed in the following section. Figure 1 shows various strategies and methods, and their relationships (relevancy between ends/means).

These categories are not intended to be mutually exclusive or to suggest cause and effect relationships. They do show major positions within each component and the applicability of each to various combinations of nonnuclear conflict. For example, it is possible that a state may engage in "support" using "surrogate force" in one area, while following a "quick strike" strategy using "direct military intervention" in another. Combinations depend upon the particular political-military environment and the policy pursued by the various states.

FIGURE 1

Strategy and Method in Nuclear and Nonnuclear Conflicts

	Strategy						
	Method						
	Low		(Intensity and visibility)				High
	Influence	Support	Quick strike	Revolution C/revolution	Limited war*	Major war	Nuclear war
S. Force	X	X	X	X	X	-	-
Ind. Int.	X	X	-	X	X	-	-
Dir. Int.	X	X	X	X	X	X	X
Mul. Int.	X	X	X	X	X	X	X
UN/Reg	X	X	-	-	X	-	-

Key:
X = Relevant or likely posture
- = Unlikely posture or irrelevant
S. Force = Surrogate force
Ind. Int. = Indirect intervention (unilateral)
Dir. Int. = Direct intervention (unilateral)
Mul. Int. = Multilateral intervention
UN/Reg = United Nations and/or regional association intervention

*A separate category for limited nuclear war has not been included. We are not convinced that such a distinction is realistic, since few powers (with possibly the exception of the United States) accept the idea that the use of nuclear weapons can in any way be categorized as limited war.

Source: Constructed by the author.

STRATEGY

Revolution and Counterrevolution

We begin with this strategy, recognizing that it does not follow the order shown in the schematic. This is done for a purpose. The involvement of the United States in Vietnam surfaced many of the most important issues likely to be faced by a democratic system involved in any type of nonnuclear conflict. Equally important, the characteristics of revolution and counterrevolution largely epitomize the political-military interactions and characteristics of all nonnuclear conflicts. Much of the discussion in this section is applicable to other nonnuclear strategies.[10]

Many scholars would agree that Mao Tse-tung's analysis of the nature of revolutionary war has served as a model—more or less—for revolutionary wars in Asia and throughout the world. The three-stage theory of revolutionary guerrilla warfare, combined with a preliminary stage (societal penetration) and a final stage (consolidation), is the basis for Mao's assessment. The essential point is political mobilization of the people is combined with armed units that are primarily political action cadres designed to overthrow the existing system or defeat an "alien" system.[11]

Revolutionary and counterrevolutionary strategy, translated into more mundane terms on the village level, creates an environment in which weapons technology and conventional tactics become generally inadequate and irrelevant, while the political-psychological aspects of the struggle become dominant. Attempts at distinguishing friend from foe are many times unsuccessful. Additionally, success at the village level normally goes to the side with the greatest political astuteness and ideological identity with the peasantry. Thus, revolutionary and counterrevolutionary forces must be sensitive and responsive to the attitudes, sympathies, and activities of the peasants.[1]

The political nature of the war means that revolutionaries are not overly concerned with real estate or with kill ratios, but with the political and psychological impact of their actions on the people. In brief, military action is multidimensional and multi-purpose: it is but one aspect—and in most instances a secondary aspect—of the total environment. Counterrevolutionary forces may need to act with considerable restraint for fear of alienating the population. As U.S. soldiers learned in Vietnam, this may mean watching comrades killed or wounded for little military reason and with few feasible countermeasures. The protracted nature of the war and the apparent inability to bring it to a successful conclusion are readily transferred into a negative domestic view of the war within a democratic society.

Public opinion, as recognized by the revolutionaries, plays an important role in the conduct of the war.[13] In the case of the external power, this can become a force militating against continued involvement while depreciating the efforts of the individual soldier on the battlefield. Thus, continued military operations that disrupt the peasant environment and gain little in the way of tangible results encourage political leaders of the intervening state increasingly to question military purpose. The ultimate result of these interactions is to undermine the military image and its professional purpose, institutionally as well as individually.

This presents limited alternatives to the democratic policymaker. The most favorable strategy under these circumstances is a "low visibility" involvement in support of existing regimes and "no visibility" involvement in counterrevolutionary warfare. The purpose would be assistance in the development of relatively stable and efficient governments in order to usurp the causes of revolution. However, once the revolutionary war commences and moves well into Phase One (strategic defensive), the success or failure of the counterrevolutionary effort is largely dependent on the indigenous government, not the commitment of external troops. Direct military involvement of an external power is a key stimulant to the development of counterpressure from nationalistic forces, though the effect of that involvement on counterrevolutionary performance is unclear. The point is succinctly made by a noted expert on revolutionary guerilla warfare. Commenting on Vietnam, he writes:

> The point to be stressed is that the war has always remained basically an insurgency, boosted by infiltration and aided, to a certain but limited extent, by both invasion and raids. . . . People's Revolutionary War is therefore, by nature a civil war of a very sophisticated type and using highly refined techniques to seize power and take over a country. The significant feature of it, which needs to be recognized, is its immunity to the application of power.[14]

Another policy alternative is to apply massive military power at the outset and in a relatively short time to attempt a quick "victory." The very conditions of revolutionary war militate against this type of policy—indeed there are few alternatives except a protracted engagement. Even in conditions in which there are major elements of the population in favor of the external power, as there were in Malaya, the external power involvement is likely to be protracted. (The emergency in Malaya officially lasted 12 years.)[15]

A protracted involvement may be possible as long as the conflict remains manageable and isolated from major power plays, as it did in Malaya from 1948 to 1960. Moreover, a purely professional military involvement (a limited number of regular military forces) may make it possible to limit the impact of the involvement on the external power's domestic society. In such circumstances, however, there must still be at least some degree of symmetry. This option presumes that the external power perceives the revolution as a "threat" or a potential threat to its security. Finally, we could easily argue that a democratic society should "never again" become involved in a counterrevolutionary war in a developing society, because there is little likelihood of success. This presumes that any society faced with revolutionary guerrilla warfare is ipso facto illegitimate and not worthy of assistance. Given the fact that most developing societies are susceptible to revolutionary guerrilla warfare, this option could easily lead to the disregard and abandonment of existing governments that may be attempting to overcome problems of development and change.

An effective military response to the revolutionary environment requires a professionally competent military institution—one based on a professionalism that includes understanding of political and social change. In other words, military professionalism must include a political element that understands the nuances of involvement in less than absolute terms. It must include an understanding of the complexities of political change, social movements, and economic modernization, as well as revolutionary struggles.[16] Given the nature of democratic society and the sensitivities of civilian leaders, it does not appear likely that this kind of professionalism will be allowed to emerge. Again, it may be easier for nondemocratic systems to engage in such conflicts.

Influence

Most states seek some control over events in contiguous areas and in important friendly or adversary states. The broader the scope of the state's interests, the greater and more important the need to have some impact on events. Influence (as opposed to the use of visible force) is the establishment of an environment and the creation of perceptions that allow the influencing state to pursue policies that promote its political-military goals.[17] In its most successful dimension, influence allows the state to accomplish its goals with little or no commitment of military resources. It is epitomized by the ability of the influencing state to pursue its policies by the use of traditional diplomacy.

This strategy is the most difficult to achieve, since it is never an absolute and is dependent upon a variety of subjectives and objective factors, ranging from considerations of military capability and perceptions of resolve, to the power projection of other states. To maintain influence the state must nurture its own image of strength and continue a pattern of purposeful policies and programs designed to affect international politics. The judicious blending of military and nonmilitary instruments of policy combined with determination and policy coherency will allow the state to condition the environment and affect the perceptions of other states. As a consequence, nonmilitary instruments of policy will be able to operate effectively with little recourse to military threats.

In the words of one scholar,

> Nuclear weapons have obviously not abolished war, they
> have displaced it. The central mechanism of the past
> was aimed at the problem of large military intervention
> by the main actors. Their restraint now depends less on
> global mechanisms than on a local one. . . . Because of
> the fear of escalation, much of the internal politics on
> the diplomatic strategic chessboard becomes a game of
> influence—less violent but more intense. There is an
> art of knowing how to deploy force rather than to use it,
> how to exploit internal circumstances to dislodge a rival.
> Whereas the traditional balancing mechanism may not
> work against war, it still functions where the stakes are
> influence, not conquest; for military strength in an area
> can deter or restrict the subtle access that influence
> requires.[18]

Influence is not only a strategy in itself; it also develops as a result of the state's ability to undertake a variety of strategies and methods. Thus, the ability of a state to adopt a policy of limited conventional war, for example, can influence the actions and policies of other states who may be potential targets for this type of conflict.

Support

This is a strategy of economic and/or military assistance, including the possible use of military advisors and cadres. The purpose is to support and develop a third state's infrastructure, not only for regime stability, but also to provide a better logistical base for indigenous military operations and possible future operations of the supporting state. Combined with military assistance in the form of money and material, this strategy can provide a substantial advantage to an indigenous government facing external and/or internal threats. Not only does the state gain access to military "expertise" and technology, but it may be able to do this with little visible connection to the supporting power. That is, a state, such as Cuba, may project an image in which it appears to retain control of its policies. A higher level of support may include military advisors and cadres directly involved in the conduct of training and operations of military units. At the minimum, there must exist political and military structures capable of absorbing and using the external assistance properly. Similarly, support may be given to forces resisting or attempting to overthrow the existing system.

This strategy has the advantage of a relatively low visibility commitment, while providing an option to withdraw with minimum loss. It is conceivable that a high level of assistance might create institutionalized and policy obligations on the part of the supporting state, locking that state into the fortunes of the state or group being supported.

Equally important, this strategy may signify to other states a commitment that many may expect the supporting state to honor, regardless of circumstances. The essential problem is, how much assistance can the supporting state give without closing off other options?

To achieve the goals of this strategy, there must be sophisticated implementation, supporting one or the other group without substituting the supporting state's military structure for that of the indigenous system. That is, the supporting state needs to be discreet in its involvement in order to insure that the indigenous state or group retains its sovereign image. This is necessary to retain a degree of freedom on the part of the supporting state and also to avoid internal and external reaction. However, a large and visible assistance group may be necessary. Additionally, if cadre groups (i.e., military teams directly involved with indigenous troop formations) are provided, then the visibility is greater and the commitment more difficult to hide or deny.

The highest level of assistance can give the supporting state the greatest political-military leverage (i.e., the ability to influence the military and affect internal politics). However, there is also an increase in the political-military risk to the supporting state. Thus, a supporting state must weigh the options carefully before implementing a policy of a higher level of assistance. Similarly, supported groups or states must also weigh their options carefully, since a higher level of external assistance brings with it a number of political-military risks that are not easy to justify or rectify if political-military strategy fails.

Quick Strike

As the name indicates, this strategy envisions an extremely limited, short-term, and highly concentrated intervention by military forces in a foreign area for a specific purpose, either military or political. Such an action, made famous by the Israeli raid on Entebbe (Uganda), is a high risk strategy with obvious political dangers. Forces required to achieve success must be highly trained and specialized in small-unit quick-strike operations and highly mobile. Perhaps the most difficult part of the operation is the withdrawal phase.

For a quick strike strategy to succeed, the objectives must be limited, and they must be clear to a domestic as well as international audience. Military objectives are of course important, but there is no denying the fact that unless strict limits are placed on the strategy and unless there is a clear and paramount political objective, such strategy can easily trigger military response by other states.

One of the major risks is that a quick strike may be viewed as a military invasion and an act of war. But given the precedence established by Entebbe and the Mayaguez affair, it seems that under certain conditions such operations may well be considered police actions rather than military operations. Yet the political consequences of failure can be quite serious, particularly if the quick-strike force is trapped in the target area. This can lead to the commitment of additional forces to rescue those trapped. The tendency toward escalation is obvious.

Limited Conventional War

Much of the attention to limited conventional war developed in the wake of the United Nations involvement in Korea. Subsequently, a great deal has been published on the subject, from which several salient considerations emerge. There are many types of limited conventional wars, differing in intensity and political purpose. These include reaction to colonial rule (such as the Indian occupation of Gao); geopolitical pressures (such as the China-India conflict in the Himalayas); historical animosities and conquest (such as the Vietnam invasion of Cambodia in 1979); and United Nations efforts to punish an aggressor (as in Korea). Moreover, the intensity of the conflict can differ from virtually a "no-battle" situation (as in the case of India and Gao) to a high intensity conflict (such as the Korean War). Conventional wars can also be limited by geographic scope, intensity, and the number of participants. Limited conventional wars may confine the actual conflict to specific boundaries. The involvement of states other than the initial protagonists may be restricted by mutual agreement so as to avoid escalation beyond the intent of the adversaries. Finally, the intensity of the conflict may be limited in terms of the kinds of weapons, targets, and tactics. In such cases adversaries may limit their military operations to clearly defined targets, using certain categories of weapons. Similarly, tactics may be constrained by geographic scope, as well as weapons and target considerations.

Conventional wars may also be limited by their duration—that is, the nature of the war presumes a limitation of involvement in time as well as commitment. This is particularly important for democratic systems. Political pressures developing within a democratic system may militate against an open-ended commitment, both in time and resources. Historically, democratic systems have sought quick solutions to limited conventional wars. Beyond a certain period of time, support for such involvement diminishes rapidly. It is true, of course, that most states seek quick solutions to any war. Yet in democratic systems this can easily become a dominant consideration. There are some states, however, that may seek to escalate the intensity of the war and prolong it for one reason or another.

As is usually the case in nonnuclear conflicts, political objectives and sensitivity to the political-social system of the target area override military considerations. Military operations on the battlefield are therefore seriously affected by the requirements imposed by these "non-military" factors. Moreover, these limitations are imposed not only at higher unit levels, but also at the lowest operational level. In simple terms, the individual pilot must know the limitations on his target choices, just as the individual soldier must know when to shoot and when not to, even if confronted by apparently hostile persons. Such rules of engagement obviously restrict military operations and limit the extent to which military forces can bring to bear their full conventional potential.

These types of wars may also be asymmetrical. While one state may limit its involvement according to the factors discussed earlier, another state may view the conflict as a matter of national survival security. Asymmetry may also develop at the local level. On the battlefield, individual soldiers may find it difficult to distinguish between major and limited wars. The number of casualties and the intensity of fighting in a given battle may make distinctions between various types of wars irrelevant. In this sense, there is asymmetry between the local battlefield environment, the military posture, and the political-military strategy. It might be added that such asymmetry is the cause of most of the tension between the military system and civilian institutions. Tension within the military itself is also related to this asymmetry.

In sum, limited conventional wars are characterized by a number of political and military considerations that, among other things, limit the scope and intensity of the involvement, and tend to create internal military tensions between the political and the military systems. Moreover, the rules of engagement between adversaries may be quite fragile, leading to serious threats of escalation. The asymmetrical nature of the war adds to this fragility.

Limited and Major Conventional Wars

The line between high levels of limited and major conventional war is thin.[19] War confined to a specific region or theater of operations may remain limited and conventional, so long as those involved in the conflict limit their objectives and geographic scope. Thus, it is conceivable, at least theoretically, that the United States, NATO, and the Warsaw Pact could engage in conventional conflict, with each group seeking only limited objectives in Europe. However, it does not seem to be possible that clashes between NATO and Warsaw Pact forces can long remain limited. Indeed, the very basis for such a conflict would in itself be serious enough to warrant a total mobilization and development of major war. The previous comments about the political aspects of major conventional as well as nuclear war are relevant here.

The state of the military institution and posture in most countries is conventional in configuration. In light of military traditions and threat perceptions, the capability of the military to engage in a conventional conflict is generally the first priority. Even in those countries priding themselves on successfully concluding a "people's" war, the priority for the military is conventional capability, reflecting the view that such a capability is necessary in light of the "hostile" foreign environment, the demands of internal order, and the stability of the political system. Thus, most systems are more prepared to engage in limited conventional war than in any other type of nonnuclear conflict. While in Western systems, it seems unlikely that limited conventional war can be initiated without high domestic political risk, non-Western systems may find it less difficult. Indeed, given the European fixation and the substitution of weaponry for manpower particularly aimed at a European scenario, there may be few situations in which the West can engage in limited conventional war without serious political and military risks.

METHOD

Surrogate Forces

A state using this method supports (and indeed may encourage)
another state to intervene militarily in the affairs of a third. Surrogate forces are used in order to influence another state without
creating a high visibility or direct link to the intervening state. Although such a method may create long-term commitments and may
embroil the state that uses it in complex political-military areas, it
has the lowest political-military risks in terms of domestic and international pressures. Thus it is particularly useful for major powers
in influencing Third World countries. Yet it does carry some element of risk since association with the surrogate state may create
problems of continuing support in an increasingly volatile situation.
All of the problems of nationalistic reaction, revolution and counterrevolution can immerse the intervening state and its supporters in a
political-military morass. Moreover, the right conditions must exist
for successful surrogate force implementation: a state willing to act
as a surrogate; a situation in which surrogate forces can be effective;
a relatively favorable political-military climate for the use of surrogate forces; and a high probability of political-military benefits.
Such a method may be particularly useful to democratic systems because of the minimum military risks involved. The political risks
for democratic systems may be great, however, since the access to
information and the existence of a free mass media can strip away
any pretense of low-visibility involvement. Nevertheless, a sophisticated and intelligent use of surrogate forces can be an extremely
useful method for achieving political-military goals.

Indirect Intervention

This method attempts to avoid direct involvement while trying
to influence the political-military environment or posture of a third
(i.e., target) state. A variety of means may be used, ranging from
arms sales to military education. Clearly this is a relatively long
range approach, since it suggests reluctance to use more visible and
direct means. Arms sales may be used, for example, to provide
modern weapons and material to the target state. Such sales can
usually be treated as business ventures with few, if any, entangling
military-political relationships. Arms sales through third parties
may also be a useful device. Additionally, nonmilitary channels
may be used to achieve political-military goals. For example, without visible military involvement, the target state may be willing to

send senior military officers to attend senior level military schools in the user state. Similarly, sons of the elite selected to enter the military may also be sent to schools in the user state.

Indirect military intervention also includes a range of military maneuvering from shows of force, regrouping of military formations, and partial mobilization ostensibly for training purposes, to military emergency drills. Many such actions can be used as diplomatic and military signals to either support or deter actions by another state or states.

The relationship between the user state and states contiguous to the target state is also important. For example, the United States' relationship with Germany may indirectly influence the political-military posture of France. Similarly, attempts by the United States to draw Lebanon into a peace accord with Israel and Egypt may also be a form of indirect intervention, attempting to influence other Arab states.

Politically, indirect intervention provides a useful procedure since the risks are low. In many instances, nonmilitary instruments can be employed. Additionally, the linkage between the user state and the target state is not so visible and strong as to suggest a positive and indefinite commitment. The state that uses indirect intervention can usually withdraw its support from the target state with minimum international and domestic repercussions. Such a procedure can also serve as a signal to the target state that the indirect involvement should be considered standard diplomacy and not necessarily an indication of the approval of the system or a commitment to support the policies of the target state.

Direct Military Intervention

This type of intervention presumes a direct involvement by ground combat units and other military contingents of a state into the target state, either for defeating the target state or for supporting it against internal or external threats. Obviously, this is a visible and clear commitment, suggesting in many instances an "open-ended" commitment on the part of the intervening state. In fact, the commitment of men and material may be substantial. It is also clear that this type of intervention can easily trigger response by other states: there is a significant risk of escalation.

Direct intervention poses internal risks for any state, regardless of the nature of the political system. Not only does the use of military force in foreign areas create problems of domestic consensus, but it raises issues of legality, credibility, and morality. For example, neither France nor the United States were immune from such matters as a result of their involvement in Indochina and Vietnam. The complexity of political-military issues and the difficulty of translating democratic values into military policy make it difficult for democratic systems to intervene directly. It is also difficult to develop consensus regarding the use of force, except in clearly perceived crises, e.g., invasion by a foreign state. This does not rule out the possibility of the use of a small force for a very limited time (e.g., the French Foreign Legion in Zaire). But most Western democracies have difficulty justifying the use of military force in foreign areas for any great length of time. Still, although it may be easier for nondemocratic systems to deploy military force or intervene, China and the Soviet Union have, for a variety of political and military reasons, been less willing to do so, except in contiguous areas.

Multilateral Intervention

By their very nature, multilateral interventions reflect a limited commitment by the participants. If such an intervention is reasonably balanced among the participants in terms of resources and purposes, then the political-military risks are minimized. A number of nations combining military resources for clearly defined political objectives are not only in a position to share success, but also to share the blame for any failure. Equally important, the "international" veneer of multilateral intervention may provide an acceptable procedure in what may otherwise be an action that is strenuously resisted by the target state or states. The international cloak can hide unilateral political objectives and hints of a more universal and unselfish purpose.

In such ventures there must be clear roles for the military forces of the various states involved and clear political-military objectives. Additionally, control, supervision, and logistics become a particularly difficult problem if any significant operation is to take place for any length of time, particularly if such operation contemplates combat.

In this respect, the difficulties in cooperation may be more pressing than the problems in the target area. In any case, multilateral intervention is a useful procedure when the political-military goals are clear. If such intervention involves major combat, then, as in cases of unilateral considerations, the military goals become paramount and it may become less difficult to develop multilateral consensus and control. The fact remains that such intervention is less onerous to the international community and less difficult to accept in democratic systems.

UN/Regional Association Intervention

This procedure is a higher form of multilateral intervention in that a formal international institution "in being" is involved. Additionally, the intervention has with it a justification and legality that flow from a recognized international association, whether it is regional (Organization of African States) or the United Nations. Success and failure occur in the name of the association and not necessarily in the name of any particular state or states. For example, the United Nations' role in Korea, although dominated by the United States, is still associated with United Nations policy and resources.

For the West an acceptable option may be UN or Regional Association intervention. For the reasons stated earlier regarding the political-military consequences, this type of intervention is best suited for states not in a political or military posture to intervene beyond the European area. Obviously, there are some serious political disadvantages. Political control can easily be lost to a large bloc of nations whose political-military objectives may be contrary to those pursued by the West. But just as success must be shared, so failure or blame is shared. The political-military risks are reduced accordingly.

The problems of command, control, and logistics are militarily and politically complex. For example, it is always difficult for the military of one state to be commanded by military men of another state, even if under United Nations or Regional Association auspices. Additionally, the political consensus to act in the name of an international organization is usually much more difficult to achieve than in other forms of intervention. The United Nations intervention in the Congo in 1960, for example, raised serious internal and institutional questions for the UN, as well as questions regarding political-military objectives in the Congo.

In the Security Council a favorable vote is required for United Nations military action, but because of the diverse and at times antagonistic ideologies and attitudes represented in the Security Council, the likelihood of favorable military action is minimal. Even when there is a favorable vote, the United Nations has difficulty in convincing states to commit military resources for international action. Such resources are occasionally committed, but usually in those circumstances that are seemingly unambiguous and "apolitical" (e.g., UN peacekeeping activities).

CONCLUSION

Events over the past ten years and an examination of the various political-military considerations as they now exist indicate that the Western powers are in a weakened position with respect to their power and influence in areas outside Europe. While this may not suggest a fundamental Western weakness, it does indicate an inability to project strength on a worldwide scale. It is argued that this inability is primarily, but not exclusively, a result of the lessened Western military capability, reduced political credibility, and questionable resolve. Furthermore, if we accept the premise that the employment of military power (actual or perceived) has an important impact on the ability to influence other areas of the world and serves as a conduit for the effectiveness of other instruments of policy, then we can only conclude that outside Europe the Western powers are in a particularly disadvantaged position.

The range of nonnuclear conflicts and the various combinations of strategy and means reinforce this conclusion. The Western political style and military posture are not in a configuration or philosophical orientation to actively engage in nonnuclear conflicts. While Western powers have a high degree of mobility and logistical capability to move military forces to most parts of the world, the political basis for "staying" power is lacking. Equally important, except for very limited and selected units, military capabilities in nonnuclear conflicts (and military staying power) are questionable at best. The fact remains that short of nuclear war or clearly perceived military crises in Europe, the West appears to be seriously limited in its ability to use military power.

There have been, to be sure, successful diplomatic initiatives and short-term gains by Western powers. But our conclusions are best summed up by an observation referred to earlier and worth repeating here: "The ability of an American secretary of state to shuttle through the Middle East in an attempt to arrange a peace should not be confused with the structures of real influence—steady purpose, geographic proximity, large arsenals, treaties of friendship—all the things which, taken together, elicit respect and fear."[20] Although success without military power and resolve can be achieved in fortuitous circumstances, the continued and systematic pursuit of political-military goals will generally require a judicious combination of all these factors.

From the point of view of non-Western systems, those in the major power category have already demonstrated their ability to use military force in a variety of nonnuclear conflicts and in a variety of ways. Even with a nuclear capability in Europe, the Soviet Union, for example, appears to have developed a flexible response to nonnuclear conflicts not only militarily, but in terms of its political credibility. On a regional basis, several nonnuclear states are capable of using military power in a variety of nonnuclear conflicts. (The Vietnamese involvement in Cambodia in 1979 is a case in point.)

Finally, as indicated by this analysis, the use of military force in international politics remains valid. While wars between major powers may have lost much of their relevance, the use of force to influence or deter remains useful and in many instances necessary. In this respect, the successful use of force requires a sophisticated leadership able to balance military and nonmilitary instruments of power.

Having noted this, however, we are also cognizant of the fact that power projection beyond the European setting may require ground troop engagement in battle, with all the political-military implications inherent in such involvement. There is no completely acceptable solution to the dilemma this poses. Can the United States, for example, pursue a policy of human rights, yet commit ground units in foreign areas to achieve certain political-military goals? Is not war itself the very denial of human rights? To put it bluntly, statesmen and military leaders are rarely faced with clear distinctions between good and evil in matters like these.

If we accept the earlier premise about the nature of international politics—i.e., that wars and military force remain a basic part of the international arena—then we are drawn to the conclusion that the Western powers, like most other states in the world, cannot neglect military force as an instrument of policy. When it is necessary, it ought to be used judiciously and decisively. Before such a policy is adopted, however, all the options must be examined, the political-military consequences weighed, and the moral and ethical dimensions understood. In particular, serious attention must be given to the achievement of political-military goals without the use of force. It is also important to understand that there may be times when long-range goals can be achieved without the use of force, even though the immediate situation seems to indicate otherwise. As we have tried to make clear, power and influence are not simply contingent upon military force. The pursuit of such goals as justice, human rights, the elimination of poverty, and economic strength may also increase the power and influence of the state. In the final analysis, the realities of international relations have not yet allowed many states to exist without recourse to such force. And, unfortunately, the effectiveness of military force as an instrument of policy depends, in most instances, upon a pattern of demonstrated and effective employment. In brief, Western powers appear to be in a position to respond only to extremes in the various categories and combinations of strategies and methods. Yet it is the middle range that is likely to characterize conflicts in the immediate future.

If Western powers wish to regain some initiative and respond to these middle-range conditions in a way that furthers state policy, several things must be done. First, coherency in policy direction and purpose must be developed. This is, for the most part, a function of leadership and the image to be projected to domestic and international audiences. Such purposes and objectives must establish a pattern of consistency that is linked to the strength of Western states. In brief, the economic as well as military strength of the West should be used, in part, to encourage stability and the promotion of values that best serve Western interests. These interests need not be, and indeed should not necessarily be antagonistic to, Third and Fourth World countries. To be sure, these considerations appear to be highly philosophical. What is being suggested, however, is the linking of philosophically-oriented policy guidelines with consistent patterns of activity and demonstrated commitments.

Second, to follow through, there is a need to establish, maintain, and (if necessary) employ military force along with other instruments of policy to achieve the purposes proclaimed by the West. With few exceptions, much of the policy of Western states (in this context, the United States seems to reflect the Western position best) tends to be declaratory and hints of the rhetorical. The fact remains that policy lacking in resolve and capability is virtually useless in affecting world events.

Finally, while the United States and other Western powers need to develop unilateral capabilities, there is an even more pressing need to develop multilateral ones. The U.S.-French cooperation in assisting Zaire in 1978 could be used as a model for such development. In this respect, serious consideration should be given to the expansion of NATO's purpose to include such contingencies.

These conclusions serve only as initial and general observations. That is, there are many other considerations that are closely related to each. For example, what kinds of forces should the United States (and other Western powers) organize to respond to nonnuclear conflicts? What are the costs involved? Under what specific conditions should such forces be committed? What kinds of command and control structures should be developed? The fact remains, however, that these initial observations can serve as a channel for the development of substantive programs aimed at linking capability and credibility with policy alternatives facing Western powers. Simply stated, either the United States (and the West) must demonstrate a pattern of purposeful action based on a judicious blend of military and nonmilitary instruments, or the sights of policy must be lowered to avoid raising expectations of both international and domestic audiences regarding United States (Western) action.

In any case, the decision to engage in nonnuclear conflict in one form or another is not simply the result of adding political credibility to military capability. A whole series of factors must be considered, ranging from the assessment of domestic and international environments to the relevance of political-military objectives and policy consequences.

After assessing the use of "coercive diplomacy" by the United States, several scholars conclude:

> Whatever the scope of scholarly disagreement in this respect, it surely excludes the simple-minded proposition that to coerce an opponent successfully is, as some imply, merely a matter of the president exercising our national resolution or guts to threaten, and use if need be, the ample military capabilities at our disposal. [21]

In a changing world order where Western hegemony is no longer operative and local and regional powers can effectively challenge major powers, it does little good to base policy on nuclear devastation or on age-worn perceptions of major power effectiveness. Yet Western interests and particularly those of the United States—interests it might be added that may be legitimate even in the eys of Third and Fourth World states—cannot be allowed to become vulnerable to the good wishes of others. In the words of Dean Acheson, quoted earlier

> No American purpose, it could be pointed out, depends on our using force against anyone. But we must be prepared to deter or meet the use of or the threat of force against our interests . . . these (conventional forces) will not act as a deterrent or moderating force unless others believe that they will be used. [22]

NOTES

1. This is not intended to suggest that somehow the West, particularly the United States, does not have a major role in many world issues. But we feel that the kinds of changes taking place in the world today and the experience and events of the immediate past signal a weakening of the Western position. As Stanley Hoffman notes:

> Even if the central balance holds, even if the American economy remains the strongest, let us not forget that the relative moderation we have enjoyed, the success of the restraints we have analyzed, have been due to features that are vanishing. . . . America's very power gives us enormous influence, and in no important arena can

anything be settled without its participation and commitment. Yet, American hegemony is over . . . we now find
the U.S., a challenger grown militarily bigger, and a
bewildering variety of actors that have taken their fate
into their own hands, and, silently or rudely, begun to
emancipate themselves from our grip. . . .

Stanley Hoffman, Primacy or World Order (New York: McGraw-
Hill, 1978), pp. 162 and 320. See also his discussion on pp. 321-22.

2. Time, September 24, 1965, p. 30. See also Robert McClintock, The Meaning of Limited War (Boston: Houghton Mifflin Company, 1967), p. 197.

3. Herbert K. Tillema, Appeal to Force: American Military
Intervention in the Era of Containment (New York: Thomas Y. Crowell, 1973), Appendix A, pp. 202-17.

4. Anatol Rapaport, ed., Clausewitz on War (Maryland: Penguin Books, 1971), p. 414.

5. Barry M. Blechman, et al., "Toward a New Consensus in
U.S. Defense Policy," Setting National Priorities: The Next Ten
Years (Washington: The Brookings Institution, 1976), pp. 59-60.
See also Klaus Knorr, "On the International Uses of Military Force
in the Contemporary World," Orbis 21 (Spring, 1977):5-27.

6. For an excellent treatment of theories of war see Lancelot
L. Farrar, Jr., War: A Historical, Political, and Social Study
(Santa Barbara, Cal.: ABC-Clio Press, 1978).

7. W. Scott Thompson, ed., The Third World: Premises of
U.S. Policy (San Francisco: Institute for Contemporary Studies,
1978), pp. 7-8.

8. The Soviet military intervention in Afghanistan in 1979 and
1980 is a clear example of the unilateral use of force to achieve a
particular political-military goal. See Fig. 1.

9. Dean Acheson, A Citizen Looks at Congress (New York:
Harper and Brothers, 1957), as quoted in Readings in American
Democracy, eds. Gerald Stourzh, et al. (New York: Oxford University Press, 1966), pp. 464-65. Interestingly enough, the current
military focus is almost solely on Europe. Not only is this evident
in the training provided in senior level military schools, but in

official literature. For example, in the Department of the Army, Field Manual 100-5, Operations, the clear intent is to prepare for battle in the Central Plains. In the first few pages, the Manual states in part,

> Battle in Central Europe against forces of the Warsaw
> Pact is the most demanding mission the US Army could
> be assigned. Because the US Army is structured pri-
> marily for that contingency and has large forces deployed
> in that area, this manual is designed mainly to deal with
> the realities of such operations. The principles set
> forth in this manual, however, apply also to military
> operations anywhere in the world. Furthermore, the US
> Army retains substantial capabilities in its airborne,
> airmobile, and infantry divisions for successful opera-
> tions in other theaters of war against other forces.

Of the 14 chapters, 13 are focused on battle in Europe. Only the last chapter is devoted to "Special Environments."

10. Adopted from Sam C. Sarkesian, "Revolution and the Limits of Military Power: The Haunting Specter of Vietnam," Social Science Quarterly 56/4 (March 1976):678-87.

11. There are a number of standard works which assess and explain the major characteristics of revolutionary guerilla warfare. See, for example, Selected Works of Mao Tse-tung, abridged by Bruno Shaw (New York: Harper and Row, 1970); Truong Chinh, Primer for Revolt (New York: Praeger, 1963); General Vo Nguyen Giap, People's War People's Army (New York: Praeger, 1962); and Douglas Pike, Vietcong (Cambridge: M.I.T. Press, 1967). See also Sam C. Sarkesian, ed., Revolutionary Guerrilla Warfare (Chicago: Precedent, 1975).

12. The general scheme of these techniques is described in Sarkesian, Revolutionary Guerrilla Warfare, pp. 1-22.

13. American public opinion and the American desire for quick decisive victories and "absolutes" in war are characteristics which created significant difficulties for American military per- formance in Vietnam. See Maurice Matloff, ed., American Military History (Washington, D.C.: Office of the Chief of Military History, 1969), pp. 14-15.

14. Sir Robert Thompson, No Exit From Vietnam (New York: David McKay, 1968), p. 45. Italics added for emphasis.

15. See John P. Roche, "Can a Free Society Fight a Limited War?" in The New Leader (Oct. 21, 1968), pp. 6-11. A distinction must be made between the American involvement in Vietnam and colonial struggles against indigenous forces. Colonial purposes, institutional control, resource control, and long-term policy provide clear contrasts to the problems and purposes behind American policy in Vietnam. One must also note that modern revolutionary guerrilla warfare is a realtively recent phenomenon—not to be compared to the pre-Maoist period.

16. For excellent discussions on these matters see Chalmers Johnson, Revolutionary Change (Boston: Little, Brown and Company, 1966) and Ted Robert Gurr, Why Men Rebel (Princeton: Princeton University Press, 1970).

17. See the discussion in Robert A. Dahl, Modern Political Analysis (Englewood Cliffs, N.J.: Prentice-Hall, 1970), pp. 14-34.

18. Hoffman, Primacy or World Order, p. 172.

19. Precise distinctions between major wars and limited wars are difficult to make. Yet some guidelines are available. Major wars usually involve more than one major power and presume that the geographic boundaries of the conflict are on a worldwide scale. It also presumes that nuclear weapons will not be utilized, but with few limits on the use of conventional weapons and targets. Thus, a major war could occur between China and the Soviet Union, conducting battles along the entire Sino-Soviet border, involving allies on both sides, and extending the battlefield to areas of the world where Chinese and Soviet interests are located. In brief, major war will probably follow the patterns of World War II. Limited conventional war will probably follow the pattern of the Korean conflict with all the limitations and constraints discussed in this paper. In a related issue, the categorization of major power also presents some difficulties. Major powers may be so designated because of their military and economic power from a worldwide perspective, i.e., the United States, the USSR, China, and possibly West Germany, France, and the United Kingdom. On a regional level, it is possible to categorize the following countries as major powers: Nigeria, Brazil, Indonesia, Japan, and South Africa. For a useful discussion of these issues, see Ray S. Cline, World Power Assessment, A Calculus of Strategic Drift (Washington, D.C.: The Center for Strategic and International Studies, 1973).

20. See note 7.

21. Alexander L. George, David K. Hall, and William R. Simons, The Limits of Coercive Diplomacy (Boston: Little, Brown and Company, 1971), p. 251.

22. See note 8.

2
THE UNITED STATES:
POLITICAL AND
MILITARY ENVIRONMENT

The political and military issues facing the United States in the post-Vietnam period make it extremely difficult for it to respond to challenges of nonnuclear warfare, although there are some military contingencies to which the United States can respond. Not only are there significant military restraints facing the United States in employing military force for most nonnuclear contingencies, but there are important political and ethical restraints as well. In this respect, the United States is best prepared to employ nonmilitary instruments of policy. Yet the military instrument is important if any credibility is to be established for defense policy. The experience of Vietnam and the resulting military and political impact prevent realistic reaction to problems of nonnuclear contingencies; internal institutional and organizational restructuring are needed. This means that attention must be given to conventional military capability, and also to a broadened conception of military professionalism that includes political-social, as well as military, concern with nonnuclear conflict. Each contingency has peculiar political, social, economic, and military factors. Leadership and organizational flexibility are needed to fashion a credible military instrument. This can be done without necessarily fashioning a military instrument for every conceivable contingency. However, extreme caution must be exercised if policy goals are not to be forced beyond military and political capabilities. The environment of the 1980s is the result of considerable change which occurred since the height of superpower influence in the 1950s and 1960s. Multi-centers of regional power and extreme nationalistic politics make it difficult to employ military power advantageously.

2

THE STRATEGIC ENVIRONMENT, U.S. NATIONAL SECURITY, AND THE NATURE OF LOW INTENSITY CONFLICT
David W. Tarr

Current Pentagon policy calls for the armed forces to be prepared "to respond effectively and simultaneously to a relatively minor
as well as to a major contingency"[1] (the so-called "one and one-half
wars" planning formula). "Low-intensity conflict" is a term currently in vogue that refers to the small war or limited contingency.
It is this "half a war," or minor contingency concept, that is the subject of this paper.

Reference to the degree or "intensity" of conflict suggests a
spectrum, continuum, or scale, ranging from low, through intermediate, to high. Some of the literature on conventional warfare
has adopted this conception, usually dividing discussion into two general categories—high-intensity or high-technology warfare, and low-
intensity or limited warfare. This language is not very precise, of
course. But it does suggest the difference between, say, an intense
large-scale battle in Europe between NATO and Warsaw Pact forces,
employing every form of advanced weapons technology, and a civil
war waged by a poorly equipped guerrilla force against the regular
armed forces of the government in an undeveloped country in the
Third World. These two situations (in addition to theater nuclear
and strategic nuclear warfare) represent the two ends of the scale of
conventional warfare for which the armed forces of the United States
are expected to be prepared.

Low-intensity warfare includes the concept of "unconventional
warfare," a type of small war in which paramilitary and partisan or
guerrilla forces are likely to be the main combatants of at least one
side of the conflict. The political contexts of such conflicts might be
characterized by such terms as civil strife, civil war, rebellion, or
revolution, but they are not confined to these. A low-intensity conflict might arise if an attempted coup results, for example, in a civil

41

war _between_ units of the regular armed forces, or a civil war between two or more small states possessing, by current standards, primitive weapons—primarily small arms, light artillery, and the like.

In any case, small wars, whether conventional, unconventional, or a mixture of both (as in Vietnam, for example), would be, from the perspective and capabilities of the United States, _limited_ wars. That is, the United States might very likely have to exercise careful restraints in types of weapons and manpower introduced, as well as in observation of territorial boundaries, etc. In all likelihood, U.S. participation in such an event would come after the conflict began and would be regarded as an act of military intervention, whether invited or not. In other words, a defense policy that requires the capacity to fight a small war implies having a limited, conventional and unconventional war doctrine and capability.

A decision to intervene is, of course, most difficult since it requires a more elaborate and convincing rationalization than is necessary when one is directly attacked and therefore reacting in self-defense. Moreover, most small war possibilities exist among states or within states that do not have the military potential to represent, of themselves, a direct security threat to the United States. Vietnam was a case in point, as are the more recent cases of conflict in Angola, Yemen, the horn of Africa, Lebanon, Uganda, and so on. Under such circumstances, the difficulty is compounded, of course, by the unpopular and unsatisfactory outcome of the U.S. experience in Vietnam. Nevertheless, quite apart from the question of intervention in specific instances, current U.S. policy requires that the military be prepared to intervene if such a contingency arises and the political leadership is convinced that U.S. security interests are at stake. Because future security risks are uncertain, the desire to be ready to respond to a broad spectrum of possibilities is a natural inclination of responsible leaders of the defense establishment.

Yet the policy objective of readiness to participate in small or low-intensity wars is especially fraught with potential problems for the United States. Surely in the post-Vietnam policy context, the U.S. government eschews the role of "world policeman." Although our political values tend to prefer peaceful change to violence, we remain uncertain, as a people, concerning what role the United States ought to play in political change throughout the world.

Moreover, the normative restraints against the use of armed force appear to have gained greater momentum in recent years in the Western democracies, especially with respect to the use of force by major powers against minor states. Klaus Knorr, reflecting on this phenomenon, observes that such restraint as exists

seems . . . to be distributed unevenly over the globe.
There is considerable evidence that this form of restraint
gained an appreciable hold in Western Europe and Japan.
Down to the beginning of the twentieth century, political
culture in the European societies still accepted war as
natural, inevitable and legitimate without making sharp
distinctions between its aggressive and defensive use. . . .
This traditional view has been subject to rapid erosion
in recent decades. At least in a substantial proportion
of the publics concerned, and in the declared credo of
political leaders, war is no longer regarded as legitimate
except in self-defense.[2]

Whether Americans ever held the "traditional" view of the
legitimacy of force as an instrument of state policy, clearly the current view coincides with Knorr's observations. Obviously, then,
U.S. participation in small wars must be combined, to be politically
supportable at home and within the alliance, with a sense of legitimate
action.

Yet, as Knorr points out, the United States "still adheres to
world order objectives,"[3] thus requiring a greater interest in and
preparation for resort to armed force. In the recent past such programs and policies were legitimized by the expressed objectives of
containment (of communism) and deterrence (of aggression). But
the consensus on which these objectives were based, as well as the
underlying political assumptions, collapsed with the failure of U.S.
military policies in Vietnam. As yet no substitutes for these doctrines have emerged.

Nevertheless, a changed world perspective is plainly visible.
The U.S. leadership of today more clearly recognizes the complexity
of the strategic environment within which foreign and military policies must operate, an environment for which Cold War formulas are
no doubt inadequate. In this sense current policy assumptions may
be more realistic and prudent, if not better prepared for unfolding
events.

THE STRATEGIC ENVIRONMENT

Any consideration of the problems posed by low-intensity warfare capabilities and policies must take into account the characteristics of the international strategic environment that largely condition
and constrain U.S. military intervention and action in small wars.

There are, it seems to me, at least five major environmental factors that will influence both the outbreak of low-intensity conflicts and the choice of (or inclination of) other powers to intervene. These are (1) the multipolar/multidimensional character of international politics (excepting the issue of nuclear weapons); (2) the altered world economy; (3) the balance of nuclear forces; (4) the revolution in conventional weapons technology; and (5) the buildup of conventional armaments in the Third World. The last three of these conditions are military in nature. The first two are not, but nonetheless require brief mention here.

First, with respect to the structure and distribution of power in the world of today and tomorrow, bipolarity is no longer an appropriate conceptualization, even though the United States and the Soviet Union remain nuclear superpowers. There are many more independent centers of decision making than ever before, and they align themselves in multidimensional ways, depending upon the issues at stake. In this context the East-West ideological division parallels the bipolarity of strategic nuclear power, but so also does the competition between China and the Soviet Union, and between the "north" and the "south." Regional political, social, and economic issues are often more salient, and these are no longer dominated by the superpowers. Territorial disputes, now an infrequent source of conflict in the industrial world, remain an important ingredient of potential conflict elsewhere. These problems are interrelated in complex ways, suggesting a greater variety of conflict conditions under less constraint than during the Cold War period.

Consider, for example, the recent effort of a scholar to summarize the complexities of the international structure in terms of the typologies in use:

> In recent times the by now almost traditional postwar trichotomization—First, Second and Third Worlds—has given way to slightly more complex formulations. . . .
> The rise of OPEC has given birth to a Fourth World of wealthy (though still nonindustrialized) and militarily weak states. The remainder of the . . . Third World monolith is now habitually subdivided to allow for a Fifth World of "basket cases" characterized by unusually low per capita incomes. Ideological and economic criteria have vied for primacy in these classifications, with the newer vogue of dependencia adding "core" and "periphery" to still earlier traditional typologies.[4]

To this the author adds a "Sixth World" typology: "the pariah state"[5] (such as Israel or South Africa) subjected to extreme isolation. The point here is that the existence of six or more "worlds" with competing power structures distribution and social and economic demands increases the possibility of conflict.

The second factor, the world economy, continues to reflect a wide gap between North and South, and in a number of situations may displace ideology as a competitive arena. The economics of the industrial powers continue to grow, though shaken by inflationary conditions and energy shortages, while the economies of the Third World remain largely inadequate to meet the needs of those populations and their rising demands and expectations. Overall, global economic growth has been slowing down, while economic interdependence is increasing. Moreover, the international economic system is now largely altered. Witness

> the collapse of the Bretton Woods monetary arrangements that symbolized the global rule of the dollar; the disturbance of the international economy due to the shift in power over oil; the urgent pressure for reordering of North-South economic relations; the systemic economic problems of the Western world; inflation; unemployment; ecological deterioration.[6]

In short, the United States is no longer able to enforce stability and cooperation, nor can it guarantee the Western industrial states' access to vital mineral deposits. Of course, an analysis of the world economy is well beyond the scope of this paper. Suffice it to observe that economic issues are a more volatile source of potential conflict within and among states today than in the previous quarter century, and the prospects are that things will get worse before they get better.

The third environmental factor that conditions the outbreak of low-intensity conflicts is the strategic nuclear balance. The nuclear forces of the United States and the Soviet Union are now roughly equivalent in overall military capability, resulting in a nuclear stalemate between them. This condition of strategic parity has existed for about ten years. Equality of status was ratified in SALT-I, and attempts to constrain subsequent competition in strategic weapons has been a major objective of SALT negotiations ever since. Current technological trends indicate a disturbing drift toward strategic instability as improved weapons accuracies increase the vulnerability of the opponent's strategic forces. Qualitative advantages upon which the United States relied to enhance its deterrent posture are diminishing in the face of significant Soviet weapon modernization. Whether the improved Soviet strategic position makes any difference at the level of low-intensity conflict is a matter for conjecture. One view is that nuclear weapons are so destructive that they are useless for anything other than deterrence; thus minor differences in capability between the two superpowers are of little consequence. In short, the Soviet Union is deterred from undertaking major military adventures, regardless of its marginal advantages (if any).

However, a number of analysts see new danger in Soviet strategic weapons advances in terms of such problems as low-intensity conflict. They see the growth of Soviet strategic power enhancing the capacity to "project" Soviet power "at the margins."[7] For example, W. Scott Thompson argues that

> the strategically superior state has enough power left
> over at the center to provide for the protection (or in-
> timidation) of states at the margin of its previous realm
> of influence. The same is true at the conventional level.[8]

In any case, according to most analysts, the existence of strategic nuclear weapons do not impose significant restraints on small-scale warfare. What many have concluded is that nuclear weapons impose restraints on the major powers, deterring their inclinations to intervene—but thus, perhaps, reducing restraint among the smaller powers. According to this hypothesis, the nuclear balance makes it more dangerous for the superpowers to attempt to regulate conflict among the smaller powers for fear of nuclear confrontation.

On the other hand, perhaps the restraints are not symmetrical. Coincident with the arrival of nuclear parity, the Soviet Union obviously has increased its capability and appears less reluctant to intervene militarily in conflicts beyond its orbit. It has enhanced its power to project military influence through such means as long-range airlift, selective military assistance, aircraft carriers, and the like; and it has used Cubans and others in advisory and fighting roles to carry out its policies in a number of instances. Whether this is due to a shift in power symbolized by Soviet arrival at nuclear parity (contrary to the above hypothesis) is problematical. Achievement of nuclear equality may appear to the Soviets to confirm their sense that the "correlation of forces" is moving in their favor.

From this perspective one should recall that until recently the United States held a position of strategic nuclear superiority in which it was presumed that the Soviet Union could be deterred from acts of aggression in most places in the world and under varying conditions. This was unilateral deterrence. It was widely presumed that nuclear supremacy gave the United States wider latitude for military action at the conventional level and even that it had "escalation dominance" in nuclear warfare. In short, the United States was once more confident that it could deter the Soviets across most of the conflict spectrum, thus permitting U.S. military intervention for a variety of purposes without unduly high risk of direct encounter with the Soviet Union. Therefore, the shift from U.S. superiority to U.S.-Soviet strategic parity has profound implications, particularly for U.S. intervention doctrine, but also possibly for the lessening constraint upon conflicts to which the United States might otherwise have applied its influence.

The fourth significant environmental factor is the "revolution" in conventional weapons technologies, a factor usually discussed under the rubric of "high-intensity" warfare, but equally applicable here. Since the early 1970s we have experienced a remarkable improvement in conventional weapons technology. Lewis S. Sorley describes the nature of the change:

> Genuinely revolutionary developments are taking place in the technology of conventional warfare. In terms of those developments which are known and extant, and thus will make a substantial difference in the next few years, none is more dramatic or challenging than the change in guidance for conventional munitions. The difference can be stated simply: throughout the history of warfare, when a gun, a bomb, an arrow, or any other projectile was aimed at an enemy, it was expected to miss; now it is expected to hit. It is virtually impossible to overstate the impact of that fundamental change. [9]

Weapons of such extraordinary accuracy will not remain exclusively in the hands of the armed forces of advanced industrial nations. Small countries are, for example, already able to obtain highly effective surface-to-air missiles to defend against attacking aircraft. And precision guidance battlefield weapons now being developed and deployed in modern armies will, tomorrow, be available to the armies of lesser powers. Thus, a future war of lowest intensity may still include the use of PGMs and other high technology weapons by either or both sides. The better equipped armed force may find that its opponent will be supplied with offsetting capabilities by a supporting third party, as was the case in Vietnam. In short, the precision guidance weaponry now being developed and deployed among the major powers may quickly see its way, also, to the nonindustrialized world. Thus, although a country like the United States may retain the advantage of more advanced technology in greater abundance, it may pay a heavy price in loss of lives and expensive equipment if it underestimates the potential role of modern weapons in the hands of adversaries in low-intensity conflict.

And this brings us, quite appropriately, to the fifth environmental factor, the growing <u>abundance</u> of conventional weapons technology throughout the world. Expenditures for armaments have grown by leaps and bounds in recent years. Moreover, the recipients of large amounts of armaments are no longer just large states, such as China or India or major bloc allies, but also many small countries. A number of them seek arms for reasons they regard as unrelated to East-West competition. Some are nonindustrialized but rich powers with vast amounts of capital to spend on arms. A significant number of new purchasers also seek arms because they perceive the United States as a less reliable ally than it was formerly. And, in any case, there are many sources of arms, as the major suppliers compete for that lucrative market and as the United States and the Soviet Union attempt to gain or preempt influence as suppliers. In short, we are witnessing a significant proliferation of conventional arms, including the introduction of some high-technology armaments to the developing countries of the world. We are, as Richard Smoke has put it, in an era of "military plenty."[10]

All five of these factors suggest that low-intensity conflict is likely to occur with great frequency, arising out of a variety of issues often not associated with East-West competition, and that such conflicts are unlikely to be dampened by nuclear deterrence. Moreover, the abundance of conventional modern armaments creates more lethal conditions, or makes those who possess more or better arms more inclined to use them against less well-defended adversaries. Finally, the states possessing the stronger arms may thereby be inclined toward interventionist policies within their regions. In any case, in the midst of increasingly unstable political conditions, especially in the Third World, it appears that the Soviet Union is becoming more interventionist at exactly the time when the United States has become more reluctant to exercise its power.

DECLINING U.S. MILITARY POWER

This analysis suggests that the strategic environment contributes conditions that promote conflict. Therefore, in a sense, the Defense Department plan to develop a limited war capability beyond its deployed commitments to NATO and Korea is prudent and realistic. On the other hand, one seeks in vain for a post-Vietnam doctrine that serves as convincing policy guidance explaining the purpose of such an interventionist instrument. After all, the United States cannot reasonably oppose all change, all conflict, all wars: it will be necessary to decide which conflicts and which conditions require intervention. In fact, though, because U.S. military capabilities, especially our limited war capabilities, have eroded, such decisions will require even greater selectivity and restraint. Thus it will also be necessary to decide whether U.S. small war capabilities should be increased to meet such potential threats.

It is remarkable how much U.S. military power and resolve have declined over the past fifteen years. The mid 1960s represent a high point of capability and optimism about international affairs. The United States had experienced a series of successes since World War II, assuming active leadership of a growing coalition of Western democracies and anticommunist governments, restoring shattered economies, containing communism, and promoting political and economic development in the Third World. Soviet expansion had been thwarted in Europe and the Middle East. Aggression had been stalemated in Korea. Europe became a zone of peace through Western strength. And though the Third World remained a zone of ideological, economic, and military competition, the United States, during most of those years, actively pursued policies to keep the peace, contain communism, and promote democracy abroad.

Fifteen years ago the United States seemed at its pinnacle of power. It enjoyed strategic superiority and a broad spectrum of military, economic, and political capabilities to cope with, stabilize, and even modify the international environment. James Reston, reflecting in 1965 on the vast U.S. involvement with affairs abroad (over two million Americans were overseas—servicemen and their families, businessmen, teachers, tourists, Peace Corps volunteers) remarked that

> no nation, not even Britain at the height of her imperial
> power, ever had such a vast company scattered across
> the world. . . . The extraordinary thing one finds in even
> a quick journey round the world is that Americans are
> everywhere, fighting or patrolling, or studying or
> trading. [11]

Numerically and qualitatively superior in strategic weapons, the United States also had more than 750,000 servicemen stationed in 30 countries abroad, with 20,000 or so performing advisory functions in 65 countries. The United States was a member of four regional defense alliances (and participated in a fifth), provided economic and military assistance to almost 100 nations, had mutual defense pacts with 42 governments, and was a member of 53 international organizations. [12] Fifteen years later, although most of this system remained intact, much had changed: strategic supremacy had given way to nuclear parity, with the Soviets posing a strong challenge toward military advantage; NATO remained intact and strong, but the Warsaw forces were even stronger; SEATO and CENTO had come apart; the U.S. military presence in Southeast Asia had ended (except for bases in the Philippines) and ended in failure; economic and military assistance programs were diminished; the number of overseas bases had declined, and access to some regions was no longer secure. The United States had even abrogated its defense treaty with Taiwan. Perhaps more important in terms of the problem addressed here, the optimism of U.S. purpose and capability had declined markedly. [13]

The critical difference over that fifteen year interval was, of course, the failure of U.S. policy in Vietnam and the loss of confidence and consensus about U.S. political objectives in the world. And while the slogan "no more Vietnams" is a manifest policy preference of the American people today, the underlying issue that troubles the American spirit has been with us since the founding of the Republic: to what extent and by what means should the United States be involved in political affairs beyond its borders and beyond this continent? This issue has bitterly divided Americans in periodic "great debate," and continues in times of lesser controversy to excite disagreement. Such cyclical shifts in moods have been described and explained by a number of scholars[14]—a task beyond the scope of this paper—but it is worth noting that insofar as such mood theories apply, we are probably in the trough of a cycle: public confidence in and support for foreign policies in general and military applications in particular are tenuous. [15]

This lack of confidence in the efficacy and to some extent legitimacy of U.S. power abroad is an important constraint on military policy and one of particular sensitivity to the problem of prospective participation by U.S. armed forces in unconventional, guerrilla or other types of limited war. Moreover, the absence of popular support is reinforced by the failure of U.S. foreign policy leadership to generate a convincing post-Vietnam rationale for such military involvement and a manpower mobilization system sufficiently responsive to emergency needs.

This is not a call for a military doctrine of intervention abroad. What I am saying is that prior to the Vietnam experience there was a strong consensus derived from U.S. global strategy that legitimized and rationalized the use of U.S. military power. This consensus no longer exists. At the level of strategic (nuclear) armaments, there once was wide support for the contention that the best way to deter Soviet (hence communist) aggression was to maintain a wide margin of military superiority. Strategic supremacy presumably deterred the Soviets from a broad range of military actions. Beneath the level of strategic weapons a corollary doctrine operated: U.S. armed forces should play an active and sustaining role in building and maintaining an international security system of alliances, bases, military and economic assistance programs, and the like, to extend military deterrence, to build up local defense capabilities, and to promote stability and peace. Deterrence and containment were linked in a global security system that explicitly included the promise to use U.S. armed forces in response to aggression.

All of this derived from assumptions and expectations concerning the nature of the communist threat to the security of the Western alliance. These have changed as the intensity of the Cold War has apparently subsided or shifted and as U.S. confidence in its capabilities and role has ebbed. These changes are reflected in a new strategic doctrine and in the collapse of coherent political-military corollaries to that doctrine. At the strategic level, the doctrine of nuclear supremacy has given way to that of strategic parity—that is, roughly equivalent, secure nuclear forces are now regarded as all that is needed to deter a major Soviet attack on the United States and/or its allies. The shift to policy rationales based on strategic parity reflects not only the fact that the Soviet Union has caught up with the United States in strategic arms, but also an acceptance of and even preference for that fact. Indeed, the official rationale promotes mutual deterrence because it is thought to be the most stable form of strategic relationship.[16] As previously noted, the implications of strategic parity for deterrence and defense below the strategic level are profound and perhaps not yet fully appreciated. At any rate, the doctrine of supremacy represented a posture of power and confidence that is no longer appropriate in terms of the current conditions of the strategic environment.

Below the level of strategic arms competition, the rationale for supporting the international security system of alliances, overseas bases and installations, widely deployed naval power, and programs of economic and military assistance is seriously wanting. Only in Western Europe, where deterrence and defense objectives remain justified by wide recognition of the nature of the Soviet threat, does the rationale of the 1960s retain validity and support. Beyond that region—exactly in those parts of the world where less intense conflicts are most likely to crop up and pose dilemmas for the West— the old Cold War rationale appears insufficient. That is, the corollary that some have labeled "Pax Americana"—which presumes that the United States must contain communism and promote stability and political and economic development in a secure environment, else the nonindustrial world will be subverted or conquered by communist forces—has seriously diminished domestic and international support.

This doctrine was supportable as long as the alternative—the forceful spread of communism that denied free expression, democratic elections and individual liberty seemed starkly unacceptable. But the Cold War appears to have moderated. Furthermore, divisions within the communist camp have undermined the U.S. conception of a Soviet-dominated system of oppression inclined toward aggression (the so-called monolithic threat). And, most important of all, the U.S. experience in Vietnam began to suggest to a growing legion of critics that many anticommunist regimes supported by the United States in the name of freedom were just as oppressive and probably more corrupt than communist alternatives might be. In other words, beneath the umbrella of nuclear deterrence, U.S. military, political, and economic programs abroad have been justified in the past by two interrelated missions—containment of communism and promotion of liberal democratic values—on the grounds that communism threatened to extinguish or preempt the development of such values. But the perception of the nature of that threat began to change at approximately the same time that serious doubts arose concerning the efficacy of U.S. efforts to promote democratic values abroad. Hence the decline of confidence as well as capability in the post-Vietnam years.

At the conventional level of armaments, the decline in capability—after taking into account the special "bulge" of expenditures, troops, and weapons associated with the Vietnam effort—is more significant perhaps than at the strategic level, because the actual combat usability of nuclear weapons is problematical at best (worst?). Surely the advent of nuclear parity serves to magnify the importance of conventional arms capabilities for all nations, from exotic new precision-guidance munitions to traditional armor, artillery, and infantry.

The relative disparity in conventional military capabilities vis-a-vis the Soviet Union has received considerable attention in the last few years, especially in the context of the buildup of Soviet forces in the European theater, where "approximately 150,000 men have been added to the Soviet forces in Eastern Europe during the past decade, including the 70,000 men and five divisions deployed in Czechoslovakia since 1968."[17] Moreover, by all accounts, the modernization process accompanying the buildup over the past ten years and more represents "impressive augmentations and improvements."[18]

But the U.S. response, while appropriate to the European theater context, appears to presume that the modernization and preparation for high-intensity conflict that would probably characterize a NATO-Warsaw Pact conventional war in Europe is also applicable in doctrine and implementation in any small war context. Note, for example, Secretary Brown's claim that improved capability in the European theater will enhance small-war capability as well;

> A possible conflict between NATO and the Warsaw Pact
> is the most demanding contingency for U.S. land forces
> and is the event for which our capabilities are primarily
> designed. These forces must also be versatile enough to

perform successfully in other areas of the world. For-
tunately, most of the programs that improve our posture
relative to a European war also enhance our capabilities
to meet other contingencies.[19]

U.S. "general purpose forces" are, in reality, equipped and deployed
to fight in Europe and in Korea, and virtually nowhere else. Their
orientation, training, and equipment prepare them for all-out, high
technology warfare. These assumptions are now established as the
official tactical doctrine of the United States Army, clearly reflected
in the latest version of the Army field manual on military operations,[20]
in which greatest stress is placed upon the mission of fighting and
winning a high-intensity war on the central plains of Europe. In its
own way this field manual is the ultimate rejection of the Vietnam
experience: the war is virtually ignored with disturbing off-handed-
ness. In short, the Army is developing weapons and doctrines suitable to the European theater and claiming that if it can cope with that
demanding mission it can also cope with any lesser circumstances.
Since the days of John Foster Dulles and Admiral Arthur W. Radford,
policymakers have sought to substitute technology for manpower and
to rely upon "superior" U.S. technology to offset manpower advantages and unconventional techniques of potential adversaries, in most
circumstances without notable success. A strategy to take care of
the cat may not be flexible enough to deal also with the kittens.
    The weakness of the Army's operational assumptions is prob-
ably recognized by the Pentagon leadership, but the alternatives may
be considered too expensive, at least in the short run. Europe has
the highest priority. As a stop-gap measure, some additional low-
intensity capabilities are being generated for other contingencies.
Last year, for example, the Secretary of Defense revealed (and,
significantly, upon visiting Saudi Arabia in the aftermath of the fall
of the Shah of Iran, repeated) that the United States was developing
a "quick strike force" of paratroopers and Marines. The reasons
for this move were explained in Secretary Brown's Annual Report:

> Although we would expect to deploy fewer forces in any
> limited contingency than in a NATO war, such contingen-
> cies differ from mobility forces.* First, we cannot pre-
> dict where such contingencies will occur. Second, we

---

*Mobility forces refer primarily to airlift and sealift forces
and pre-positioned equipment and supply programs.

> are likely to have fewer mobility assets available for a
> limited contingency. . . . There will probably be little or
> no prepositioned equipment and supplies. . . . Finally,
> operational problems will be greater. In particular, we
> may be operating over longer distances with few or no
> intermediate bases. . . . We want to have the capability
> to deploy quickly (and support) at least a small force to
> distant locations without reliance on foreign bases or
> overflight rights.[21]

The most visible and specific program recommendation the Defense
Secretary proposed in connection with limited contingency capabilities
is procurement of the KC-10 Advanced Tanker/Cargo Aircraft (ATCA),
which, while it will enhance NATO war support, is intended "primarily to improve our capabilities for limited contingencies."

> The KC-10 enhances our capability to deploy combat
> forces and tactical fighter squadrons over long distances
> without enroute stops. Aerial refueling of our airlift
> forces by the KC-10 can increase their payload and de-
> crease their dependence on foreign bases. The KC-10
> can also be used to escort a flight of fighter aircraft
> long distances and carry cargo and personnel to support
> these fighters at the same time.[22]

In short, the Secretary's argument is that with sufficient long-range
airlift U.S. armed forces can be transported anywhere. One sus-
pects, however, that transportation will be the least of our problems.

In summary, the strategic environment is conducive to low-
intensity conflicts due to inherently unstable conditions. Compared
to the mid-1960s and in relation to growing Soviet military capabilities, the United States has experienced a significant decline in military capabilities and political confidence. At the strategic level this
is symbolized by the shift from U.S. supremacy to nuclear parity
with the Soviet Union. Below that one sees a decline in forces deployed abroad; a shrinking base structure, manpower, and alliance
system; an eroding consensus with respect to U.S. power and purpose beyond Europe and Northeast Asia; and a questionable reliance
upon weapons modernization and high-intensity tactical doctrine to
cover what the Pentagon calls "limited contingencies."

LIMITED CONTINGENCIES

What are the possibilities for "limited contingencies" in which
U.S. armed forces, such as the "quick strike force," might be

considered? In the absence of doctrinal guidance, we are free to speculate as follows on the basis of general considerations of U.S. interests abroad.

There are at least two types of low-intensity conflicts in which U.S. military power might be actively employed (i.e., beyond demonstration or show-the-flag operations). The first is the "rescue mission." U.S. armed forces may be inserted (1) to rescue beleaguered U.S. (or other) citizens caught up in civil strife and in danger of annihilation; and (2) anti-terrorist operations to rescue hostages, preempt the destruction of facilities, etc. Such rescue missions probably come within the repertoire and capabilities of U.S. armed forces, especially the "quick strike force" concept. Operations of this kind are likely to occur in conditions of extreme emergency, with high public support, and with the expectation that the whole operation will be brief—long enough only to extricate persons from the conflict or to defeat a single terrorist group. In short, this first type of limited contingency, while it may require delicacy of operation and selectivity of intervention, does not pose insurmountable political and military problems for U.S. policymakers.

The second type of limited contingency, on the other hand, does represent much more serious political and military difficulties for the United States. It might best be labeled the "military incursion" mission. In this category a vast number of identifiable situations can be reduced to four possibilities: U.S. armed forces might be sent to (1) seize, protect, or recapture vital assets that are subject to imminent capture or destruction by hostile forces (e.g., oil fields, airfields, secret high-technology military equipment); (2) intervene between combatants in a civil war in an attempt to restore the peace, mediate, etc.; (3) support one side or the other in a civil war or rebellion in an effort to determine the outcome; and (4) turn back an invasion, most likely of an ally. The United States has already experienced each of the four types of limited incursion contingencies, although in almost every case with mixed and controversial results. For example, the recapture of the Mayaguez from Cambodia (1975) serves as an example of the first category (or, perhaps, the failure to rescue the Pueblo—seized by North Korea—serves as an example of the problem). In the second category, the United States alleged that it inserted forces into the Dominican Republic (1965) to stop the fighting (although this claim is at variance with evidence that it in fact took sides to determine the outcome). The third category is most memorably represented by the Vietnam intervention, and the fourth by the Korean War. All these examples illustrate the extraordinary range of problems, the potential complexities, and the difficulty of achieving quick, easy, or even decisive results.[23]

The most easily imagined limited contingency of the future is likely to arise as a result of U.S. security commitments and arrangements, whether formal or informal, with a variety of nations throughout the world. In the past these commitments have been regarded as interconnected, so that a failure to respond in one case was thought to reduce the credibility of U.S. response elsewhere. Moreover, failure to respond to military events associated with communist activities (such as Soviet-inspired Cuban actions in Africa), whether or not involving a challenge to a U.S. ally, has been regarded as eroding the credibility of U.S. commitments.[24] Thus, in the post-Vietnam context, the perceived capacity of the United States to intervene has declined, not only in terms of changed military capabilities, but also and especially in terms of changed intentions and resolve.

At the same time, there is increasing interest and concern expressed about Soviet capabilities and activities. Although the Soviet Union does not have the base structure and deployed armed forces to project its military power beyond its orbit with anything approaching the military capabilities of the United States, it has nevertheless exercised its influence in an opportunistic and often effective manner. Donald S. Zagoria identifies seven instances since 1975 in which pro-Soviet communists have, with Soviet assistance, used armed force to seize power: Vietnam, Laos, Angola, Ethiopia, Afghanistan, South Yemen, and Cambodia. In addition, he identifies two abortive armed coups (Somalia and Sudan) and other activities linked to the Soviet Union.[25] Although Zagoria does not attribute these events to a "master plan," he does suggest that the Soviets have embarked on a "new strategy for expanding their power and influence in the Third World."[26] And while this same author does not think that a U.S. military intervention is necessarily the remedy in these cases, he and others have expressed concern that "the credibility of American power has been shaken by these developments and our apparent lack of response to them."[27]

Whether or not one accepts interpretations of this kind, there is an obvious potential for U.S.-Soviet confrontation in such cases. Indeed, throughout the regions of highest political instability—Mediterranean Europe, the Middle East, and Africa, in particular—the multiplicity of problems and the high probability of conflict highlight not only the limited capabilities of the United States, but also the vacuum of policy guidance. There is a serious danger that U.S. policy may swing wildly, from its currently demoralized, unresponsive, post-Vietnam posture, to an overreactive or impulsively activist posture wherein an Administration seeks to improve America's image and credibility. The basic U.S. problem is (as trite as it sounds) political and not military. U.S. military capabilities are not an appropriate substitute for sound strategy and prudent policy.

Neither high technology nor unique organization will provide the answer to the fundamental issues at stake. U.S. policy needs to comprehend the basic political forces at work in the world, to identify and define an appropriate role for this country compatible with its basic traditions, and to formulate guidelines for military action when such action is deemed necessary.

Yet we have perhaps learned from the Vietnam experience that the programs and preferences of the organizations assigned such "incursion" missions are in a position to determine the methods subsequently employed. The types of low-intensity combat techniques that need to be tailored to the special conditions of civil strife and revolution, for example, are hardly the same as those that might be implemented in a war in Europe. The military is highly resistant to imaginative responses to such special conditions. Hackneyed as this observation is, none of the services appear especially interested in developing specialized approaches to unconventional warfare environments. They appear, instead, to have again riveted their attention on the problems associated with NATO defense. Lawrence E. Grinter, in one of the best brief critiques of the U.S. military experience in Vietnam, argues that a basic inadequacy of the U.S. approach was that it was "conventionally military":

> That tells us something about why U.S./GVN responses to the multi-leveled Communist challenge proved relatively inflexible, and often ineffective. . . .
>
> The Vietnam experience does not foster much confidence . . . that the Army can tailor its capabilities very well to unconventional warfare environments. The Army never wanted a counterinsurgency/stability operations mission in the first place—witness what happened to the Special Forces in the early 1960s.[28]

It is hardly surprising, therefore, that the Secretary of Defense claims that improvements in U.S. forces in NATO will enhance U.S. limited contingency capabilities. The conventional approach continues to dominate military thinking. This tendency is reinforced by the following observations: (1) NATO defense problems appear more urgent, although a war in Europe is not probable; (2) the Vietnam experience was distasteful, so putting it behind is tantamount to putting it out of mind; and (3) the desire to avoid "another Vietnam" can be subtly transformed into a choice not to prepare for another unconventional war. Yet, in terms of probabilities, the United States is much more likely to become involved in a limited conflict outside Europe than inside, and more likely, still, to be faced with a complex, unconventional political and military environment.

Military intervention is usually a technique of last resort. Other instruments of policy are available and quite likely preferable in most circumstances. No matter how well informed, how wise and influential U.S. foreign policy is, this country cannot have absolute control over events. Many things will happen that are opposed to our interests and may have to be accepted for what they are. Not all radical movements or all revolutions constitute a threat to us. Not all gains by the Soviets are necessarily losses on our score sheet. Moreover, neither gains nor setbacks are likely to be permanent.

When U.S. armed force is used for rescue or deeper incursion, the decision had better be based on unambiguous purposes, a reasonable probability of success, a thorough understanding of the local political situation, and a flexible, responsive military apparatus capable of working with indigenous forces. This is a lot to ask of policymakers, intelligence organizations, military planners, and the soldiers themselves. That is why unconventional warfare is so demanding and why U.S. involvement should be carefully tailored to the special circumstances each situation presents.

In short, most contingencies in which a U.S. military incursion might be considered are highly politicized and require extraordinary military restraint and political resourcefulness. Hence the low intensity of the military campaign must be matched by the high intensity of the political effort.

NOTES

1. U.S. Department of Defense, Annual Report, Fiscal Year 1979, p. 9.

2. Klaus Knorr, "On the International Uses of Military Force in the Contemporary World," Orbis 21 (Spring 1977):20-21.

3. Ibid., p. 25.

4. Robert E. Harkavy, "The Pariah State Syndrome," Orbis 21 (Fall 1977):623.

5. Ibid.

6. Richard J. Barnet, "U.S.-Soviet Relations: The Need for a Comprehensive Approach," Foreign Affairs 57 (Spring 1979):791.

7. W. Scott Thompson, "Toward a Communist International System," Orbis 20 (Winter 1977):850.

8. Ibid.

9. Lewis S. Sorely, "Technology, Mobility, and Conventional Warfare," in The Limits of Military Intervention, ed. Ellen P. Stern (Beverly Hills, Ca.: Sage, 1977), p. 189. For a balanced assessment of this "revolution" see Robert Kennedy, "Precision ATGMs and NATO Defense," Orbis 22 (Winter 1979):897-927.

10. Richard Smoke, "Analytic Dimensions of Intervention Decisions," in Stern, op. cit., p. 27.

11. New York Times, December 24, 1965, p. 15.

12. See U.S. Congress, Senate, U.S. Commitments to Foreign Powers, Hearings, Committee on Foreign Relations, 19th Cong., 1st Sess., 1967, especially pp. 52-71; U.S. Congress, Senate, Worldwide Military Commitments, Hearings, Preparedness Investigating Sub-Committee, Committee on Armed Services, 89th Cong., 2nd Sess., 1966, Pt. 1 and 2; Ronald Steel, Pax Americana (New York: Viking Press, 1967), p. 10; and Paul C. Davis and William T. R. Fox, "American Military Representation Abroad," The Representation of the United States Abroad, rev. ed., ed. Vincent M. Barnett, Jr. (New York: Praeger, 1965), pp. 129-83.

13. Two of many reportable measures of change are (1) the decline in armed forces personnel stationed abroad, from the 1964 (pre-Vietnam) peak to the current level of 472,000 personnel (Department of Defense, Annual Report, Fiscal Year 1980, p. 23), and the even more remarkable decline in military personnel assigned to security assistance (MAAG) missions, from over 7,000 in FY 1960, to 2,109 in FY 1974, and 854 in FY 1978 (as reported by David J. Louscher in testimony before the Subcommittee on International Security and Scientific Affairs, Committee on Foreign Affairs, House of Representatives, February 23, 1979).

14. The classic study is Frank Klingberg, "The Historical Alternation of Moods in American Foreign Policy, World Politics 4 (January 1952). See also Michael Roskin, "From Pearl Harbor to Vietnam: Shifting Generational Paradigms," Political Science Quarterly 89 (Fall 1974); and Bruce Russett, "The American's Retreat from World Power," Political Science Quarterly 90 (Spring 1975).

15. For recent data on American attitudes toward military power, see John E. Rielly, ed., American Public Opinion and U.S. Foreign Policy, 1979 (Chicago: The Chicago Council on Foreign Relations, 1979).

16. See Donald Brennan, "Commentary," International Security 3 (Winter 1978/79):193-98, for some telling implications of such assumptions and arguments.

17. Department of Defense, Annual Report, FY 1979, p. 74.

18. Ibid., p. 76.

19. Department of Defense, Annual Report, FY 1980, p. 142.

20. Department of the Army, Field Manual 100-5, Operations.

21. Department of Defense, Annual Report, FY 1980, p. 202.

22. Ibid., p. 207.

23. Consult Herbert K. Tillema, Appeal to Force: American Intervention in the Era of Containment (New York: Thomas Y. Cowell, 1973), for an informative analysis of interventions since 1945, including interesting data and discussion of situations where the U.S. did not intervene.

24. For a systematic argument, see James L. Payne, The American Threat (Chicago: Markham, 1970).

25. Donald S. Zagoria, Foreign Affairs 57 (Spring 1979): 233-54.

26. Ibid., p. 737.

27. Ibid., p. 741.

28. Lawrence E. Grinter, "Nation Building, Counterinsurgency and Military Intervention," in Stern, op, cit., p. 241 and 250.

3

THE UNITED STATES:
MILITARY AND
POLITICAL PERSPECTIVES
Lawrence Grinter

There is very little long-range analysis in the United States
government about the nature of the future international system, the
kinds of threat environments that are likely to develop, or what U.S.
military strategy and force structure should be. Without attention to
these long-range trends (10- to 30-year projections), future U.S.
strategy and force procurement programs risk irrelevance. This
chapter does not develop long-range projections or scenarios of global
or regional conflict situations. It does suggest likely kinds of global
change and related threat environments in the foreseeable future and
their consequences for strategy and force structure.

The chapter first examines the changing global threat environment from the perspective of the general diffusion of power and the
various interpretations of what it means, or does not mean, for U.S.
national security. U.S. general purpose forces and mobility/inter-
vention capabilities are analyzed for their relevance to the changing
threat environment. The chapter concludes by drawing the implications for U.S. security policy of the new threats when compared to
threat and readiness assumptions in the Carter Administration's current defense policies, especially those regarding nonnuclear conflict.

In the 1890s, when Prime Minister Benjamin Disraeli commented on the relative success of nearly a century of British balance
of power policy, he said that Great Britain had no permanent allies,
only permanent interests. Britain's interest was to prevent war on
the European continent by preserving stability and precluding power
shifts, and her policy was always to side with the weaker party. The
task for U.S. policy over the next fifty years is more complex than
was Britain's, because America's sphere of influence is not just
Europe but the entire world, and because certain critical power shifts
cannot be controlled by the United States or other major powers,

including the Soviet Union, China, Japan, and Western Europe. The fundamental task for U.S. policy is to exercise its influence in order to preserve stability, deflect or constrain power shifts inimical to U.S. interests, and encourage democratic/capitalistic systems of government that improve human welfare. Such a policy requires courage and sophistication. And unless U.S. military forces and strategy serve that policy, the United States is in trouble.

The second thesis is that current U.S. defense policy and general purpose force structure are increasingly irrelevant to the global power shift and the new threat environments, because they concentrate almost exclusively on NATO. We need to refocus our general purpose forces toward capabilities that can better influence political-military outcomes in resource-rich and strategically located Third World areas. In essence this means reallocating resources from the short, intensive European war scenario to power projection (mainly naval and air), while increasing our security assistance to critical Third World countries.

THE CHANGING THREAT ENVIRONMENT

The Diffusion of Power

In 1945 the U.S. economy accounted for almost 45 percent of world GNP, while Soviet GNP was one-seventh that of the United States—less than 7 percent of the world GNP. By the mid-1970s the U.S. snare of world GNP was down to about 24 percent, and the Soviet Union's had grown to approximately 15 percent. Japan and Western Europe were rebuilt after World War II with the help of U.S. money, and by the mid-1960s were challenging the United States in trade and investment. By 1965 there were some $80 billion in foreign-held exchange reserves floating around European financial centers—the Eurodollar market—essentially independent of U.S. control. In 1971 the global financial system unraveled when the United States tried to pull money back from Europe, and West Germany raised its interest rates. Two years later OPEC's oil embargo and quadrupling of prices staggered the world with a massive inflationary whiplash. Western (particularly U.S.) financial predominance eroded.

In military affairs, the world has remained essentially bipolar at the strategic nuclear level, although the United States, starting from a monopoly of atomic and hydrogen weapons after World War II, has seen its lead challenged and then overtaken by the Soviet Union in several areas of strategic power. However, nuclear bipolarity is complicated by Chinese, British, French, and Indian nuclear weapons inventories, and by the threat of many other states gaining the bomb. In conventional armaments, a vast array of weaponry has spread across the world to small and medium powers and into the hands of private groups. Conventional arms control negotiations are underway between the United States and the Soviet Union, but the likelihood of their seriously controlling the global weapons flow is meager.

Political power, traditionally a product of arms, money, and industrial development, has become less certain and is fluctuating rapidly from one year to the next. Separatist movements, reflecting breakdowns of central control, are prevalent. Media attention fastens on change rather than stability. Global hierarchy is eroding: small states that were previously dependent now act autonomously, and divisive tendencies are prevalent in both Western and communist alliances. The communist world has experienced the East Berlin riots of 1953, the Hungarian uprising in 1956, China's defection from Soviet orthodoxy in the late 1950s, and the Warsaw Pact invasion of Czechoslovakia in 1968. On the Western side, there was lukewarm support for U.S. policies in Vietnam, difficulties in NATO over defense payments and weapons standardization, trade and monetary disagreements among allies, the shock of the Nixon opening to China, the reluctance of NATO to allow U.S. use of European bases during the 1973 Arab-Israeli war, and tension with Latin American friends over the Panama Canal.[1]

These developments have produced a highly complex international system in which countries align and realign around shifting geopolitical and functional issues. The forecast is for more pluralistic, selfish, unilateral behavior by nation-states. Regional and local wars fueled by spreading arms are prevalent. New combinations of proxy war and guerrilla war, using precision-guided weapons, are likely. Nuclear proliferation (and the possibility of nuclear theft) is a concern.

As a result both the United States and the Soviet Union operate in a more fluid and complicated world than during the Cold War era. Global structure has fractured and diffused, changing the locations and types of conflict environments and threats, as well as the reliability of allies.[2] Powerful new trends have begun to overlay traditional international security calculations. They include

1. The constraints that the diffusion of power places on both superpowers and their alliances.
2. The effects of scarce resources and interdependence on both the West and the East.
3. The impact on national policy of the new maritime regime (exclusive economic zones, offshore and seabed resources).
4. The Soviet Union's uneven but determined emergence as a global power.

These new realities have complicated policy for the United States. The shifting interplay of economic, political, and military factors and the fluid nature of state commitments are critical. The potential for conflict involving military forces of nonindustrial states has increased.[3]

U.S. security policy must adjust to and try to give positive direction to these new global realities. The task is both conceptual and managerial, and weakness in one effort will produce sterility in the other. East-West competition, while still critical to U.S. interests, is more diffused and complex than it used to be. Our first requirement, then, is to understand the enormous changes under way in the global distribution of power. The second is to assess the likely threat environments foreseeable over the next 20 to 50 years. Third, we must reexamine our current and projected military forces—especially our general purpose forces and intervention capabilities—as instruments for projecting influence and managing these new global realities.

Lack of Consensus in the United States

Obstacles: There are powerful impediments to undertaking such a reassessment. Political, perceptual, and bureaucratic constraints, fragmentation of public positions, and the reluctance to undertake serious long-range planning and forecasting have combined to prohibit consensus on the shape of the international system, the likely threat environments, and the aims of U.S. military strategy. There is little consensus in the country at large and there are clear disagreements within the Carter Administration. On the Soviet issue, for example, witness the differences between the Administration's Secretary of State and the President's Assitant for National Security Affairs, or between the National Security Assistant at the Defense Department and the Ambassador to the United Nations on the Soviet/Cuban role in Africa. Debates over Soviet objectives on SALT and related arms control issues, and different levels of concern about the Soviet military build-up among Joint Chiefs of Staff, the Office of the Secretary of Defense, the Department of State, and Arms Control and Disarmament Agency are other examples. Some, probably most, of these disagreements are inevitable in the bureaucratic jungle of Washington. However, no agreed upon conceptual scheme for dealing with the changing threat environment has come to the fore. On the matter of Soviet intentions, opinion divides sharply in the United States on the degree to which the Soviets remain a central threat to the United States, and on how far the world has moved from an East-West to a North-South structure. Figure 3.1 depicts positions on a quadrant constructed from two axes: degree of perceived Soviet threat is vertical; assumptions about Global structure are horizontal. Each axis is a continuum.

FIGURE 3.1

Assumptions about Global Structure

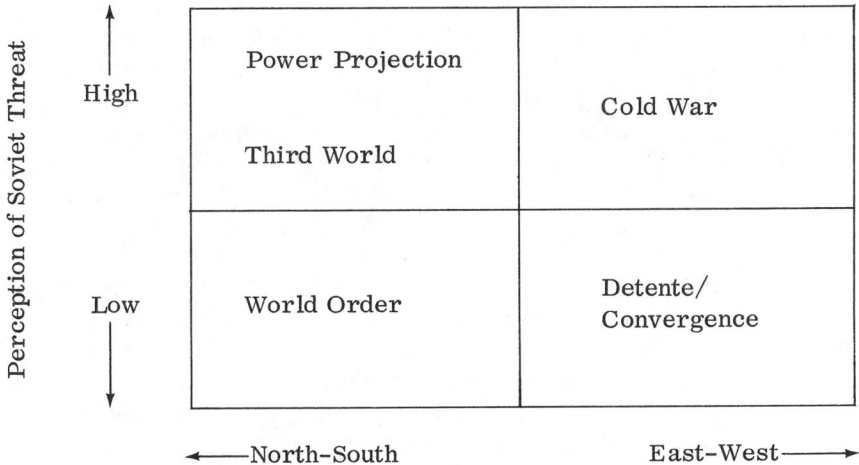

People who believe that the Soviet Union is a strong threat to U.S. security, and who also assume that global power remains structured on an East-West, bipolar basis are positioned in the top right quadrant. These are the strong defense advocates. We have labeled this quadrant "Cold War." It is a sine qua non that all senior U.S. military officers fall into this position, as do interest groups with strong defense affiliation, such as the Committee on the Present Danger.

The bottom left quadrant represents the opposite position from the Cold Warriors. Those who doubt or downplay the salience of the Soviet threat and who emphasize the diffusion of power away from bipolarity to a multipolar and North-South basis are labeled "World Order" proponents. Academics like Stanley Hoffman of Harvard, Robert Keohane of Stanford, and Joseph Nye, currently of State, articulate this school's position.[4] World Order proponents within the Carter Administration naturally tend to deal with international economics, trade matters, loan and assistance issues, and United Nations policy. C. Fred Bergsten, Assistant Secretary of the Treasury for International Affairs, has been one of the most articulate spokesman in this field.[5]

The bottom right quadrant is called "Detente/Convergence." This school believes that the Soviet challenge is substantially less threatening than the Cold Warriors suppose. They may also feel the United States has no choice but to get along with the Soviets. Detente has been the official policy of the last three U.S. Administrations, but interpretations differ over what detente really means. Convergence theorists take detente assumptions even further: they believe that the United States and the Soviet Union are becoming similar, that both are conservative, status quo, nonrevolutionary societies whose need to cooperate in an increasingly unmanageable world clearly outweighs the desirability of conflict.[6]

The top left quadrant represents those people who see U.S.-Soviet competition as continuing and critical, but increasingly blended into North-South issues because of the diffusion of power. For these people, the resource-rich developing areas are the major arena for the struggle between communism and capitalism. Superpower projection of influence into Third World situations becomes the new and single most important factor in international relations.[7]

Though it ignores many of the subtleties, this shorthand method categorizes the vast spectrum of opinion in the country and in government on current security issues. Trying to pull it together into a cohesive conceptual basis for threat analysis has proved beyond the means of recent U.S. governments. However, if the preceding analysis on the diffusion of power is correct, and if the emergence of Soviet power on a global scale is not accidental but represents a deliberately implemented forward strategy, then the Power Projection concept is the direction toward which influential U.S. thinking and government response must shift in the short to medium term. And that kind of conceptual reorientation will have serious implications for U.S. military strategy and force posturing.

The Carter Administration's View: The Carter Administration's response to global complexity and the new threat environment is not easily categorized. The Administration calls it a "policy of constructive global engagement." American national security," in the Administration's view, "means the effective and morally responsible management of change." U.S. national security "depends on giving positive direction to this turbulent process of worldwide political awakening and worldwide redistribution of power." The Administration calls for a "renovation of the international system" in which the United States can play "a genuinely creative role in shaping a world community no longer built on the domination of any sector or culture—a community which respects global diversity as the basis for a cooperative and increasingly just world order."[8]

Within this context the Administration posits seven goals for U.S. foreign policy:

1. to enhance U.S. military security;
2. to reinforce ties with key allies and other states to promote a cooperative world system;

3. to respond in a positive way to economic and moral challenges of the North-South relationship;
4. to improve East-West relations;
5. to help resolve the more threatening regional conflicts and tensions;
6. to cope with emerging global issues such as nuclear proliferation and conventional arms dissemination;
7. to reassert traditional American values—especially human rights.[9]

The accent, then, is on managing change and coping with or adjusting to trends, many, perhaps most, of which are assumed to be beyond U.S. control. This is a fundamental change from the confident policies of the Kennedy, Johnson, or Nixon Administrations with their assertive efforts to shape international conditions. Intractable global complexity and a modest U.S. role in world affairs are the working assumptions of the Carter Administration's foreign policy. It is a foreign policy philosophy that borrows elements from each of the quadrants in Figure 2.1, but that tends to alternate back and forth between the World Order and Cold War concepts. The Brzezinski statement is philosophically lodged within the World Order block, but Brzezinski himself is an acknowledged hardliner on Soviet activities. There are of course times when any Administration must alter its approach, depending on the issue. The question is whether the foreign policy articulated above is in practice rooted in a conceptual base, or dictated by expediency; and whether it is a realistic response to the changing security conditions and threats of the current and foreseeable future.

Two documents in particular show how the administration sought to translate its foreign policy goals into military strategy: Presidential Review Memorandum (PRM) 10 and Presidential Directive (PD) 18. PRM 10, "Comprehensive Net Assessment and Military Force Posture Review," was undertaken in the first six months of the Administration. A compilation of bureaucratic views of U.S. national security objectives, strategies, and force structure, rather than a long-range analysis of likely threat trends, PRM 10 was, in the words of the Secretary of Defense "one of those essential, occasional reviews."

> One part of it, the comprehensive net assessment, looked at the world in general, and the evolving relationship between the United States and the Soviet Union in particular. The second part assessed the capabilities of the current US defense posture under various assumptions and constructed a range of defense postures for the United States, along with rough estimates of their costs and what they could accomplish.[10]

One of the more comprehensive media accounts of the contents of PRM 10 appeared in The New York Times (January 6, 1978). The article, based on a copy of the top secret study, obtained by the Times, was captioned: "US Doubts Ability to Defend Europe in Conventional War/Confident of Atomic Parity/Study Reported Linked to Carter's Stress on Building up Regular Units, Not Strategic Arsenal."[11] It reported that PRM 10 made these points:

> At the strategic level neither side could win a major nuclear war, a preemptive strike against an opponent's ICBM forces would leave the attacker "significantly worse off" in terms of surviving numbers of missiles and warheads, American nuclear missile submarines have a clear advantage over the Soviets, and the US must retain the ability to inflict "unacceptable damage" on the USSR if it launches a first strike.
>
> The analysis of European security apparently focuses on the insufficiency of conventional forces for defending NATO Europe against a concerted Warsaw Pact attack. In a 30-day conflict the Warsaw Pact could muster 86 to 92 divisions, in a longer war, over 130 divisions. The report also mentioned NATO's critically low ammunitions and parts inventories, the allied need to threaten escalation to tactical nuclear weapons despite the risks of Soviet reprisals, and lack of enthusiasm by NATO allies for increased defense spending.
>
> On the Middle East and Africa, the study reportedly compared US and Soviet intervention capabilities and concluded that the US had several advantages—a highly effective combat ally in Israel, the ability to project and sustain forces more quickly than the Soviets into the Middle East as well as into the interior of Africa. Less optimism was the case in assessing the results of a Soviet surprise attack on the Sixth Fleet in the Mediterranean.
>
> The Administration's outlook for East Asia was reported to be gloomy—the value of American access to bases in Japan and Korea was "offset by the difficulty of establishing effective antiair and antisubmarine barriers in the face of internal Soviet opposition." In Korea PRM 10 reportedly conceded that North Korea outguns South Korea "in all categories," but did not question the President's policy of withdrawing ground forces. The outcome of a new Korean war, assuming that the US troop withdrawal is completed, would depend on the ability of the

United States to reinsert major forces—five carrier task
forces, two marine amphibious forces, one army division
and up to 24 fighter squadrons to a Korean conflict.[12]

In summary, the PRM 10 study, a collection of government
inputs, fell into place with the overall philosophy of the Administration when it argued that "essential equivalence" maintained U.S.
ability to inflict "unacceptable damage" on the Soviets after they had
struck first. But on two other critical issues the study acknowledged
the insufficiency of NATO conventional forces to beat back a communist invasion of Central Europe without relying on nuclear weapons,
and acknowledged that North Korea's advantages, as U.S. ground
troops were withdrawn, would grow to the point where only a massive U.S. air, sea, and ground reinsertion could turn the tide in
event of war.

Secretary of Defense Brown was quick to point out that, in
contrast to much of the press's speculation, PRM 10 was a study, not
policy—a discussion of alternatives and options, not a decision document. The decisions that reflected the actual policy choices are
found in Presidential Decision (PD) 18, August 24, "US National
Strategy" (August 24, 1977). The acknowledged thrust of PD-18 is
revealed in the same September 15, 1977 speech by the Secretary of
Defense. The Secretary's public summary of the President's decision was as follows:

Global Trends

U.S.-Soviet relations would be marked by both competition and cooperation. The U.S. has enormous advantage
in nonmilitary aspects of the competition (i.e., industrial, agricultural, and technical capabilities). The USSR
is suffering from major internal problems. Many international trends and issues develop independently of East-
West rivalry or control. The USSR nonetheless remains
the United States' "principal national security problem—
not the only one, but the biggest one."

The Strategic Balance

The Administration pledged itself to maintain "a strategic nuclear equilibrium" with the Soviets. Acknowledging
the Soviet weapons momentum, the Secretary said that
the United States had to be able to inflict unacceptable
second strike damage on the Soviets, implement a range
of selective options, maintain command and control, hold

a secure force in reserve, and permit adequate control and surveillance of U.S. airspace.

General Purpose Forces

The Secretary mentioned the need for "tactical balances" region by region and the simultaneous need to be ready to respond to minor as well as major contingencies. But he put his emphasis on improving NATO's ability to fight and sustain defense. For non-NATO contingencies he cited the need for a limited number of "relatively light" land combat forces (three Marine divisions and one Army division), and strategic mobility forces with a range and payload to minimize U.S. dependence on overseas staging and logistical support.

There seems to be an ambivalence in the Administration about whether the non-NATO contingencies are really critical enough to warrant significant reallocations of monies from general purpose forces. The Secretary stated in his FY 1980 Report that "Many of the most serious international crises of the post-war era have arisen . . . from regional threats and instabilities."

Because the United States cannot escape worldwide involvement, our security and our defense needs are a function of these developments and of the success of our foreign policy in dealing with them.[13]

The Secretary's Report mentioned the recent turmoil in Iran, North Korea's expanding military capabilities, the spread of Sino-Soviet-Indochinese violence, instability in the Mideast and South Asia, and 37,000 Cuban troops in Africa. Analysis of these events and programs at the conventional and non-NATO level took up 23 pages, or only about 7 percent, of the 354-page document.[14]

Thus, despite comments by Ford and Carter Administration spokesmen that the United States must be prepared for a wide range of conflict in a variety of environments, priority and flexibility in U.S. force structuring seem to lie almost exclusively at the upper levels of the conflict spectrum.[15] The increasing mechanization of U.S. Army divisions and the minimal attention given to doctrine and training for conflicts outside Europe give the impression that the Government does not adequately appreciate how serious these non-NATO threats can be to U.S. security. A potentially dangerous situation may now exist as a gap widens between our NATO-oriented force posture, ongoing Soviet and Soviet-proxy involvement in Third World conflicts, and the probability that these conflicts will harm U.S. interests.

DOD spokesmen have met this kind of criticism with the rejoinder that our general purpose ground and air forces, while structured to fight primarily in Western Europe, are relevant for use elsewhere, especially the developing world:

> Fortunately, most of the programs that improve our
> (force) posture relative to a European war also enhance
> our capabilities to meet other contingencies.[16]

Considering the terrain, climate, society, and infrastructure in various non-NATO areas, one may be skeptical about this assertion, especially in the light of recent U.S. experience. Indeed, outside Europe and North America, only in Korea and some areas of the Middle East is the heavy NATO-style force structure of the U.S. Army and Air Force appropriate. The effectiveness of U.S. operations in Vietnam was clearly hampered by their mechanized, conventional nature and the huge logistical and administrative apparatus that Army and Air Force units required. All this contrasted with the Vietnamese communists, whose flexibility and adaptability were legendary.[17]

What we have been saying, then, is that developing a U.S. military strategy relevant to the changing international distribution of power and new threat environments depends on accurately and objectively assessing the future threat environments, and adapting our force structure accordingly. It will not be easy. Army Secretary Bo Callaway's testimony before the Senate Armed Services Committee in 1975 was revealing:

> It is difficult to prove with mathematical precision, the
> absolute need for any specific number of divisions. There
> are too many uncertainties—uncertainties in enemy
> strengths and weaknesses, in capabilities of allies, in
> our own ability to see into the future.[18]

It is precisely those uncertainties that must be analyzed and clarified if the United States is going to have a relevant force structure in the 1990s and into the twenty-first century.

GENERAL PURPOSE FORCES: MISSIONS, CAPABILITIES, AND ASSUMPTIONS

Force Structure

All forces not specifically tasked for a nuclear war come under the definition of General Purpose Forces. These include ground, naval, and tactical air forces. General Purpose Forces consume a majority of the annual defense budget—about 67 percent—as contrasted with strategic forces which take about 8 percent of the DOD budget."[19]

The extraordinary U.S. emphasis on preparing for a NATO contingency to the significant exclusion of other regional conflicts is particularly evident in the United States Army. U.S. Air Force tactical capabilities are also heavily oriented toward NATO. The Navy and the Marines are exceptions: their missions and force postures are more balanced, although the size of the Navy has dramatically decreased in the last ten years, especially in power projection and intervention capabilities.

U.S. Ground Forces: In 1979 the United States Army had 16 active divisions on duty of which four were armored, six were mechanized infantry, four others were regular infantry, one was airborne, and the other was air assault. In addition the Army had nine major nondivisional units including four infantry brigades, one armored brigade, three armored cavalry regiments, and one cavalry brigade. The Marine Corps had three divisions, essentially infantry, which also could be employed as elements of Marine Amphibious Forces. This gave the United States a total of 19 active ground divisions. Four of them were stationed in Europe, along with other special regiments and brigades. Two divisions were deployed in Asia or the Pacific—the 2nd Infantry Division in South Korea, understrength and being redeployed to the United States, and the 3rd Marine Division on the Japanese Island of Okinawa. All the other forces were stationed in the continental United States (CONUS), Hawaii, Alaska, or the Panama Canal Zone.[20] Most of the CONUS-based divisions were trained and equipped for the European theater. The heavy concentration on Europe, with backup reserve forces in CONUS also dedicated to a European conflict, has been argued by the Secretary of Defense this way: "No other contingency places so great a demand on land forces, and no other, short of an attack on the U.S., is so critical to the vital interests of the United States."[21]

Thus a Warsaw Pact invasion of Western Europe is the event for which U.S. ground force capabilities are primarily designed. In detailing the status of U.S. combat capabilities for Europe, the Secretary spoke to a number of deficiencies and recommended the following improvements:

1. Enhancing initial combat capability against a Pact threat by upgrading howitzer, helicopter, and tank firepower, increasing and re-positioning U.S. maneuver batallions, and introducing the new XM-1 main battle tank and other equipment.
2. Improving overall unit readiness.
3. Improving air defense capabilities with improved high to medium altitude missiles, and short-range missiles.
4. Improving combat longevity by building up pre-positioned war reserve stocks of end items, spare and repair parts, and fuel, and increasing these items standardization and interoperability with NATO allies.
5. Improving electronic warfare capabilities, and command, control, and communications.
6. Enhancing chemical warfare capabilities and protection against nuclear, biological, or chemical warfare.

In summary, the Army's principal modernization emphases are geared to a fight in Europe, with some transferability to Korea or possibly the Sinai Desert. But these developments are of highly questionable relevance to the other areas of the Middle East, Africa, East Asia, or Latin America.

In 1972 President Nixon and the Congress established a 13-division structure with a manpower ceiling at just under 800,000. In 1975 then Secretary of Defense James Schlesinger presented a reorganization plan to Congress for an Army of 16 active combat divisions squeezed out of a manpower ceiling of 793,000.[22] By 1979 U.S. active Army forces were down to 772,000, but the 16 divisions were retained. The Carter Administration has continued the Schlesinger/Ford expansion plan: the three additional divisions are being filled out. In 1975, estimates of the five-year cost for procurement and operational maintenance of the three new divisions was approximately $1.9 billion. This figure escalated to $3.5 billion by the end of 1977.[23] By mid-1979, it may be $4 billion.

These changes in force structure and program trends are also reflected in Army doctrine. Between 1974 and 1976 the Army revised its basic operational doctrine. Field Manual 100-5, "Operations" (July 1, 1976), was introduced as the "foundation for what is taught in our service schools and the guide for training and combat developments through the Army."[24] FM 100-5 concentrates almost exclusively on fighting a Soviet/Warsaw Pact conventional invasion of Western Europe. It is a detailed, tightly argued, performance guide for operational commanders.

Placing its emphasis on Europe, the Army draws on examples from the October 1973 Middle East war, with its many lessons (and nonlessons) about offensive and defensive technology, range and precision of new weapons, and coordinated air-ground tactics. Mobility, accuracy, firepower, and defensive advantages will have to offset a Warsaw Pact invasion.[25] The Vietnam War and the Army's experience there are not mentioned in FM 100-5.

What remains of Army thinking on unconventional operations and counter-guerrilla warfare (called "Internal Defense and Development") has to be pieced together from dated manuals and statements. "The primary purpose of U.S. Army assistance (in internal defense and development activities)," states FM 100-20 (November 1974), is "to increase the capabilities and efficiency of host country armed forces."[26] Furthermore:

> Advice may be the least desired assistance offered (by
> US advisors) and only tolerated to obtain material and
> training assistance. Even when accepted, host country . . .
> leaders may not immediately act upon advice given by their
> US advisors.[27]

That the Army was truncating its intervention capabilities in non-NATO areas showed, ironically, that it had learned what to expect from these operations.

The decline of interest in non-NATO conflict situations has been evident in the armed forces school systems. By 1975 the senior service colleges—the National War College; the Industrial College of the Armed Forces; the Army, Navy, and Air War College; and the State Department's Senior Service Seminar—had only a handful of course offerings left on the developing areas and conflict there. Yet these service colleges graduate nearly 950 military and civilian officers each year into jobs that elevate some of them into senior ranks of government.

The decline has been most pronounced in the middle-level service schools where field grade officers are trained. For example, when broad comparisons are made of Army school instruction, the trend away from attention to non-NATO regional threats and conflict situations is striking. As Figure 3.2 indicates, all instruction in internal defense and development (IDAD) has been dropped from the Army Officer basic course at the Infantry School, the Armor School, and the Field Artillery School. Meager instruction time—up to 4 percent—continues at the Intelligence School and in the Infantry School's advanced officer course. These curricula changes have occurred despite belief among student officers that violence in the developing areas, not Europe, is the most likely to occur, and that it is also the kind the United States is going to have to address.[28]

The thrust of the Carter Administration ground force policies, therefore, has been to accelerate preparation for a short, intensive,

FIGURE 3.2

Decline in Low-Intensity Conflict Instruction in Army School Systems

The table reflects in broad terms comparisons of selected school courses time devoted to internal conflict and is offered in support of my contention that the trend is away from studying low-intensity conflict.

US ARMY ARMOR SCHOOL

Total academic hours   1969—1186   Hours devoted to IDAD—5.4
Officer Advanced Course   1975— 986   Hours devoted to IDAD—0
    Percent of total hours reduction 16.8   Percent of IDAD reduction 100

Total academic hours   1971— 409   Hours devoted to IDAD—20
Officer Basic Course   1975— 552   Hours devoted to IDAD—0

US ARMY INFANTRY SCHOOL

Total academic hours   1972—1072   Hours devoted to IDAD—34
Officer Advanced Course   1976— 845   Hours devoted to IDAD—34

NOTE: Of the 34 hours, 7 are devoted to planning a battalion IDAD (Internal Defense and Development) operation and 12 to execution of a battalion strike mission in an IDAD environment. These instructional elements are mechanical in nature offering minimal understanding of the nonmilitary aspects.

Officer Basic Course   1972— 401   Hours devoted to IDAD—
                                    elective only
                              1976— 557   Hours devoted to IDAD—none

US ARMY FIELD ARTILLERY SCHOOL

Total Academic Course   1974—1347   Hours devoted to IDAD—5.1
Officer Advanced Course   1975— 893   Hours devoted to IDAD—0
    Percent of total hours reduction 33.7   Percent of IDAD reduction 100
Officer Basic Course   1972— 532   Hours devoted to IDAD—2
                              1975— 350   Hours devoted to IDAD—0

US ARMY INTELLIGENCE SCHOOL

Total Academic Hours   1974—1052   Hours devoted to IDAD—22
Officer Advanced Course   1975— 829   Hours devoted to IDAD—31
    Percent of total hours decrease 21.2   Percent of IDAD increase 40.9
Officer Basic Course   1972— 338   Hours devoted to IDAD—2
                              1975— 361   Hours devoted to IDAD—4

NOTE: As in the case of the infantry advanced course, significant portions of IDAD instruction are functional/technical (for example, the US Army Security Agency support in IDAD operations), instruction which does not increase basic understanding of IDAD operations.

Source: LTC Donald B. Voight, USA, Military Review, May 1977, p. 30.

mechanized war in Central Europe, largely to the exclusion of other regions and other contingencies. The Ford Administration, while placing emphasis on NATO and modernization of ground forces following the Vietnam years, sought to strengthen U.S. armed forces across the board. The Carter Administration is attempting to do this within a level budget by taking funds from Navy shipbuilding, tactical air force programs, and strategic weapons systems.[29] It has been estimated that perhaps 47 percent of the entire U.S. defense budget (80 percent of our land mobility and tactical air forces and 50 percent of our naval force costs) is NATO-related.[30]

By the early 1980s the Army's mechanization efforts could result in twelve "heavy" divisions (eight mechanized and four armored) and four "light" divisions (two infantry, one air assault, and one airborne). This contrasts with the pre-Vietnam force of 16 divisions with equal numbers of heavy and light divisions.[31]

U.S. Air Forces: The United States Air Force has 26 active and 10-1/2 reserve fighter attack wings. These wings usually consist of 72 aircraft. Fighter/attack squadrons, under these wings, are generally equipped with 18 or 24 aircraft. Supporting aircraft are organized into squadrons of from 12 to 24 aircraft. Table 3.1 shows current U.S. tactical airforce structure.[32] Like the Army, the Air Force deploys the majority of its overseas forces in Europe—eight fighter/attack wings compared to three in the Pacific. These

TABLE 3.1

Active U.S. Air Force Structure

Fighter/Attack Wings	End-FY 1979	End-FY 1980
Total	26	26
A-7	1	1
A-10	2	2
F-4	14	13
F-15	5	5
F-16	--	1
F-111	4	4

Source: Department of Defense, Annual Report FY 1980 (Washington, D.C.: 25 January 1979), p. 185.

11 fighter/attack wings represent 42 percent of the USAF total. The other 15 wings are stationed in the United States.

Naval air and Marine Corps air assets add approximately 696 and 333 fighter or attack aircraft respectively, augmenting by about 1029 the Air Forces' 3744 fighter/attack aircraft expected by the end of FY 1981.[33] U.S. Air Force Reserve and Air National Guard aircraft are in a high state of readiness. They are the most modernized and best-trained reserve force in the armed services. Many air guard and air reserve units participated in the Vietnam War, and have deployed to Europe or the Pacific on training missions. Figures 3.3 and 3.4 compare active and reserve Air Force and Navy/Marine aircraft, both current and projected.

The major program initiatives under way in aircraft procurement are:

1. Expansion of the active Air Force to 26 fully-equipped fighter/attack wings.
2. Modernization of U.S. tactical aircraft through additions of A-10 and F-16 aircraft.
3. Modernization of active and reserve Navy and Marine tactical aviation with additions of the F/A-18 aircraft.
4. Maintenance of high readiness and continuance of intensive training programs like the Red Flag operation in Nevada.
5. Increase in electronic warfare capabilities to counter potential adversary capabilities.
6. Improvement of target acquisition, surveillance, and reconnaissance capabilities.

Like the Army's modernization programs, all these air efforts are designed to increase the ability of tactical air forces to combat the Warsaw Pact's major advantages—at least 2500 aircraft—in a European scenario. In addition, three critical aircraft are being developed: the high-performance and expensive F-15, the less sophisticated F-16, and the A-10 close support attack aircraft.

The Air Force plans to buy about 750 F-15 aircraft, 1390 F-16s, and about 735 A-10s; and each program has experienced serious cost inflation. Moreover, the Carter Administration has reduced the projected Air Force budget for FY 1979-83 by about $6 billion in general purpose forces. Thus, because of higher costs and reduced budgets, the Air Force has slowed down its introduction of F-15s and A-10s.[34]

U.S. Naval Forces: Recent Chiefs of Naval Operations (CNOs) have stated that the Navy's primary missions are to protect critical U.S./Allied sea lines of communication (sea control) and to maintain U.S. maritime superiority (power projection). Within those general guidelines there are strong debates about Navy priorities. Navy

FIGURE 3.3

U.S. Air Force Active Fighter/Attack Aircraft

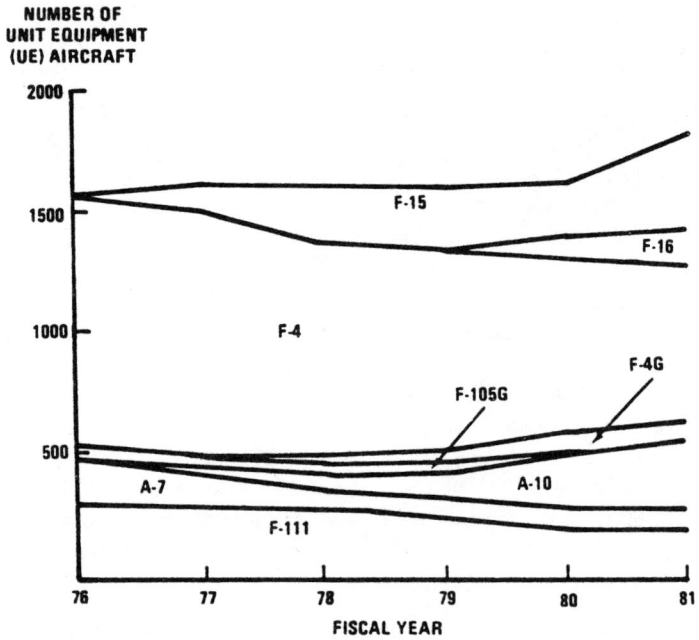

U.S. Air Force Reserve and Air National Guard Aircraft

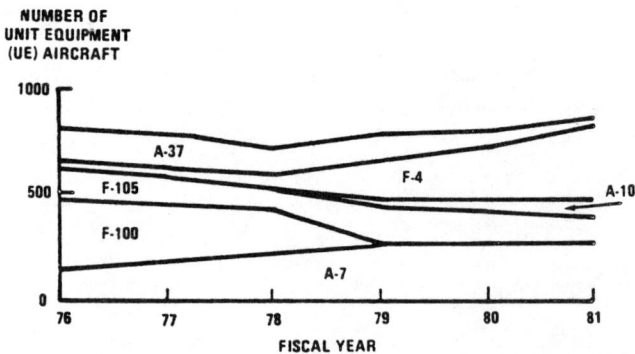

Source: Secretary of Defense, Department of Defense, Annual Report, Fiscal Year 1980 (Washington, D.C.: 25 January 1979), p. 185.

FIGURE 3.4

Department of the Navy Active Fighter/Attack Aircraft

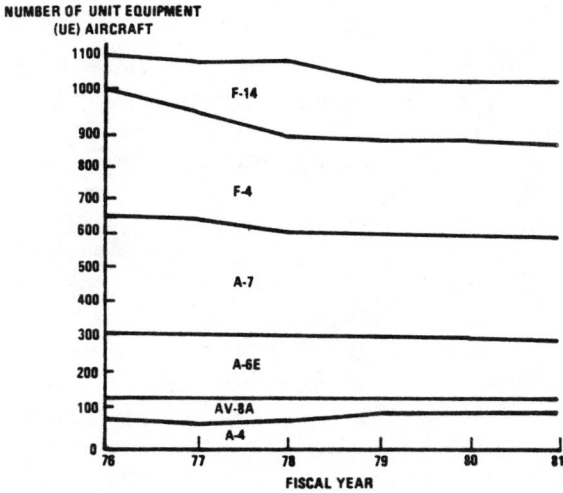

NUMBER OF UNIT EQUIPMENT
(UE) AIRCRAFT

1100
1000   F-14
900
800
700   F-4
600
500
400   A-7
300
200   A-6E
100   AV-8A
0   A-4
76   77   78   79   80   81
FISCAL YEAR

Department of the Navy Reserve Fighter/Attack Aircraft

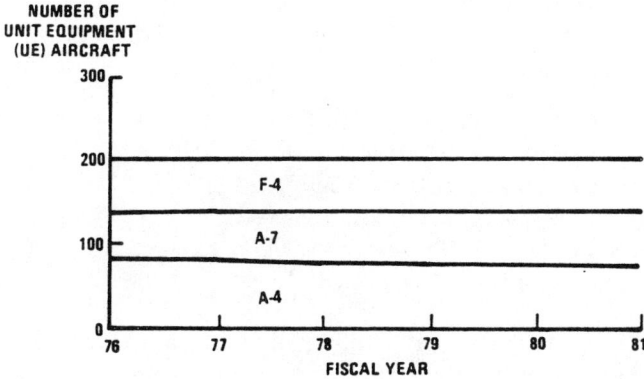

NUMBER OF
UNIT EQUIPMENT
(UE) AIRCRAFT

300

200
        F-4
        A-7
100
        A-4

0
76   77   78   79   80   81
FISCAL YEAR

Source: Secretary of Defense, Department of Defense, Annual Report, Fiscal Year 1980 (Washington, D.C.: 25 January 1979), pp. 189-90.

doctrine does not exist in any single document as do Army or Air Force doctrine. Instead it corresponds to the prime operating divisions under the office of the CNO. Implementing instructions and technical annexes fill out the bases of these essentially separate domains. But the Navy sees its mission in global terms and appears more sensitive to the changing distribution of power and new threat environments than do the Army and Air Force. The principal debates within the Navy, however, are not doctrinal: they are about its ship programs. There is disagreement about whether to favor high-technology craft (nuclear-powered aircraft carriers and ballistic missile submarines) or low-technology capabilities (conventional-powered destroyers, assault ships, patrol and coastal surveillance ships, and sea planes). U.S. Naval intervention in regions other than NATO would involve capabilities at the middle to lower end of this technological spectrum. Naturally the Marine Corps, whose principle mission remains amphibious operations, has a strong interest in seeing the Navy retain and enlarge its capabilities in the lower technological areas of sea control and sea-power projection.

The U.S. Navy has 398 vessels in its active fleet, including 13 aircraft carriers, 165 surface combatants (cruisers, destroyers, and frigates), and 77 nuclear-powered submarines. Naval reserve and fleet auxiliary forces (especially destroyers and mine warfare ships) bring the total of operating ships to 479.[35]

Under normal peacetime conditions, about 30 percent of the Navy's active operating force is deployed overseas. In contrast to the Army and Air Force, which deploy or task principally for Europe, the Navy places a majority of its overseas surface combatant ships, attack submarines, and support ships in the Western Pacific and the Mideast.[36] General Purpose Forces account for about 90 percent of all the Navy's ships, 95 percent of its service personnel, and the greater part of the Navy Department's budget.

One recent analysis found that "The size and structure of the U.S. Navy today is, in large part, a result of earlier choices about budgets and forces."[37] Ship building programs require long lead times—and some units in the current inventory were acquired up to 30 years ago.

Table 3.2 displays the number of active ships in the Navy's General Purpose Forces for the past 10 years, and shows a Navy projection of these force levels to 1982. Table 3.2 illustrates several important points:

1. As maritime threats have grown, the number of general purpose ships in the active U.S. fleet has declined by over 50 percent.
2. Proportionally, the reduction in ships has been highest in the types of craft most useful in intervention operations: amphibious assault ships and mine warfare ships.

TABLE 3.2

Composition of the U.S. General Purpose Fleet

	1967	1972	1977	1982
Aircraft carriers	23	17	13	13
Cruisers, destroyers, and frigates	296	225	155	190
Attack submarines	105	94	77	94
Amphibious ships	162	77	62	66
Patrol ships	7	16	7	6
Mine warfare ships	83	31	3	4
Underway replenishment ships	78	59	39	42
Auxiliary ships	169	89	62	47
Command ships	2	0	0	0
Total general purpose ships	925	608	418	462

Source: Kassing, op. cit., p. 65. For 1967, 1972, and 1977, U.S. Navy Historical Budget Data, March 1977. For 1982, information provided by the Chief of Naval Operations to the Senate Committee on Armed Services, Hearings on Fiscal Year 1978 Authorization, Part 2, February 3, 1977, p. 1010.

3. Support forces—replenishment ships and auxiliaries—have been reduced almost 60 percent.

The major reductions have been in antisubmarine carriers, surface combatants, and amphibious ships. Most of these retirements were older, World War II ships. Some planned expansions by 1982 will concentrate on destroyers, frigates, and attack submarines. Reserve ships also have been reduced in the last ten years, but not as severely as the active ships.

The readiness of the Navy to perform its fundamental tasks is not easy to assess. "Trends in the sizes of ship and aircraft forces do not capture many important—but not readily measurable—factors that make up naval capabilities."[38]

Chiefs of Naval Operations are prone to analyze publicly the Navy's capabilities in a worldwide war with the Soviets, especially in keeping sea lines open, but leave other scenarios vague. The emphasis is on the battle for the North Atlantic and resupply of Europe. To quote Admiral James C. Holloway (in April 1977):

> Today, the US Navy has a slim margin of superiority over the Soviets in those scenarios involving the most vital US national interests. In the event of conflict, the US could retain control of the North Atlantic sea lanes to Europe, but would suffer serious losses to both US and allied shipping in the early stages. The Navy's ability to operate in the eastern Mediterranean would be uncertain at best. US fleets in the Pacific would hold open the sea lanes to Hawaii and Alaska, but shortages of sea control and mobile logistic support forces could cause the US to have difficulty in protecting its sea lines of communication into the western Pacific.[39]

Since 1967 the Marine Corps has also experienced significant reductions, averaging 30 percent in manpower, Hawk Battalions, and some aircraft types. Amphibious assault ships in the Navy have declined 62 percent since 1967, further cutting into Marine intervention capability.[40] Marine aviation has improved in quality since 1967 with new or improved F-4s, A-4s, and AV-8s. But the major changes in USMC capability have been undertaken to gear them for a high-threat, mechanized environment such as Central Europe. This results from growing pressure (across all services) to make forces contribute to NATO defense. Thus in the Marines two new tank companies, increased numbers of TOW and Dragon missiles, and other capabilities have been added. New Navy acquisitions include:

1. One new aircraft carrier capable of supporting all of the Navy's current aircraft, including the S-3, F-14, and E-2c.
2. AEGIS air defense system.
3. Antisubmarine warfare capabilities, including new attack submarines and patrol craft, towed arrays, helicopters, and sensors
4. New surface combatant construction to make up for retirements of older classes. This includes a new guided missile frigate modernization of guided missile destroyers.

The Marine Corps is the only service organized, manned, and equipped to perform quickly in areas other than NATO. (The Army's last remaining airborne division, its small special forces and ranger units, and the Navy's seal teams constitute the rest of the U.S. rapid-reaction intervention forces.) But like the other services preoccupied with European contingencies, the Marines are also being pressured to heavy up for mechanized warfare. There have been moves in Congress and the Executive branch to transform the Marines from a light infantry, light armor, amphibious force to an armored heavy infantry service tasked to fight alongside the Army.[41] This is the basic thrust of a broadly circulated 1976 Brookings Institution study that concluded the amphibious forces and related aviation are too vulnerable to precision-guided missiles and the ground/air defense of most communist countries.[42] The study questions

> whether Marine ground units, short on firepower and cross-country mobility, could stand up to the sophisticated, heavily armored forces that can be fielded by the Soviet Union and its allies—and, if not, what should be done about it.[43]

However, a 1978 study of the Marine Corps had this to say:

> Adding more armor and vehicular mobility to offset Soviet capabilities, overlooks the higher probability of requirements for Marine Corps employment in Third World confrontations during the 1980s and 1990s, where strategic mobility, tactical flexibility and immediate availability will be critically important.[44]

Although the debate continues, the Marines' primary mission remains amphibious operations—the complex coordination of ground, air, and seaborne assault forces at the land-sea interface. Marine Corps force structure and operating doctrine are flexible: vehicles and heavy equipment are minimized; weaponry is lightweight; space requirements are reduced; readiness is high; and mobility is excellent. The Marines use force packages that mix infantry, light armor, and heliborne capabilities for different kinds of threats. They are able to move quickly and adjust rapidly to tactical situations. These are precisely the kinds of capabilities that will be required for effective U.S. responses to non-NATO challenges.

The General Deemphasis on Intervention Capabilities Dilemmas

Intervention per se has a bad name—in the West. Most accepted legal and public definitions imply that intervention is an

unsolicited interference by one state in another state's affairs.[45]
All governments say that they are committed to nonintervention. The
problem, of course, is that states are always involved in each other's
affairs, in economic, military, and political ways, openly and sec-
retly. Just when involvement becomes intervention is a matter of
opinion. Were the Soviets intervening or were they invited in when
Warsaw Pact forces crossed the borders of Czechoslovakia in 1968?
Did the United States intervene or involve itself in South Vietnam's
affairs? What about the Vietnamese military move into Cambodia in
1978, when the Pol Pot government collapsed? In an era of growing
interdependence and regional conflicts, the prospects for intervention would seem to have increased. The whole point of national foreign policy is to influence the behavior of other states. Just where
influence becomes involvement and involvement becomes intervention
is not an easy question.

Nonintervention is a universally declared policy that is everywhere violated. Take, for example, the Carter Administration's
policies. When President Carter was asked, in his second month in
office, about U.S. policies in various regions, he stated that "we
can't impose our will on other people." He promised good offices,
but said that the nations in conflict areas would have to carry the
main burden of their problems.[46] However, when reporters suggested that Washington, with UN Ambassador Andrew Young in the
lead, was meddling in South Africa's internal affairs, the President
denied it, contending that deploring blatant violations of human rights
does not constitute intervention by U.S. standards.[47] The Soviets
with their Cuban surrogates have shown no hesitancy to intervene in
Africa, but they deny that they are doing anything questionable, since
they are on the side of the "revolutionary" or "progressive" (i.e.,
anti-Western or anti-Chinese) forces.

For the United States to combat external intervention requires
much more of a political risk than for the communist regimes that
do the intervening. Accordingly, U.S. foreign policy under the Nixon,
Ford, and Carter Administrations has increasingly curtailed the
scope and degree of U.S. military intervention. Direct U.S. combat
involvement is generally ruled out, although arms sales have served
as a kind of substitute. In May 1977 President Carter declared that
under his Administration the United States would significantly curtail
its arms sales, making them an "exceptional" instrument of policy.
However, because Soviet/Cuban intervention gains in Africa during
1977-78 threatened to destabilize major areas, the President declared
in March 1978: "We will match any threatening power through a combination of military forces, political efforts and economic programs."[4]

Thus the Carter Administration, despite its declarations of
nonintervention, has found that effective influence requires interventio

In Africa, Washington pressured both Rhodesia and South Africa to take radical steps to transfer power to blacks, while it has also sent military aid and transport planes to Zaire to help combat attacks from Marxist Angola. The U.S. has given military assistance to Somalia and North Yemen in their struggles with communist neighbors and provided sophisticated aircraft to Israel, Egypt, and Saudi Arabia. In Asia the United States has tightened its basing arrangements with the Philippines, has partially substituted air power for ground power in Korea, and has looked kindly upon Thailand's request for more military aid. Regarding Latin America the Administration has stated that it will refuse to resume U.S.-Cuban relations until Havana withdraws its troops from Africa. It also has objected to the transfer of nuclear capabilities between West Germany and Brazil, and negotiated a new Panama Canal Treaty. In June 1979, the Carter Administration called for the resignation of the Somoza government in Nicaragua. And in Europe the Administration put pressure on the Soviets by the means of the Helsinki human rights agreements, pledged increased support of NATO, and opposed the spread of Eurocommunism.

So influence and intervention are common currency in international politics—the very stuff of foreign policy—and their necessary exercise usually overrides philosophic goals.

Mobility Forces and Security Assistance

Several years ago the Secretary of Defense began including a section on "mobility forces" in his annual report. Loosely defined, mobility forces include all logistics airlift and sealift capabilities necessary to support a substantial U.S. overseas deployment or supply operation. Figure 3.5 shows these forces. The critical elements are the C-5A Galaxy and the C-141 Starlifter transports. They are the largest long-range military cargo aircraft in the world. These strategic airlift forces, stationed in the United States, are held for major refueling and resupply requirements. The tactical airlift forces (C-130, C-1, C-2, CT-39, C-9, and CH-47 and CH-53 helicopters) are split about evenly between the European/Mediterranean theater, and Asia and the Pacific. A composite reaction force lifted by the C-5As or C-141s would most likely include the Army's 82nd Airborne and 101st Air Assault Division, and one or more Marine divisions. The Secretary of Defense has alluded to the employment of such a quick-strike force in the Persian Gulf or Korea, for example.

Moreover, DOD is emphasizing the need to be able to deploy and support forces in limited contingencies "without reliance on intermediate bases or overflight rights"[49]—a clear reminder of how seriously constrained our resupply of Israel was in the October 1973 conflict. Major program improvements under way are:

1. Increased pre-positioning of equipment, weapons, and fuel.
2. Conversion of all C-141As to the C-141B (stretch model).
3. Development of wide-bodied cargo convertible aircraft in the reserve fleet.
4. Deployment of the KC-10 tanker-cargo aircraft.
5. Development of more ready reserve fleet ships.
6. Earmarking of more NATO-allied ships for rapid improvement.

Figure 3.6 illustrates some of these improvements in strategic airlift capabilities.

"Soviet projection capability," writes the British journal Strategic Survey, "still cannot match the absolute capability of US forces. Their significance lies in their improvement in recent years, in the use to which they have been put, and in the Soviet willingness to use them in the future."[50] Soviet airlift can carry only about one-half of what the U.S. can. Soviet sealift carries only about one-third of the U.S. single-lift capacity. Soviet marines are less than one-fifteenth the size of the USMC. Nevertheless, Soviet projection capabilities have vastly improved in the last 10 years, relying on the Il-76 transport aircraft with its cargo capacity of 44 tons (twice that of the An-12 it replaces). Three new airborne divisions, new armored vehicles, amphibious ships and roll-on/roll-off ships are also important. But the real punch to Soviet power projection involves low-risk operations by surrogate forces: the Cubans. Despite the casualties, Cuba maintains over 37,000 troops in Africa, situated mainly in Ethiopia and Angola. The 1975-76 Angolan operation was massive: airlift and sealift brought 15,000 Cuban combat troops into the country. Similar operations supported the Horn of Africa in 1977 and 1978.

A second aspect of U.S. intervention capabilities focuses on security assistance.[51] The U.S. government has viewed security assistance from several perspectives: strengthening U.S. collective defense arrangements; maintaining regional military balances; securing base and operating rights; compensating for U.S. force withdrawals; and strengthening bilateral political relations.[52] In the Persian Gulf, U.S. security assistance tied Washington closely to the Iranian and Saudi governments, which—until the replacement of the Shah with Khomeini—were the two largest, richest, and most conservative states in the area. Both governments had acted to block radical activity. In East Africa, U.S. security assistance and bilateral defense ties to South Korea and the Philippines, and the massive trade relationship and security tie with Japan, helped anchor U.S. policy interests. In Latin America, Mexico, Venezuela, and Brazil have been the primary focus of U.S. security policies. Africa, only recently returned to prominence in U.S. policy under the Carter

FIGURE 3.5

Strike Force Composition

Strategic Airlift

Active US Air Force	Civil Reserve Air Fleet (CRAF)
70 US C-5A aircraft	272 passenger aircraft
234 UE C-141 aircraft	113 cargo/convertible aircraft

Pre-positioned Material Configured in Unit Sets (POMCUS)

2 brigades from each of 3 divisions plus an armored cavalry regiment (equivalent in total to 2-1/3 division sets), plus nondivisional support units.

Sealift

27 military sealift command ships	273 US flag merchant fleet ships
152 national defense reserve fleet ships	192 non-US NATO vessels

Tactical Airlift

Active US Air Force	Active US Navy
218 UE C-130 aircraft	20 UE C-1 COD aircraft
	10 UE C-2 COD aircraft
	2 UE C-9 aircraft
	16 UE CT-39 aircraft
	7 UE C-130 aircraft
Air Force Reserve and Air National Guard including 376 aircraft	Reserve US Navy including 64 aircraft

Logistics Support Helicopters

Active US Army	Active US Marine Corps
358 CH-47s	126 CH-53s
36 CH-54s	
Army Reserve/National Guard	Reserve US Marine Corps
including 131 helicopters	including 18 helicopters

Source: Secretary of Defense, Department of Defense, Annual Report, Fiscal Year 1980 (Washington, D.C.: 25 January 1979), pp. 196-197.

FIGURE 3.6

Total Strategic Airlift Aircraft Inventory and Capability

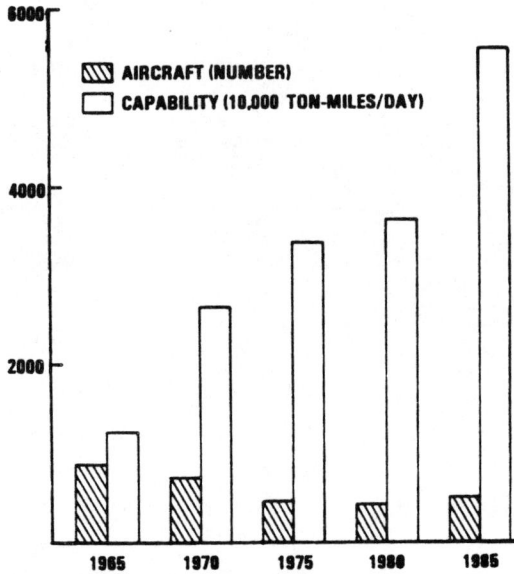

Trends in Total U.S. Strategic Airlift Capability

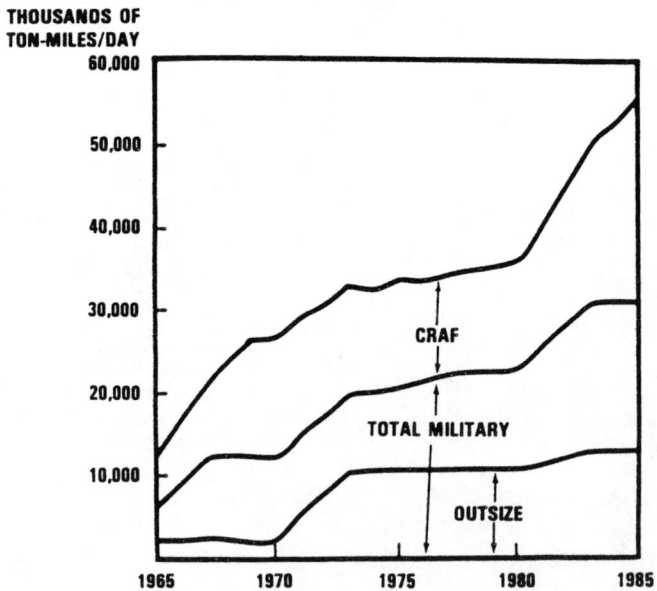

Source: Secretary of Defense, Department of Defense, Annual Report, Fiscal Year 1980 (Washington, D.C.: 25 January 1979), p. 200.

Administration, still receives the smallest amount of U.S. military assistance or sales credits of any region in the world, while the Soviets are now the dominant external arms supplier to the continent.[53]

Under the Nixon Administration, the United States contracted its overseas force presence. The financial drain of the Vietnam War and depletion of military equipment stocks to resupply Israel in 1973 had strapped U.S. defense programs. "Self-reliance" for our allies became a conceptual underpinning of the Nixon Doctrine. A second aspect of the doctrine was regionalism: certain countries were fastened onto as "stabilizers": Brazil and Venezuela in Latin America; Iran and Saudi Arabia in the Middle East; Nigeria in sub-Sahara Africa; and Japan in East Asia. It was defended by the Nixon and Ford Administrations as a method of promoting "regional balances." The same logic has appeared in later Carter Administration statements.[54] Since 1974, U.S. arms sales have steadily incteased, while grant aid has been drastically reduced. (See Figure 3.7.)

FIGURE 3.7

Grants and FMs Deliveries (Millions FY 78 Dollars)

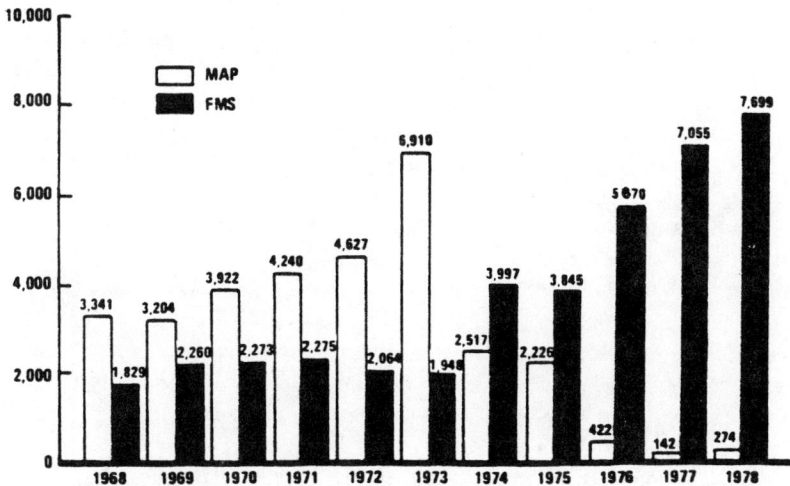

NOTE: Yearly totals often include deliveries under agreements reached several years previously.

Source: Secretary of Defense, Department of Defense, Annual Report, Fiscal Year 1980 (Washington, D.C.: 25 January 1979), p. 225.

During the period 1965 to 1974, the United States provided some $32 billion in arms, equipment, and military support to other nations—and the developing areas received approximately 78 percent. By 1976 the majority of U.S. arms sales were still going to members of the traditional "containment tier": South Korea, the Philippines, and Saudi Arabia. The Soviet Union's documentable arms transfers were approximately $19 billion during this period, of which 71 percent went to developing countries in 1974. Asia and the Middle East/ Persian Gulf absorbed the majority of the superpowers' arms transfers: 64 percent of U.S. exports, 52 percent of the Soviet Union's. Chinese arms transfers were comparatively small and heavily concentrated on North Vietnam and North Korea.[55]

President Carter's campaign promises and statements once in office that he would get control of and then reduce U.S. arms sales[56] came up against previous commitments and DOD accounting practices that made an actual reduction of arms sales very difficult. Despite statements by the Chairman of the Joint Chiefs in 1977, 1978, and 1979 that security assistance was an integral and essential element of U.S. collective security policies, little systematic attention was given to security assistance until recently. Detailed analysis of the purposes and ingredients of the various programs was scarce.

Under the Carter Administration, U.S. security assistance was in part explained from the perspective of human rights performance by governments asking for U.S. aid. United States military assistance "can be used to promote human rights by altering the size or functions of our military representatives, the level of training grants, and the quantity and types of arms transfers."[57] Then, beginning in mid-February and continuing through the spring of 1978, as Soviet and Cuban-braced Ethiopian forces wrecked Somalia's army and cleared the disputed Ogaden region, the Administration changed emphasis. On March 17, 1978, the President warned the Soviets about what he termed Moscow's "ominous inclination" to use its growing military power to intervene with its own and "proxy forces." In early May, the President called attention to Soviet "racism" in Africa. In late May, the President, clearly concerned with Soviet and Cuban intervention in Africa as Zaire's Shaba province deteriorated, said he would oppose any further legislative restrictions on U.S. military and economic aid to friendly and nonaligned countries. This was followed by the President's address to the NATO Summit Conference about the threat to Africa.

The President has pledged FMS and MAP "ceilings" each fiscal year and modest reductions on the dollar volume of new commitments to "nonexempt" (nonallied) countries. He has established an Arms Export Control Board and entered into conventional arms transfer talks with the Soviet Union. Several factors account for the

Administration's difficulty in reducing U.S. and global arms sales: among these are a backlog of over $44 billion in undelivered orders; balance of payments problems; local arms races; and reluctance of other arms sellers to restrain their actions.[58]

In summary, the U.S. position on security assistance seems to have come full circle. For a number of years, Washington deliberately built up anticommunist and conservative governments through military assistance and arms transfers. Then came the Nixon-sponsored jump in arms sales to offset oil payments. Then the Carter Administration reexamined the arms sales policy from moral and security points of view.[59] This stance shifted in the face of increasingly bold communist tactical intervention in Third World conflicts and the admitted difficulties of obtaining cooperation from other arms sellers to reduce arms. The Administration's call for restraint of conventional arms transfer is commendable. Its willingness to continue advancing arms to responsible governments whose interests coincide with the United States is also commendable.

CONCLUSION

The most important future security challenge for the United States, after maintaining our strategic deterrent against the Soviet Union and our conventional-nuclear deterrent in Europe, is to improve the U.S. crisis management and intervention capabilities for non-NATO, nonnuclear conflicts. The vast global diffusion of power under way for at least a decade is creating and accelerating rivalries and conflicts in the non-NATO areas that bear on U.S. national security interests and military strategy. U.S. security policy must be highly flexible, capable of doing many things simultaneously, but it must also be guided by a central conceptual foundation. Without that conceptual foundation, the whole will be simply the sum of its parts.

If, as Prime Minister Disraeli once said about the relative success of nearly a century of British balance of power policy, Great Britain had no permanent allies, only permanent interests, then Britain's major interest was to prevent war on the European continent by preserving stability and precluding power shifts. The task for U.S. policy over the next ten to thirty years is more complex than was Britain's, because the U.S. sphere of influence is considerably larger and because critical power shifts are occurring independently of U.S. control—and the control of other countries as well. (The latter include the Soviet Union, China, Japan, and the nations of Western Europe.) If the United States is to exercise its influence in order to preserve stability, deflect or constrain power shifts inimical to its way of life, and encourage democratic/capitalistic systems of government that improve human welfare, then it must develop a policy based on courage and sophistication. U.S. military strategy and military forces must serve that policy. Current U.S. defense policy and general purpose force structure and modernization programs, by focusing so heavily on a NATO contingency, are becoming increasingly inappropriate to the global power shifts and the new threat environments in non-NATO areas. The United States should partially reorient its forces and policies away from such exclusive concentration on NATO in order to better influence political-military outcomes in resource-rich and strategically located Third World areas. This means shifting some resources and program emphases from the short, intensive European war scenario to power projection and intervention capabilities, while continuing and in some instances increasing security assistance and arms transfers to critical Third World countries.

The specific requirements are as follows:

1. Halt further mechanization of U.S. Army units not explicitly tasked to NATO, because it is making them increasingly ill-suited to non-NATO areas.
2. Increase the mobility and theatre flexibility of the remaining light Army units.
3. Terminate all programs designed to mechanize Marine Corps divisions.
4. Reexamine the extensive tactical airpower modernization programs (Air Force, Navy, Marines) to determine if they have not gone too far in inhibiting U.S. ability to respond to less intensive non-NATO conflicts.
5. Begin new Navy ship building programs that concentrate on rebuilding amphibious assault, mine warfare, and auxiliary ships, and other mobility/intervention capabilities.
6. Accelerate the modernization and expansion of U.S. mobility forces, both airlift and sealift.
7. Continually reexamine U.S. security assistance and arms sales programs for relevance to shifting power balances and surrogate reliabilities.

It is highly doubtful that these efforts can be undertaken without an increase in the defense budget, since the United States has no choice but to compete with Soviet strategic and Warsaw Pact conventional military spending. The Carter Administration's defense decisions have been designed to enhance NATO preparedness while foregoing some strategic programs (the B-1 decision) in order to try and maintain a level defense budget. It is not possible under a level defense budget to continue the NATO modernization programs, make the necessary improvements in strategic modernization efforts (the MX missile and mobile ICBM basing mode), and also arrest the decline in this country's non-NATO crisis management and intervention/ mobility forces.

NATO preparedness and strategic weapons modernization programs must continue, and improvements in our intervention capabilities must begin. The changing threat environment and the diffusion of power will force these requirements on U.S. defense planning sooner or later. U.S. policy would do well to anticipate them and make the commitments now.

NOTES

1. A powerful summary of these alliance trends is in Seyom Brown, New Forces in World Politics (Washington, D.C.: The Brookings Institution, 1974). Extensions of Brown's reasoning with focus on economic affairs, interdependence, and inequalities are, Robert Keohane and Joseph Nye, Transnational Relations and World Politics (Cambridge, Mass.: Harvard University Press, [972]; Robert W. Tucker, The Inequality of Nations (New York: Basic Books, 1977); and Robert Keohane and Joseph Nye, Power and Interdependence (Boston: Little, Brown, and Co., 1977).

2. An extensive inventory of the many interpretations of global structure is found in Joseph L. Nogee, "Polarity: An Ambiguous Concept," Orbis (Winter 1975):1193-1224.

3. See, for example, Geoffrey Kemp, "The New Strategic Map," Survival (Jan/Feb 1977):50-59.

4. Robert O. Keohane and Joseph Nye, Power and Interdependence (Boston: Little, Brown and Co., 1977); Stanley Hoffman, Primacy or World Order (New York: McGraw Hill, 1978).

5. While he was a Brookings Institution Fellow, Mr. Bergsten wrote extensively on trade and assistance problems, emphasizing Third World-Western relations. See, for example, C. Fred Bergsten, ed., The Future of the International Economic Order: An Agenda for Research (Lexington, Mass.: Lexington Books, 1973); Managing International Economic Interdependence: Selected Papers of C. Fred Bergsten, 1975-1976 (Lexington, Mass.: D. C. Heath and Co., 1977); and his many Foreign Policy articles.

6. For the more conservative view of detente, see Secretary of State Henry Kissinger's testimony before the Senate Foreign Relations Committee in October 1974. A more liberal interpretation with implied assumptions of convergence is Lawrence T. Caldwell, Soviet-American Relations (Atlantic Institute, 1976).

7. For examples of this view see Avigdor Haselkorn, The Evolution of Soviet Security Strategy, 1965-1975, Strategy Paper (New York: National Strategy Information Center, November 1977); W. Scott Thompson, Power Projection: A Net Assessment of U.S. and Soviet Capabilities, Agenda Paper (New York: National Strategy Information Center, April 1978); and Donald S. Zagoria, "Into the Breach: New Soviet Alliances in the Third World," Foreign Affairs (Spring 1979):733-54.

8. See Zbigniew Brzezinski, "American Foreign Policy in a Rapidly Changing World," The Atlantic Community Quarterly (Spring 1979):6-13. Also see President Carter's 1977 Notre Dame University and 1978 Annapolis speeches.

9. Brzezinski, op, cit., p. 8.

10. Secretary of Defense Harold Brown, "Today's National Security Policy," speech to the National Security Industrial Association, Washington, D.C., September 15, 1977.

11. Richard Burt, The New York Times, January 6, 1978, pp. A1, A4.

12. Ibid.

13. Secretary of Defense Harold Brown, Department of Defense, Annual Report, Fiscal Year 1980 (Washington, D.C.: U.S. GPO, January 25, 1979), p. 45.

14. Brown, Annual Report, FY 1980.

15. See, for example, Secretary of the Army Martin Hoffman, "The Army at 200 Years: Visible, Capable, Ready," Army (October 1975); Secretary of Defense Donald H. Rumsfeld, Department of Defense Annual Report, Fiscal Year 1977, Washington, D.C., January 17, 1976; and General George S. Brown, Statement on the Defense Posture of the United States for FY 1978, and FY 1979, January 20, 1977, and January 20, 1978, respectively. In his posture statements General Brown concentrated almost exclusively on Strategic Nuclear

Forces and General Purpose Forces. With the exception of one page devoted to Security Assistance and five pages devoted to Mobility Forces, his FY 1979 124-page report did not allude to unconventional warfare or intervention requirements. General Jones' 1980 report devoted a bit more attention to analyzing subversive and guerrilla war threats in the developing areas, and international terrorism. General David C. Jones, United States Military Posture for FY 1980, January 1979.

16. Brown, Annual Report, FY 1980, p. 142.

17. Relevant is Robert W. Komer, "Bureaucracy Does Its Thing: Institutional Constraints on US-GVN Performance in Vietnam," Rand Corporation Memorandum R-967-ARPA, August 1972; and Lawrence E. Grinter, "How They Lost: Doctrines, Strategies, and Outcomes of the Vietnam War," Asian Survey (December 1975).

18. Cited in The Defense Monitor, "U.S. Ground Forces: Inappropriate Objectives, Unacceptable Costs," VII/9 (November 1978):2.

19. Lawrence J. Korb, "The FY 1979-1983 Defense Program: Issues and Trends," AEI Defense Review, 2/2: 25 and 35.

20. Brown, Annual Report, FY 1980, pp. 140-41.

21. Brown, Annual Report FY 1980, p. 1400.

22. The Defense Monitor, "U.S. Ground Forces: Inappropriate Objectives, Unacceptable Costs," VII/9 (November 1978):2-3.

23. Ibid., p. 3.

24. U.S. Department of the Army, Field Manual 100-5, Operations (Washington, D.C.: Department of the Army, July 1, 1976), p. i.

25. For an example of skepticism about the manual's tactical and technical thinking, see William S. Lind, "Some Doctrinal Questions for the United States Army," Military Review (March 1977).

26. U.S. Department of the Army, Field Manual 100-20, Internal Defense and Development: U.S. Army Doctrine (Washington, D.C.: Department of the Army, November 1974), Ch. 8, p. 11.

27. U.S. Department of the Army, Internal Defense and Development, Ch. 7, p. 6. Compare the particulars on this document with earlier manuals, for example, Army, FM 31-21, Special Forces Operations, June 1965; Army, FM 31-23, Stability Operations: U.S. Army Doctrine, December 1967; and Army, FM 31-23, Stability Operations: U.S. Army Doctrine, October 1972.

28. Voight, pp. 16-34.

29. Korb, "The FY 1979-1983 Defense Program," p. 41.

30. Ibid., p. 44.

31. Ibid., p. 42.

32. Though there are 26 active fighter/attack wings currently organized, they are underequipped. Brown, Annual Report FY 1980, p. 178.

33. Naval air fighter and attack assets are distributed across 12 carrier air wings. Marine naval air assets are organized into 3 active wings. See Brown, Annual Report, FY 1980, p. 182.

34. Korb, p. 41.

35. Brown, Annual Report, FY 1980, p. 160.

36. Ibid.

37. David B. Kassing, "General Purpose Forces: Navy and Marine Corps," in Francis P. Hoeber et al., Arms, Men and Military Budgets: Issues for Fiscal Year 1979 (New York: Crane, Russak, 1978), p. 64.

38. Kassing, op. cit., p. 71.

39. Quoted from CNO Report, A Report by Admiral James C. Holloway, Chief of Naval Operations on the Posture of the U.S. Navy, April 1977, pp. 45-46, as cited in Kassing, op. cit., p. 71.

40. Hoeber et al., p. 72.

41. In early 1979, the Secretary of Defense commented that "United States land forces (Army and Marine Corps) are needed first of all to counter Soviet/Warsaw Pact ground forces in Europe as part of the NATO alliance." Brown, Annual Report, FY 1980, p. 140.

42. Martin Binkin and Jeffrey Record, Where Does the Marine Corps Go From Here? (Washington, D.C.: Brookings Institution, 1976). See pp. 87–88.

43. Ibid., p. vii.

44. LTC John Grinalds, USMC, "Structuring the Marine Corps for the 1980s and 1990s," National Security Affairs Monograph (Washington, D.C.: National Defense University, Research Directorate, May 1978).

45. See the analysis by Colonel Richard W. Smith, USMC, in his "Military Intervention in a Changing World," The National War College Strategic Research Group, Washington D.C. (October 1974), pp. 9–16.

46. The President cited in The New York Times, February 24, 1977, as quoted in Doris A. Graber, "Intervention Policies of the Carter Administration: Political and Military Dimensions," in Defense Policy and the Presidency: Carter's First Years, ed. Sam C. Sarkesian (Boulder, Colo.: Westview Press, 1979), p. 207.

47. The President, quoted in The New York Times, October 28, 1977, as cited by Graber, op. cit.

48. See the Wake Forest University Speech, The New York Times, March 18, 1978.

49. Emphasis is by the Secretary of Defense, FY 1980 Report, p. 198.

50. IISS Strategic Survey, 1978, p. 12.

51. Since 1972, all U.S. security-related aid and government arms sales are now included under the label of "security assistance": the military assistance program (MAP), foreign military sales through government channels (FMS), credits and loans, provision of excess defense articles, security supporting assistance, and training programs. See Secretary of Defense Harold Brown, Department of Defense Annual Report, Fiscal Year 1979, February 2, 1978, p. 244.

52. Ibid., p. 94.

53. Ibid., p. 250.

54. U.S. Congress, House, Committee on International Relations, International Security Assistance Act of 1976: Hearings, Testimony of Secretary of State Kissinger, 94th Cong., 1st sess., 1976, pp. 1-6; and Secretary of Defense Harold Brown, Department of Defense Annual Report, Fiscal Year 1979, p. 94.

55. U.S. Arms Control and Disarmament Agency, World Military Expenditures and Transfers, 1965-1974 (Washington, D.C.: Arms Control and Disarmament Agency, 1976), interpreted by Caesar D. Sereseres, "U.S. Military Assistance to Non-Industrial Nations," in The Limits of Military Intervention, ed. Ellen P. Stern (Beverly Hills: Sage, 1977), p. 235.

56. See, in particular, his May 19, 1977 statement in which the President announced that henceforth his policy would be to regard arms transfers as an "exceptional" instrument of U.S. policy and that in the future the burden of proof for a particular sale would rest on those proposing it.

57. Brown, Annual Report, FY 1979, p. 252.

58. Brown, Annual Report, FY 1980, pp. 223-33.

59. Of interest is Leslie Gelb, "Arms Sales," Foreign Policy (Winter 1976-77):3-23; and Emma Rothschild, "Carter and Arms Sales," The New York Times, May 10, 1978, p. 35.

4
NONMILITARY INSTRUMENTS OF
DEFENSE POLICY
Lewis S. Sorley

Although the military instruments of development and application of national power have in recent years received disproportionate attention bordering on preoccupation, the nonmilitary aspects of national power are in fact far more diverse, pervasive, and hard to deal with. This paper will delineate the range of nonmilitary instruments available to large and small nations in the present era, analyze the usefulness and hazards inherent in their application, and discuss the central policy issues involved in prospective application of such factors by the United States in the near term.

The paper will suggest three general conclusions concerning nonmilitary aspects of national power that presently pertain to the United States:

1. Nonmilitary aspects of power are complementary to, not substitutes for, military capability.
2. Nonmilitary aspects of power can in some cases achieve results that are simply not attainable through the use of military force; in other cases they can achieve results more quickly, cheaply, or surely.
3. The United States lacks an effective mechanism for coordinated planning and employment of nonmilitary elements of national power.

We must recognize that we are faced with a new conception of national security. There are today virtually no aspects of relations

The views expressed in this paper are the author's and do not necessarily represent those of any governmental element or agency.

among nations, and precious few domestic considerations, that lack a national security component. Helmut Schmidt, addressing the "new dimensions of security," cited "the economic, the social and the internal aspects of Western security." His observations on social and internal aspects of security are particularly interesting, since these represent novel challenges to security—challenges to which we have yet to find adequate responses. Foremost among the social requirements he cited are "the necessity to achieve and maintain social peace at home." One could easily extend the list to include the need to combat subversion, illegal trafficking in narcotics, organized crime, corruption in government, and other actions that serve to erode the effectiveness of government and to undermine the confidence of the public. In terms of domestic security, he placed first "the necessity to strengthen and defend our society against terrorists whose sole aim is to destroy its fabric with acts of brutal killing and kidnapping."[1] This list, too, could be extended. There is, for example, the threat of irresponsible domestic policy making: it is not hard to understand the corrosive effects of setting up an impossible array of goals in some realm, then watching the multitude of governments that are quite naturally unable to succeed fully in meeting those goals undermined in the esteem of their populaces and perhaps driven from office.

A frequently discussed element of the contemporary strategic environment has been what the late Alastair Buchan called "a characteristic of the present state system which differentiates it sharply from that of the late nineteenth or early twentieth centuries, namely the ability of the small to defy the great."[2] Others have spoken of a "diffusion of power" as one of a number of dramatic changes in the international system that have resulted in a changed security environment.[3] Stanley Hoffmann has remarked on the frustration of the great powers, observing that they are now often reduced to preventing others from imposing their wills, while being similarly inhibited in imposing their own.[4] Although there are serious limitations to the theory that military force lacks utility in such an environment, it is nevertheless true that effective use of nonmilitary instruments of national policy is at a premium in these areas. In addition to providing lower risk, lower cost, and often more efficacious means of bringing national power to bear, such measures have the additional virtue of being backed by resort to military force if they should fail, whereas failure in the use of military means can seldom be redeemed by the application of less violent measures.

Brian Crozier recently argued that we are in the midst of World War III, and that it is a war whose major instruments are "insurgency, terrorism, and detente." In particular, he observed, "the Communist powers are waging this war utilizing such non-military techniques as subversion, disinformation, terrorism, psychological warfare and diplomatic negotiations."[5] Some of these techniques are among those which the United States has foresworn, but the necess:

of protecting itself against their use by hostile powers nevertheless means that they cannot be ignored. And since the effective use of diplomatic and economic measures depends heavily upon an international environment conducive to negotiation and reasoned agreement and cooperation, control of actions that tend to produce chaos is of critical importance not only to preserving the effectiveness of such nonmilitary instruments, but even more fundamentally to protecting basic national security. Yet few would argue that at present the United States possesses effective and comprehensive means of countering the threats posed by hostile use of the combination of techniques described by Crozier.

Further support for the use of nonmilitary aspects of national power and for learning how to defend against their use by unfriendly foreign states is provided by Lincoln Bloomfield and Harland Cleveland:

> The most compelling new connective between arms and the global community arises from the changing ways in which security is defined. In a world where nobody is in charge, non-military activities—energy, food, economic collaboration, multinational enterprise, information systems, monetary policy, global technologies, even voting in international organizations—now have to be ranked along with military preparedness as relevant forms of power in international relations.[6]

Of particular concern is that substratum of especially dangerous and insidious threats to national security that includes terrorism, illegal trafficking in narcotics, and political subversion. To the extent that nations provide support for such activities directed against other states, or tacitly approve when they have the capacity to intervene, they may be said to manipulate these factors for security purposes. Conversely, a nation's inability to deal with them constitutes an obvious security hazard. The proposition demonstrates, among other things, the critical importance of internal stability and security to a nation's security in the international framework.

Fred Ikle, having spent many years attempting to improve national security by means of negotiated arms limitation agreements, reflected recently that "our experiment in unilateral restraint ended in sad failure." He went on to conclude, in part because of the relative military weakness of the United States resulting from prolonged persistence in this approach, that

> the U.S. government must construct—or reconstruct—a wider range of instruments to exert influence abroad. With the military balance moving against us, we will have to compete more effectively, for example, in the information and propaganda battle, with more sophisticated

communication throughout the world. We will have to
compete vigorously in providing financial and organizational assistance to our friends and in defending our
interests through other overt and covert actions abroad. [7]

In the following pages we consider some of the nonmilitary
means either presently or potentially available, and then the mechanisms required for their successful employment. As a final preliminary observation, the notion advanced by some analysts of the
declining utility of military force needs to be approached with some
caution. It seems to be based, at least in part, on failure to understand and differentiate between those things that military force can
and cannot be expected to achieve, and on incorrect conclusions as
to its utility derived from observation of inept attempts by the United
States to employ military power in recent times. It would be difficult to convince such international actors as the North Vietnamese,
the Palestinians, the Israelis, the Arabs, the Soviets, and many
others who have good reason to believe otherwise of the declining
utility of military force. Another whole class which includes all of
Western Europe, South Korea, Taiwan, Japan, and many others, has
reason to believe that the possession of military force for its deterrent effect is another reason to continue to believe that it has contemporary utility and relevance.

THE RANGE OF NONMILITARY INSTRUMENTS

During the predominantly bipolar period of international relationships in the postwar era, there came to be a kind of militariza-
tion of outlook, resulting in overemphasis on the military aspects of
national power and neglect of nonmilitary factors. Now that military
parity has come to characterize—at least transitionally—the superpower relationship, this neglect has come to be markedly less sus-
tainable. Just as, in strategic arms limitation negotiations, constraint of quantitative factors in the balance served to deflect force
improvement efforts in the qualitative realm, so a kind of stalemate
in the military sphere of national security is accelerating interest
in nonmilitary aspects.

There is always a question, in thinking about nonmilitary
measures, of where to draw the definitional line. Military and nonmilitary elements of national power are not entirely separate enti-
ties; rather there is a spectrum of aspects of national power, elements of which can be employed singly or in combination, and which
may be considered more or less military. Many of the economic or
political steps that might be taken impact upon military forces or the
ability to employ them, for example. Certainly the events of recent

years have underscored the critical importance of energy supplies to the viability of military forces, just one illustration of the links between those forces and realms which we have customarily not considered to be primarily military in nature.

For the purposes of this discussion we will consider nonmilitary instruments of national power to consist primarily of economic, political, and psychological aspects, with an additional category, which we might call quasi-military, utilized to discuss some of the ambiguous instruments on that borderline. It is clear to experienced practitioners that employment of various elements of national power in judicious combination, either at once or sequentially, can markedly increase their effectiveness, so that the element of coordinated and comprehensive planning that will be addressed later is of central importance in obtaining the maximum benefit from available instruments of power.

If we are to talk meaningfully of instruments of defense policy, whether military or nonmilitary, it is necessary to have some notion of the concerns of defense policy in general. Max Lerner once told an audience at the Army War College that the national purpose of the United States was "to survive—and perchance to flourish." In today's world, survival implies the means to deter or defeat external and internal threats to the sovereignty, political freedom and economic viability of the nation; beyond that, the opportunity to flourish involves a range of trade, cultural, scientific, and intellectual interactions in a world that is not fundamentally hostile to the survival of American values and interests. Clearly no single instrument would suffice to ensure survival, much less flourishing, in a world as complex and dynamic as that of the late twentieth century; rather, a range of instruments, both military and nonmilitary, is required. Their effectiveness in turn depends upon coordinated employment, discerning selection, and wise implementation. Given the inherently ambiguous, imprecise, and delayed impact of many nonmilitary instruments of national power, it is a challenge of sufficient magnitude for the most ambitious of governments.

ECONOMIC INSTRUMENTS

It is fashionable to talk today of the growing interdependence of the nations of the world. What is usually meant is economic interdependence, the implication being that there are reciprocal dependencies that result in a mutuality of interests among the states involved. In the context of peaceful solutions to international disputes, such interdependence seems desirable. Yet this model fails to account for the historical frequency with which trading partners have gone to war with one another. Furthermore, in many cases the pattern of modern interdependencies is more accurately described as a network of unilateral dependencies in which reciprocal elements are often lacking. Thus the massive dependency of the industrialized nations on the oil supplied by the petroleum-exporting countries is not balanced by any reciprocal dependency even remotely approaching it in magnitude or importance. While some have professed to see such reciprocity in the supposed need of the oil producers for markets for their oil, the saturation of their ability to absorb the massive payments for oil shipped has meant that, if anything, the problem has been to find investments for the surplus until development opportunities can be created in the producer economies. Clearly, production of oil could be maintained at markedly reduced levels without hampering the economic plans of producing states.

If unilateral dependencies occur more often than genuine interdependencies, one of the economic applications of nonmilitary instruments of national power is to create and where necessary exploit reciprocal dependencies on the part of nations upon which the United States is in significant measure dependent. The reciprocities need not be confined to the nonmilitary realm, of course, and thus the coordination of planning for use of nonmilitary instruments must not only be internal, but must extend to harmonization with the use of military instruments as well.

For a nation such as the United States, which has not only abundant natural resources but also extensive capacity to produce finished goods of every kind, the range of economic measures is extensive. Trading relationships with other nations are perhaps the most obvious, from enactment of a total trade embargo on the one extreme to extension of most-favored-nation treatment on the other. By combining economic and political (or diplomatic) measures, U.S. leadership in international trade negotiations can have an important effect on the ability of the United States to utilize economic elements of its national power. The selective export of goods, such as armaments or high technology items where loss of the advanced technology is a concern, is an example of economic means by which national power can be brought to bear, either to strengthen other nations by providing goods or technology (either as quid pro quo because we have important shared interests that will be furthered by assisting the recipient nation), or to weaken them by withholding such benefits.

A special case concerns foodstuffs, which are one of the most attractive U.S. exports. The idea of manipulating the export of foodstuffs for reasons of national power application or security is unattractive to many. But few nations in the world are in a position, even just from the national security standpoint, to fail to provide for the basic food requirements of their population. Thus a case can be made that providing foodstuffs to meet shortfalls in the domestic production of unfriendly nations enables them to divert domestic resources from the production of food to other more threatening purposes.

Where dependencies exist for critical raw materials obtainable only or principally from foreign sources, strategic planning would presumably be directed to developing means of assuring continued access to those supplies, or applying technology to the task of devising alternate sources or substitute materials. Again energy provides a case in point, since the idea of energy independence is an appealing but so far elusive goal. Beyond that, of course, are the continuing strategic implications of allies who are unable to develop such independence regardless of the application of resources, at least in the near and mid-term. The contingent liabilities of major powers that derive from vulnerabilities of their allies often complicate the direct effects. The nature of the international system and the current status of relations among states helps to explain why this is so.

As we have observed, there is substantial overlap between military and nonmilitary factors. Arms collaboration between France and West Germany provides an example. The economic imperatives that dictated spreading the overhead costs of military production were key to the evolving coproduction arrangements between the two countries, as was the necessity to restrain the competition for export markets for arms, which was hampering the efforts of each to maintain an independent production capacity. Working together, they have been able to share the costs, develop the markets jointly, and maintain arms production capability that, if not independent in the strictest sense, is at least independent of the United States.

Such developments are shaped by the perceptions of the nations involved. Cultural and traditional political outlooks, conditioned in turn by geographic factors, have served as important determinants of national security perspectives and, to some extent, strengths and vulnerabilities. Thus France has in recent years tended to think of security primarily in military terms, whereas the West Germans have emphasized economic aspects, particularly since their opening to the East some years ago. Recently, however, perhaps influenced by the diminishing credibility of the U.S. strategic guarantee, the views of these two European nations have tended to converge, so that each has a more balanced view of the underpinnings of security, with military and economic factors considered complementary.

This is an approach that ought to be compatible with U.S. views, where a massive reallocation of resources from military expenditures to domestic purposes has taken place over the past decade. In fact, as far back as the Eisenhower admininistration, key national figures were emphasizing the interrelationship of military and economic factors as joint determinants of national security. Probably no chief executive in modern times has made this connection more explicit than did Eisenhower himself, when he explained the reductions in defense spending in his budget for Fiscal Year 1955 by asserting that "we cannot afford to build military strength by sacrificing economic strength. We must keep strong in all respects."[8] If that were true in 1954, when the United States enjoyed a substantial advantage in military power of every kind over any potential adversary and was also far more preeminent economically than at present, it is arguably more so by orders of magnitude in the world of today.

As nonmilitary factors take on greater importance as means of bringing national power to bear in an era in which the United States no longer enjoys a clearly dominant military position, so economic factors continue to gain in importance in the nonmilitary realm. One of the key implications for effective formulation and execution of policy in this area is the need for greater cooperation, rather than an increasingly adversarial relationship, among government, business, and labor, so that trade policy, technology transfer, international monetary policy, and the like are in harmony with, and advance the interests of, the national security as broadly conceived.

Such prescriptions are of course far more easily formulated than implemented. Just as scholars are coming to realize that general purpose force issues are more difficult aspects of national security policy than the strategic force issues on which so much attention has been lavished over the past thirty years, so they may come to appreciate that the effective use of nonmilitary instruments of national power is in some ways more challenging than the use of force. Some of the reasons are obvious. Control of military forces is direct, and is the exclusive province of the state. Economic means are diffused throughout the nation and—in cases of multinational corporations— throughout many parts of the world. Thus they are susceptible to government manipulation only by exception, or where specific provisions have been enacted. The application of military force is also reasonably direct, and the results generally apparent. Application of economic, diplomatic, and psychological measures is often ambiguous and delayed in impact. Other differentiations could probably be articulated, with the majority tending to substantiate the comparatively greater difficulty in using nonmilitary means skillfully.

A further distinction is made by Vincent Davis, who suggests that military threats create a unifying effect, whereas economic threats are disunifying. The corollary is that the United States is ill-prepared to deal with national security problems other than those of a military nature.[9] Since a major shock would be required to overcome the disunifying effect of an economic threat, diffuse threats at lower levels of intensity can pose even more dangerous challenges. Perhaps the clearest recent substantiation for this view may be found in the disarray of the Atlantic Alliance in the wake of the 1973 oil embargo, when disparate dependencies on Middle East oil split alliance partners and resulted in markedly different assessments of the strategic imperatives and the resultant proper course of action in dealing with the Arab-Israeli crisis. The point is not to criticize various allies for reacting in different ways, for their critical vulnerabilities are easy to understand and must be accommodated, but rather to illustrate the point that economic threats can be inherently disunifying. As with other aspects of threats and their particular characteristics, of course, this can at times be turned to advantage in skillful use of nonmilitary instruments of national power.

Political and economic approaches to application of national power come together in many ways to include arrangements by which allied nations assist one another in bearing economic burdens that are the result of shared security interests. The offset payments and purchases of military goods that West Germany undertook for a number of years to help the United States reduce the impact on its balance of payments caused by stationing troops in the Federal Republic is one case in point. Another is widespread use of coproduction arrangements to reduce the economic impact on allied nations that purchase U.S. defense products, like the F-16 fighter aircraft. The F-16 will be manufactured by four different NATO nations, thereby increasing the economic feasibility of European acquisition of the U.S.-designed system. In order to restrict the growing economic-military independence of an ally, a different approach can be taken, as when the United States used provisions of an agreement with Israel to prevent that nation from selling, for export, aircraft that included a U.S.-designed engine. Provision or withholding of economic assistance to other nations has already been cited as an important means of applying nonmilitary aspects of national power. Here, as with military assistance, the economic and political aspects interact extensively, since the presence of U.S. military and civilian personnel who provide assistance in foreign nations often leads to creation of relationships that later prove useful in facilitating joint responses to international events in which the two nations have a shared interest.

POLITICAL USES OF NATIONAL POWER

Several manifestations of international politics affect national security, and their potential impact is increasing. Voting patterns in international organizations can be significant, particularly when they result in constraints on action which are not uniformly advantageous. Negotiations on such matters as law of the sea, which may involve restrictions on passage of warships and on commercial development of the ocean's resources, provides an example of obvious and direct impact on security interests. Another is multinational agreement on allocation of broadcast frequencies for international use. In fact,

spacecraft communications and satellite relay increasingly involve
international economic, military, and psychological aspects of
national security, in addition to the obvious military applications.
On a broader plane the whole pattern of alliances and preferential
relationships among nations can serve to enhance security of the
participants (or of some of them), or to lead to a more threatening
and risky global environment. Alliance politics, in particular, have
been a central determinant of the evolving nature of the international
system in the postwar years, affecting political, economic, and
military aspects alike.

Specific examples of how this can work are provided by recent
international negotiations. According to one analyst: "Three conferences of government weapons experts sponsored by the ICRC [Inter-
national Committee of the Red Cross] in conjunction with the 1974,
1975, and 1976 sessions of the Diplomatic Conference generally were
little more than battles of rhetoric between the 'haves' and the 'have
nots,' with at least one developing nation changing its position over
the course of the sessions once it had acquired its own arsenal of the
weapons it previously had condemned."[10] Likewise, agreements
such as the new Law of the Sea will have some asymmetrical impacts,
particularly on "political cohesion and security in a maritime alliance like that of the Atlantic."[11] No doubt many such cases could be
catalogued in which a nonmilitary instrument of power (such as an
international negotiation) is used to enhance the security of some
states, perhaps at the expense of others that on purely military
grounds could not be so disadvantaged. In effect, the nonmilitary
instrument has been used to preempt military means in the hands of
other states, at least insofar as those other states continue to abide
by the agreements to which they are parties.

On this level of macrostrategic approaches to the application
of national power, political initiatives designed to shape the international environment within which specific instruments of national
power are brought to bear provide both hazards and opportunities.
When international negotiations such as those sponsored by the Red
Cross result in limitations on the use of certain forms of weaponry,
and when the effect of the limitations is to impose disproportionate
disadvantages upon some states (whether because of their heavy reliance upon weaponry of the type constrained, asymmetries in tactical
mission, or whatever) to the benefit of other states, those negotiations
may be described as exercises in the application of nonmilitary instruments of national power. Even more generally, political initiatives
that succeed in dealing with threatening or disruptive developments
in international affairs are among the most important examples of
nonmilitary instruments.

Perhaps the most arresting example in recent years has been the attempt to limit the proliferation of nuclear weapons. While the acquisition and use of nuclear capabilities is, in the main, a military aspect of national power, diplomatic efforts to restrict the proliferation of such capabilities involve a number of nonmilitary instruments. These include the development of a treaty or agreement; diplomatic efforts to obtain adherence to it by other states not yet possessing nuclear weapons (this may involve assurances of protection against use of nuclear weapons by those states that have them, economic quid pro quo, or a combination of inducements); and monitoring of the international environment to determine compliance by signatories.

PSYCHOLOGICAL FACTORS

Ideology is far from dead as a determinant of national and international behavior: witness recent events in Iran. Upon his return from exile, Ayatollah Khomeini's first act was to "beg the Almighty to cut off the hands of foreigners."[12] In his subsequent successful attempts to bring down the Bakhtiar government, which the Shah had left in place upon his departure into exile, the Ayatollah told the Iranian people that it was a "religious obligation" for them to demonstrate in opposition to the existing government. [13] Nationalism, religious zealotry, postcolonial resentment, racial and tribal antagonisms of long standing—all seem certain to compound economic and military rivalries and fears to provide more than sufficient grounds for conflict in many regions in the years ahead. To whatever extent fear of escalation and retribution constrain the direct use of military force, nonmilitary instruments of national power can be expected to increase in importance. Psychological instruments can play a major role.

Nonmilitary measures are often useful in achieving results that cannot be brought about by military force—or that cannot otherwise be achieved as quickly, cheaply, or neatly. Nonmilitary means frequently have the character of persuasion rather than coercion, which means that the side effects of their use are likely to be less bitter, and the development of residual antagonisms may be avoided or reduced. While military means seldom involve any quid pro quo for the unlucky recipient, at least until after the fact, economic, political and other nonmilitary means can often be applied on conjunction with an element of reciprocity that, even when the other party has little choice but to go along, can make the going less objectionable. For example, international political negotiations that result in agreement on use of certain waterways by ships of every nation can achieve rights of access for the major powers that they could probably force through application of military power, but only at much higher cost in resentments created, support and fielding of the necessary military forces, and constant fear of interference. Key votes acquired in such negotiations may be compensated by trade or economic assistance concessions. Similarly, landing rights in certain foreign nations could probably be forced by the more powerful nations, but obtaining them voluntarily in exchange for assistance, commercial airline routes, or some other form of quid pro quo is not only mutually beneficial, but far less disruptive to the fabric of international life. Where application of military force comes to be one of the first, rather than one of the last, resorts of any nation, the range of possibilities is greatly narrowed and the effectiveness of the military option may also be diminished.

In certain cases it may be argued that military force simply cannot achieve the desired end, no matter how ample that force may be. This may result from the fact that military force is simply inapplicable in a given case, as in forcing the majority of nations in an international organization to vote in a particular way, or from lack of domestic political support for the use of military force to bring about some outcome, even one that would be welcomed if achieved through nonmilitary means. This derives in part from the fact that military means are usually the most expensive, both in terms of men and monetary resources, and in terms of the traumatic effect on international relations and the domestic self-concept. While the nation may hold many goals worthy of attainment, not all are worth the same expenditure of assets. Thus, most goals are considered worthwhile only if they can be achieved by something less than ultimate military involvement.

Lincoln Bloomfield, observing that a large percentage of effective "violence-controlling policy activity" takes place before an identifiable conflict even emerges, has stressed the importance of perceptions as an element of national power, given that the perceptions held by others are key to their responses to other nations.[14] That extends from determining whether defense preparations are required in advance of anticipated military conflict to the desirability of currying political favor with a powerful neighbor whose good will is important to future well-being. It is essential that the United States effectively shape the perception of other nations regarding U.S. strength and the will to use it.

Obviously, there must be a fairly close relationship between actual power and the perception of it that one seeks to engender in other nations, lest discovery of too great a disparity undercut the effect being sought. Efforts must be made to ensure that real power is not undervalued or overlooked by others. Such efforts may include judicious heightening of those perceptions in selected instances. This is a realm that may prove fruitful for the United States, which has in the past too often tended to describe its own power in terms of unfavorable numerical comparisons, while neglecting to find means of dramatizing its very real economic power and qualitative military advantages.

QUASI-MILITARY FACTORS

In this borderline category where military and nonmilitary factors are difficult to sort out, there are a number of aspects of the application of national power that are of particular current concern. Among these are arms transfers (economic and military aspects); support for or toleration of international terrorism (military and psychological-political aspects); proliferation of peaceful nuclear energy technology (economic and, potentially, military aspects); active participation in or passive acceptance of illegal trafficking in narcotics (economic and security aspects); and manipulation of domestic developments in foreign countries (political, psychological, and possibly military aspects).

Each of these manifestations involves both opportunities and hazards. Whether any one of them is considered a legitimate means of bringing national power to bear is in part a function of the national ethic and in part of the previous success or failure of particular means. But each represents a serious security concern for every major nation, for even when a nation chooses not to employ such means itself, it must be prepared to counter their effects when they are used by other nations. Sometimes this is done (as it is in the case of the flow of illegal narcotics) even in the absence of certain knowledge of which nation or nations are responsible.

THE SPIRITUAL ELEMENT OF NATIONAL POWER

Discussions of this kind are usually concerned solely with concrete considerations of economic and political matters. But there is another aspect that is equally, and perhaps much more, important: for the purposes of this analysis, I will call it the spiritual element. I am using the term spiritual to imply a complex of factors that underlie the ability of a nation to maintain and employ the other elements of its power, and to do so with consistency, energy, and endurance. National morale is a part of this dimension, and it stems in part from belief in the rightness and value of the strategic goals, the legitimacy of the larger purpose, and the utility of a chosen strategy as a means of accomplishing its objectives. It involves essential agreement as to the role the nation should play in world affairs and the means it should employ. Such agreement must be based on the political and ethical values that have contemporary meaning for that particular society.

Recognition of this spiritual dimension is implicit in the widespread agreement that a national strategy acceptable to Americans must be based upon and give expression to national values and political ideals, an agreement that appears to approach unanimity in this post-Vietnam, post-Watergate era. Thus an essential nonmilitary element of the exercise of national power—particularly at times when those values and ideals are in flux or have been called into question—involves reformulating central values and demonstrating their validity in determining, and finally in achieving, worthy strategic goals.

The spiritual dimension also has to do with national will—not just the will to use force when necessary (which is the formulation usually encountered), but also the will to accept responsibilities appropriate to the nation's means and principles, and to play a consistent and reliable part in shaping the global order even when this involves risk and sacrifice. The exercise of power in this fashion requires confidence, which is derived from an overall strategic concept that is viewed as sound and workable.

Whatever the means, whether military or nonmilitary, they have little utility in the absence of the will to employ them, the wisdom to do so to good advantage, and the values that cast that advantage in ethical and humane terms. The attributes of a nation that has its bearings, knows what its obligations are, and is determined to live up to them are not so difficult to define, however challenging they are to achieve. Churchill may have epitomized them best: "In war: Resolution. In Defeat: Defiance. In Victor: Magnanimity. In Peace: Good Will."[15] That Americans will respond to appeals to their patriotism, generosity, and responsibility has often been demonstrated. That they will do so only when convinced of the value of the cause and the possibility of success is equally clear. In the absence of such conviction, no democracy can long sustain a major effort, military or otherwise.

The interaction of the spiritual aspect of national power with aspects of military capability and the political, economic, and psychological factors of nonmilitary instruments is thus of central importance, for in a sense it determines the energy and dedication that will be devoted to developing and applying those more tangible qualities. The national self-concept and the role in world affairs engendered by it could thus be viewed as the elements governing the use of instruments of national power.

ENHANCEMENT AND DENIAL ASPECTS

Nonmilitary instruments of national power, like military instruments, can be used both offensively—to deter or disable a hostile power—and defensively. While offensive uses of power receive considerable attention, as they ought, defensive uses are sometimes insufficiently considered. In fact one might argue that the primary value of nonmilitary instruments have in the main been defensive—as, for example, in rebuilding the economies of war-devastated allies through the Marshall Plan and sustaining friendly governments in Third World nations through economic and advisory assistance.

There seems to me to be even greater opportunities in the future for security enhancement through use of nonmilitary instruments. The scientific, technical, and industrial capacity of the United States provides the means. The approach might well be to examine key strategic vulnerabilities of the United States and its primary allies, then set about using these competitive advantages to devise means of removing or offsetting those vulnerabilities. One need not look far for an example of great current relevance. Although the supply of imported petroleum is of great importance to the United States, it is even more important to our West European allies, and absolutely critical to Japan. Development of a viable alternative source of energy, one that would be economically competitive with petroleum and that could be made available in significant amounts within a reasonably short time, would simply redesign the strategic map. And, it should be noted, it would not be necessary to deny access to such technology on the part of hostile states: it would be enough simply to remove the reliance upon foreign sources of petroleum that constitute strategic vulnerabilities for friendly states. In fact, making the technology more generally available might even remove a potential source of conflict by easing the energy requirements of states that would otherwise be tempted to undertake aggressive actions to secure foreign oil.

Such a strategic initiative employing a nonmilitary instrument of national power—scientific and industrial capabilities—would need to be planned and undertaken within the context of a broader consideration of the probable impacts and their effects on national security. Replacement of petroleum as the world's primary source of energy, for example, would have a tremendous effect on the principal suppliers of petroleum, who have come to depend on oil revenues to fund their development and security programs. Likewise, replacement of oil with a markedly cheaper source of energy, should it prove possible, would have important effects on patterns of world trade, relative positions in earning foreign exchange, and the political and economic

leverage enjoyed by certain states or groups of states. While energy
may provide the clearest example of the enormous strategic impact
of security enhancement, careful study might yield many others.
Advanced means of transportation that make reliance upon certain
routes no longer necessary, communications facilities that do not
rely on ground facilities in various locations abroad, and development
of alternatives to other critical raw materials or even finished goods
are examples of possible application of this approach. It is not new,
of course. During World War II, artificial rubber replaced natural
rubber when supplies of that essential material were interrupted.
The resulting technological progress opened up a whole range of other
possibilities and improved performance products. To anticipate such
problems and apply the necessary developmental efforts to their solution in advance of the need promises even more important impact in
the future.

PLANNING AND USING NONMILITARY INSTRUMENTS

In presenting the proposed foreign assistance program for the
current (1979) fiscal year to the Senate Foreign Relations Committee,
Secretary of State Vance observed that "we need the cooperation of
the Third World to deal effectively with such pressing global problems
as economic instability; population growth; adequate food and energy
production; environmental deterioration; nuclear proliferation; terrorism; and the spread of narcotics."[16] Two conclusions of central importance to our topic seem inescapable. The first is that this range
of problems is directly related to the national security of the United
States. The second is that military power seems largely inapplicable
as a means of dealing with them. Nonetheless, it seems fair to say
that we are a long way from developing nonmilitary instruments that
deal with them effectively. Foreign assistance, proposed by Secretary
Vance as one such instrument, is clearly not going to resolve problems of such magnitude and complexity by itself, particularly given
the quite modest levels provided by Congress in recent years. The
task of devising and utilizing a package of nonmilitary instruments
for dealing with these and other pressing security problems not amenable to military solutions is, I would suggest, almost entirely before
us.

The Secretary of Defense recently acknowledged that many of
the "newer vulnerabilities" that face the United States "are economic
and social in character and do not lend themselves to military reme-
dies." In this context, Secretary Brown defined national security for
the Council on Foreign Relations:

Most of us . . . would consider the United States reasonably secure if we are able to go about our business without major external infringement on our internal affairs, and without damage to our society as a whole from outside. By that static criterion, the problem may seem simple. It becomes much less so when we consider what we ought to be doing in the present to give reasonable assurance of having that ability in the future. [17]

A mechanism that systematically defines and plans for the acquisition and employment of those future means, particularly in the nonmilitary realm, is critical. As though in confirmation, Geoffrey Kemp has spoken of our "extraordinary vulnerability to forms of conflict short of war." [18] While this is in part the unavoidable lot of a highly industrialized society, surely one of the primary reasons for this vulnerability is the lack of a mechanism for planning and utilizing our own nonmilitary elements of national power, and for countering the use of such means by hostile nations. This deficiency is rendered all the more troublesome in that there is no shortage of nonmilitary means available to the United States, which possesses at least in potential a richer mixture of economic, diplomatic, and psychological means than virtually any other nation.

Samuel Huntington recently pointed out, in a discussion of economic diplomacy, that over a recent six-year period the Soviet Union imported some $6 billion worth of machinery and equipment from the West, 30 to 40 percent of it involving advanced technology. Many of the imports were made possible through provision of official credits that were sometimes offered at below market rates. As a result, according to an estimate cited by Dr. Huntington, Soviet production of petroleum would now be 10 to 15 percent less were it not for the imports of Western technology. Arguing that economic detente cannot continue to coexist with Soviet military adventurism, he observes nevertheless that

harnessing economic power to foreign policy goals presents formidable obstacles: bureaucratic pluralism and inertia; congressional and interest group politics; the conflicting pulls of alliance diplomacy; and most important, in dramatic contrast to military power, a pervasive ideology that sanctifies the independence, rather than the subordination, of economic power to government. [19]

This useful essay concludes with a plea for legislation that would permit the President to engage in "economic diplomacy," and the obser-

vation that "it would be truly ironic, even tragic, if it should turn out
that the nature of the American political system prevents this nation
from capitalizing on its very real economic advantages."[20] Inherent
in this commentary is the recognition that the United States has not
succeeded thus far in capitalizing on this strength, a realization
coupled in the article with a discussion of the inadequacy of present
coordinating mechanisms to permit such actions to be undertaken.
That assessment must be given particular consideration in view of
the author's recent association with the staff of the National Security
Council, where, one presumes, whatever may be done to accomplish
these tasks is now being attempted.

Perhaps underlying the inadequate mechanisms is an American
reluctance to manipulate nonmilitary factors to strategic advantage.
There may be cultural antecedents for such reluctance: manipulation
may be seen to go against the grain of native generosity and good will.
If so, this could be a disabling trait in the more subtle but no less
dangerous contemporary strategic environment. Observing that the
United States has historically tended to view all challenges in military
or diplomatic terms, one commentator has suggested that "this problem renders U.S. policy-makers insensitive to the magnitude of the
conflict and unprepared to cope with innovative Soviet non-military
actions against Western spheres of influence which pass unrecog-
nized."[21]

Dealing with such a problem can never be easy—Tocqueville
noted that "once the American people have got an idea into their head,
be it correct or unreasonable, nothing is harder than to get it out
again"[22]—but a viable planning mechanism would be helpful in starting
the process of reshaping U.S. attitudes toward effective nonmilitary
action.

There is, as these examples suggest, much evidence that the
United States presently lacks an effective mechanism for planning
and utilizing nonmilitary elements of national power. Such a deficiency
in planning capacity is particularly disabling in view of what was once
characterized as, "for a mixture of constitutional and behavioural
reasons, . . . the most complex decision-making process since
Byzantium."[23] Partly, of course, this is the inevitable result of a
pluralistic society and a transitory government. Not only has the
United States lacked any sustained controlling vision of the nature of
the international system and the role of the nation in that system, but
there has been no consistent grand strategy that could be said to em-
body even a de facto manifestation of such a role or vision. In the
absence of enduring touchstones, the policies and actions of the government in office have necessarily been geared to the vicissitudes of
the moment, fragmented and at times incompatible in objective or
effect, and more often reactive than anticipatory.

Beyond this capstone problem, there is the range of difficulties deriving from the very nature of the political and economic systems, which are in many other ways great strengths of the nation. The absence of governmental control over commercial interactions with the world at large (except in a few special cases, such as arms transfers), though it works as a powerful incentive to entrepreneurship, also compounds the problem of implementing the economic aspects of nonmilitary national power in a systematic way. Likewise the domestic political power of special interests can often override any longer-term interests of the nation as a whole, defeating attempts to implement long-range solutions to complex problems in favor of short-term advantage to those special interests. (This is illustrated by the protracted wrangles over development of an effective national energy policy.) Other culturally-induced aspects of the national outlook on international problems also contribute to the difficulty of effectively employing nonmilitary instruments of power. The longing for noninvolvement runs strong and deep in the American subconscious and repeatedly manifests itself in neglect of external affairs until they have deteriorated to the point where they can no longer be ignored, nor dealt with by other than military means. Thus many opportunities to head off or ameliorate international problems before they demand military involvement are lost because of this antipathy. The tendency is by no means consistent, of course, as evidenced by such creative U.S. actions as development of the Marshall Plan, a leading role in creation of the United Nations, foreign aid to a variety of recipients, and the formation of defensively oriented international political alliances. But the key here, as in terms of a viable overall concept of the nation's role, seems to lie in effective political leadership, which can engender a sense of international obligation sufficient to overcome the ingrained tendency to disengagement. These are, at base, political and indeed philosophical problems of long standing.

But, while development of a compelling vision of a U.S. role that could coalesce and energize the American people is a task beyond the charter of the working bureaucracy, there remains much that could be done to ameliorate the problems involved in using nonmilitary instruments of national power. Most important, it seems to me, is a lean, competent, and properly organized policy-planning mechanism. Essential to its success are at least these attributes:

1. Backing of senior policy officials, specifically the President and other members of the National Security Council. Nothing is more futile than a policy-planning staff that lacks access to and the confidence of the policy-making official it ostensibly serves. This is dramatically illustrated by the varying fortunes of the NSC staff under successive Administrations. To be effective in anticipatory and not just reactive terms, the policy staff must have insight into the

principal concerns of national leaders, opportunities to brief them on impending problems, and visible impact on decisions. This is the key to attracting and retaining the talented staff required.

2. The acquisition and retention of people with a high level of both administrative and technical competence. An effective planning staff is no place for on-the-job training, or cross training, or whatever other euphemisms are from time to time used to gloss over the absence of detailed knowledge and sustained professional involvement with the central problems that occupy such a staff. To be effective a policy staff must be kept small (a few dozen persons at most). Thus there is no problem finding enough fully qualified people. The key lies in attracting and retaining them by providing meaningful work, which means work that is genuinely contributory to the formulation of national policy.

3. Stability and continuity of such a staff, once assembled, are indispensable if there is to be real long-term impact. While military instruments of power can occasionally be resorted to on a short-term basis, with results achieved quickly and within a relatively unchanged policy context, the nature of nonmilitary instruments is such that their effects are usually slower to develop and more subtle in impact, and thus necessitate more sustained planning and implementation. This is also the nature of anticipatory (as opposed to reactive) planning, so that on both counts it is imperative that the constant shuffling of people, accounts, and organizational arrangements that characterizes so many other elements of government be excluded from policy planning. This implies a professional staff not subject to automatic replacement when the political leadership changes. A professional staff deals with problems, develops options, and devises means of implementing the decisions of the political leadership. It does not itself choose the options, although naturally its outlook tends to shape the options deemed most responsive to the problem at hand.

4. Access to detailed data and planning support from the government and the civilian academic and analytical communities. This implies authority to ask governmental elements to provide studies, members of task forces, review services, and the like. It also implies sufficient funds to contract for whatever outside assistance is deemed useful, and a very small study management staff to orchestrate the support program inside and outside government.

5. Insulation from political pressures as determinants of what issues are to be considered, the range of options developed or their relative rankings, and other decisions properly residing in the realm of professional judgment. This is not to say that considerations of domestic or international politics ought not have an impact on a policy planning staff, but they should be filtered through the senior policymakers served by the staff, instead of being communicated by

distracting and highly competitive direct access to such a staff on the part of those who wish to gain added prominence for their particular concerns. This objective also implies that privileged status be accorded the results of the planning staff's deliberations, both to avoid having them become political issues in their own right and restricting the President's freedom of action in considering them, and more basically to avoid undercutting proposed courses of action by informing other nations in advance of U.S. intentions. Here the parallel to military strategy is instructive.

The lack of an effective coordinating mechanism for any major element of governmental operations is of course nothing new. Ours is to a frightening extent an ad hoc government, one that responds to crisis by convening on the spot a temporary mechanism for dealing with the situation at hand, and which has then to devote its first and best efforts to organizing itself and establishing communications with the various elements involved. Perhaps it is an inevitable result of our Puritan heritage that we cannot bear to see anything go to waste, and thus mechanisms for crisis management are not maintained in readiness, to begin functioning when needed. Whatever the reason, the lack of an appropriate mechanism for dealing with a given problem is a common phenomenon. But when that problem involves coherent planning for application of a complex range of approaches to international problems, the lack of such a mechanism is very close to disabling.

Alastair Buchan has remarked on the "unpalatable" advantages possessed by nations "with a strong central government that need not make short-term promises, as democratic politicians must, and can make plans and execute them over a considerable period of time."24 For the United States, throughout much of its history, the principal counterbalance to that advantage has been a high degree of unanimity as to the goals to be pursued, and even the means by which to pursue them. That is not to say there have not been partisan differences, even heated ones, but only that they have been concentrated in a fairly narrow part of the broad spectrum of possible approaches. This has resulted in far more continuity of both purpose and program than might otherwise have been expected. But there remains the inherent disadvantage of not having more centralized control and greater administrative tenure, whatever the attendant disadvantages such arrangements might also entail. A planning mechanism of the kind here advocated could provide a useful vehicle for sustained treatment of persistent and long-range problems that would confront any Administration of whatever party.

For the United States, a structured approach coupled with increased understanding could significantly strengthen the ability to use nonmilitary instruments of national power, while at the same time protecting against adverse impacts of their use by hostile powers.

NOTES

1. "The 1977 Alastair Buchan Memorial Lecture," Survival (January-February 1978): 3.

2. Alastair Buchan, The End of the Postwar Era (New York: Saturday Review Press, 1974), p. 130.

3. For example, Geoffrey Kemp in U. S. Military Academy, Arms Transfers: A Senior Conference, 1976, p. 24.

4. "No Choice, No Illusions," Foreign Policy (Winter 1976/77): 110.

5. Quotations are from Frances S. Wright's summary of Crozier's Strategy of Survival in Friday Review of Defense Literature, August 18, 1978, p. 4.

6. "A Strategy for the United States," International Security (Spring 1978): 34.

7. "What It Means to Be Number Two," Fortune (November 1978).

8. As quoted in The Washington Post, October 15, 1978, p. A17.

9. "The U.S. Military in Foreign Policy in the 1980's," Panel Discussion, Inter-University Seminar on Armed Forces and Society: Southwest Regional Conference, Dallas, April 27-29, 1978.

10. W. Hays Parks, "The 1977 Protocols to the Geneva Convention of 1949," Naval War College Review (Fall 1978): 21.

11. Elizabeth Young's review of New Strategic Factors in the North Atlantic, ed. Christoph Bertram and Johan Holst, in Survival (January/February 1978): 42 (quoting the editors).

12. The New York Times, February 11, 1979, p. E17.

13. The Washington Post, January 17, 1979, p. 17.

14. Lincoln P. Bloomfield and Amelia C. Leiss, Controlling Small Wars: A Strategy for the 1970's, pp. 26 and 33.

15. Winston Churchill, The Gathering Storm (Boston: Houghton Mifflin, 1948).

16. "Statement: U.S. Foreign Assistance Programs for Fiscal Year 1979," Department of State, March 2, 1978.

17. Address of September 13, 1978, as extracted in Selected Statements #78-9, Department of the Air Force, October 1, 1978, p. 20.

18. U.S. Military Academy, Arms Transfers, p. 37.

19. "Trade, Technology, and Leverage: Economic Diplomacy," Foreign Policy (Fall 1978): 68-70.

20. Ibid., p. 76.

21. Michael J. Deane, "The Soviet Assessment of the 'Correlation of World Forces': Implications for American Foreign Policy," Orbis (Fall 1976): 636.

22. Alexis de Tocqueville, Democracy in America, J. P. Mayer and Max Lerner, eds. (New York: Harper and Row, 1966), p. 186.

23. Buchan, The End of the Postwar Era, p. 195.

24. Ibid., p. 293.

3
THE UNITED STATES: PROBLEMS AND POLICY

This chapter examines the broad guidelines for U.S. policy in nonnuclear conflict. Reviewing the changing policy conditions from the World War II era, the chapter points out that there are a number of lessons to be learned from the experience of the past generation. These include the need to understand how the United States projects its power internationally—and sometimes fails to do so—and the need for caution in a variety of nonnuclear situations. In a number of instances, the best policy posture for the United States is to project its power indirectly, without the commitment of troops or military maneuvering. Using the Vietnam experience, the chapter focuses on the limitations imposed upon the United States in nonnuclear (low-intensity) conflicts and the policy constraints that all policymakers should appreciate. Particularly important is the observation that the Vietnam experience remains an important factor that affects the perceptions of military men and civilian policymakers. Military intervention, as a broad policy guide, requires specific types of military forces. As the chapter points out, the configuration of military forces to respond to every contingency is a difficult policy to adopt, requiring significant resources in both manpower and money. Preconfiguration of forces can serve as a useful symbol to project credibility; but, in a liberal democracy, military intervention requires, at the very minimum, popular support. Without such support, no amount of military planning and manpower can successfully carry out a policy of military intervention. Finally, intervention in low-intensity conflict (nonnuclear situations) is essentially a result of presidential wars—wars that can be initiated by the President with little, if any, Congressional or public input. The problem faced by the President is the reaction of Congress and the public after the fact, particularly if military intervention does not accomplish its goals. The chapter discusses the restraints on the President and the various policies that the President may adopt to intervene militarily. In the final analysis, U.S. involvement in nonnuclear conflict requires public support, as well as that of a variety of institutions. The experience of Vietnam has injected a high degree of caution, indeed skipticism, regarding a policy of military intervention. Moreover, even if the political will should develop, military forces are inadequately prepared to exercise military staying power in areas outside Europe.

5
POLICY PROPOSALS:
U.S. POLITICAL AND
MILITARY RESPONSE
Edwin Fedder

Patience may well be a virtue that goes unrewarded when practiced by political leaders. The threat to use force and, indeed, its
actual use are hallmarks of superpower status globally and even of
the petty principalities who may be number three. Super- and regiona
powers may be distinguished by the extent of their reach. Conceived
of as concentric circles, superpower influence may radiate globally,
whereas regional powers are more limited.

Superpowers tend to assume that all areas within reach are
subject to their control. This assumption is seductive, and accounts
for claims that certain policies have succeeded when in fact their
influence on events has been slight. This may be seen in the alleged
success of U.S. policy in the revolution against Sukarno and America
prowess at Sadat's eviction of Soviet personnel.

The purpose of this essay is not to re-examine the details of
U.S. policy as a superpower, nor its fall from grace. The intent is
to comment on the nature of U.S. policy in the decade of the 1980s,
based on the relative success or failure of its policy in the post-
World War II period.

AN OVERVIEW

Having reached superpower status following World War II, the
United States was virtually alone until the USSR began expanding her
role in the mid-1960s. Starting rather hesitantly with the Truman
Doctrine (1947) and the Containment Policy (1947), we followed with
NATO (1949). The Korean War (1950-54) demonstrated the fragility
of America's domain, which was subsequently shored up under

Secretary Dulles' alliance expansion policy. NATO was to be cloned as CENTO, SEATO, ANZUS and a myriad of siblings in the guise of bilateral alliances and mutual assistance pacts with Japan, Taiwan, Israel, South Korea, Iran, etc.

Soviet reluctance to challenge U.S. policy directly provided the United States with a clear road. U.S. policy was only to be limited by logistical requirements and latent nationalism in the areas concerned, and this was hardly an effective barrier to U.S. military power. Officials of the Eisenhower Administration learned that Soviet power could be contained by the threat of U.S. nuclear superiority, while demonstrably weak conventional military forces were sufficient for the tasks of intervening in distant places. Iran (1954), Suez (1956), and Lebanon (1958) proved that a relatively small mobile force could regulate the defense perimeter so that the U.S. strategic and military position could be advanced cheaply and without bloodshed.

This is not to say that there were not frustrations: France's refusal to ratify her own proposal for creating a European Defense Community (EDC), the debacle of French policy in Indochina, Indian hostility to creating a South Asian Treaty Organization, and Egyptian opposition to a Middle East Treaty Organization were signal defeats for U.S. policy. But the United States recovered from each setback with what was considered skillful aplomb. It virtually restored Vietnam to ante bellum status, replacing the French; the Baghdad Pact replaced the projected METRO only to be replaced by CENTO, headquartered in Turkey. Though the plan had been to forge an Arab equivalent to NATO, no Arab states joined. (Iraq withdrew following her revolution in 1958.) The projected South Asia Treaty Organization was to be a NATO-like entity organized around Nehru's India. But SEATO's linch pin was Pakistan, leading Nehru to conclude that it was targeted against India, not the USSR or China.

EDC's defeat, following immediately upon Dulles' "Agonizing Reappraisal" speech, helped pave the way for nationalist resurgence in Europe. Coupled with the Anglo-French debacle in Suez, the end to French and British imperial designs was hastened by a U.S. policy that had not set out to discourage those designs.

U.S. NUCLEAR SUPERIORITY AND DIMINISHED UNCONVENTIONAL CAPABILITY

Between 1953 and 1960, U.S. military capability for engaging in low-intensity conflict was declining at the same time that its nuclear superiority was apparently increasing. But appearances can be deceptive, and Americans tended to believe they were uniquely safe from serious challenge because of their overwhelming nuclear superiority in terms of instruments and delivery systems. That the Soviets were not all that far behind the United States was made crystal clear with the launching of Sputnik in 1957, demonstrating the Soviet ability to better the Americans in space and signalling an end to America's unique position.

The Kennedy Administration took office in 1961 with the self-proclaimed mandate to restore U.S. prominence (close the "missile gap") and to develop the technology and skill for (1) combatting Soviet "indirect aggression" by means of counterinsurgency warfare, and (2) promoting liberation wars to build nations who would be friendly to the United States. Though still concentrating on its burgeoning nuclear stockpiles, the Administration launched a massive space program (NASA, and others), increased expenditures for conventional weapons and forces, initiated combat operations in South Vietnam, created the Green Berets (patterned after the French Algerian forces), developed its laboratory for counterinsurgency warfare in Vietnam, undertook the task of building a new nation in South Vietnam, and launched the invasion of the Bay of Pigs. This is only a partial list of developments in 1961.

The missile crisis in Cuba (1962) proved to the Administration that it was on the right track. It spread the word that, had the gauntlet been thrown by the Soviets during the previous Administration, the United States might not have been able to mount a blockade since the U.S. military were in so low a state of readiness as to preclude chances for a limited response to limited challenges.

Eisenhower's reliance upon nuclear deterrence posited threat escalation to the nuclear threshold to compel Soviet acquiescence to limits set by the United States. Thus, John Foster Dulles became known for his brinksmanship, and the favored account of his term was titled Duel at the Brink. "Brinksmanship" became the fashionable topic of discourse among policy and academic elites. Such discourse included mathematically sophisticated games of chicken and multiple prisoner dilemmas, demonstrating the choices available given limited information about an adversary's intentions and capabilities.

INTERVENTIONIST ORIENTATION

While it is still too early to size up the Carter Administration, it might be said that each U.S. Administration since World War II has been interventionist. Still, since the styles, modes, scales and loci for the various interventions have differed, it is hard to generalize intelligently from them. It may well be that, like "war" and "peace," "intervention" is too broad a term to be studied with precision.

Comparing one Administration's interventions with another is somewhat like comparing apples and oranges. Changed conditions make each case almost unique. Still, it may be possible to discern trends. It is important to bear in mind that foreign policy makers may be accountable for what they do, not what they say they do—and especially not while they are doing it. Official statements made at the time of an incident must always be considered self-serving, mis-leading, and dissembling. Such statements are public relations events, not analytically meaningful documents. If one wishes to study Truman-Acheson foreign policy, one must examine what they did, not what they claimed to do. Examining speeches may be rhetorically interest-ing; it rarely tells much about events.

From the standpoint of their rhetoric, presidents from Truman through Ford exhibited remarkable similarities; however, the simi-larities tend to fade when the rhetoric is put aside. The triumph of Truman–Acheson policy—the North Atlantic Treaty Organization (NATO)—was largely a European creation designed to compel U.S. participation in a European renascence to (1) deter the Soviet Union, (2) police Germany, and (3) guarantee an American hegemony expected to be more beneficent than any likely European hegemony. The Tru-man Doctrine, stripped of its rhetorical flourishes, becomes merely the first in a long line of military and economic assistance programs entered into by the United States in succeeding decades. The fading away of Greek communist activity resulted more from serendipity than from U.S. acuity. Even the Marshall Plan now appears to have accompanied European recovery rather than caused it.

Aside from Korea, which would have been an unqualifiedly suc-cessful intervention had the Chinese not been drawn in, Truman's interventions had a largely indeterminate influence upon events. Eisenhower's policies were similarly indeterminate, save for Guate-mala, Iran, and Suez. In Guatemala, leftists were overthrown and have been denied a governing role since their ouster in 1954. In Iran, the ouster of Mohammed Mossadegh may have contributed significantly to recent events. Twenty-five years later, ouster of Mossadegh's protege, Bakhtiar, in favor of Khomeini, was certainly not an outcome preferred by the United States. Restoring the Shah to his throne in 1954 marked the triumph of anachronism. That the Shah was over-thrown eventually was not remarkable: his survival for 25 years was. King Khaled, Prince Fahd and the sheiks of Kuwait, Dubai, Abu Dhabi, etc., should tremble, for they too are anchronistic in this epoch.

In Suez, the United States intervened against two allies (Britain and France), and promised a client state (Israel) far more than it would or could deliver. Israel's voluntary withdrawal from Sinai rested upon U.S. guarantees of free navigation through the straits of Tiran and the Suez Canal. As Israel should have known, such guarantees are rhetorical flourishes, not policy indicators. They are statements of hope, not intent. The effect upon Britain and France may have been even more serious than upon the Middle East.

Suez proved the vacuousness of the much vaunted "special relationship" of Britain and the United States. Prime Minister Anthony Eden's political position was destroyed, and the Anglo-French attempt to undermine Nasser's control of Egypt was frustrated by the U.S. government, which had encouraged it. The French government survived, but not for long. The coup de grace had been delivered to the Fourth Republic. The seeds of what was to be called Gaullism were planted, to be fertilized by de Gaulle himself in 1958. Since then France had been a most contentious ally.

INDOCHINA AND VIETNAM

The Kennedy, Johnson, and Nixon Administrations came to be dominated by U.S. involvement in Indochina. This involvement has proved counterproductive, since South Vietnam has been absorbed by the North, which also controls communist Laos and Cambodia, successors to the neutral governments in place when U.S. interventions began. One is tempted to suggest that the domino principle was stood on its head. Only the intervention in the Dominican Republic can be proclaimed an unqualified success. U.S. intervention in Cuba (1961 and 1962) helped to solidify Castro's position, not weaken it.

SOVIET INTERVENTIONIST POLICIES

Real changes have occurred in Soviet foreign policy since World War II. Until his death, Stalin pursued a very sober, conservative policy resulting in a net withdrawal of Soviet military forces (Iran, 1946, and Korea, 1948). Stalin avoided intervening in Greece, Turkey, and, most significantly, Yugoslavia. To be sure, the coup de Prague in 1948 was aided and abetted by the USSR, but Soviet troops had remained in occupation since the war, and Soviet hegemony was acknowledged de facto by the Western powers.

The Soviets did intervene in East Berlin (1953), Poland (1956) and Hungary (1956); however, each was within the sphere of influence conceded by the West. Significantly, Albania's split did not result in Soviet military involvement, despite the bitterness of the dispute. And the USSR did not intervene in China, despite the potential danger posed by Chinese disaffection.

The Cuban missile incident (1962) was the watershed. For the first time, the USSR intervened in a place that was not only distant but in an American sphere. While they failed to obtain bases or to station missiles in Cuba, the Soviets secured U.S. acquiescence in Cuban territorial integrity and sovereignty. Certainly this was the primary goal of her intervention. Kennedy's triumph was shared by Khrushchev.

It remains somewhat unclear whether the Soviets led or were pushed by their Warsaw Pact allies to intervene in Czechoslovakia in 1968. In any case, the outcome was unambiguous. Dubcek's regime offered no resistance and was replaced by a more compliant government.

Soviet interventions beyond her sphere have had rather more indeterminate results. Soviet military personnel were evicted from the Sudan (1971), Egypt (1972), and Somalia (1977), and it might be presumptuous to assume that the Soviet-Cuban roles in Ethiopia and Angola are unambiguous. It is too soon to conclude that Neto and Mengitsu are "safely" in the Soviet camp; they may discover, as Somalia and Egypt did earlier, that Soviet-Cuban support is dispensable. Indeed, it is most unlikely that Soviet influence will overcome national pressures in any of the areas affected by Soviet and/or Cuban troops. Afghanistan, South Yemen, Iraq, Syria, Ethiopia, Angola, and so on, are ruled by men who—if push comes to shove—will place their national self-interest above Soviet or Cuban or any nonnational interest.

REASONS FOR INTERVENTION

If the results of intervention are as indeterminate as this review indicates, why do nations intervene in the affairs of other nations? The range of answers is perhaps unlimited, but would seem to include the following:

1. Modified machismo. States intervene to reassure themselves and others that they are there. They have little concern for matters of cost, benefit, risk. The Mayaguez Affair is an example.
2. Capability. States intervene because they can intervene. U.S. involvement in South Vietnam in 1961 is an example.
3. Inverted machismo. States intervene to deprive an adversary of a modified machismo intervention—for example, the Dominican Republic in 1965.
4. Displaced animosity. States intervene against a target to punish or frustrate an adversary not participating in the fighting. China intervened in Vietnam in 1979 to discredit the USSR.

5. Control. States intervene to determine specific political choices in the target—for example, the USSR in Hungary, 1956.
6. Deflect dissent. States intervene to deflect criticism from political leadership to an adversary. The Mayaguez affair also illustrates this point.
7. Camouflage. States proclaim hostile intervention to justify "retaliation." North Vietnam's "attack" on the Maddox and the Turner Joy in 1964, for example, resulted in the Gulf of Tonkin Resolution.

LOW-INTENSITY CONFLICT

Low-intensity conflicts (limited wars) are risky enterprises for all parties because they are easily protracted, and they may become unlimited. The conflict can be protracted if the adversaries are not exhausted by the struggle (as, for example, the United States and North Vietnam, 1961-74; and Israel and Egypt, Syria, Jordan, etc., since 1948). It was apparent to many that the Vietnam War as fought from 1965 to 1968 or after 1969 could have continued indefinitely with indeterminate results—neither side winning or losing. Resources available to the United States and to Vietnam would have permitted indefinite continuance so long as the conflict remained limited.

Similarly, resources available to Israel and her Arab adversaries permit an equally protracted conflict. Left to their own resources, the parties would long since have exhausted their resources and would have been more restricted in the level of fire-power available. Indefinite Soviet and U.S. resupply promoted renewed and intensified hostilities.

The homily that all wars must end is but a homily. It is not accurate historically to conclude that wars always result in an end that permits maintenance of the integrity of each adversary in whole or in part. Wars may result in the virtually complete eradication of a nation or even of a civilization.

Low-intensity conflicts may even be more dangerous for superpowers than for less powerful targets. This follows because the superpower projects its global role and may be drawn into multiple conflicts. Such conflicts may deplete resources or propel escalation to unlimited warfare. Given the U.S. predisposition to assume that the USSR ordered or enticed North Korea to invade South Korea, had China chosen that moment to attack India and the USSR to invade Yugoslavia, U.S. officials might well have concluded that the United States must go to war against the Soviet Union. Committing large military forces to war in Korea and Vietnam heightened U.S. vulnerability to hostile actions, to which the response would likely have been either inadequate or excessive.

INTERVENTION BY PROXY

It is always dangerous for political leaders to provide adversaries with options that may back them into corners. This is why it is better for superpowers to find proxies to front for them. Thus the USSR could terminate its support for Angola with little embarrassment for Cuba. Indeed, Cuban forces could (hence might) be abandoned at scattered points in Africa if such abandonment were necessary or useful for Soviet purposes. Such action by the USSR would be consonant with her status as a superpower and with the use of the Cuban proxy. Obviously, abandonment would not occur capriciously, but if and only if such abandonment were deemed necessary by reason of Soviet national interests. Such considerations may be seen in Soviet abandonment of communist parties in China in the 1920s and in Western Europe during the Nazi-Soviet pact in 1939, Iranian abandonment of the Kurds in Iraq (1977), and Yugoslav abandonment of Greek communist guerrillas in 1947.

Abandonment should not be viewed as dysfunctional; indeed, inherently reserving the option to abandon a proxy justifies the use. After all, the Soviets were not fighting in Angola and the Ogaden: Cubans were. The USSR can assume a posture of innocence with some degree of credibility, low though it might be. Were a major Islamic rebellion in Central Asia to occur, the Soviets might find that they need their transport, supplies, and personnel at home. This would undermine the logistic support of Cuban activities in Africa. Obviously, though, Cuba is aware of the risks involved in playing her role and considers them worth taking.

LESSONS FOR U.S. POLICY

In light of these considerations, what lessons can be applied to U.S. policy as we enter the 1980s? Neither relatively nor absolutely has U.S. military power diminished significantly, despite the Vietnam war and events in Africa and Iran. Perceptions of U.S. power have diminished, as have the bluster and swagger of U.S. deportment. Nurtured by Truman's and Dulles' oratory and Kennedy's adventurism, domestic and foreign publics tended to view the United States as well-nigh invincible. Czechoslovakia, China, and Korea should have proved the lie to such perceptions, but it took Vietnam and Iran to make the point, and U.S. prestige plummeted from its fancied position. It had to fail: only the timing was in question.

Exaggerated notions of a state's influence and control interfere in planning, implementing, assessing, and understanding its foreign policy. Thus the Truman Doctrine has been judged an astounding success, even though such claims are baseless and ill-informed. It suited presidents and satraps to pay homage to the claim, and the myth continued to grow until the success became part of conventional wisdom, to find its place alongside NATO's salvation of a Europe that likely was not even threatened by Stalin's hordes. Similarly, the United States conceded monolithic Soviet control over East Europe before such control was "established." Americans then exaggerated such influence by thinking of the Eastern European states as satellites, a rather preposterous notion politically.

The limitations of policy facing the United States today are not appreciably different from those it faced in the 1950s and 1960s. To control events in one's own jurisdiction is not easy. Khrushchev, Johnson, Nixon, and the Shah learned this lesson but recently. Controlling events abroad, beyond the reach of jurisdiction, is a will-o'-the-wisp, a fantasy, an invitation to self-deception. U.S. policy can exert some influence upon foreign leaders, but usually such influence is so slight as to be difficult to detect. If it were not, the United States could compel Israel and Egypt to make choices they otherwise would not make. And Somoza would have departed Nicaragua sooner.

Perhaps a sign of maturity, experience has finally demonstrated that U.S. policy is not so controlling or influential as Americans have pretended it to be. Such a lesson can have salutary effects if the sights of U.S. policy are lowered and if Americans do not pretend to what they cannot achieve. If the newly found American humility is excessive, adventures to restore U.S. pride and prestige may prove too tempting to resist.

American power is best projected indirectly, since indirection optimizes flexibility while offering some protection against over-extension and overexposure. Maintaining flexibility is of paramount importance in political situations if actors are to control events. Politics is an eclectic process in which ad hoc decisions are made on the basis of information that is only occasionally reliable, and that competes with much that is less reliable and more that is simply wrong. The scarcity of reliable information makes it necessary to maximize flexibility, thereby permitting modifications of policy to fit events. The Soviet shift from Somalia to Ethiopia may prove to have been an adroit response to shifting events, but it might also have resulted from inadequate or unreliable information. Somalia's eviction of Soviet personnel may similarly prove to have been adroit or inept.

It is quite easy for states to overextend their resources by intervening in diverse disputes. Relatively, all resources are scarce and should be managed prudently, else the consequences may prove more disadvantageous to the intervening state than to that in which it intervenes. Had Nationalist Chinese troops played the role taken by the United States in Vietnam, costs to this country would have been substantially reduced, even if U.S. financial and material support had been provided. Most American goals in Vietnam could have been accomplished better by Chinese than American forces. More importantly, policy failures that were legion and probably inevitable would not have been borne directly by the United States, and that will-o'-the-wisp, prestige, would not have plummeted so radically. Additionally, of course, shocks to the American economy and psyche would have been reduced significantly.

The implications for Taiwan would have been significant but would have resulted from Nationalist policy and would have had less profound significance for world politics. U.S. economic and military resources would have been husbanded and flexibility maintained. As things developed, the United States became ensnared in a trap largely self-constructed, leading to a general buffeting by events beyond its control. Americans maneuvered themselves into an indefinite war that virtually monopolized their attention and diminished their resolve. Of course a proxy war by ROC forces might well have drawn direct Communist Chinese involvement, thereby intensifying the war. The rational choice for the PRC would have been to remain aloof, permitting the Nationalist Chinese to become mired in South Vietnam as the United States eventually sank into the bog.

In addition to maintaining flexibility and avoiding overextension, states should avoid overexposure. An empirical term, overexposure is used here to mean the repetitive use of political devices that generate expectations for specific performance that may be inappropriate. The readiness of the United States to dispatch military and economic aid to Greece and Turkey eventually led to mutual assistance agreements with 42 states in the Dulles era. States such as Iran, Korea, and Israel were encouraged to build relatively massive military establishments without regard to the fact that such investment and consumption of resources tends to foster inflation and destabilize local economies and politics. And overexposure has made the United States hostage to local officials who seek aid for private as well as political gain. During the Dulles era, the Shah would occasionally threaten to turn to the Soviets if the United States refused his requests. Tom Mboya, then Vice President of Kenya, told the author that Third World leaders had but to invoke the communist spectre to obtain what they wished from the United States. More recently, states have developed expectations of U.S. intervention, or at least assumed the right to

threaten such intervention when it suited their policies. Thus it
seemed that the credibility of U.S. intervention policy would depend
on American willingness to intervene on call. More recently, Congressional initiatives, such as the War Powers Act, and Carter's
articulated nonintervention policies (particularly concerning Iran,
Ogaden, and Vietnam) appear to have reversed policies pursued by
previous Administrations. The shock of U.S. nonperformance would
have had less noticeable impact had images of American omniscience
not been so overblown.

Obviously, the United States cannot permit its credibility to be
determined by client or target states. The notion that such states can
determine American response actually stands logic on its head: here
the United States is de facto client; the ostensible client becomes
master. After the Treaty of Paris and during Watergate, Kissinger's
importunings about U.S. credibility implied that the test of credibility
was exertion of such force as clients may require or demand. Kissinger moved far beyond the strides made by his immediate predecessors,
who failed to distinguish between allied and nonallied states. Dean
Rusk proclaimed South Vietnam an ally when no alliance had been
executed. This caused chagrin among some of our other allies.

It is important to bear in mind that an alliance is quite a specific instrument of policy. An alliance is formed when a limited set
of states act in concert to increase their military security against a
common enemy. It represents a contractual arrangement entered into
by the parties according to their constitutional practices, requiring,
from the United States, approval by at least two-thirds vote of the
Senate. No alliance substitutes for or supersedes any constitutional
practice of a member, nor does it diminish sovereign independence
or national self-determination. Typically, alliance treaties provide
that in the event of an enemy attack, each allied party will respond as
it deems appropriate, according to its national decision-making practices. No alliance diminishes discretionary powers by government
officials in crisis situations. Official pronouncements justifying
actions by reference to alliance are always dissembling. Such statements are designed to blunt criticism by pretending limited choice.
Rusk's statement that we had to assist South Vietnam because we
would otherwise betray an ally was untrue. In fact there was no alliance; and even if there had been, U.S. options would still have been
free.

If alliances or client state dependency constrained U.S. policy
so effectively, such policy would be more system-determined than
the policies of most other states. But this is logically untenable. As
a superpower the United States is system-dominant, not system-
dependent, and U.S. policymakers act appropriately even if they do
not always speak appropriately. Appropriate behavior requires maxi-

mizing discretionary power and avoiding entanglements that diminish flexibility or that deplete resources. U.S. military power, or Soviet military power for that matter, are most effective instruments of policy when held in reserve. Large-scale commitment of military forces to low-intensity conflicts signals a failure of policy.

Vietnam had serious consequences for the United States not because South Vietnam became communist or because Vietnam as a whole became unified, but because the economic and political-military costs were excessive. Principal economic consequences include inflation and the dilemma of the U.S. dollar. In the political-military sphere, North Vietnam demonstrated that the emperor had indeed no clothes—or at best transparent ones. Emperors' garments are always superficial artifacts, but wise emperors do not expose themselves in public.

LESSONS LEARNED

The lessons of the past do not always enlighten future behavior, though frequently they provide a guide to future responses. We do not tend to respond rationally, even when perfect information is available; rather we tend to respond as we or our predecessors responded to analogous situations in the past. Despite their mocking of incumbents while campaigning for office, candidates, once elected, tend to mimic those who served before them.

Learning from the past requires scrupulous honesty in evaluating prior events and in drawing analogies. Our historical lessons must be free from cant and our analogies must contain isomorphic behavioral properties. The Truman Doctrine did not stem the tide of Soviet expansion in Greece, but coincided with Stalin's opposition to communist Greek insurrection. And the experience of the Vietnamese boat people bears little resemblance to the plight of the Jews in Nazi-occupied Europe. Had Hitler driven the Jews into the sea, many more would likely have been rescued.

Learning correctly from the past is not impossible: it requires investigation nurtured by skepticism. We must learn to distinguish what really happened from conventional wisdom that is but rarely wise.

6

STRATEGY LESSONS FROM AN
UNCONVENTIONAL WAR:
THE U.S. EXPERIENCE IN VIETNAM
Richard Shultz

From the standpoint of political and military policy, U.S.
involvement in Vietnam presents the analyst and policymaker with
several complex questions. However, because of the pervasive guilt
and sensitivities that have gripped this nation as a result of our Vietnam experience, the serious analysis of such questions has not been
undertaken. Perhaps the most crucial of these questions concerns the
political and military lessons of the U.S. intervention and how these
lessons can be applied to a coherent policy to be utilized in future
low-intensity conflicts. Instead of such a systematic assessment of
the lessons in Vietnam, the literature has been dominated by tracts
that draw "one absolute lesson" from that experience—the United
States should not consider any involvement in future low-intensity
conflicts: all such engagements are "no win" situations.[1] In effect,
we have returned to the post-Korean War "never again" syndrome in
the political realm, while in terms of our current military posture,
the reaction has manifested itself in the refusal seriously to consider
any strategy devised for low-intensity conflicts.

This study will go beyond such explanations to examine the
various counterinsurgency strategies devised to respond to the unconventional situation in Vietnam. It will focus, as well, on the social,
political, economic, cultural, and historical factors that constrained
these strategies. From this analysis we shall deduce lessons concerning the operation of various counterinsurgency strategies and
their impact on future low-intensity policy. In addition, we will identify lessons that should not be drawn from the Vietnam experience.

U.S. counterinsurgency strategies reveal two general approaches
that directly contradict each other.[2] However, interestingly enough,
each approach has as its primary goal the separation of the insurgents

from the populace they depend on for recruits, supplies, etc.
The essential difference hinges on how this separation is to be
achieved. Bluntly stated, the populace is either "courted" or "co-
erced" by the counterinsurgents. The former is based on what might
be termed the welfare reform approach, arguing that the support of
the populace can be acquired only through social improvement programs, while the latter relies on the use of coercive force in a
rationally calculated, cost-benefit equation. In terms of scope, this
study will divide the U.S. counterinsurgency experience in Vietnam
into three periods: (1) the 1961-63 social reform strategy; (2) the
1965-68 cost-benefit or suppressive approach; and (3) the 1968-72
Vietnamization policy. The analysis of each period will follow the
same format, but separate lessons will be drawn from the various
assessments. Finally, the conclusion will sum up the more general
lessons from the Vietnam experience and suggest how these lessons
should influence future planning for low-intensity conflicts.

THE STRATEGY OF REVOLUTIONARY WARFARE

Before we can proceed with this reassessment, the strategy
and tactics of the insurgents must be briefly identified.[3] The development of revolutionary warfare as a systematic theory can be traced
to the writings of Mao Tse-Tung. Mao divides his strategy into two
interrelated parts: (1) three general military stages; and (2) socio-
political reform measures.[4] However, the military elements do not
dominate this strategy. For Mao, the political considerations of
Revolutionary Warfare are the critical factors, the most essential of
which concerns the relationship between the insurgents and the populace. He considers the support of the populace essential, if the
insurgents are to establish the base areas that are critical to his
overall program. With respect to this point Mao uses his often quoted
fish/water analogy.[5] The way the insurgents succeed is through the
establishment of a competing ideological system and political structure. The goal is to perpetuate the moral isolation of the regime and
to substitute a system of parallel hierarchies. The major task is not
to outfight, but to out-administer, the regime. Thus, ideological
thrust, organizational form, and programmatic content are essential,
for the insurgents must demonstrate to the populace that there is an
alternative system to that of the regime in power. Only through such
a process are the insurgents able to socialize and mobilize the populace into backing their cause. No less an authority than the late
Bernard Fall, one of the few Western analysts to understand Revolutionary Warfare, noted that "it can . . . be postulated that no revolutionary war can be won without at least a measure of popular

support."[6] In summary, it is Mao's contention that Revolutionary Warfare must be a constructive as well as destructive process.

With respect to these negative factors, Mao and other proponents of Revolutionary Warfare are apprehensive about the use of such measures against the populace.[7] In fact, there is general agreement that coercive force and terrorism are purely ancillary techniques "to be used cautiously and selectively in revolutionary warfare. The rationale derives from the fact that this form of warfare requires strong support from the populace, which cannot be obtained if terror is employed against the populace."[8]

Essentially, this was the strategy employed by the Viet Cong.[9] In fact, the great strength of the VC derived from their organizational infrastructure in the South Vietnamese countryside. Dating back to the 1940s, this infrastructure enabled the VC to support and carry out its military activity. An effective U.S. response would most certainly have had to take this process into account.

THE SOCIAL REFORM MODEL
OF COUNTERINSURGENCY: 1961-63

During the period of direct U.S. involvement in the Vietnam War, the first attempt to employ counterinsurgency took place during the Kennedy Administration. This initial experiment with counterinsurgency involved the implementation of the social reform or "hearts and minds" variation. This model was based on the belief that revolution in the Third World resulted from the instability and heightened tensions that accompany the passage of traditional society and the rise of expectations involved in modernization. Furthermore, the Kennedy Administration believed that the crushing social, political, and economic deprivations that existed in these areas were being exploited by Soviet-influenced indigenous insurgents.[10]

In 1961, the White House view was that such upheavals might prove contagious and that the United States was largely unprepared to prevent or terminate them. For the Administration, the solution to this dilemma was the social reform model of counterinsurgency. The focus of this approach was directed toward the development of benevolent programs designed to ameliorate instability and tension, and win the support of the populace. Accepting the arguments of Chalmers Johnson and others that "the irreducible characteristic of successful guerrilla warfare is the close cooperation between full-time guerrillas and a population almost wholly in sympathy with the guerrilla's goals," this approach to counterinsurgency was directed toward "stealing their [the insurgents'] thunder."[12] In other words, its advocates concluded that the loyalty and support of the populace must be won if the insur-

gents were to be defeated. This line of reasoning is apparent in the
following statement by Rutherford Poats, a senior AID official involved with counterinsurgency during the Kennedy years:

> this kind of war depends heavily upon the psychology of
> the peasant. . . . If we can quickly demonstrate . . .
> the prospects of improvement in his livelihood . . . then
> he will not be vulnerable to the propaganda of the insur-
> gents. [13]

To achieve this end, the model envisaged a combination of military,
paramilitary, social, economic, political, and civic action operations.

In spite of the enthusiasm and euphoric pronouncements sur-
rounding the development and operation of this approach, it failed to
turn the tide in South Vietnam. With the removal of Diem by a military
coup in November, 1963, the strategy came to an end. What follows
is a critical examination of this initial unsuccessful counterinsurgency
program.

The Social Reform Model

The theoretical literature pertaining to the social reform
approach to counterinsurgency is quite extensive. However, for purposes of strategy specification we will rely on the more standard
works of Thompson, McCuen, Galula, Fall, Lansdale, and Trinquier,
to name the most important. [14] Each of these counterinsurgent strategies devised somewhat different step-level approaches to meet the
threat of guerrilla warfare. For example, Galula divides counterinsurgency into an eight-step process, Thompson identifies five principles, while McCuen specifies six. [15] In this brief overview of the
strategy, we have synthesized these similar approaches into the following seven principles: (1) separation of the populace from the insurgents; (2) government reform; (3) social reform; (4) role of coercion;
(5) military tactics; (6) external support; and (7) unity of principles.
Taken together, these principles were devised, according to McCuen,
"to parry the revolutionary weapons, adopt them, improve them for
one's own uses, and then turn them against the revolutionaries."[16]
Thus counterinsurgency is not regarded simply as a military effort,
but as a complex political-military problem.

In an insurgency situation, the advocates of this strategy argue
that the security of one's own base is the first step. Therefore, the
population in these areas must be physically and psychologically separated from the insurgents. In order to achieve this psychological
separation, the government must develop a cause or program with

which the populace can identify. While most strategists argue that the cause or program must reflect the local context, Thompson, on a broader scale, states that "there are three main forces which influence the people of a country: nationalism and national policies, religion and customs, material well-being and progress."[17] With regard to physical separation, a variety of procedures have been developed, the most frequently recommended being resettlement and village security. Through such procedures the government secures its bases and then begins to spread security outward "by osmosis, leaving behind firmly controlled strategic bases."[18]

Once security is achieved, the government moves to carry out various reforms beginning with its own administrative and organizational structures. For Thompson and others, a centralized, unified, and functional government administration is essential to the overall strategy.[19] The social reform measures and other vital functions will not be achieved if the government is not reorganized and cleansed of corruption. Based on the view that insurgent success is the result of organizational expertise, McCuen argues that the government must "oppose organization with counter-organization."[20] Paralleling these developments are the social reform measures, the central ingredients of the strategy. Given the assumption that social inequities breed revolution, the social reform segment of the strategy is crucial to the overall design.[21] According to Lansdale, government support derives from reform measures that increase "social and economic progress at a more rapid pace in villages."[22] Such measures were to reflect local needs.

Up to this point we have been concerned with the more positive aspects of the strategy. With regard to the role of government coercion vis-a-vis the populace, the theorists of this approach delegate such measures to a strictly ancillary status. While they argue that harsh measures are likely to be necessary, they must be "employed rationally and with clear understanding that they are emergency measures."

The role of the military is divided into the two categories consisting of counter-guerrilla military operations and nonmilitary civic action operations. While political considerations take precedence over military operations in this approach, the combat forces nevertheless have an important dual function. In terms of combat tactics, the military must be reoriented to operate in unconventional situations.[24] Emphasis is placed on the development of local self-defense forces to maintain secured areas.[25] The military is also very involved in the process of civic action. In this role the indigenous military forces are used in a variety of developmental projects ranging from agriculture, public works, and transportation, to sanitation and public health.[26] In effect, the military is called upon to assist substantially in modernization.[27] Finally, the proponents of the strategy agree

that a government faced with an insurgent situation should seek outside aid (but not military forces).[28]

In conclusion, the proponents of this strategy note that while
each of these principles is important, an effective effort will result
only if they are drawn together into a coordinated plan.[29]

THE IMPLEMENTATION OF THE STRATEGY
IN VIETNAM: 1961-63

The failure of the 1961-63 strategy cannot be attributed to any
single violation of the seven principles of the strategy, but can be
traced to a number of interrelated errors. In the first place, the
Diem government was never able to achieve either the physical or
psychological separation of the rural populace from the Viet Cong.
Although Diem devised a state philosophy—personalism—it did not
mobilize and unify the populace behind the regime.[30] In fact, given
its abstractness and lack of coherence and direction, personalism,
according to the Pentagon Papers, "limited Diem's political horizons,
and almost certainly impaired his government's ability to communicate with the peasantry."[31] With respect to physical isolation, resettlement during this period was carried out through the strategic
hamlet program. While the failure of this program is clearly recognized, many U.S. officials involved attribute it to the overextension
of the program and the unrealistic and uncoordinated pace of its execution.[32] While these were certainly contributing factors, the reasons
for the failure go much deeper.[33] From a sociological point of view,
the strategic hamlet program faced a very difficult situation in that
the communities it sought to resettle were established ones whose
residents had strong ritualistic and community ties. Kahin and Lewis
point out that necessary precautions were not taken; rather, "the
peasantry involved were dragooned into compliance" and "bitterly
resented the sacrifice of their ancestral homes and fields."[34] In
addition, the program was plagued by widespread corruption, which
translated into very poor conditions in the resettlements.[35] Taken
together, these developments resulted in the violation of the initial
principle of the strategy.

In the area of governmental and social reform, the Diem regime's performance was equally unimpressive. In fact, the evidence
suggests that Diem continually blocked attempts at government administrative reform in order to buttress his personal position. Therefore,
the civilian government was saturated with political appointees who
owed their positions to factors other than expertise. Many important
military appointees were based on the same criteria. Structurally,
Diem destroyed the village council system and replaced provincial

heads and other local officials with appointees loyal to the GVN. As if this were not dysfunctional enough, he also fragmented the power of various government agencies in such a way as to make cooperation impossible.[36] Such tactics were particularly aimed at the armed forces, as the Pentagon Papers explain:

> the chain of command problem was that control . . . in the provinces was divided between the local military commanders and the Province Chief, a personal appointee of Diem, reporting directly to Diem.[37]

The purpose was to limit the ability of the military to play an active role in Vietnamese politics. In sum, the regime was willing to sacrifice urgently needed administrative reforms in order to consolidate its own power base. This only further weakened the government's ability to deal effectively with the insurgency.[38]

Social reform factors are, then, the central ingredients of the strategy. But the history of the Diem regime is one of unyielding opposition to these crucial elements. To initiate such policies would have antagonized major elements of Diem's narrow power base. Even in the face of continual U.S. pressure, the regime refused to broaden its political base,[39] and was equally unyielding on the issue of economic reform. The latter was especially reflected in the land reform issue. Rather than initiating a land reform policy aimed at the peasants, Diem permitted landlords to reimpose control in areas where Vietminh land redistribution had occurred.[40] Such policies not only added to the unpopularity of the government, but, according to one Rand report, were often cited as a reason for joining the opposition.[41]

The Diem government also violated the stipulations placed on the role of coercion. Rather than relegating these tactics to an ancillary status, the regime came to rely on them. In fact, it was apparent even during the initial years that Diem intended to repress all opposition.[42] As the insurgency and other forms of opposition intensified in the 1960s, Diem came to rely more and more on such measures.[43]

The military tenets of the strategy—counter-guerrilla operations and civic actions—were also violated. In the first place, a major over emphasis was placed on military to the exclusion of political and social factors during this period. This over-militarization of the war can be traced, according to Komer, "to such institutional factors as the dominant role of the military in the U.S. aid and advisory structure."[44] The effect was the development of an approach that was not just militarily oriented, but of one that emphasized conventional military strategy. Finally, the South Vietnamese army became "more a reflection of the U.S. military establishment than of the type of threat or terrain" it faced.[45] In sum, the counter-guerrilla military operations, as well as civic action programs, were never developed beyond the superficial level.

There were also fundamental mistakes made concerning external support. From the perspective of the strategy, the following criticisms can be made: (1) the type of aid sent to South Vietnam was entirely too military-oriented; (2) the U.S. advisory group was dominated by those who advocated a conventional military approach;[46] (3) the training of ARVN emphasized conventional tactics; and (4) the decision to broaden the U.S. role violated the stipulation that outside elements ought not be substituted for indigenous ones.

Finally, given the above developments, it is apparent that no unified and coordinated counterinsurgency plan was implemented during the 1961-63 period. The diffusion of authority, fragmentation of command, conflicting views over strategy, and organizational disunity that characterized both the U.S. and GVN efforts go a long way in explaining why it proved so hard to translate the counterinsurgency policy of the Kennedy Administration into practice in South Vietnam.

IN RETROSPECT: 1961-63

While the failure of the 1961-63 counterinsurgency strategy is not attributable to any one source, certainly the Diem government played an instrumental part. Aside from its feeble administrative capabilities, inadequate armed forces, and declining economy, the GVN operated under serious political constraints. It fragmented the armed forces and civilian authorities, playing them off against each other. It refused to carry out much-needed reforms, and instead relied on repression to maintain control.

A second factor contributing to this failure can be assigned to the various U.S. agencies involved. Their understanding of the conflict and of counterinsurgency varied greatly. The result was a very disjointed and contradictory approach to the insurgency, rather than a unified counterinsurgency policy. This was particularly reflected in the emphasis on conventional military tactics. In the conflict over the way the war should be fought, the conventionally oriented JCS and DOD won out over those advocating counterinsurgency. Furthermore, this conventional focus was carried over into the training of ARVN. So while the Administration claimed to be employing counterinsurgency strategy in Vietnam, in reality the U.S. and GVN forces were geared for a conventional engagement.

As a result of these developments, the 1961-63 counterinsurgency strategy failed to improve the rapidly deteriorating situation in South Vietnam. While in retrospect, this can be attributed to the fact that it was never seriously employed, nevertheless, at that time it was perceived as ineffective. Thus, with the removal of Diem, the United States began to search for a new approach.

THE COST-BENEFIT MODEL OF
COUNTERINSURGENCY: 1965-68[47]

Following Diem's assassination the Johnson Administration faced a rapidly deteriorating situation in which the GVN continually demonstrated its inability to achieve political stability and military success.[48] Faced with impending disaster, the Administration opted for the cost-benefit or suppressive counterinsurgency strategy.[49] The advocates of this approach argued for the use of force to modify and control behavior, rather than attempting to win support through social reform. In doing so they went beyond the traditional military concepts of seizing and holding, disarming and confining, penetrating and obstructing, and emphasized factors that have generally "received less attention in Western military strategy."[50] According to Schelling:

> The power to hurt can be counted among the most impressive attributes of military force. . . . It is measured in the suffering it can cause and the victims' motivation to avoid it . . . For the United States modern technology has drastically enhanced the importance of pure, unconstructive, unacquisitive pain and damage. . . . Military strategy can no longer be thought of . . . as the science of military victory . . . It is now equally, if not more, the art of coercion, of intimidation, and deterrence.[51]

The 1965-68 approach to counterinsurgency, reflecting Schelling's notion of employing "pain and violence" to make resistance "terrible beyond endurance,"[52] appears to be derived from deterrence logic as it has been applied to strategic thermonuclear warfare. In fact, George and Smoke argue that the basic aspects of deterrence theory have greatly influenced U.S. military policy not only at the strategic but also at the conventional and unconventional levels.[53] However, they further note that while the abstract-deductive logic of deterrence has been employed effectively at the strategic level, at the conventional and unconventional levels "a multitude of variables, many . . . subjective, that fluctuate over time and are highly dependent upon the context of the situation,"[54] make the employment of an abstract-deductive strategy,[55] based on the use of coercive force in a rationally calculated, cost-benefit equation, complicated and problematic. The cost-benefit counterinsurgency strategy, employing coercive force to control behavior, reflected these problems.

In Vietnam, this strategy was implemented in the summer of 1965 and culminated in the shock of the 1968 Tet offensive. In order to see why it failed, we must understand first how it worked.

The Cost-Benefit Model

Specification of this model was most concisely articulated by Charles Wolf of the Rand Corporation. It was first publicly articulated in a 1965 Rand Memorandum, [56] with a much more detailed theoretical account appearing in 1970 under the title Rebellion and Authority (co-authored with Nathan Leites). [57]

Leites and Wolf begin with the assertion that insurgent success results from the effective use of coercive force to gain the compliance of the populace. Based on this assertion they advise that the more effective use of such tactics by counterinsurgents will result in the defeat of the guerrillas. [58] Focusing on the assumption that individuals behave in a rational manner, "calculating costs and benefits . . . to different courses of action," it becomes the objective of the counter-insurgent to estimate this ratio for the insurgents and their supporters, and then to employ coercive force at a level that exceeds the point where participation and/or support for the insurgency is beneficial. [59]

The insurgent movement is viewed as an operating system requiring inputs and producing outputs. These inputs—recruits, supplies, information, etc.—are obtained in varying amounts from either the internal environment (endogenous inputs) or external environment (exogenous inputs). [60]

From the above propositions a four-part strategy is devised for defeating insurgent movements:

1. Raise the costs to R (insurgents) of obtaining inputs, or reduce the inputs obtained for given costs: the aim is input denial.
2. Impede the process by which R converts these inputs into activities—that is, reduce the efficiency of R's production process.
3. Destroy R's outputs.
4. Blunt the effect of R's outputs on the population and on A (government). . . . Increase A's and the population's capacity to absorb R's activities. [61]

The aim of these tactics is to disrupt the process by which inputs are obtained and converted into outputs. The effective use of coercive force is the essential factor underlying this model, as Leites and Wolf frequently state.[62] In essence, the objective is to raise the "costs" of producing insurgent activity.[63] This is achieved through the following steps. First, reduce insurgent resources through interdiction of exogenous sources and through limitation of endogenous inputs via control of the behavior of that portion of the populace supporting the insurgents. With respect to the latter, the goal is to raise the cost of support to the point where it becomes rationally unbeneficial.[64] Second, disrupt the insurgent conversion mechanism (infrastructure) through various harassment programs.[65] Third, reduce insurgent force levels. And fourth, develop government programs that separate the insurgents from the populace.[66]

In sum, the suppressive strategy takes a position diametrically opposite the social reform approach. In fact, those advocating the suppressive approach flatly reject the argument that pure preference is the reason underlying popular support of insurgent movements.

Operationally, the strategy emerged in the wake of a continuing series of coups following Diem's assassination. It recognized that the bombing of North Vietnam (designated Rolling Thunder) was not sufficient to turn the tide, and it anticipated a National Liberation Front (NLF) offensive that could very well have resulted in the collapse of the Government of Vietnam (GVN).[67] The decision was made in the summer of 1965 to initiate a strategy that relied on U.S. troops and firepower to defeat the enemy.[68] This meant direct pressure against North Vietnam, which was intended to raise GVN morale and "reduce the flow and/or increase the costs of the continued infiltration of men and supplies," thus breaking Hanoi's "will."[69] This was coupled with the attrition tactics of "search and destroy," which aimed at separating the NLF from its endogenous sources and destroying the insurgent infrastructure. The aim was to deny the enemy freedom of movement, and through superior firepower to deal the enemy the heaviest possible blows.[70] Destroying supplies, eliminating the protective cover of nature, forcing urbanization as a consequence of saturation bombing, implmenting the Phoenix program, and similar tactics were intended to raise the costs of participation and/or support for the insurgency to an unacceptable level.[71] With the merging of Rolling Thunder and the attrition tactics of search and destroy, a suppressive strategy based on cost-benefit logic was implemented.[72] From this point until the reassessment of U.S. policy following the 1968 Tet offensive, this was the principal strategy employed by the U.S. military in Vietnam. It is to this strategy and its implementation that we now turn.

IMPLEMENTING THE COST-BENEFIT STRATEGY:
1965-68

In order to explain why the 1965-68 strategy fell short of its
goals, it is important to examine the strategy's theoretical structure,
as well as its implementation.

Strategy Misspecification

Theoretical misspecification of a model occurs, in the broad
sense of the term, whenever one or more of its underlying assumptions is incorrect. With respect to the strategy under examination,
the following assumptions appear problematic: (1) governmental
coercive force assures the quelling of dissident resistance and civil
strife; (2) the Western economic concept of rationality is applicable
cross-culturally in insurgency situations; and (3) insurgent success
(especially of the NLF) results from social compliance gained through
coercive force.

To begin with, the central proposition that coercive force will
guarantee control of collective behavior ignores a large body of evidence that suggests that government repression "may" result in the
opposite response. This counter-position is typified by Gurr's assertion that "force threatens and angers men, especially if they believe
it to be illicit . . . angered, they want to retaliate."[73] This proposition is based on social-psychological research that supports the
frustration-aggression hypothesis.[74] Stated probabilistically, the
hypothesis suggests that frustration may elicit an aggressive response,
given certain other factors.[75] A variation of the hypothesis, which
concerns this study, suggests that negative physical sanctions increase
the probability of aggression.

Experimental animal and individual human studies present conclusions in explaining the relationship between force and obedience.[76]
A review of this literature points to the tenuousness in the proposition
that punishment automatically inhibits aggressive behavior. The same
is true at the level of collective group behavior. At this level the
literature that relates to the use of coercive force to deter aggression
centers around studies of collective violence within national politics.[77]
In reviewing this literature, Snyder notes that "explanations of collective violence attributes some regular importance to the actions of
governments. In particular, 'coercion' . . . is generally considered
to affect the frequency, magnitude and intensity of violent action."[78]
The work of Gurr, the Feierabends, Bwy, and Passos, among others,
present empirical support for the proposition that governmental coercion may induce collective violence.[79]

If evidence exists to support the argument that endogenous governmental coercion may result in collective violence, the frequency of a violent response is high when an exogenous government is involved (e.g., the French in Algeria). There are numerous examples of invading foreign armies being met with stiff popular resistance as a result of their reliance on coercive force.[80] Thus when the French initiated a brutal coercive campaign against the Algerian populace, the response was unyielding resistance.[81] Such evidence raises serious questions about this critical tenet of the suppressive strategy. While aggression does not automatically result from governmental coercion,[82] neither does compliance. The problem with the strategy lies in the fact that its proponents do not appear to take into account the speculative nature of the proposition that coercive force will result in social compliance. They never discuss the probabilistic nature of this proposition or how to calculate its implementation.[83]

The rationality concept and the related process of estimating an opponent's cost-tolerance level are also tenuous.[84] Those who employ these concepts in counterinsurgency strategy assume that the enemy and those who support him evaluate the costs of their actions in a rational-value maximizing fashion and that the enemy's (and his supporters') cost-tolerance level can accurately be estimated by the counterinsurgents. The former notion, based on Western economic theory, assumes that individuals make decisions through rational calculation of the costs and benefits of various potential choices. However, the transition from the economic to the political sphere may not be as smooth as the cost-benefit strategists assume, especially when it cuts across cultures. This would seem particularly true in an insurgency situation that has evolved over several decades and is characterized by a high degree of emotion and ideological commitment. In such situations, a willingness to sacrifice for the sake of one's goals may raise one's cost-tolerance level well above the point at which a purely rational calculation would predict capitulation. Under such circumstances, the behavior of insurgents (and their supporters) is not the result of a single factor, but of a number of variables that may not be easily understood by counterinsurgents. When they disregard these factors, advocates of this counterinsurgency model are unable to discern that negative payoffs frequently reinforce existing dedication in the calculations of personal choice.[85] Additionally, given the complexity and magnitude of the factors involved in such situations, the problem of estimating the enemy's cost-tolerance level becomes much more difficult than the advocates of the strategy suggest.

Finally, this proposition assumes that if insurgents rely on coercive force to effect social compliance, then counterinsurgency strategy must be predicted on the more effective application of coercive force. It is an assumption imbued with conceptual difficulties.[86] One could argue that, on the contrary, coercive force has not been the primary tactic employed in various successful insurgencies to gain support from the populace. In a previous study this point was argued with respect to the strategy of the Viet Cong.[87]

From a theoretical standpoint, Revolutionary Warfare proponents agree that terrorism should be relegated to an ancillary status and employed selectively, since insurgents require a commitment from the populace, and this cannot be secured through sheer coercion. Apparently the Viet Cong complied with this stipulation, and employed coercive tactics in a selective manner against carefully chosen targets. Coercion and terror were employed by the NLF in conjunction with other, positive, tactics, and were accorded a secondary position in their overall strategy. The principal components of this strategy combined ideology, organization, attractive policies and programs, nationalistic goals, and coercive techniques. The decisive factor in this design was the overall social, political, and economic strategy, not coercion and terror per se. These propositions were confirmed in a prior study that used a variety of sources including the "Rand Interviews in Vietnam" series,[88] and reports based on these materials,[89] as well as the written records, messages, orders, and assignments of the Viet Cong and studies based on these documents.[90] In sum, these findings expose a third theoretical weakness in the specification of the strategy.

It is apparent, then, that some serious specification errors exist in the conceptual logic of the cost-benefit approach to counterinsurgency. The remainder of this study will explain how these specification problems seriously limited the effectiveness of U.S. strategy in Vietnam.

Implementing the Strategy—The Exogenous Factors

The exogenous aspect of the 1965-68 strategy was contained in the bombing program carried out against North Vietnam. It was expected that this aspect of the strategy would contribute to the defeat of the insurgents by denying them the external logistical support deemed essential to their survival and growth. However, in spite of the extensiveness of the bombing program, the major objectives were never realized. These objectives, as noted above, were threefold: (1) to reduce the flow and/or increase the costs to Hanoi of continuing the infiltration of men and supplies; (2) to lower the morale of their populace and break the will of the North's leadership; and (3) to raise the morale of the GVN.[91]

Evidence of this policy began to appear as early as the fall of 1965 in the form of various intelligence reports.[92] While space does not allow for an examination of all these reports, it should be noted that the two most comprehensive critiques were completed by the Jason Division of IDA.[93] These two reports, completed in 1966 and 1967, constitute a powerful repudiation of the bombing program.[94] They evaluated the bombing on the basis of three of the program's goals. With regard to the first objective, the conclusions were emphatically negative.[95] Due to foreign aid and effective countermeasures, disruption and other difficulties were effectively neutralized.[96] In terms of the second objective, the second Jason study concludes that there was "no evidence that possible war weariness among the people of NVN had shaken the leadership's belief that they can continue . . . and outlast the US in a protracted war."[97] Finally, the bombing was unable to raise GVN morale.[98]

In sum, it becomes evident how the previously identified theoretical problems affected the implementation of the strategy. The assumption of rationality resulted in a disregard for factors like dedication and will; the DRV's cost-tolerance level was not estimated accurately; and the strategy ignored the fact that such tactics might stiffen the determination of the enemy. Finally, the problems created by bombing in a rural society were not addressed.

Implementing the Strategy—Endogenous Factors

The endogenous component was contained in the attrition strategy of search and destroy. The objectives were two-fold: (1) to deny the insurgents their political bases and support in the countryside; and (2) to destroy the insurgency system (NLF infrastructure). To accomplish this, it was expected that the greater mobility of U.S. troops and their massive firepower capability would be utilized to defeat the enemy, while the GVN would take responsibility for pacification.[99] In fact, the strategy failed to eliminate and even to demoralize the opposition forces in the South. The evidence presented below, which very briefly summarizes a much larger study,[100] illustrates the failure of the strategy to achieve either of its objectives.

In spite of the introduction of 500,000 U.S. troops and massive firepower, the VC/NVA force levels were never seriously drained. Evidence to this effect appears throughout the Pentagon Papers.[101] The futility of the process is summarized in the following passage from the "A to Z Reassessment" ordered by Secretary of Defense Clifford: the enemy is not only able to offset losses but to "match the U.S. buildup in SVN with their own buildup."[102] Finally, the Phoenix program proved ineffective in neutralizing the enemy cadre.[1]

The attrition strategy also aimed at the psychological demoralization of enemy forces.[104] But evidence from the Rand interviews and various reports based on them clearly show the inability of attrition strategy to alter the enemy's behavior on the battlefield. The most pertinent of these reports consists of a series concerned with VC/NVA troop morale and motivation compiled during 1965-68.[105] According to the final report in this series (1968), the morale of the enemy remained essentially the same: psychological attrition proved unattainable.[106]

Finally, the strategy aimed at separating the insurgents from that segment of the population in the South that supplied them with recruits, intelligence, information, food, and other logistical supports. It was expected that this objective, too, would be accomplished by raising the costs to those indigenous elements supporting the insurgents to the point where costs outweighed benefits.[107] The evidence nonetheless suggests that the linkage between insurgents and rural populace was never broken. The ability of the VC to recruit effectively in rural areas is one good indication of this.[108] Additionally, the extensive use of firepower, refugee resettlement, and the poorly run GVN pacification program resulted in a great deal of disaffection that the Viet Cong could effectively manipulate. For example, one Senate report cites numerous examples of how the Viet Cong used these situations to make inroads into large segments of the populace.[109] The Rand Interviews and Reports, as well as other evidence, strongly corroborates these findings.[110] Thus, by 1968 it was apparent that the objectives of the suppressive counterinsurgency strategy aimed at the enemy in the South had failed.

IN RETROSPECT: 1965-68

In the aftermath of the Tet offensive, President Johnson, no longer believing military victory was possible, began to search for a way out of Vietnam.[111] In retrospect, it would appear that Tet demonstrated the probabilistic nature of the cost-benefit model of counterinsurgency. The logic of the model, based on the use of coercive force in a rationally calculated, cost-benefit equation, constitutes the principal underlying cause of the failure of the 1965-68 strategy. The application of these assumptions to an insurgency conflict is dubious and may result in a stiffening of resistance and willingness to undergo further hardships. In sum, the strategy does not take into account the situational context, but assumes that coercive force will result in compliance on the part of the enemy. The abstract-deductive character of the logic, as well as the emphasis on coercive force, economic rationality, and cost-tolerance estimation all appear to be theoretically questionable aspects of this strategy. The limits to the applicability of these concepts were not recognized by those who devised the cost-benefit counterinsurgency strategy. The inability to perceive these limitations and the problems arising from them led to the implementation of a strategy that was incapable of achieving its primary objectives.

THE STRATEGY OF VIETNAMIZATION: 1968-72

It was observed previously that the Tet offensive of 1968 had a devastating political and psychological impact on the U.S. approach to the war in Vietnam. While the question as to whether Tet was a victory or defeat has stimulated conflicting interpretations (including Brodie's persuasive argument that the offensive resulted in both a strategic victory and tactical defeat for the VC/NVA[112]), what is clear is that it greatly altered the U.S. approach to the war, bringing to an end the cost-benefit counterinsurgency strategy.

The final U.S. approach to the conflict was characterized by the deescalation and gradual withdrawal of U.S. forces, while the GVN was transformed, through the process of Vietnamization, into an effective political-military system that could legitimatize itself with the populace and maintain a favorable balance of forces against the VC/NVA. While it would be inaccurate to characterize this approach as a complete reversion to the counterinsurgency strategy of the 1961-63 period, essentially because certain conventional-main force military concepts continued to be employed, it nevertheless shifted the focus back to the "other war." This was particularly the case with regard to the pacification and civic action programs, which had been greatly deemphasized during the 1965-68 period. This dramatic reversal in strategy was marked by two important changes in U.S. civilian and military leadership. First of all, General Creighton Abrams was appointed Commander, U.S. Military Assistance Command, Vietnam (COMUSMACV). Unlike his predecessor, Abrams supported the deployment of U.S. forces in a manner that concurred with a pacification-civic action approach. In early 1969, he approved a new "Military Assistance Command, Vietnam—Strategic Objectives Plan," which was based on the concept of "area security." The aim was to provide continuing security for the Vietnamese population in expanding areas of increasingly effective civil authority. In effect, the area security concept was to blend combat operations with pacification and civic action. [113]

In the civilian sector the appointment of Robert Komer to coordinate and supervise nonmilitary programs in Vietnam was equally important. A persistent advocate of the social reform approach to counterinsurgency, Komer was instrumental in organizing the Civilian Operations and Revolutionary Development Support (CORDS) program. CORDS was responsible for the pacification–civic action aspects of Vietnamization. It was a unique experiment in civil–military organization in that all aspects of pacification were subsumed under the military command (MACV), while CORDS personnel were drawn from a variety of civilian sources, in addition to the military services. While CORDS was actually initiated prior to Tet, it was only in the aftermath of the offensive that it became significant. During the pre-Tet period, Komer, who was appointed to the post of deputy to COM-USMACV for CORDS, encountered several problems in developing the programs that would come to be included under the rubric of Vietnamization. These bottlenecks included the U.S. military's insistence on employing the attrition strategy and ARVN's continued low performance in pacification. After the offensive, the situation changed rapidly because the military concept of area security was linked to the various pacification programs developed by CORDS. It is with regard to the final U.S. attempt at counterinsurgency that this section is concerned.

The Vietnamization Model

The design of the Vietnamization strategy closely paralleled the 1961–63 approach. The aim was to develop a governmental system that could "hold its own" against the Viet Cong infrastructure and VC/NVA forces. Guy Pauker, in one of the more concise explanations of the underlying tenets of the 1968–72 strategy, defined the process as follows:

> Vietnamization is . . . much more than transfering of
> equipment to the South Vietnamese and training them to
> use and maintain it. It involves the consolidation of the
> emerging politico–military system in South Vietnam . . .
> to face the challenge of Vietnamization the GVN must
> pursue a correct rural strategy and gradually increase
> its popular acceptance by demonstrating that . . . it is
> able and willing to offer tangible, immediate benefits to
> the masses. It must also follow a policy of military
> "sufficiency." The GVN should aim at maintaining at
> all times a favorable military balance of forces while
> accepting the fact that communist violence will continue
> and that it cannot secure total control of territory in
> the short run . . .[114]

In effect, the war would be turned over to a revitalized and properly prepared South Vietnamese government and army, and U.S. forces would gradually withdraw.

In the concluding portion of this study, the implementation of this strategy will be examined to determine how successful it was in terms of winning the "other war." However, it will be necessary first to identify the specific conceptual components of the strategy; next, to review the system that was devised to evaluate the strategy once it was implemented; and finally, to present the official U.S. government evaluation of the Vietnamization process.

Conceptually, Vietnamization was designed to achieve three specific aims: (1) to provide security and protection for the rural population (area security); (2) to develop rural support for the GVN through political, social, and economic reform (pacification); and (3) to destroy the Viet Cong infrastructure. Within each category specific civil and military programs were to be developed and integrated together.

With respect to area security, the ARVN would require significant upgrading, and other elements of the Republic of Vietnam Armed Forces (RVNAF), particularly the local Popular Force (PF) and Regional Force (RF) elements, would be enlarged and improved. Given the above definition of area security, the primary role of the RVNAF would no longer be the destruction of VC/NVA main forces.[115] Accordingly, "each segment of the RVNAF" was to have "a distinct mission and area of operation."[116] The area security concept divided the four zones of South Vietnam according to degree of security offered. In areas that were at least nominally secure[117] the PF and RF forces were primarily charged with guaranteeing hamlet security. ARVN units might also be assigned to such areas, depending on the level of threat. In sum, the area security concept, according to official documentation, "emphasizes pacification and population, and resource control operations."[118]

To implement area security RF and PF force levels were to be raised to over 500,000. Functionally, they were to be trained and equipped primarily for defensive security situations. In effect, these were to be the paramilitary auxiliaries of ARVN.[119] The regular ARVN forces, on the other hand, were to be involved in the offensive aspects of area security. This entailed a certain degree of role redefinition in terms of unconventional tactical capabilities. However, ARVN also had to maintain the ability to thwart any future VC/NVA main force attacks. Therefore, this would require not merely an increase in force levels, but a qualitative upgrading of ARVN in the specific areas of leadership, training, equipment, and commitment. According to official estimates, in order to implement the area security program successfully, ARVN and other RVNAF elements would require an increase to between 1.13 and 1.18 million troops (with appropriate qualitative improvements).[120]

The second aim of the Vietnamization strategy, pacification and civic action, had a long and checkered history in South Vietnam. Komer notes that "these attempts had many names . . . Civic Action, Agrovilles, the Strategic Hamlet Program of 1961-1963, the 1964-65 Hop Tac campaign . . . and Revolutionary Development (RD) during the 1965-67 were only the most prominent."[121] However, as Komer points out, while "grandly designed," all of these were "small-scale efforts compared to what was going into the conventional war."[122] The Vietnamization strategy sought to reverse this situation. In conjunction with area security, this new approach sought to establish a fully developed civic action program. The proposed measures included the following:

1. Revival of a functioning rural administration program (including hamlet self-government).
2. Rural economic revival to provide pragmatic incentives to farmers (including land reform).
3. Providing essential rural services, including medical, educational, refugee care, etc.[123]

Each of these factors was to make an important contribution to the process of rural organization, mobilization, participation, and identification with the GVN. Through such programs the GVN would establish legitimacy with the rural populace.

In sum, security through various unconventional, paramilitary, and limited conventional tactics would isolate the rural population from the insurgent infrastructure, while the various civic action elements would allow the GVN to compete directly with the VCI. Finally, the third element of the Vietnamization process aimed at the destruction of the infrastructure. Two specific programs were developed to accomplish this—Chieu Hoi (Open Arms) and Phung Hoang (Phoenix). The former sought to induce members of the Viet Cong to rally (surrender) to the GVN, while the latter aimed at neutralizing (kill or capture) VCI members. These programs, taken together, aimed not at outfighting, but out-administering, the VCI through ideological thrust, organizational form, and programmatic content.

Monitoring the Vietnamization Strategy

One factor that distinguished this counterinsurgency strategy from the two that preceded it was the evaluation instrument developed for operational management purposes by those from the Defense Department and other agencies involved. The techniques devised for measuring Vietnamization were basic quantitative computer-oriented ones. Given the scope of the strategy, which was directed at some 44 provinces, 250 districts, 2000 villages, and 12,000 hamlets, some means for periodically determining effectiveness had to be devised. Further complicating matters, as Komer notes, was the fact that such systems "had to be designed realistically for input by relatively unskilled field advisers."[124] Given these and other limitations, the systems devised for evaluation were fully automated to compile hamlet level data on a monthly basis.

The most comprehensive of the measurement procedures was the Hamlet Evaluation System (HES). HES was designed to be employed monthly by U.S. district advisory teams, using a standard format questionnaire. This consisted of 18 evaluative categories that were to be rated on a six-point scale (A through F). The 18 factors were divided into three categories: six for hamlet security (measures of insurgent activity and penetration); six for social and economic factors (rural development measures); and six for political factors (measures of local self-government and administration). Once each of the 18 categories was evaluated, the average was determined. This averaged score was the measure of how effective or ineffective the Vietnamization process had been in a particular hamlet for a given month. The grade could range from A (secure) to F (VC-controlled).[125] This was employed monthly for over 12,000 hamlets.[126]

While HES was the most ambitious of the evaluation systems, there were "also . . . over a dozen specialized data reporting systems all closely related to each other and to HES for comparative purposes."[127] It was through these data systems that trends in the various aspects of Vietnamization were measured.

A Feat of Political Alchemy—Official Evaluation
of the Vietnamization Strategy

"A feat of political alchemy" were the words chosen by Guy Pauker to describe the results of the Vietnamization strategy.[128] It would not be an exaggeration to argue that Pauker's conclusion was shared by many U.S. officials connected with Vietnamization. This was certainly true of Robert Komer, who claims that Vietnamization "spurred . . . a GVN-sponsored rural revolution. Politically, socially, and economically the traditional face of the countryside was transformed . . . by radical land reform, economic revival, new transportation networks, mass communications, revived local autonomy, and other measures."[129] With regard to rural security, Komer notes that "the figures for the end of 1971 rate about 97 percent of South Vietnam's 17.9 million population as 'relatively secure,' and 3 percent as 'contested,' and only about 7,000 people still under VC control."[130] When success in other programs such as RF/PF development and Chieu Hoi were added to these developments, the result was, in Komer's words, "GVN domination of the countryside . . . at the expense of the Viet Cong."[131]

In light of the 1975 collapse, how valid is the Komer thesis? Until recently, data have not been available to make such judgments. Therefore, although there was speculative criticism, and a few localized studies that pointed out problems that might have a larger importance, no comprehensive analysis (outside official circles) was undertaken.[132] However, two recent studies have addressed the Vietnamization strategy. The first, by Douglas Blaufarb, relies primarily on Komer's analysis. Accordingly, he states that "by 1970 a considerable measure of security had been restored and the ability of the insurgency to affect events . . . had been eroded to the point where it was a manageable threat . . . the population had substantially abandoned the VC."[133]

In the other recent publication, Guenter Lewy, using new information, identifies important weaknesses in the Vietnamization program.[134] However, in explaining the 1975 defeat he attributes it not to a failure of Vietnamization, but to critical military mistakes on the part of Thieu. These miscalculations were profoundly destabilizing and resulted in a panicked chain reaction of cumulative defeats. The final defeat was not inevitable.[135] Others attribute the defeat not to miscalculation, but to the ability of the NVA army to overpower an inferior foe in a conventional engagement. The VC, according to this view, played little part in the final defeat.

The Strategy of Vietnamization: A Reassessment

Was Vietnamization as successful as Komer and other officials associated with it claim? To answer this we must first determine the reliability of the quantitative measuring systems and the data collected. The analysis presented in this section is based on this line of investigation.[136] While these findings are preliminary, with further research still in progress, they do raise serious questions about Komer's position.[137] The reassessment that follows will focus on four factors: (1) the accuracy and relevance of the Hamlet Evaluation System; (2) the effectiveness of Chieu Hoi and Phung Hoang; (3) ARVN and RF/PF development; and (4) the establishment of political reform and community.

SECURITY AND PACIFICATION

Given that HES was the principal means for evaluating the Vietnamization strategy and that those officials who proclaimed the strategy
a success relied on HES data, we begin our reassessment with a close
scrutiny of that system. The question that must addressed is this:
did HES identify and measure those factors that allowed for an accurate evaluation of Vietnamization, or was performance evaluated
simply by whatever factors HES could most easily measure?

According to HES documentation, the system was devised for
measuring security and control, and not GVN legitimacy in the rural
areas. [138] This measure, based on the averaging of the 18 file indicators, signified the degree of overt GVN control and presence of
overt VC/NVA military or political activity. This resulted in the
development of the following rating system:

"A"   Adequate security forces, infrastructure eliminated, public
      projects underway, and economic programs improving.
"B"   VC threat exists but security is organized and partially effec-
      tive, infrastructure partially neutralized, self-help programs
      underway and economic improvement programs started.
"C"   Subject to frequent VC harassment, infrastructure identified,
      and inhabitants participate in self-help programs and local
      government.
"D"   VC activities reduced but still an internal threat. Some VC tax-
      ation and terrorism. Some local participation in hamlet govern-
      ment and economic programs.
"E"   VC are effective although some government control is evident.
      VC infrastructure intact.
"VC" Under VC control. No government officials or advisors enter
      except on military operations. Populace willingly support Viet
      Cong. [139]

In effect, these measures were based primarily on the capacity of
U.S. and GVN defense forces to check local enemy forces and overt
party apparatus activities. This process was officially explained in
the following terms: "control indicators assigned the population of a
hamlet to GVN . . . control if the military and political strength of
the GVN control organization in that hamlet is sufficient to administer
the hamlet effectively while preventing the other side from doing so."
Therefore, if the GVN has "both military strength . . . and political
and administrative control," the hamlet is secure. [140] If a hamlet
were physically occupied and under GVN control, was it necessarily
the case that all VC influence and legitimacy had been eliminated?

Would such a situation result in long-term identification of the hamlet populace with the GVN, or was this only short-term control based on physical presence?

To answer this, one must take the VCI procedures for maintaining control and influence, and compare them with the HES measures of security. VCI influence and control were, in many instances, covert. However, as was noted in the introduction, such a presence should not be interpreted as less effective than physical occupation, given the roots of the movement. Understanding this difference is critical to explaining why hamlets labeled relatively secure (A-B-C) could still experience both covert VCI activities (taxation, recruitment, propaganda, intelligence, and the like) and guerrilla violence.[141] What does this mean in terms of hamlet security? From a preliminary investigation, some interesting patterns emerge. For instance, a hamlet that receives an A or B rating for a given year may, during one or two months of that year, receive a low score on those HES indicators that are concerned with VCI or guerrilla activities. While this would have some impact on the end-of-year score, it may only be marginal. This is particularly true if the VCI action was low level and covert. However, in terms of continuing VC influence, such action was very important. [142] This may very well have been the way the VCI retained veto power in an occupied area until they could formally return. Preliminary examination of the data does support the assertion that this type of periodic insurgent activity occurred. [143] Additionally, it indicates how resilient the VCI was in hamlets rated secure, once the GVN or U.S. forces moved out. This development is noted in the following excerpt from a September 1971 report concerned with the problem: "The VCI . . . is showing considerable staying power, and has previously shown its capability to resurge strongly. This could lead to an intensified, protracted struggle which the GVN may well lose; only the introduction of U.S. forces saved the GVN in the last struggle."[144] In fact, initial examination of HES-based analysis and other reports indicate a trend in VCI resiliency upon the withdrawal of GVN forces. For instance, a 17-province study in the fall of 1971 notes a clear relationship between ARVN and/or U.S. troop redeployment from an area, and the rise of overt VC activity. [145] This is corroborated by the end-of-tour reports of U.S. senior district advisors connected with province Vietnamization. [146] By the end of 1971, with the United States rapidly pulling out of South Vietnam, the critical question was whether ARVN and RF/PF could maintain security in the countryside. [147]

Thus, two very different conceptions of control can be seen to emerge from these data. On the one hand, the HES measures "military presence (and to some extent, geographical control) and known enemy activity."[148] Based on ARVN presence, this can change rapidly. Thus, a village could be pacified one day and VC the next day. What this suggests, as the following excerpt from the Office of the Assistant Secretary of Defense (Systems Analysis) SEA Analysis Reports notes, is a situation quite different from that presented by the HES figures alone:

> The HES system represents a snapshot of security and development at one point in time. The monthly statistics merely provide a series of these snapshots and creates an impression of steady progress and widespread GVN influence among the people of South Vietnam. But security and development are dynamic, not static events; and much of the movement and interaction in pacification is not reflected by the summary HES reports.[149]

VC influence and control, on the other hand, were maintained through a different type of presence that had developed during a period of time extending back into the 1940s. The nature of this difference is explained in the OASD(SA) report:

> A large percentage of the South Vietnamese . . . live in areas that are subject to VC domination or influence for at least one month out of the year. These people simply cannot afford to openly support the GVN knowing that an active VC infrastructure still operates in their village and that enemy troops will return one day soon . . . the bulk of the South Vietnamese people live in a . . . contested status at least once a year.[150]

While the above analysis explains how a hamlet rated A or B could quickly become VC,[151] the more important insight to be drawn concerns the questionable validity of the instrument used to evaluate an important part of the Vietnamization strategy. This uncertainty is further compounded by other information that contradicts the HES ratings. For example, an early 1970 MACV (Military Assistance Command, Vietnam) review of hamlet security concluded that among the rural inhabitants only 20 percent were not subject to VCI taxation and only 29 percent lived in hamlets with no platoon-size enemy forces nearby.[152] Additionally, in only 39 percent of the hamlets had no VC forces entered.[153] By the end of 1970 these security ratings had improved so that 95.1 percent of the hamlets were rated A-B-C, with 84.6 percent of these in the A-B categories.[154] Contradicting these scores were the results from the Pacification Attitude Analysis System (PAAS). According to the responses of the rural inhabitants sampled during this period, 59 percent "said VC personnel could enter their hamlet at night and 62 percent said that their hamlet was not secure enough to take down fortifications."[155] Journalistic reports during the Vietnamization period also raised serious questions about how reliable the security data really were. For example a July 1971 story in the Washington Post notes that "trips over the past month to all four military regions revealed a widespread disquiet, a feeling that security in many areas is still extremely fragile."[156] The story goes on to quote John Paul Vann's assessment of the situation. Vann, one of most astute U.S. advisors, stated: "the majority of the people still oppose the government . . . Military occupation is only the first step to pacification, and if the government never gets beyond that then they won't be viable."[157]

Other important factors that raise doubts about the validity of the security ratings include the process of HES indicator averaging and the application of the evaluating instrument in the field. With regard to the former, we noted previously that the final monthly rating for a hamlet was the result of an averaging of the individual scores on the 18 HES indicators. From a methodological perspective, this was not very sound, and the results could be misleading. For example, a "hamlet with indicators rated as one A, two B's, nine C's, five D's, and one E would be given an over-all rating of 2.83 . . . a C category hamlet."[158] Such averaging is deceptive, for it might well mask certain developments that present a very different picture. It is important to recognize that all data collected in the field were susceptible to advisor subjectivity. While a number of problems can be identified, only the most pertinent will be noted. In the first place, many of the U.S. advisors had no particular political, economic, or sociological skills to draw on in assessing hamlet developments.[159] In addition, because the advisory teams were small, they did not always visit every hamlet each month. This meant that they had to rely on other sources in determining their ratings. There was also the problem of the short tour of duty.[160] In addition, one needs to recognize that these advisors were evaluating their own work. Finally, if we turn our attention to the hamlets themselves, there is the problem of whether the local people provided U.S. and GVN officials with an accurate picture of the local situation.

This preliminary analysis, then, raises some important doubts about the proposition that the GVN won the "other war," and were defeated only by an invasion from the outside. These doubts will be discussed further once this reassessment is completed. In concluding this section we would argue simply that a reliance on HES data to evaluate the success of the pacification aspect of Vietnamization is problematic. The reliability of the evaluating instrument is suspect, and this certainly affects the validity of the findings. Perhaps the seriousness of the problem can best be put into focus by citing the experience of one former U.S. district senior advisor (DSA) involved in Vietnamization during 1971-72:

> I inherited a village that was rated B and had even been
> an A . . . This village was looked upon by two DSA's
> before me as the model village. All the answers to the
> HES made it B and I carried it B for some months before
> I found out the horrible truth about this village and two
> others that were like it. For, you see, my best village,
> which also had the best village chief, village administra-
> tive office, etc., was also the best VC run village I had.
> The village chief was hard core VC, and all of his staff
> were VC. So, if this village was so infested with VC,
> how was it able to pass as a B on the HES? Think about
> this . . . if a village were completely VC and knew how
> to play the game with RVN, and they knew how, i.e.,
> no overt or covert (VC) tax collection was needed, since
> after all they had the village, and the villagers would not
> say a word about the setup . . . The VC had this village
> locked up so they really didn't need to cause trouble . . .
> Run or establish a VC hamlet with a complete infra-
> structure that plays the game . . . and see if the hamlet
> would not come out B . . . I have seen it work and work
> very successfully. [161]

While further analysis is obviously necessary, one must seriously question the conclusion that by 1972 the GVN had won the "other war."

THE MILITARY ASPECTS OF VIETNAMIZATION

A crucial aspect of Vietnamization was the capability of the RVNAF to guarantee security and repel VC/NVA probes. With the culmination of the U.S. withdrawal, these developments were a major question mark. By 1971, RVNAF troop strength was considered ade-quate, as were their equipment and supply levels. [162] However, the real issue was not one of troop levels or equipment but of "will." While there were those officials who claimed that the RVNAF, and particularly ARVN, had achieved the ability to stand on their own, there were important warning signals suggesting that ARVN was not appreciably different from what it had been during the pre-Vietnami-zation period.

One such signal was that of desertion. For instance, by 1971, after three years of Vietnamization, the annual average desertion rate for GVN forces was over 140,000.[163] What was even more disturbing, according to a 1971 Defense Department study, was that the "desertion problem . . . is concentrated in the ground combat units."[164] Comparatively the desertion rate for ARVN combat units was "4 times the RF . . . 7 times the PF . . . and 13 times the rate for ARVN non-combat units."[165] This desertion problem was further compounded by the fact that only "14% of all deserters . . . returned."[166] Furthermore, there was no indication at that time that things were going to improve. Certainly such factors could greatly affect morale and, as one report suggests, "cast further doubt on the RVNAF's ability to sustain operations."[167]

A second and continuing problem, according to OASD(SA) SEA Analysis Reports, was poor ARVN leadership,[168] and as with desertion, poor leadership was much more prevalent in combat units.[169] Good leadership is undoubtedly of major importance, for the foundation of any army is its officers corps. Additional ARVN handicaps included lack of training time;[170] reliance on heavy weapons firepower, use of conventional tactics, and inability to fight an unconventional war;[171] and various forms of corruption.[172] Finally, many of the same problems also plagued the RF/PF forces.[173]

In sum, the capability and will of the ARVN and other RVNAF forces was suspect. The impact of this on Vietnamization and the 1975 defeat will be addressed in the conclusion of this reassessment.

THE CHIEU HOI AND PHUNG HOANG PROGRAMS

These two programs, designed to cut into insurgent strength, constituted the psychological operations elements of the 1968-72 strategy.[174] Despite the increased attention each received, preliminary findings indicate no major achievements from either program. Although first initiated in 1963, it was only during Vietnamization that Chieu Hoi attracted large numbers of defectors. For example, the number for 1969 (47,088) was almost three times that of 1968 (17,836).[175] While impressive initially, these figures are deceptive due to the special rewards attached to Chieu Hoi. The most notorious of these was the "Third Party Inducement Program." Under it a person who induced a VC/NVA member to surrender received a reward that varied with the defector's rank. While defectors from previous years came mostly from the lower ranks, under this reward program it was discovered that many defectors were not VC/NVA at all. A 1969 report on Chieu Hoi notes that the program became a money-making enterprise for many South Vietnamese, including GVN officials.[176] Additionally many of those who defected did so more than once.[177]

Likewise, the results of the Phung Hoang or Phoenix program were very suspect.[178] Directed specifically at the VC infrastructure, the program presented results that appeared to be impressive. For example, 13,000-14,000 "eliminations" were reported for 1968. However, when non-VCI were removed, actual losses were estimated to be "as low as 5200."[179] Furthermore, of these, "less than 1% . . . held positions of top leadership" in the VCI. This was considered "too low to cause the VCI any serious problems."[180] There were many reasons why Phoenix was not successful in 1968,[181] and they continued to plague the program in subsequent years. For example, an analysis of 1969 "eliminations" concluded that these not only had "little impact on the strength of the infrastructure . . . but the estimated VCI strength increased."[182] Finally, a 1971 report notes "Phung Hoang has changed very little . . . no one seems to be able to improve it."[183] In sum, the infrastructure remained intact. The implication for the successful implementation of the Vietnamization strategy is obvious.

RURAL DEVELOPMENT—POLITICAL COMMUNITY

Once the hamlets were secured and VCI control broken, the final goals of Vietnamization were rural development and political community. With respect to the former, land reform and civic action programs were important initial steps. By 1972, over 400,000 farmers had acquired 1.5 million acres under the Land to the Tiller Law (March 1970). This lowered tenancy from 60 percent to 34 percent.[184] We would concur with Lewy that this not only weakened the landlords, but also began to change "the perceptions of the government as simply the protector of the rich."[185] With respect to other elements of rural development, the United States understood that this simply provided a large quantity of goods (and services) earmarked for rural areas. This was a questionable strategy for development, even aside from the problem of making sure such aid was properly distributed.

In the area of political reform, the GVN reestablished locally elected village councils and chiefs. The goal was to create a healthy village political structure that would act as a base of support for GVN. However, no such developments occurred because, as Popkins explains "Thieu's purpose had not been to enact major reforms giving the peasants a role in government, but to develop a power base outside ARVN."[186] This had a debilitating effect on political reform. Further blocking this development, according to Blaufarb, was ARVN's influence and manipulation of local government. "ARVN was . . . a political cabal whose first priorities were to perpetuate the system and to protect . . . those who controlled it."[187]

With respect to the development of political community, most analysts who have seriously addressed this issue agree with the following conclusions by Lawrence Grinter:

> The failure to fashion a political community tells why South Vietnam ultimately collapsed after marked successes against the communists in the early 1970's. . . . Pacification was the core of the problem. . . . From 1954 until about mid-1968 Saigon failed to adequately address the communist challenge . . . But after the 1968 Tet offensive the situation changed radically. The Thieu government's political-military strategy . . . became more relevant to the challenge, and, under better priority and management began to involve the people in the task. This had three principal effects: (1) . . . long-term protection of the villages was greatly upgraded; (2) local self-government . . . ; (3) economic redistribution. . . . But to have set the seal on these efforts the Thieu government needed more time, continuing American military and economic assistance . . . and less pressure. . . . Still, as late as the Spring of 1974, it appeared the Thieu government could hold out, provided it received enough ammunition to defend the country. [188]

While we would agree that political community was never forged, Grinter and others seem to suggest that the Thieu government came close to it through the 1968-72 strategy. [189] But these preliminary findings suggest that this is not true. Furthermore, they appear to refute theories that explain the demise of South Vietnam because of lack of time for completing Vietnamization, continuing North Vietnamese military pressure that took the form of a full scale invasion in 1975, or lack of supplies and ammunition to halt the invasion.

VIETNAMIZATION—SUCCESS OR FAILURE?

In closing, two questions remain: first, how successful was the Vietnamization strategy; and second, what effect did the strategy have on the events of 1975? Conceptually, as a counterinsurgency strategy, Vietnamization was sound. Given the Revolutionary Warfare approach of the opposition, Vietnamization focused on the problem areas and the requisite counter-steps. However, our preliminary findings cast serious doubt on the assertion that Vietnamization "brought significant security and development to the rural population" and that a "People's

War of National Liberation' had been defeated."[190] Basically, such conclusions reflect Komer's evaluation of Vietnamization. However, given the data base, it is our position that no such conclusions should be drawn. It is doubtful that the HES instrument allowed for an accurate evaluation of who controlled the countryside. In effect, the instrument did not accurately measure the VC style of politics and insurgency. Therefore, the conclusions drawn from the HES data may in no way reflect who was winning or losing. As we noted above, monthly security ratings could very well mask the real power balance in a hamlet. The HES conclusions are based on factors like the 1968-71 lull in intense VC/NVA actions and on the equation of security with military occupation. But to conclude from this that the VC were defeated is empirically unsound. Certainly the evidence presented above contradicts the HES conclusions and demonstrates the effectiveness of VC activity as late as 1972. In sum, this highly oversimplified quantitative evaluation was bound by a series of constraints that greatly biased any conclusions derived from it.

In addition to the issue of security, there is evidence that the other elements of the Vietnamization strategy were not successfully implemented. This was certainly true in terms of the RVNAF, Chieu Hoi, Phung Hoang, and rural development-political community. Thus, one is led to the preliminary conclusion that this final attempt at counterinsurgency also resulted in failure. Many of the problems that blocked prior attempts to employ similar approaches also stood in the way of Vietnamization.

The broader question is what impact these findings have on the popular explanations of the events of 1975. Although preliminary, they raise serious doubts about the success of Vietnamization. Only a powerful argument would attribute the swiftness of the NVA success not merely to the superiority of the North Vietnamese military, but to the fact that the Vietnamization strategy was not successfully implemented by the GVN.

PAST LESSONS—FUTURE PROSPECTS

Although the Vietnam war ended in 1975, the essential lessons regarding U.S. involvement have still to be clearly drawn. In this final section we attempt to draw those lessons and to determine what impact they should have on future planning for low-intensity conflicts.

The first lesson is derived from the sharp difference between the enemy the United States faced and the regime it supported. Both the VC and DRV were strongly motivated foes who effectively applied the tenets of revolutionary warfare. In fact, only the Chinese Communists under Mao have employed the strategy as effectively. On the other hand, the various regimes supported by the United States were weak and ineffective either in fighting the enemy or in governing the nation. Given this asymmetrical situation, the United States found itself in a unique and highly unfamiliar conflict environment, supporting a client with little chance of success and unwilling to reform. In the future, the United States must avoid such commitments, for they are "no win" situations. A more realistic assessment of one's client is essential.

The second lesson has to do with the strategies employed in low-intensity conflicts. In explaining how strategy is developed, Beaufre states that "we are dealing with a problem of dialectics; for every action proposed . . . enemy reactions must be calculated and provision made to guard against them. . . . Each successive action planned, together with the counter to the corresponding enemy reaction, must be built up into a coherent whole, the objective being to retain the ability to pursue the plan in spite of the resistance of the enemy."[191] In effect, Beaufre argues that one must know the enemy and understand the situation within which the conflict occurs. Contextually, we did not understand Vietnam. Our strategies ignored or misunderstood the historical setting, the culture, and the nature of the opposition. These misperceptions resulted in strategies based on prior U.S. military experiences or faulty interpretations of contextual factors. Future U.S. involvement in low-intensity conflicts should be predicated on sound situational assessment. This will permit the United States to circumvent unmanageable situations. In sum, strategy development is a "context-dependent problem."[192]

A related problem is that of evaluating the strategy once it has been implemented. In the case of Vietnamization the pitfalls of a faulty evaluative instrument were identified. As with strategy development, the instruments employed to measure effectiveness are "context dependent."

The third lesson has to do with the relationship between political and military factors in unconventional situations. A client can only succeed militarily if it develops an indigenous political base from which support can be mobilized. Thus the United States cannot substitute itself for its client: it cannot stand in place of those indigenous elements who must win the conflict for themselves. The outside support for our client can only supplement and not replace him.

This in turn suggests a fourth lesson, that there are limits to the effective use of military force and intervention. The Vietnam involvement demonstrates that sheer U.S. military power cannot resolve all conflicts, and that it is not applicable in all situations. The lesson to be learned is that regardless of America's military superiority, U.S. policymakers cannot manipulate every situation.

The dangers of the precipitate use of military force to solve complex political problems is now apparent.

A fifth lesson derives from the bureaucratic and organizational constraints on effective policy implementation. Komer points out in his study Bureaucracy Does Its Thing . . . that the impact of institutional factors or bureaucratic constraints seriously limited U.S. effectiveness. [193] Certainly organizational factors underlie the unrelenting emphasis on conventional military procedures. Likewise, interagency conflicts resulted in severe constraints. The reluctance of large organizations to change their preferred way of functioning and their resistance to interagency cooperation were major obstacles to developing policy that reflected the local context.

Additional lessons include the need to recognize the close relationship between domestic politics and U.S. foreign policy; more precise definition of U.S. goals in low-intensity conflicts; and knowledge of when to disengage from irretrievable situations. First of all, the Vietnam intervention demonstrates the limitations on long-term, large-scale military involvement, unless the national interest is challenged. Insuring sustained popular support for extended interventions seems unlikely. Given these restraints, future involvements must avoid open-ended commitment, as well as the absence of precise, short-term goals that characterized Vietnam. Goals must be adequately defined, clearly communicated, and understood at the public level. Finally, the United States must learn when to disengage from a situation in which it cannot succeed. Vietnam demonstrates how costly it can be to ignore the early warnings.

On the other hand, it would seem empirically unsound to draw the general conclusion that all low-intensity conflicts reflect the Vietnamese context, which was in many ways unique. The insurgents employed the tenets of Revolutionary Warfare with exceptional proficiency. The organizational structure was resilient, efficient, and deeply rooted; its foundation was firmly established, dating back to World War II. The insurgency was supported by generations of strongly motivated guerrilla fighters. On the other hand, the side we supported sorely lacked many of these attributes. To summarize, we would argue that very few insurgent situations in the post-World War II period have been similar to Vietnam. Certainly today, the various low-intensity conflicts are not similar to that in Vietnam. However, this uniqueness has not been understood by policymakers or the public. Such misunderstanding is certainly reflected in the "no more Vietnam" syndrome, which regards all low-intensity conflicts in terms of the U.S. experience in Vietnam.

Disillusionment with Vietnam has resulted in a military posture that focuses on the U.S.-USSR strategic balance and the NATO-Warsaw Pact balance, to the complete exclusion of a third security concern for the United States—the proliferation of low-intensity conflicts and local crises throughout the world.[194] In fact, in a recent exploratory discussion of the possible implications of such threats for U.S. security planning, defense and international affairs experts concluded:

> Low-level conflict, including international terrorism, may well be the kind of conflict that will increasingly confront the United States; the outcome of such conflicts may directly affect national facilities and interests, such as sources of raw materials and the sea-lanes for transporting them. The outcome of such conflicts may also affect the perceived strength of the United States.[195]

Although this group of experts is not the first to recognize that such crises will persist and will directly and indirectly affect the United States, the Carter Administration has been unwilling to take any steps to develop a capability to respond to them. For example, no single organization is presently assigned to direct the U.S. response to low-intensity conflicts. Furthermore, this lack of will and organizational direction is accompanied by a lack of force capabilities for such situations. Retired Col. Donald Vought, in a recent article titled "Preparing for the Wrong War," marshals strong evidence showing how unprepared the United States really is in the area of low-intensity conflict. According to Vought, "the U.S. Army is preparing vigorously for the wrong type of war to the near exclusion of the more probable forms."[196] Of course, there is also little contingency planning, identification of range options, intelligence gathering, and so on.

In conclusion, the critical question facing the present Administration is what lesson it will draw from the Vietnam experience and how it will deal with the continuing proliferation of low-intensity conflicts.

NOTES

1. Low-intensity warfare is one in which theoretically the United States does not fully mobilize, restrains its military power, adopts a posture to engage in conventional as well as unconventional warfare, and limits the geographical boundaries as well as the intensity of the conflict. This definition is borrowed from Professor Sam C. Sarkesian.

2. There is no theoretically detailed summary of these competing approaches. For the most useful, shorthand summary see Roger Hilsman, "Two American Counterstrategies to Guerrilla Warfare:

The Case of Vietnam," in China's Policies in Asia and America's Alternative, ed. Tang Tsou (Chicago: University of Chicago Press, 1969). For a general inventory of the Vietnam case, the only presently published account is Lawrence Grinter, "South Vietnam: Pacification Denied," Southeast Asian Spectrum (July 1975): 49-78; and Grinter, "How They Lost: Strategies and Outcomes of the Vietnam War," Asian Survey (December 1975): 1114-32.

3. This overview is drawn from Richard Shultz, "The Limits of Terrorism in Insurgency Warfare: The Case of the Viet Cong," Polity (Fall 1978): 67-91.

4. See Mao Tse-tung, "The Problems of Strategy in Guerrilla Warfare," in his Selected Works of Mao Tse-tung, Vol. II (Peking: Foreign Languages Press, 1967). For an interpretation see Bard O'Neill, D. J. Alberts, and Stephen Rossetti, eds., Political Violence and Insurgency: A Comparative Approach (Boulder, Colorado: Phoenix Press, 1974).

5. Quoted in Samuel Griffith, ed., Mao Tse-tung On Guerrilla Warfare (New York: Praeger, 1961), p. 44.

6. Bernard Fall, Street Without Joy (New York: Shocken, 1964), p. 371.

7. Shultz, pp. 75-76.

8. Ibid., p. 76.

9. For good secondary accounts of the Viet Cong strategy, see William Andrews, The Village War (Columbia: University of Missouri Press, 1973); Michael Conley, The Communist Infrastructure in South Vietnam (Washington, D.C.: The Center for Research in Social Systems, 1967); Bernard Fall, Street Without Joy (New York: Shocken, 1964); idem, The Two Vietnams (New York: Praeger, 1967); idem, Viet-Nam Witness 1953-66 (New York: Praeger, 1966); Francis Fitzgerald, Fire in the Lake (Boston: Little, Brown, 1972); Douglas Pike, Viet Cong (Cambridge, Mass.: M.I.T. Press, 1966); idem, The Viet Cong Strategy of Terror (Cambridge, Mass.: M.I.T. Press, 1970); Jeffrey Race, War Comes to Long An (Berkeley: University of California Press, 1972); and Robert Sansom, The Economics of Insurgency (Cambridge, Mass.: M.I.T. Press, 1970). For an excellent summary overview, see C. L. Cooper, J. E. Corson, and L. J. Legere, The American Experience with Pacification in Vietnam, Vol. II (Arlington, Va.: Institute for Defense Analysis, 1972).

10. Any of the major biographies on John Kennedy discuss this. See Roger Hilsman, To Move a Nation (New York: Delta Books, 1964). For a critical view see Bruce Miroff, Pragmatic Illusions (New York: David McKay, 1976).

11. Chalmers Johnson, "Civilian Loyalties and Guerrilla Conflict," World Politics (July 1962), p. 649.

12. Charles Bohanman, "Antiguerrilla Actions," The Annals (May 1962): 20.

13. Foreign Assistance Act of 1961, Hearings before the Committee on Foreign Affairs, House of Representatives, 88th Congress, 2nd Session, April 1964, p. 208.

14. David Galula, Counterinsurgency Warfare (New York: Praeger, 1964); Edward Lansdale, In the Midst of War (New York: Harper and Row, 1972); Fall, Street Without Joy; John McCuen, The Art of Counterrevolutionary War (Harrisburg, Pa.: Stackpole, 1966); Robert Thompson, Defeating Communist Insurgency (New York: Praeger, 1966); and Roger Trinquier, Modern Warfare (New York: Praeger, 1961). These are only the more standard works.

15. Galula, pp. 107-35; McCuen, pp. 50-75; Thompson, pp. 50-63.

16. McCuen, p. 50.

17. Thompson, p. 63.

18. McCuen, p. 198.

19. Thompson, pp. 71-72.

20. McCuen, p. 53.

21. The theoretical roots of the reform aspects of this strategy are derived from the large volume of modernization and development literature that emerged in the late 1950s and early 1960s.

22. Edward Lansdale, "Vietnam: Do We Understand Revolution," Foreign Affairs (October 1964): 84.

23. Peter Paret and John Shy, Guerrillas in the 1960's (New York: Praeger, 1964), p. 47; McCuen, p. 56.

24. Special Operations—Operations Against Guerrilla Forces—FM 31-20 (Washington, D.C.: Department of the Army, 1961).

25. McCuen, p. 108.

26. Civic Affairs Operations—FM 41-10 (Washington, D.C.: Department of the Army, 1969).

27. Robert Slover, "This is Military Civic Action," Army (July 1963). Also see Edward Glick, Peaceful Conflict (Harrisburg, Pa.: Stackpole, 1967).

28. McCuen, p. 67; Thompson, p. 164. The general consensus is that such aid can supplement, but an outside force cannot replace indigenous ones.

29. McCuen, pp. 72-73.

30. For a discussion of personalism, see Fall, The Two Vietnams, pp. 246-47.

31. United States Congress; House Committee on Armed Services, United States-Vietnam Relations, 1945-1967, 92nd Congress, 2nd Session (Washington, D.C.: Government Printing Office, 1972), IV.A.5. Tab 2, p. 17.

32. William Nighswonger, Rural Pacification in Vietnam (New York: Praeger, 1966), pp. 124-25.

33. See United States-Vietnam Relations, 1945-1967, IV.B.2., p. 36. Also see Cooper, Corson, and Legere, The American Experience with Pacification in Vietnam, Vol. III.

34. George McTurnan Kahin and George Lewis, The United States in Vietnam (New York: Delta, 1967), pp. 140-41.

35. Milton Osborne, Strategic Hamlets in South Vietnam (Ithaca, N.Y.: Department of Asian Studies, Cornell University, 1965), pp. 54-55.

36. United States-Vietnam Relations, 1945-1967, IV.A.5., Tab 2., pp. 1-71.

37. Ibid., IV.B.a., pp. 9-10.

38. Ibid., IV.A.5., Tab 2., pp. 14-15.

39. Ibid., IV.B.1., p. 61.

40. U.S. House Committee on Government Operations, "Land Reform in Vietnam," 90th Congress, 2nd Session, Report No. 1442, p. 8.

41. F. H. Denton, Volunteers for the Viet Cong (Santa Monica, Calif.: Rand, 1969), pp. x-xi.

42. Fitzgerald, Fire in the Lake, p. 88.

43. Joseph Buttinger, Vietnam: A Political History (New York: Praeger, 1972), Ch. XVII.

44. Robert Komer, Bureaucracy Does Its Thing: Institutional Constraints on US-GVN Performance in Vietnam (Santa Monica, Calif.: Rand, 1972), p. 38.

45. United States-Vietnam Relations, 1945-1967, IV.A.4., p. 41.

46. Two general views emerged among U.S. agencies involved: (1) the conventional military view (JCS and DOD), which understood the insurgency in terms of security and search and destroy; and (2) the political view (State and CIA), which saw the situation in terms of social, political, and economic reform.

47. What follows is a much shortened version of two previous research papers. See Richard Shultz, "Breaking the Will of the Enemy During the Vietnam War: The Operationalization of the Cost-Benefit Model of Counterinsurgency Warfare," Journal of Peace Research, 2 (1978); and Shultz, "Coercive Force and Military Strategy: Deterrence Logic and the Cost-Benefit Model of Counterinsurgency Warfare," Western Political Quarterly (December 1979).

48. United States-Vietnam Relations, 1945-1967, IV.A.5., Tab 2., pp. 1-71.

49. The cost-benefit terminology is taken from various works by Charles Wolf, who at the theoretical level most concisely articulates this model. See Charles Wolf and Nathan Leites, Rebellion and

Authority (Chicago: Markham, 1970); Wolf, United States Policy and the Third World (Boston: Little, Brown, 1967). The term "Suppressive Model" is borrowed from Jeffery Race, "Vietnam Intervention: Systematic Distortion in Policy-Making," Armed Forces and Society (Spring 1976).

50. Thomas C. Schelling, Arms and Influence (New Haven: Yale University Press, 1966), p. 2.

51. Ibid., pp. 2, 33-34.

52. Ibid., Chapter 1 contains an extended discussion of this argument.

53. This argument is borrowed from Alexander George and Richard Smoke, Deterrence in American Foreign Policy: Theory and Practice (New York: Columbia University Press, 1974), Ch. 2.

54. Ibid., p. 54. This point is nicely brought out in the author's checklist of varying characteristics of deterrence at each of the three levels. Here we will list a portion of the responses to clarify the author's point that when you go below the strategic level to the conventional and unconventional levels, "a multitude of variables . . . that fluctuate over time . . . dependent on the context of the situation" greatly affect the employment of strategic deterrence logic at these levels. One, the objectives (many, rarely clear, and hard to determine commitment to these objectives). Two, opponents means (unclear and hard to determine quantity and usefulness). Three, ability to determine effectiveness of deterrence of the enemy (considerably difficult). Four, ambiguity of the situation (usually very great). Five, possible outcomes to the situation (a great many). Six, the nature of "rationality" in dealing with the situation (considerably problematical). Seven, degree of uncertainties (enormous). pp. 52-53.

55. For a useful discussion of the abstract-deductive nature of deterrence and the pitfalls involved from the fact that "contemporary deterrence theory has developed substantially as a deductivist product of the field known as 'decision theory,'" ibid., pp. 66-83.

56. Charles Wolf, Insurgency and Counterinsurgency: New Myths and Old Realities (Santa Monica, Calif.: Rand, 1965).

57. Leites and Wolf.

58. According to Leites and Wolf, the answer lies in what they term "damage-limiting" and "profit-maximizing decisions." We call "behavior based on fear of the consequences . . . damage-limiting, and behavior based on considerations of gain profit-maximizing . . . To the extent that the population responds to damage-limiting motives, R's (insurgent) strength may derive directly from its harshness toward uncongenial behavior . . . To the extent that the population responds to profit-maximizing, R should stress rewards . . . R may envoke the behavior it desires by methods that combine considerations

of damage and gain. . . . The same pattern applies symmetrically to behavior desired by A (counterinsurgents)." Ibid., pp. 11-13.

59. Ibid., p. 29.

60. Ibid., pp. 32-33.

61. Ibid., p. 36.

62. Ibid., p. 56.

63. Ibid., pp. 37-38.

64. In other words, if counterinsurgents make the situation unpleasant enough, through the use of varying degrees and types of coercive force, the populace will move to desist in their support. For the rational decision maker, the need to avoid today's damage or pain will override any considerations of preference he/she may have over the long run. Thus, one will choose today's safety rather than gamble on the future achievement of long-range preferences.

65. According to Leites and Wolf, "A can use various measures to reduce the productivity of R's resources, as well as force R to divert resources from producing offensive operations to more defensive, productive activities." Examples of the former would include measures that "cause R's forces to lose sleep, to be on the move at times and places of A's choosing" while the latter would focus on "targeting the production mechanism directly—for example, by destroying crops that are relied upon to provide food for R's forces." Leites and Wolf, pp. 78-79.

66. Ibid., p. 82.

67. United States-Vietnam Relations, 1945-1967, IV, C.5., p. 1.

68. Prior to this the goal had been to deny the enemy victory or to ride the GVN/ARVN to victory. Now the United States was going to take over the war and win it for the GVN.

69. Prior to the strategy, the administration had hoped to improve the situation by bombing the North. Designated Rolling Thunder, the goals were the three listed above. United States-Vietnam Relations, IV.C.7.(B), pp. 12-13. This had little effect as DOD Deputy Assistant Secretary McNaughton noted in the "April 1 Reassessment." According to McNaughton, "the situation is bad and deteriorating. The VC have the initiative." Ibid., IV.C.3., p. 82. Due to this, the administration felt something dramatic had to be added to the bombing. Under the cost-benefit strategy, the goals of the air war remained the same.

70. Ibid., IV.C.5, pp. 84-94.

71. To accomplish this, the tactics implemented by the United States took on a variety of forms, the most prevalent being saturation bombing and free-fire zones. Such tactics were used to destroy the enemy's main force, as well as clear the regions of civilians who might be supporting the NLF. In addition to the massive bombing

and artillery fire that characterized the saturation and free-fire zone tactics, attrition took other forms as well. For example, antipersonnel weaponry such as cluster bomb units, napalm, white phosphorus, and the like, were heavily relied on. Defoliation and crop destruction tactics were used to deny the enemy effective concealment as well as to destroy the enemy's supply of food at the source. By the same token, measures of success came to be seen in terms of body counts and kill ratios, acres of crops destroyed and defoliated, and percentages of the population displaced.

72. United States-Vietnam Relations, 1945-1967, IV.C.5., pp. 124-26.

73. Ted Robert Gurr, Why Men Rebel (Princeton, N.J.: Princeton University Press, 1970), p. 232.

74. This was originally by John Dollard et al., Frustration and Aggression (New Haven: Yale University Press, 1939).

75. Leonard Berkowitz, Aggression: A Social-Psychological Analysis (New York: McGraw-Hill, 1962); "The Frustration-Aggression Hypothesis Revisited," in Roots of Aggression, ed. L. Berkowitz (New York: Atherton, 1969); "Whatever Happened to the Frustration-Aggression Hypothesis?" American Behavioral Scientist (May/June 1978), pp. 691-708. For a number of related propositions have been proposed about other factors that affect aggression. See Russell Green and David Stonner, "Reaction to Aggression," Journal of Psychology (January 1973), pp. 95-102.

76. For a review of some of this literature, see Shultz, "Breaking the Will of the Enemy . . .," pp. 111-15.

77. Among the most important contributions, we would include: Douglas Bwy, "Political Instability in Latin America: The Cross-Cultural Test of a Causal Model," Latin American Research Review (Spring 1968): 17-66; Ivo Feierabend and Rosalind Feierabend, "Aggressive Behavior Within Politics, 1948-1962: A Cross-National Study," Journal of Conflict Resolution (September 1966): 249-71; "Systemic Conditions of Political Aggression: An Application of the Frustration-Aggression Theory," in Anger, Violence, and Politics, ed. by Ivo Feierabend, Rosalind Feierabend, and Ted Robert Gurr (Englewood Cliffs, N.J.: Prentice-Hall, 1972), pp. 136-83; Gurr, Why Men Rebel; "A Causal Model of Civil Strife: A Comparative Analysis Using New Indices," American Political Science Review (December 1968): 1004-24; "Psychological Factors in Civil Violence," World Policies (June 1968): 245-78; "A Comparative Study of Civil Strife," in Violence in America, ed. by Gurr and H. Graham (New York: Signet, 1969), pp. 544-605; James C. Davies, "The J-Curve of Rising and Declining Satisfactions as a Cause of Some Great Revolutions and Contained Rebellions," in Violence in America, pp. 671-709.

78. David Snyder, "Theoretical and Methodological Problems in the Analysis of Governmental Coercion and Collective Violence," Journal of Political and Military Sociology (Fall 1976): 278.

79. Ted Robert Gurr, Ivo Feierabend, Rosalind Feierabend, Douglas Bwy, and Alaor Passos, "Development Tensions and Political Instability: Some Hypotheses Concerning Latin America," Journal of Peace Research (1968): 70-88.

80. For a discussion see Shultz, "Breaking the Will of the Enemy During the Vietnam War . . . ," pp. 113-14.

81. Peter Paret, French Revolutionary Warfare from Indochina to Algeria (New York: Praeger, 1964); C. Melnik, The French Campaign Against the FLN (Santa Monica, Calif.: Rand, 1967); John Ambler, The French Army in Politics 1945-1962 (Columbus: Ohio State University Press, 1966), especially chap. 11; ALF Andrew Heggoy, Insurgency and Counterinsurgency in Algeria (Bloomington: Indiana University Press, 1972).

82. See Alexander Dallin and George Breslauer, Political Terror in Communist Systems (Stanford, Calif.: Stanford University Press, 1970). For a good discussion of the limits of "Aversive Techniques of Control" see A. E. Fredman, The Psychology of Political Control (New York: St. Martin's Press, 1975), Chapter 3.

83. Rosen notes that "the science of power measurement is not very well developed, and even if it were, and parties knew what matters and what does not, the difficulties of assessing the value of each variable are immense. The result is a highly conjectural process of reasoning." See Steve Rosen, "A Model of War and Alliance," Alliance and International Politics, ed. Rosen, Julian Friedman, and Christopher Bladen (Boston: Allyn and Bacon, 1970), pp. 229-30.

84. Rosen devises a "War Power Ratio" which is divided into two fundamental categories (or components). He notes that "the most visible component of a nation's power is its ability to harm its opponent by destroying his assets. This destructive capacity . . . called 'strength,' is composed of manpower and weaponry, and is based on economic productivity, strategic inventiveness, and other facts which maximize the . . . ability to harm" . . . to achieve a goal; we will call this . . . 'cost-tolerance.'" As will be demonstrated in this study, one of the major problems in operationalizing the cost-benefit insurgency strategy in Vietnam was the inability of the United States to measure the cost-tolerance of the North Vietnamese and NLF. Ibid., pp. 215-37.

85. It should also be noted that the rationality assumption contains an ethnocentric bias.

86. See Shultz, "The Limits of Terrorism . . ."

87. Ibid., pp. 79-91.

88. The Rand Vietnam Interview series is composed of a number of parts of which we have relied on Series AG (649 interviews), Series PT (285 interviews), Series K-KO (87 interviews), and Series PIE (102 interviews). The entire series is available through NTIS and Rand has put out a User's Guide to the Rand Interviews in Vietnam (Santa Monica, Calif.: Rand, 1972).

89. W. P. Davison, Some Observations of Viet Cong Operations in the Villages (Santa Monica, Calif.: Rand, 1968); F. H. Denton, Volunteers for the Viet Cong (Santa Monica, Calif.: Rand, 1968); J. C. Donnell, G. P. Pauker, and J. J. Zasloff, Viet Cong Motivation and Morale: A Preliminary Report (Santa Monica, Calif.: Rand, 1965); D. W. P. Elliott and M. Elliott, Documents of an Elite Viet Cong Delta Unit: The Demolition Platoon of the 154th Battalion—Part One-Five (Santa Monica, Calif.: Rand, 1969); Konrad Kellen, Conversations with Enemy Soldiers in Late 1968/Early 1969: A Study of Motivation and Morale (Santa Monica, Calif.: Rand, 1970); Kellen, A View of the VC: Elements of Cohesion in the Enemy Camp (Santa Monica, Calif.: Rand, 1969); Victoria Pohle, The Viet Cong in Saigon: Tactics and Objectives During the TET Offensive (Santa Monica, Calif.: Rand, 1969); and J. J. Zasloff, Political Motivation of the Viet Cong: The Vietminh Regroups (Santa Monica, Calif.: Rand, 1968).

90. Vietnamese Documents, translated and released by the U.S. Mission in Saigon and distributed by the Office of Media Services, Department of State, Washington, D.C. (LC number: DS557 .A5 V58). Also, the study by Stephen Hosmer, Viet Cong Repression and Its Implications for the Future (Lexington, Mass.: Heath Books, 1970), is based on the use of such documents, which were identified, logged, and translated at the Combined Document Exploitation Center (CDEC), a joint U.S.-GVN installation that was located on the outskirts of Saigon.

91. United States-Vietnam Relations, IV.C.7. (B)., pp. 122-30.

92. Shultz, "Breaking the Will of the Enemy . . .," pp. 117-18.

93. Several factors combined to give this study powerful credibility: (1) many of the country's most distinguished scientists were part of this group; (2) the reports were well documented; and (3) they gave added confirmation to the intelligence community studies.

94. In addition to presenting a powerful repudiation of the bombing, the Jason report had an important impact on the reordering of Defense Secretary McNamara's view of the air war. It was at this time that McNamara adopted the "infiltration barrier" concept. United States-Vietnam Relations, IV.C.7. (A), pp. 144-45.

95. Ibid., IV.C.7. (B), pp. 123-25.

96. Ibid., p. 125. Also see Alain Enthovan and Wayne Smith, How Much Is Enough? (New York: Harper and Row, 1971), pp. 293-306.

97. United States-Vietnam Relations, 1945-1967, IV.C.7. (B), p. 126.

98. Ibid., pp. 126-27.

99. This is a good indication of how unimportant pacification had become.

100. Shultz, "Breaking the Will of the Enemy . . . ," pp. 119-22.

101. Ibid., pp. 119-20.

102. United States-Vietnam Relations, IV.C.6. (C), p. 29.

103. United States Assistance Programs in Vietnam. Hearings before the Subcommittee on Foreign Operations and Government Information, House of Representatives, 92nd Congress, 1st Session, July-August, 1972. In the section on Vietnamization, the Phoenix program is dealt with more thoroughly. It is included here because its origins lie in the 1965-68 period. However, it was carried over into the 1968-72 period. "The majority of the people classified as VC under Phoenix were captured as a result of sweeping operations . . . A huge dragnet was cast out . . . and whatever looked good . . . was classified as VC." Nomination of William Colby, Hearings before the Armed Services Committee, U.S. Senate, 93rd Congress, 1st Session, July 2-25, 1973, p. 59.

104. Shultz, "Breaking the Will of the Enemy . . . ," pp. 120-21

105. The reports in this project include: Donnell, Pauker, and Zasloff, Viet Cong Motivation and Morale: A Preliminary Report; Konrad Kellen, A Profile of the PAVN Soldier in South Vietnam (Santa Monica, Calif.: Rand, 1967); Kellen, A View of the VC: Elements of Cohesion in the Enemy Camp; and Kellen, Conversations with Enemy Soldiers in Late 1968/Early 1969: A Study of Motivation and Morale.

106. Kellen, Conversations with Enemy Soldiers . . . , p. 101. My own examination of other interviews strongly supports these findings. Shultz, "Breaking the Will of the Enemy . . . ," pp. 121-22.

107. Ibid., p. 121.

108. Ibid.

109. Civilian Casualty and Refugee Problems in South Vietnam, Findings and Recommendations of the Subcommittee to Investigate Problems Connected with Refugees of the Committee on the Judiciary, U.S. Senate, 90th Congress, 2nd Session, May 1968.

110. See Rand Interviews and Reports.

111. United States-Vietnam Relations, 1945-1967, IV.C.6. (C), p. 28.

112. Bernard Brodie, "The Tet Offensive," in Noble Frankland and Christopher Dowling, eds., Decisive Battles of the Twentieth Century (London: Sedgewick & Jackson, 1976).

113. F. J. West, Area Security: The Need, the Composition, and the Components (Santa Monica, Calif.: Rand, 1968).

114. Guy Pauker, An Essay on Vietnamization (Santa Monica, Calif.: Rand, 1971).

115. While the RVNAF was supposed to be involved in pacification from 1965 to 1968, they in fact continued to focus on conventional operations.

116. Much of the primary documentation in this section is drawn from special reports compiled in the Office of the Assistant Secretary of Defense (Systems Analysis) during 1968-72. They will be cited as OASD(SA), Southeast Asia (SEA) Analysis Reports with the appropriate file and page number. This particular one was file 610, p. 90.

117. In addition to materials cited in the preceding note we are working with the primary data gathered in the field to evaluate Vietnamization. This is all on computer tape and is accompanied with codebooks. It is available through the national archives. For a useful explanation of the measures of security see the documentation accompanying the Hamlet Evaluation System File (HAMLA).

118. OASD(SA), SEA Analysis Reports 610, pp. 90-91.

119. James L. Collins, The Development and Training of the South Vietnamese Army 1960-1972, Vietnam Studies (Washington, D.C.: Department of the Army, 1975).

120. OASD(SA), SEA Analysis Reports 612, pp. 274-80.

121. Robert Komer, "Was There Another Way," in Lessons of Vietnam, ed. W. Scott Thompson and Donaldson Frizzell (New York: Crane, Russak, 1977), p. 213.

122. Ibid.

123. Robert Komer, "Impact of Pacification on Insurgency in South Vietnam," Asian Survey (August 1970): 6.

124. Ibid., p. 8.

125. See codebook to the Hamlet Evaluation System File (HAMLA).

126. The data tape cited in the preceding note is only one of a number of files that the National Archives has under the title "Records of the Office of Secretary of Defense—Vietnam War Records."

127. Komer, "Impact of Pacification . . . ," p. 9.

128. Pauker, p. iv.

129. Komer, "Was There Another Way," p. 222.

130. Ibid., p. 220.

131. Ibid.

132. Samuel Popkins, "Pacification: Politics and the Village," Asian Survey (August 1970); Allan Goodman, "South Vietnam and the New Security," Asian Survey (February 1972).

133. Douglas Blaufarb, The Counterinsurgency Era (New York: Free Press, 1977), pp. 270-71.

134. Guenter Lewy, America in Vietnam (New York: Oxford University Press, 1978), especially chapters 1-6.

135. Ibid., see his Epilogue, pp. 419–41.

136. With the exception of the OASD(SA), SEA Analysis Reports no critique of these measuring instruments outside government circles has been undertaken. Recent bibliographical searches by NTIS and DDC have turned up newly declassified DOD reports. For further information please contact me.

137. As one can imagine, with such a volume of material, the data stage is a long one that we are only in the initial stages of.

138. OASD(SA), SEA Analysis Reports 317. This file contains various reports discussing this issue.

139. Taken from codebook to the Hamlet Evaluation System File (HAMLA), pp. 8–10.

140. OASD(SA), SEA Analysis Reports 316, p. 226.

141. In HES there is a procedure for ranking VCI activity and guerrilla violence on a scale of intensity. So, a single terrorist incident is not nearly as bad as a military attack. This will then tell you the latter security situation is much worse than the former. In revolutionary warfare this does not hold up.

142. Terrorism indicators show this pattern. What is interesting is that as you go from military attacks to incidents of terrorism this was understood as a sign of insurgent weakness. This is a faulty assumption. Also, it did not tap covert VC actions. See OASD(SA), SEA Analysis Reports 314 for reports to this effect.

143. Ibid.

144. OASD(SA), SEA Analysis Reports 316, p. 240.

145. Ibid., pp. 243–46.

146. Some of these reports are available through NTIS and DDC. However, most are located at the Current History Branch, U.S. Army Center of Military History, Washington, D.C. I have seen only a few of these. Lewy cites a number of them in his America in Vietnam. However, I have interviewed some of these advisors, and I'm presently involved in developing a questionnaire to be administered to former district senior advisors I've had contact with. The only study that really examines their views on Vietnamization is by Albert C. Bole and K. Kobata, An Evaluation of the Measurements of the Hamlet Evaluation System (Naval War College Center for Advanced Research, 1975). This is, to my mind, a very important report.

147. OASD(SA), SEA Analysis Reports 609, p. 217.

148. OASD(SA), SEA Analysis Reports 313, p. 36.

149. Ibid., pp. 37–38.

150. Ibid.

151. West, in his previously cited monograph, calls this the "We'll be back (in force)" syndrome. See pp. 2–4.

152. OASD(SA), SEA Analysis Reports 316, p. 153.

153. Ibid., p. 152.

154. Ibid., p. 218.

155. Ibid., p. 168. The Pacification Attitude Analysis System is part of the Records of the Office of the Secretary of Defense—Vietnam War Records. I have the data tape but have not yet worked with it. It contains 26,180 respondents.

156. Washington Post (July 19, 1971), p. 15.

157. Ibid.

158. Erwin Brigham, "Pacification Measurement," Military Review (May 1970): 50.

159. Ibid., p. 51; Blaufarb, p. 249.

160. John Paul Vann argued in early 1970s that in Vietnam "We don't have twelve years' experience. . . . We have one year's experience twelve times." Cited in Lewy, p. 118.

161. Bole and Kobata, pp. 50-51.

162. However, from 1968 to 1971 the U.S. forces were heavily involved in helping ARVN with security measures. So ARVN's effectiveness was in doubt.

163. OASD(SA), SEA Analysis Reports 162.

164. Ibid., p. 49.

165. Ibid.

166. Ibid., p. 70.

167. Ibid., p. 74.

168. Ibid., 313, pp. 32-34.

169. Ibid., 315, p. 165.

170. Ibid., 612, p. 15.

171. Brian Jenkins, The Unchangeable War (Santa Monica, Calif.: Rand, 1972).

172. Lewy, pp. 180-81.

173. OASD(SA), SEA Analysis Reports 162, pp. 140-234.

174. For a general discussion of the psychological operations failure, see Barry Zorthian's comments in Thompson and Frizzell, pp. 108-10. Zorthian served for four years as head of the United States Information Service (USIS) in Saigon.

175. OASD(SA), SEA Analysis Reports 613, pp. 53-90.

176. Ibid., pp. 88-89.

177. Ibid., pp. 88-90.

178. This program was one of the most controversial of those developed by the United States. For a criticism see Fitzgerald, Fire in the Lake, pp. 411-14.

179. OASD(SA), SEA Analysis Reports 317, p. 61.

180. Ibid., pp. 61-75.

181. Shultz, "Breaking the Will of the Enemy . . . ," p. 120.

182. OASD(SA), SEA Analysis Reports 317, p. 80.

183. Ibid., pp. 94-102.

184. U.S. Senate, Committee on Foreign Relations, "Vietnam: May, 1972," a staff report (Washington, D.C., 1972), p. 29.

185. Lewy, p. 188.

186. Popkins, p. 670.

187. Blaufarb, pp. 244-45.

188. Lawrence Grinter, "How They Lost: Doctrines, Strategies and Outcomes of the Vietnam War," Asian Survey (December 1975): 1115-16.

189. Blaufarb makes the same argument, pp. 72-78.

190. This quote is from Stephen Young, a member of AID who worked in CORDS. Contained in Thompson and Frizzell, p. 114.

191. Andre Beaufre, Introduction to Strategy (London: Faber and Faber, 1965), Ch. I.

192. See George and Smoke, ch. 2-3.

193. Komer, Bureaucracy Does Its Thing . . .

194. See George Tanham et al., "United States Preparation for Future Low-Level Conflict," Conflict, 1 and 2 (1978): 1-20.

195. Ibid., p. 4.

196. Donald Vought, "Preparing for the Wrong War?" Military Review (May 1977): 16.

7
MILITARY INTERVENTION FORCES
William P. Snyder
Roger A. Beaumont

The meaning of U. S. involvement in Vietnam between 1965 and 1973 remains to be fully assessed.[1] Yet almost all of us have drawn some tentative conclusions from that experience. One conclusion shared by most observers is that military intervention is risky business, to be avoided in all but the gravest cases. At the same time, as recent events suggest, an unwillingness or inability to threaten or to undertake intervention has its costs as well. Based on the proposition that there is a middle ground between these two positions, this paper considers the adequacy of military forces the United States maintains for intervention purposes. Specifically we are concerned with the nature of forces required for intervention in places other than Western Europe or Northern Asia--and on a smaller scale than intervention in these areas would imply. In addition, we explore some of the implications for civil-military relations of maintenance and use of intervention forces.

Thanks are due the following for assistance in providing information for this paper: Colonel William L. Hauser, Director, Army Research Institute; David Fulghum, Publicity Director, Georgetown University; Roger Spiller and Victor Stemberger of the U. S. Army Command and General Staff College; and Paul Bracken of the Hudson Institute.

PRELIMINARY ACTIONS

Military intervention is normally preceded by a number of preliminary actions. That is, intervention generally occurs only if, and
usually only after, preliminary activities have failed to resolve the
crisis. The actions that normally precede intervention include:
diplomatic negotiations; demonstrations of resolve, such as a change
in the alert or readiness status of selected forces; and a show of force,
generally involving naval or air units. The time span during which
these preliminary actions take place may vary considerably. When
these actions fail to resolve the crisis, commitment of military forces
may follow. If military forces are able to resolve the crisis quickly,
policymakers are then free to withdraw the force or to institute other
policy actions. If the desired objectives are not achieved, however,
policymakers may then be faced with what has come to be termed a
"half-war."

Originally a force-planning concept, the "half-war" is analytically useful in distinguishing situations of greater severity and
duration than are encountered in most military interventions. Half-wars
have the following general characteristics: (1) political-military
circumstances that, if unresolved, would have serious implications
for the United States; (2) quick or potential involvement of U.S. military forces of significant size; (3) uncertain prospects for an early or
short-term settlement of the crisis; and (4) some potential for escalation to a broader, more intense regional conflict. As noted above,
the conflict occurs in areas other than Western Europe or Northeast
Asia.

There are many gradations of effort in military interventions;
the rubric "half-war" refers only to more serious and lengthy situations. Blechman and Kaplan examine some 215 cases in the period
1946-75 in which the United States used armed forces as a political
instrument. [2] Over 60 percent of these cases were relatively minor--
almost half involved only naval forces--and the duration of military
involvement was, with few exceptions, generally short-term. Only
four can be considered true half-wars--Korea (1950-53); Lebanon
(1958); Dominican Republic (1965); and Vietnam (1961-73).

We do not wish to suggest that military intervention or half-war
situations will occur with the same frequency in the future: Conflicting trends are present. The U.S. experience in Vietnam has
counselled caution in the use of military force. At the same time,
however, the United States has become more deeply involved in
African affairs over the past decade, and the recently concluded
Middle East peace accords assign the United States a central peacekeeping role in that politically unstable and faction-ridden area. In
addition, the United States has grown increasingly dependent on

energy resources and raw materials from these and other areas. In these circumstances, the possibility of military intervention leading to a half-war is far from remote; and the consequences of not having an adequate or suitable half-war capability may be greater than in the past.

LEGAL AND POLITICAL FRAMEWORK

Before considering the adequacy and suitability of U. S. military forces for intervention and half-war situations, it is essential to recognize how the legal and political framework of military intervention has changed over the past decade. Prior to Vietnam, authority to order military intervention resided largely, if not solely, in the hands of the President. That authority was sharply circumscribed by Congressional actions early in this decade, notably by the War Powers Act, and is now shared by the President and Congress. [3] Perhaps more important than this new legal restriction is the diminution in the political standing of the executive branch: the judgments and initiatives of the President and his principal foreign policy advisors remain important, but are no longer accepted uncritically by Congress. Thus, a crisis serious enough to warrant military intervention involves the Congress, too. The structure and style of that body suggest caution and restraint; these qualities are strengthened by the "lessons" of the intervention that followed hasty Congressional action after the Gulf of Tonkin incident. Major segments of the public, also influenced by the Vietnam experience, would almost certainly oppose recourse to military intervention, although the intensity of their opposition would be influenced by the nature and management of the crisis.

Strategic relationships, which provide the larger setting in which military intervention takes place, have changed significantly in recent years. Between 1945 and 1972, the United States held strategic nuclear superiority over the Soviet Union. Throughout most of this period—even as late as 1969 or 1970—U. S. strategic superiority was massive and unquestioned. But the Soviets have drawn even with the United States in recent years and now possess strategic forces of equal or greater capability. Many analysts now believe that if present trends continue the Soviet Union will achieve overall strategic superiority by the mid-1980s. [4]

Nuclear power was not brought to bear in most of the crises that precipitated earlier U. S. military intervention. In every instance, however, nuclear superiority remained in the background, a trump card that could be brought into play if necessary. The loss of this trump card may now dictate greater caution and discretion than was evident even in Korea and Vietnam, both of which involved numerous constraints on both sides in deference to the special dangers of the nuclear age.

As the legal, political, and strategic dimensions of military intervention have changed, so too have the conventional military dimensions. Three major developments have gradually taken place over the last two decades. First, U. S. access to overseas bases has shrunk, thereby reducing our ability to support military intervention. Second, the principal instrument of intervention, the U. S. Navy, has decreased sharply in 'size—from over 1,000 ships in the mid-1950s to about 450 at present. These changes do not make intervention impossible, but they do multiply the problems associated with staging and supporting military operations abroad. Improved air mobility capabilities offset to some extent the loss of overseas bases and naval capabilities. [5] But some flexibility has nevertheless been lost, and, as supply operations during the 1973 Yom Kippur War demonstrated, strategic airlift can be seriously impaired when overflight rights are withdrawn. As a recent R—paper noted, the world's airspace sovereignty is being preempted rapidly again, to the disadvantage of the United States. Finally, for the first time since World War II, the Soviet Union has naval forces in sufficient quantity to impede or oppose U. S. military intervention in many geographic areas. [6]

The new legal and political framework, the loss of strategic superiority, and changes in conventional forces and base facilities serve to make military operations more complicated and risky than in the past. These changes imply that U. S. military intervention will be less frequent in the future. But they do not mean that there will be no threats to perceived vital interests or even that such threats will go unanswered.

MILITARY FORCES

Most of the situations in which the United States intervened with military forces ended quickly and favorably. But the more serious encounters--the half-war situations--suggest that the kinds of military forces required for the contingency at hand were not available at the outbreak of the crisis. Certainly that was the case at the beginning of the Korean War: units initially deployed to Korea were poorly trained, improperly equipped, and understrength. Military forces trained for counterinsurgency operations were available in small numbers and in various levels of proficiency as the U. S. involvement in Vietnam move beyond the advisory level. These quickly proved inadequate to the task of conventional combat, however, and were engulfed by the thousands of conventionally trained troops that followed them to Vietnam. In the

Lebanon and Dominican Republic crises, intervention forces were
more suited to the essentially preventive and symbolic roles they
played. It now seems to many that policymakers overreacted in both
crises: the forces were larger than necessary and military intervention may not have been necessary at all. In any event, the large
number of troops available and the rapidity of their deployment made
it unlikely that organizational and other shortcomings of the intervention forces would be apparent.

The U. S. experience in these earlier crises supports the proposition that military intervention involves extraordinary uncertainties.
These can be grouped into two categories. The first concerns require-
ments--that is, the size and type of military forces to be maintained
for intervention and half-war situations. The second involves decisions
about which military forces to use in a given crisis.

Requirements

The many interests of the United States around the world derive
from alliances, political ties, markets, resource dependencies, and
defense needs, which in turn create an array of possible contingencies.
Translating such a range of contingencies into specific statements of
requirements that can guide decisions on forces, weapons, and tactics
involves three basic problems. The first is deciding on the importance
to the United States of any given area or country and is related to the
thorny paradigm of "national interest": Is a particular area or country
"vital" to the United States, i. e. , is it closer to the realm of defense
than strategy? Responsible officials, as well as citizens, journalists,
and academicians, can be expected to disagree over this and the related question of whether military intervention should be planned.
Moreover, judgments on the importance of an area and on the character and capabilities of governments in the region can also change,
sometimes almost overnight, as the recent Iranian crisis demonstrated. [7] The superstructure of policy is built on sand, not concrete,
and the tides are not cyclical. Second, even if there is agreement
that certain situations warrant military intervention, policymakers are
likely to disagree on the size, composition, mission, and rules of
engagement of the military forces dispatched to meet the contingency.
The debate within the Kennedy Administration in 1961 and 1962 over
the appropriate actions for the United States to take in Vietnam is a
case in point. Finally, even if planners anticipate a particular contingency, it is usually impracticable to maintain forces tailored to the
special circumstances of that contingency except for a short time. As
a practical matter, elements of the overall force will be earmarked

for intervention purposes and adapted, as time permits, to the requirements of the specific contingencies that do occur.

Careful political and military planning can serve to define more
precisely where and under what circumstances intervention might take
place. Scenario generation, war gaming, and maneuvers can help to
delimit force requirements for various contingencies, and shape their
design, organization, and training. But however careful and prescient
the planning, it cannot guarantee congruence between needs and capabilities in the actual situation. As Ralph Strauch notes:

> [There is] a need for considerable flexibility to react to
> contingencies. . . . That this need can be met ade-
> quately by detailed pre-planning . . . no matter how
> extensive, seems doubtful. . . . [What is required is]
> a high institutional tolerance for ambiguity, a tolerance
> which must be carefully nurtured and developed, since
> the normal tendency for any organization is to attempt
> to structure and perform its function in a way minimizes
> uncertainty and ambiguity. [8]

Deployment

A second set of uncertainties emerge during a crisis, when military intervention becomes a possible response. The most important is
how officials define the crisis. One shaping factor is the way information is reported. The sophisticated command and control systems
that link Washington with most likely trouble spots make rapid,
timely, reporting possible, or at least probable. Yet rapid communications do not insure accurate reporting of the political and military
dimensions of the crisis. Moreover, rapid, easy communications may
induce among policymakers a false sense of accuracy. The most valuable information in many crisis situations concerns political relationships and outlooks; evaluation of the nuances of these relationships
depends on the judgment of officials on the scene. During periods of
crisis and stress, as Graham Allison and others have noted, there is
a marked tendency for policymakers to simplify drastically. [9] Also
important in shaping policymakers' definition of a crisis is the way in
which information is processed and handled within the foreign policy
community. Finally, the outlook and prior commitments of senior
officials influence the way the crisis is perceived. All these factors
are involved in crisis definition, but not necessarily in a helpful way.
Yet it is the crisis <u>as defined and perceived by Washington officials</u>
that is the basis for decisions regarding size, composition, and

tasks of military intervention forces. It is hardly necessary to add that the actual circumstances at the scene may differ significantly.

Contingency plans prepared in anticipation of a possible crisis normally indicate the size and composition of the intervention force. In many situations, military units may already have been alerted for possible deployment before a final decision is reached. But the fact that certain types of forces have been earmarked for deployment does not mean that these forces will actually be used. At this point, further complications may arise. If the situation as perceived by policy-makers differs significantly from the circumstances hypothesized by planners, officials will be tempted to modify existing contingency plans. Other problems may also dictate changes: military units ear-marked for intervention missions may not be available because of training activities or other commitments. A second, perhaps unre-lated, crisis may force reconsideration of the initial plan. The air-craft and ships needed to move forces to the crisis area may also not be available, for similar reasons. The reactions of allies, and the restrictions they impose, such as limits on overflying privileges or the use of bases, can also dictate last minute modifications. The area of proposed intervention and the conditions there may, for a variety of reasons, produce varying reactions among some members of the armed forces. Subsidiary tasks, such as evacuation of military dependents and other U. S. citizens from the crisis area, may delay the deployment of intervention forces. Finally, selection of units for deployment can be influenced by the tempo of crisis development and by the sensitivity of particular groups to the special context of the crisis. A problem emerging slowly over time may permit an orderly revision of earlier plans. If the crisis develops suddenly or involves unanticipated dimensions, policymakers may be forced to improvise. Vietnam emerged incrementally, and Mayaguez in a flurry, and one may not be able to generalize about the relationship of tempo and policy.

FORCE STRUCTURE

The many uncertainties and complexities outlined above suggest that there is no obvious or optimum approach to the problem of designing forces for intervention and half-war situations. Careful planning is necessary and can define more precisely the capabilities these forces should possess. But detailed contingency plans are often inapplicable, and forces assigned such missions can not always be made available during actual crises. Moreover, detailed planning may induce a false sense of confidence among officials regarding the ability of U. S. military forces to handle the crisis. Such caution is particularly relevant at this time because of the limitations of present U. S. military forces for intervention and half-war missions. These limitations result from recent policy, organizational, and doctrinal changes that affect the size, flexibility, and staying power of U. S. military forces.

Size

Between 1968, the peak of the Vietnam War, and 1975, the active duty strength of U. S. armed forces fell from 3.6 million to 2.1 million. Active duty strength has remained at that level since 1975, and is expected to stay at or near the 2.1 million level in the future. The present and projected force is smaller—some 400,000-500,000 fewer personnel--than the force available in the period between the Korean and Vietnam wars. The defense civilian work force and ready reserve forces, both of which contribute greatly to overall combat capabilities, have each declined by roughly 20 percent from the pre-Vietnam levels.

As might be expected, this decrease in overall size has required cutbacks in the number of tactical units in the force structure. Army and Marine Corps maneuver battalions now number 202, a 9 percent reduction from the 222 battalions available in 1963; tactical fighter and air defense squadrons have experienced a 20 percent decrease from 244 squadrons in 1963 to 194 at the present time. [10] As noted above, an even sharper reduction has taken place in naval forces, which makes it more difficult than in the past to provide logistical support and sea control forces for other than short-term token commitments. Cutbacks in logistical and support units, while more difficult to measure, appear to be of even greater magnitude.

Despite the reductions in size, the present force structure is sufficiently large and contains appropriate types of military units to undertake intervention missions. A small contingency involving three to six maneuver battalions and supporting units could probably be sustained for an extended period without significant impact on other commitments. But as we move from small, short-term interventions to true half-war situations, the adequacy of U. S. forces drops markedly. [11] In a contingency requiring one or more divisions plus supporting troops drawn from Army and Marine Corps units stationed in the United States, the difficulties mount quickly. Four of the Army divisions most likely to be involved in half-wars have a National Guard unit as their third brigade. In addition to these brigades, 11 reserve battalions are designated "round out" forces. These same active Army forces also depend heavily on some 20 reserve units of battalion size for augmentation. [12] The two Marine divisions located in the United States are reduced by those forces required to maintain "BLTs afloat," i.e., battalions deployed aboard helicopter carriers. The net force available for immediate use, then, is about 4-1/3 divisions—rather than six divisions.

Logistical and Personnel Considerations

Beyond the restrictions inherent in this mixture of active and reserve units, logistical support for the intervention force would present a problem. Some logistical units are, of course, available for such missions. Should these prove insufficient, as would be the case if the intervention force were large, two alternatives are available: support units in the active establishment could be switched from existing missions; or logistical units from the reserve components could be activated. Neither solution is very satisfactory. In the first, other active units, including some deployed overseas, would lose support and readiness; in the second, there would be a time delay before the reserve unit could perform the mission satisfactorily. The same dilemma would exist in terms of personnel support. Replacements for the intervention force could be obtained from other units in the active establishment or from the reserves, including the Individual Ready Reserve. Maintaining the intervention force would therefore cause a loss of readiness among active units or involve sending inadequately trained personnel to the intervention force. Managing the personnel shortage so as to prevent a serious loss of capability among units assigned other missions (NATO, for example) would be more difficult than at any time since the Korean War. In short, although the existing force structure may be able to support intervention missions, it cannot easily undertake half-war operations.

Beyond such quantitative problems, there are a number of qualitative limitations. One set relates to the splayed pattern of training and possible roles, dominated now (or once again) by the image of the next major involvement coming in Western Europe. A second is the continuing tendency to keep tactical units heavily involved in administrative activities, which tends to blunt the deft tactical sense essential in half-wars. Finally, the relative absence of high-quality enlisted personnel in the all-volunteer force seems certain to affect the military performance of what is typically a difficult and sensitive mission.

The severity of the short-run support problems and the ability of the armed forces to resolve those problems depend largely on the size of the intervention force. The larger the force, the more difficult it would be to support. In a situation involving a division or more and accompanying support units, early difficulties could be expected to give way to even more serious problems. In general there are three constraints that limit the ability of the armed forces to sustain a

half-war force over time. The first is that the present active duty
force has a relatively higher ratio of combat to support units than was
the case in the recent past. Put in other terms, there is now less
"fat" in the administrative and support components that can be shifted
from these duties to tactical units. [13] In becoming more "efficient,"
the armed forces have sacrificed flexibility and staying power.
Closely related is the increasing number of women in the military
service. Women now comprise 7 percent of the force, and this is
expected to increase over 11 percent by 1983. Because they are not
permitted by law to engage in combat, and for other reasons as well,
women tend to be concentrated in support or administrative units. [14]
In fluid situations, in which headquarters and logistical units are vulnerable to attack, some of these units might not be deployable until
women were replaced by men. This shift of personnel would not only
delay deployment but would absorb men who would otherwise be
available to tactical units as replacements. Furthermore, the
services, especially the Army, would face another classic problem
immediately: Should such personnel as can be made available be used
as replacements for losses in deployed units, or should these personnel become the cadre for new units to replace those committed to
the crisis? Training and lesson transfer into doctrine are also vital if
not immediate tasks that compete with other personnel requirements.

Reserve Forces

The second constraint on our intervention capabilities is the size
and quality of the nation's reserve forces. Except for personnel
shortages, the reserve components have improved somewhat in recent
years. But the tasks of the reserve components—early reinforcement
of the active forces—has become more demanding. Beyond the important question of whether political leaders would be willing to order a
reserve call-up, and despite a wide range of improvements, concern
properly centers on reserve component capabilities, especially the
time required to ready units for combat. Most measures of readiness
and training proficiency remain generally unsatisfactory: in the Army--
the service most likely to require augmentation--many units are below
authorized strength. Training and equipment deficiencies in many units
reduce further the number that can be deployed quickly. The quality of
recent enlistees in organized reserve units has dropped markedly since
the end of the draft and is well below that of their active duty counter-
parts. [15] These developments prompt additional doubts about the combat effectiveness of reserve units, especially in a limited war context,
when shrewdness, initiative, and sophistification at all levels are at a
premium. The strength of the Individual Ready Reserve (IRR), which

is supposed to provide replacements for losses in active units in wartime, has declined by about 200,000, about one-seventh of its Vietnam era strength. And while most of the individuals in the IRR are readily available for military duty, few have adequate or up-to-date training. [16]

Personnel Problems

Third, the end of the draft and the switch to the all-volunteer force in the period 1970-73 have made it difficult for the services to acquire new personnel quickly or easily. Indeed, the armed forces are now barely able to meet active duty personnel requirements with volunteers. Even if a half-war crisis triggered increased enlistments or prompted Congress to reinstate the draft, it would take roughly six months for replacement personnel to become available to tactical units. In these circumstances, the only available sources of replacement personnel would be from units assigned other missions, e. g., NATO or from the reserve forces. For the reasons outlined above, neither is an attractive alternative, militarily or politically.

Summary

To summarize, reductions in size have sharply reduced the capability of U. S. military forces to carry out half-war missions. The two qualities that have been sacrificed but which are critical in most situations are flexibility and staying power. President Johnson created a Vietnam intervention force by adding draftees to the active duty force; in the foreseeable future a President would need to seek early Congressional support for a substantial reserve call-up or reinstitution of a selective service system. Approval of these steps which directly affect the lives of many Americans, may be more difficult to obtain than the Congressional authorization required under the War Powers Act.

Reduced flexibility and staying power are the most significant limitations on present or projected U. S. capabilities for half-war situations. But other developments, especially growing mission and doctrinal specialization, are also of consequence and deserve brief comment.

NATO AND CONVENTIONAL WAR

The most important, although perhaps least probable, mission assigned to U. S. armed forces is the NATO commitment in Western Europe. As the conventional military balance in Western Europe has shifted in favor of the Warsaw Pact over the past decade, military planners have attempted to improve the capabilities of NATO forces. The U. S. response has been fivefold. First, the number of personnel in NATO Europe has been increased slightly. Second, conventional or "leg" infantry units, both those stationed in Europe and those earmarked for NATO reinforcement, have been converted to mechanized or armored units. Third, precision-guided munitions (PGMs), especially antitank guided weapons, have been introduced in large numbers. These weapons, it is believed, provide the only hope of blunting and eventually halting a Warsaw Pact attack. Fourth, stocks of ammunition and equipment are now being increased to meet the logistical requirements of an intense conventional conflict. Finally, improvements in strategic airlift capabilities to permit more rapid reinforcement of NATO forces are planned. Other problem areas— equipment standardization and force location—present more difficult problems but are also beginning to receive attention. [17]

Accompanying these changes are two others: a new conventional war doctrine and increased organizational specialization of military units. The doctrinal change is best summarized by the language of the Army's new operations field manual, FM 100-5, Operations:

> We cannot know when or where the U. S. Army will again be ordered into battle, but we must assume the enemy we face will possess weapons generally as effective as our own. And we must calculate that he will have them in greater numbers than we will be able to deploy, at least in the opening stages of a conflict. Because the lethality of modern weapons continues to increase sharply, we can expect very high losses to occur in short periods of time . . .
>
> Therefore, the first battle of our next war could well be its last battle: belligerents could be quickly exhausted, and international pressures to stop fighting could bring about an early cessation of hostilities. The United States could find itself in a short, intense war-- the outcome of which may be dictated by the results of initial combat.
>
> . . . .
> Today the U. S. Army must, above all else, prepare to win the first battle of the next war . . .
>
> Battle in Central Europe against forces of the Warsaw Pact is the most demanding mission the U. S. Army could be assigned. Because the U. S. Army is structured primarily for that contingency and has large forces deployed in that area, this manual (FM 100-5) is designed mainly to deal with the realities of such operations. [18]

The organizational change involves a higher degree of weapons specialization in military units. The trend is toward smaller tactical units, each designed to employ only one or two complex weapons systems. One proposal now being considered, for example, would reorganize the infantry rifle battalion, reducing its size from 848 to 581 personnel and limiting its armament to individual weapons, machine guns, antitank guided weapons, and fighting vehicles. [19] Such specialized military units, it is believed, have greater combat effectiveness, are more mobile, and can be controlled more easily. Training and personnel economies, important in a small force, are other possible benefits of organizational specialization.

In short, the trend is to organize, equip, and train a major segment of U. S. general purpose forces for a single military mission--central Europe. The ability of U. S. forces to operate successfully in that area has undoubtedly been improved because of these changes. At the same time, forces so equipped are ill-suited to the circumstances likely to exist in many intervention situations. Some units and items of equipment--air cavalry troops, for instance-- may be quite valuable; but tank and self-propelled artillery units, precision-guided munitions, and intelligence organizations equipped with the latest collecting devices are clearly designed for mobile, rapidly moving warfare. Thus, shaping the bulk of our conventional land forces for the anticipated requirements of central Europe may further reduce their flexibility and utility in half-war situations, most of which have occurred in more exotic environments. [20] If such forces are used against less well-equipped adversaries, we provide domestic and foreign observers an additional basis for criticism of our actions. Beyond the question of the suitability of these forces for intervention or half-war missions, the fact that we have assigned such high priority to NATO suggests that stripping those forces to support units engaged in half-war situations will be more vigorously opposed than was the case during the Vietnam era.

To this list of constraints on the capabilities of U. S. forces, another possible limitation must be added: a low level of combat effectiveness among U. S. ground combat units. A number of observers believe that U. S. Army units became relatively ineffective in the later stages of Vietnam, as evidenced by combat refusals, a sharp increase in disciplinary incidents, a high rate of drug abuse, and "fraggings" of officers and NCOs. [21] The most persuasive explanation of this phenomenon centers on the low level of cohesiveness in ground combat units, caused by rapid rotation of personnel, short command tours, and the emergence of a managerial ethic within the officer corps. Some of the conditions that led to the loss of combat effectiveness in Vietnam have been corrected; short of fairly radical changes in organization and policy, and an increase in training resources, serious deficiencies are likely to persist.[22] Thus to the objective limitations on U. S. capabilities must be added serious concern about the combat performance of U. S. ground force units.

U. S. POLICY AND CAPABILITIES

The argument is that the United States has sufficient military capabilities to undertake small-scale, short-term military intervention but not, given other missions, adequate forces for a half-war. In particular, U. S. forces lack the flexibility and staying power needed for such operations. These last two deficiencies cannot, under existing circumstances, be easily overcome.

The Carter Administration has acknowledged this problem. In his March 1978 speech at Wake Forest the President noted the need for "forces to counter any threats to our allies and friends in [sic] our vital interests in Asia, the Middle East, and other regions of the world. " The President also announced that "the Secretary of Defense at my direction is improving and will maintain quickly deployable forces--air, land, and sea--to defend our interests throughout the world. "[23]

Thus far, the Defense Department has taken some steps to improve U. S. intervention and half-war capabilities. The following are among the most important:

1. Strategic mobility capabilities are being expanded through procurement of new tanker aircraft, modifications to C141 and C5 aircraft to increase their capacity and utilization rates, and an increase in the number of ships in the Ready Reserve Force.
2. Programs have been initiated to reduce shortages in war reserve stocks of munitions and secondary items of equipment.
3. A service-wide exercise (NIFTY NUGGET), intended to assess partially the adequacy of plans and procedures for full mobilization, was carried out in fall 1978.
4. New programs designed to improve recruiting for and training levels in the reserve components have been initiated.
5. Major ship and aircraft fleet readiness has been improved and equipment arrears in ground force units have been reduced.[24]

Although these initiatives serve to improve U. S. capabilities, it is hardly necessary to point out that they fall far short of those needed for an effective half-war capability. Two problems in particular require early attention. The first is the method of personnel procurement. The volunteer force has significant limitations: it cannot provide sufficient personnel to maintain the armed forces, active and reserve, at authorized strength levels; and it cannot furnish the sudden influx of personnel required in an emergency.[25] Thus far, the Administration remains optimistic about the all-volunteer force, and has avoided even "trial balloons" regarding an alternative method of personnel procurement or modifications to the present all-volunteer framework. Related to this, the Administration has also been reluctant to endorse upgrading of the Selective Service System. The second problem is reserve forces. As presently organized, significant elements of the reserves cannot provide effective units or well-trained filler personnel to support the active forces.[26] Certain expenditures on reserve forces have increased only slightly above inflationary offsets, and equipment shortages in the reserves are as serious as ever.[27] The Administration, however, has been unwilling to address this issue head-on.

Nonmilitary Instruments

The Administration has also been uncertain in regard to other U.S. capabilities. This is especially true in the case of nonmilitary instruments whose effective use would reduce the likelihood of a crisis developing to a point where military intervention was indicated. Three nonmilitary instruments are involved: foreign assistance programs, arms transfer policies, and intelligence operations.

U.S. foreign assistance programs are intended to promote economic and social development, to further regional security and stability, and to contribute to the advancement of human rights. Although the Carter Administration has increased foreign assistance by roughly 15 percent, the program remains modest in size and scope—just over $6 billion in FY 1978. Over 40 percent of U.S. assistance goes to multilateral lending agencies. Contributors have only limited control over these agencies and virtually no leverage in regard to recipients of such aid. The same point can be made in terms of contacts with local military elites: military assistance grants for training and weapons procurement have declined to below $1 billion per year.[28] To be sure, foreign assistance programs provide only limited influence for the United States; yet recent Administrations have done little that would increase the effectiveness of this policy instrument. Larger and more strongly supported assistance programs might both reduce the possibility of crises and give the United States a strengthened mediating posture if crises do develop.

Arms Transfers

Arms transfer policies have been a major concern of the Carter Administration. In general, it has aimed at reducing the volume of arms transactions. By so doing, the Administration had hoped to reduce regional tensions, to make additional local resources available for economic development, and to prevent local arms races. [29] Commendable as these objectives are, the execution of new policy has been characterized by contradictions: the volume of sales and transfers has increased, not declined. Almost every request for weapons has been considered a special case, warranting an exception to policy. Finally, the Administration has not been successful in persuading other arms suppliers of the merits of a policy of restraint. The consequences have been twofold: in some cases the United States has been replaced by other suppliers, with a corresponding reduction in its influence in buyer nations; and the many exceptions to announced policy have created uncertainty abroad about U.S. intentions and reliability. These uncertainties may serve to intensify, rather than attenuate, regional insecurities.

Intelligence Services

The most glaring shortcoming, however, has been the inability of the Carter Administration to resolve the intelligence tangle. Two key capabilities are at issue: the ability of the intelligence community to provide adequate and timely intelligence on developments abroad; and the extent to which the United States should engage in covert operations.

The intelligence tangle, of course, was inherited by the Carter Administration. The involvement of Congress has complicated the task of defining appropriate roles and controls for the intelligence community. But senior Administration officials are sharply divided on the issue and have thus far been unable to define a workable and effective approach. The overthrow of the Shah of Iran illustrated dramatically the consequences of inadequate intelligence. More accurate and timely intelligence or even extensive covert operations would probably not have changed the eventual outcome in Iran. Nevertheless, the failure to predict the crisis weakened the Administration's response, contributed to an image of U.S. incompetence and uncertainty held by other nations in the Middle East, and, with the loss of communications facilities, weakened the prospects for early ratification of SALT-II. [30]

Given the limits of U.S. military capabilities, there is clearly a need for effective programs to provide early warning or, better yet, to prevent crises from developing at all. Foreign assistance and arms transfer policies complement and must be related to military intervention capabilities; timely and accurate intelligence is essential to decisions regarding military intervention.

CONCLUSIONS

One must conclude, given the available evidence, that the present Administration, while dealing with some subordinate if not cosmetic details, has not compensated for the decline in military response capacity. This is particularly noticeable with respect to intelligence capability, and contradictions reflected in attempts to balance foreign assistance, arms sales, and technology transfers with political military policy. If brought into phase with each other and with policy, these programs offer opportunities for improvement. Chaos in the intelligence community, evident throughout the crisis in Iran, is unhappily an indicator that military force might be called upon to fill the gap created by the lack of a covert capability. Another complex of subtle problems, as yet unaddressed, is the stress on the defense budget created by mounting personnel costs, the need to upgrade strategic forces, the energy crisis, and the enhancement of the Navy. The enthusiasm, long dormant, for a balanced budget, could exacerbate the turbulence generated by these other problems.

Beyond this set of policy, organizational, and resource problems is the qualitative dimension of civil-military relations. Limited war blurs traditional civil-military boundaries and creates moral ambiguities of a kind that have been swallowed up or reduced in impact in modern general wars. An uncensored news media and the hunt for scapegoats in various eighth-, quarter-, and half-wars since 1945 both identifies and intensifies these ambiguities. Beyond that, the need for a close fusion between social remedy and military operations in half-war situations introduces complexity and subtlety—if balance is not adequate—and makes resort to military power as much a danger as an advantage.

One source of possible tension in civil-military relations concerns the willingness to resort to force and the manner in which military forces should be used. The gradualism strategy employed in Vietnam, most evident in the air campaign against the North, produced serious disagreements between civil and military elites in the 1965-68 period. Since in any future crisis military leaders are likely to be acutely sensitive to the limitations of existing forces and to remember the experiences of Korea and Vietnam, their posture may involve an extraordinary reluctance to employ force, coupled with an insistence that, if employed, force be used massively.

Political leaders, more concerned with domestic and international reactions and less sensitive to the deficiencies of the forces then available, could be expected to believe a gradualism strategy more appropriate. In a future crisis, then, sharply divergent civilian-military perspectives on the commitment and use of U. S. military forces might emerge. [31]

Also relevant to the military perspective is the fact that the Vietnam cohort is moving up and into the tier of power in the U. S. hierarchy. Unlike the professionals of World War II and Korea, their "imprinting" is nonlinear. They are less prone to acceptance of the "can do" ethic—busyness for busyness' sake—than were their predecessors. They are more sensitive to ethical questions and to an awareness that civil authority may not understand the limits of military power; they recognize that elected leaders may tamper with the military system to meet short-range political goals. Compared to those military generations blooded in World War II and Korea, the Vietnam cohort may show considerably greater sophistication in regard to establishing preconditions for intervention, and shy away from becoming apologists for policy at variance with professional military opinion and interests. [32]

This is not as remote a problem as it may seem. During the Watergate crisis the question of legitimacy came under discussion within the U. S. military. Whether or not the military should respond to civil authority was considered at the same time that some in the civilian hierarchy were purported to have altered the definition of constitutional authority. The fear that a crisis might be manipulated to provide a distraction from the President's political problems permeated well down into the rank structure of the Army at least, as well as up into the civilian hierarchy. [33] In view of Vietnam and Watergate, then, future crises might be affected by the perceptions of military leaders of hidden agendas, of the domestic political climate, and of the fear of becoming a heat-sink or a scapegoat in a situation where failure seems as likely as victory.

The importance of this new dimension in U. S. civil-military relations would not be clear short of another limited war. But some sort of new dimension there is: in military interventions and limited wars, the corporate integrity, mystique, and morale of the regular forces are involved to a greater degree than in a large-scale war. In several such cases, e. g. , the Philippine Insurrection, Nicaragua in the late 1920s, and Vietnam, the dislike of many Americans for the military became operational and affected political decisions regarding the military's mission. Contingency planning cannot avoid this possibility. When Shakespeare wrote of the soldier seeking the bubble reputation in the cannon's mouth, he drew a good analogy with the durability of reputation. It may seem rash to suggest that interests beyond those related to executing orders duly given may influence the action or doctrine of military planners and commanders. Would that the world were so simple! The shapers of the Constitution did not foresee the intensity of factionalism or the complexity of the nation and its foreign policy two centuries in the future. The only legitimate basis for suggesting a self-consciously limiting role is that the military must do what it can to assure that its civil masters understand possible outcomes, which means that sophisticated contingency planning is needed, along with orders far more specific than in major wars. Win, lose, or draw, after a limited war an Army in a democracy must live for a long time with the effects on habit, customs, and experience, while the body politic, rejuvenated by fresh goals and new political leaders, moves on to other purposes.

While it constrasts sharply with both mythology and events, such a position on the part of the nation's military leaders can easily be rationalized by historical experience. The value of history as an aid to effective projection and policy formulation has long been debated among historians; that has not, as Ernest May suggested in "Lessons" of the Past, [34] stopped history from influencing perceptions in crises, or in policy formulation in general. Most recent analyses of the intervention problem have focused on historical cases and extrapolations of trends and principles. [35] The latter may be more useful, but are subject to the same kinds of abuses that one finds in respect to the "principles of war." Ignoring the historical aspect would be imprudent, but the use of history is always selective, and any process of analysis idiosyncratic.

With these caveats in mind, an overview of American's major half-wars shows some interesting consequences:[36] all caused major political turbulence; all saw relief of major commanders in the field; and all required the military structure to modify sharply the mode of employment it had expected to use. In most of the cases the political party of the Administration that began the conflict was removed from power in the next election.

While the instances are few in number, even if one includes the British cases of the Boer War and the Irish Troubles and the French in Vietnam and Algeria, it does raise the question about the ability of liberal democracies to maintain military effort in quasi-wars. The "n" may be small, but who would be eager to fly in an aircraft of a type in which three of the last four takeoffs ended in a crash?

There are other questions related to the issue of military intervention. Perhaps the most important now is: Should the United States preconfigure military intervention forces beyond the scale of Special Forces, SEALS, Air Commandos, and Rangers? Or should intervention capabilities beyond emergency forces designed for counterterror and similar very short-term surgical roles be left unspecified within the general force structure? If one chooses to preconfigure intervention forces, several problems emerge. First, how much would formal structuring in itself fulfill predictions and arguments of insurgents? Given the broadly held perception of America as a nation implementing moral goals through the use of force, if the U. S. structures forces for such contingencies and then uses them, does the act itself constitute a propaganda defeat ipso facto? Or must the United States recognize that it is only another nation bent on self-interest in an amoral or immoral world of competing states? Thus, intervention raises the spectre of a contradiction between force and moral loftiness difficult to transcend by expressions of sentiment or rhetoric. Second, while such ethical and philosophical problems may seem merely academic, certain mechanical problems in the design of intervention forces touch on the question as well. Given the symbolic nature of limited wars and the fragility of public sentiment, there is greater significance in weapons choice (e. g., CNS gas, cluster bombs, stratgic bombers, napalm), and in force composition (e. g., minorities, reserves, political factions) than in a full-scale war in Europe. Recalling public anger that attended the North Vietnamese threat to try U. S. pilots as war criminals in 1965, and the subsequent agony over their maltreatment, one can ask, for example, how public opinion would respond to the plight of female personnel in the hands of enemies whose treatment of prisoners fell far outside the Geneva Convention. Conversely, how would respective parts of the polity react to an enemy subtle enough to treat POWs well and to parole draftees (or enlisted men) or certain minorities; or to try only officers for "crimes against the people"? In the Age of Skinnerianism, intervention forces may not always confront sadists and thugs.

Concern for such what-ifs and nuances is implicit in half-war contingency planning and decision making, for the long-range consequences of seemingly trivial choices have come to haunt interventionists, military and civilian alike. Decisions on personnel policy, force mix, tactics, weapons, definition of interests, and alliance relationships are often hurried expedients, made in the heat of crisis. The subsequent collision of events with policy and intention can set up oscillations in the manner of an unbalanced feedback circuit. A crisis atmosphere may generate a tendency to action, thereby gaining a sense of relief through commitment of force of the kind described by Mrs. Johnson in her diary, as, for example, the air strikes launched after the Gulf of Tonkin incident, and a similar feeling noted in the Nixon memoirs in respect to Linebacker II. [37] Unhappily, the U. S. response may make the form of high-technology solutions, which may be tactically successful or buy time, but which may also be perceived as the actions of a technological bully or heavy-handed imperialist, long a theme of provocateurs who see in such tactics a means of galvanizing their support. At the same time, the ability to perceive grassroots impact is screened from the decision-makers by several levels of bureaucracy, as well as conflicting advice from "experts," all of whom see only part of the loaf.

The tendency to "pile on" and the "can do" reflex are not exclusive to the military. The hunger of Americans for clear, quick solutions and achievements is proverbial. Within the armed services, of course, there is an urge to get into combat before a brief or low-level conflict is over, the "it-ain't-much, but-it's-the-only-war-we-got" syndrome. The tendency, not exclusively a product of careerism, should not be viewed as something unusual, but should be kept in mind by controllers and policymakers, especially since the question of the amount of force and the rapidity of its application was a major source of controversy in both Korea and Vietnam.

Preconfiguration of intervention forces, therefore, serves as more than a weapon in the scabbard; it is also a symbol of capability, suggesting that the military leads policy in predisposition towards intervention. The first wave of U. S. commitment to Vietnam and the Dominican Republic was in the form of elite units, i. e., Special Forces, Marines, airborne, airmobile. The situation in Vietnam began to change dramatically as increasing numbers of draftees arrived. The reliance on designated elite forces for intervention, however, creates a problem spotted by Lord Slim, who suggested that overspecialization of units leads to a drain of morale and motivation in the general forces. The end result, he noted, could be such diversified units as a Royal Corps of Tree Climbers, which implied that all soldiers would not be capable of climbing trees, when, indeed, they should be. There is a tension between such elitization and compartmentalization, insomuch as it drains leaders rom the general forces and concentrates them. It also contributes to a symbolic aggressiveness on the part of the military, which may not generate support at home, and which can play into the propaganda hands of an enemy in a limited war. Beyond that, if elites are committed and lost, what then? Such a loss assumes a value beyond the original intent and policy. What was designed to serve as a limiting boundary may turn into a catalyst in the uncertain atmosphere that builds around crisis and military operations. [38]

Popular support is the essential element underlying the question of whether intervention is a valid strategy in other than the short run. Starting a half-war has brought down two Administrations since 1945, and Nixon's bombing of North Vietnam did not stand him in good stead when the Watergate storm broke. The question of legitimacy is elemental to the decision to intervene for more than a moment: President Ford's use of force to release the crew of the Mayaguez is still criticized by some observers. The gap between strongly commited elites and a lukewarm public must be kept in mind in considering intervention. In view of that, the current state of U. S. policy and intervention forces may be a fairly close reflection of the dissension that would greet a decision to intervene and the durability of public suppor in cases of extended and frustrating involvement.

NOTES

1. The literature is extensive and growing. Some of the important recent items include Douglas Kinnard, The War Managers (Hanover, N. H.: University Press of New England, 1977); Guenther Levy, America in Vietnam (New York: Oxford University Press, 1978); W. Scott Thompson and Donaldson D. Frizzell, eds., The Lessons of Vietnam (New York: Crane, Russak, and Co., 1977); and Leslie H. Gleb with Richard K. Betts, The Irony of Vietnam: The System Worked (Washington: The Brookings Institution, 1979).

2. Barry M. Blechman, Stephen S. Kaplan, et. al., Force Without War (Washington: The Brookings Institution, 1978), pp. 23-5'

3. For a useful analysis of the War Powers Act, see Graham T Allison, "Making War: The President and Congress," Law and Contemporary Problems, 40 (3) (Summer 1976): 86-105.

4. John M. Collins, Imbalance of Power: Shifting U. S. -Soviet Military Strengths (San Rafael, California: Presidio Press, 1978, pp. 65-96.

5. Ibid., pp. 193-226.

6. Ibid., pp. 180-91.

7. For a discussion, see Herman Nickel, "The U. S. Failure ir Iran," Fortune, March 12, 1979, pp. 94ff.

8. Ralph E. Strauch, "Winners and Losers: A Conceptual Barrier in Our Strategic Thinking," Rand Paper P-4769, June 1972, p. 21.

9. Graham T. Allison, Essence of Decision: Explaining the Cuban Missile Crisis (Boston: Little, Brown and Company, 1971), pp. 71-72.

10. See Department of Defense, Annual Report for Fiscal Year 1963 (Washington, USGPO, 1964), pp. 107, 252-54, and 318-19; and International Institute of Strategic Studies, The Military Balance 1978-79 (London: IISS, 1978), pp. 6-7.

11. For a descriptive scenario of a possible Middle East intervention, see Juan Cameron, "Our What-If Strategy for Mideast Trouble Spots," Fortune, May 7, 1979, pp. 154ff.

12. John T. Fishel, "The Army Reserve Components in the 1980s," paper presented at Southwestern Social Science Association, March 1979, p. 22.

13. On the importance of "fat," see Herman Kahn, On Thermonuclear War (Princeton: Princeton University Press, 1960), pp. 160-62.

14. See George Gilder, "The Case Against Women in Combat," The New York Times Magazine, January 28, 1979, pp. 29ff.

15. U. S. Congress, Senate, Committee on Armed Service. Achieving America's Goals: National Service or the All-Volunteer Armed Force? by William R. King, Committee Print (Washington: 1977), pp. 23-25.

16. Fishel, "The Army Reserve Components in the 1980s," pp. 8-9.

17. For a brief discussion of the NATO-Warsaw Pact balance, see Collins, Imbalance of Power, pp. 227-306.

18. Department of Army, FM 100-5, Operations (Washington: 1976), pp. 1-1 and 1-2. Italics added in the last sentence.

19. William E. DePuy (General, USA Ret.), "U. S. Army: Are We Ready for the Future?" Army (September 1978): 24ff.

20. Roger Beaumont, "Geographical Patterns of Conflict," Military Review (February 1969): 73-76.

21. The most extensive discussion is in Richard A. Gabriel and Paul L. Savage, Crisis in Command: Mismanagement in the Army (New York: Hill and Wang, 1978).

22. See Richard A. Gabriel, "Modernism vs. Pre-Modernism: The Need to Rethink the Basis of Military Organizational Forms" and William L. Hauser, "Adapting the All-Volunteer Situation." Both papers were presented at the Air University-Inter University Seminar Conference on Armed Forces and Society, Maxwell Air Force Base, Alabama, June 3-5, 1979.

23. Department of State, News Release, March 16, 1978, pp. 3-4.

24. Harold Brown, Department of Defense, Annual Report, FY 1980 (Washington: January 25, 1979), pp. 207-208, 263-64, 268, 284-89.

25. William P. Snyder, "Military Personnel Procurement Policies: Assumptions--Trends--Context" in John B. Keeley, ed., The All-Volunteer Force and American Society (Charlottesville: University Press of Virginia, 1978), pp. 4-5, 32-33.

26. John B. Keeley, "United States Reserve Forces: A High-Cost, Low-Return Investment in National Security," in Ibid., pp. 166ff.

27. Fishel, "The Army Reserve Components in the 1980s," p. 24.

28. Department of State, "US Overview of Foreign Military Assistance," March 2, 1977.

29. Department of State, "US Conventional Arms Transfer Policy," November, 1977.

30. Nickel, "The U. S. Failure in Iran," pp. 94ff.

31. For other views on this issue, see Samual P. Huntington, "The Soldier and the State in the 1970s" and Franklin D. Margiotta, "The Changing World of the American Military," in The Changing World of the American Military, ed. Franklin D. Margiotta (Boulder, Colorado: Westview Press, 1978), pp. 26-29 and 425-30.

32. For a similar but more generalized argument, see Lawrence J. Korb, "The Role of the Military in the National Security Decision Making Process During the 1980s: Some Prospects and Problems," paper presented at Southwestern Social Science Association, March 1979.

33. The problem is hinted at in press reports of the transition between Presidents Nixon and Ford. See New York Times, August 6, 7, 8, 1974.

34. Ernest R. May, "Lessons" of the Past (New York: Oxford University Press, 1973).

35. E. g. , Blechman, Kaplan, et. al. , Forces Without War.

36. The "major" American half-wars occurred in Mexico, the Philippine Insurrection, Korea, and Vietnam.

37. Lady Bird Johnson, A White House Diary (New York: Holt, Rinehart and Winston, 1970), p. 188, and Richard·M. Nixon, The Memoirs of Richard Nixon (New York: Grosset and Dunlap, 1978), pp. 717-58 and especially pp. 733-41.

38. Roger A. Beaumont, Military Elites (New York: Bobbs-Merrill, 1974), pp. 171-85.

8
POLITICAL CONTRAINTS ON
PRESIDENTIAL WARS
Allan Ned Sabrosky

Few nations come easily to the task of waging war successfully. The United States is certainly no exception. It is readily apparent that no other form of conflict places greater political demands on a democracy than those posed by a so-called "limited" or "small" war with its attendant restrictions on means and ends alike. The oft-stated belief that democracies go to war at their peril applies with particular force to the prospective involvement of the United States in such situations. The American experiences in the Korean and Indochinese conflicts clearly raise a number of fundamental questions about the ability of the United States to counter similar challenges in the future. [1] In itself Vietnam provides a textbook example of how such a war should not be waged, and the political consequences attending the ensuing failure. [2]

Perhaps the most notable domestic political consequence of the U. S. defeat in Indochina has been the dissolution of the basic foreign policy consensus that had taken shape with the onset of the Soviet-American Cold War. Before the Vietnam War, that broad national consensus served as a unifying theme in whose name commitments could be undertaken, alliances structured, and U. S. armed forces deployed overseas and--when the need to do so arose--sent into battle. [3] Differences existed within that consensus, of course, and opposition to specific policies was commonplace in various circles. Rarely, however, did such differences and opposition call into question the basic tenets of that consensus, key provisions of which were the justifiability of armed intervention in defense of our interests and allies, coupled with the acknowledgement in principle of Presidential primacy in foreign affairs. [4] Even the intervention in Indochina itself, decried later as a wholly unnecessary conflict into which the United States had been misled by the President, [5] had been undertaken initially with the general encouragement of the majority of the American people and the specific support of an overwhelming majority of both Houses of Congress. [6]

All of that changed as the U. S. misadventure in Vietnam progressed. The postwar foreign policy consensus was broken and has yet to be persuasively recast. [7] The human rights campaign so prominent in the early part of the Carter Administration, while fully consonant with the strong element of moralism so prominent in U. S. foreign policy over the years, appears inadequate to the task. [8] Agreement no longer exists on the proper role the United States should assume in world affairs, the definition of legitimate U. S. interests abroad in whose name we should be willing to intervene militarily if necessary, or even the preferred locus of governmental authority for the effective and legitimate exercise of influence in the world. It has even been suggested that

> We may simply have to learn to conduct foreign policy
> for a very long time without a single unifying theme on
> which to base a broad national consensus. [9]

These reservations notwithstanding, certain pertinent facts cannot be overlooked. First, military power retains political utility in world politics, a point that some countries seem to understand better than the United States. [10] The resort to war as an instrument of national policy is certainly more precarious a venture now than in the past, even for a major power. But it is equally certain that the controlled use of military force for political purposes is essential in the nuclear age if nations are to avoid a nuclear holocaust that may moot all principal political questions. At the least, the lack of such a capability cannot enhance American interests and prestige, and could well be politically (and perhaps militarily) catastrophic.

Second, the fact that "small" or "limited" wars remain possible means that U. S. involvement in such conflicts is also a possibility, however remote that might now seem to some. The memory of Vietnam may well serve to inhibit U. S. military intervention abroad, at least for the immediate future. [11] But our formal commitments overseas remain extensive, even after the demise of the South-East Asia Treaty Organization (SEATO), and this country's informal commitmenst are also considerable. It would be unwarranted to assume that selective intervention in support of some of those commitments might not be needed. It would also be most unwise for the United States to foreswear such an option in the first place. [12] It is appropriate to recall that

Although nearly every American President and Secretary of State have pledged support for the rule of nonintervention, the United States has always included intervention among its foreign policy options. [13]

Third, and finally, whatever the strategic feasibility or desirability of military intervention in certain carefully defined situations, the political constraints on the exercise of that option may well be considerable. The maintenance of an adequate base of political support is essential for effective intervention, especially in the event of a protracted limited war. [14] Yet the U. S. experience in Vietnam raises serious doubts about the political feasibility of assuming that such support will be forthcoming or maintained long enough to permit success. Some have seen Vietnam, for example, as a "quagmire" into which this country blindly stumbled. [15] Others concede the accuracy of the "quagmire" metaphor, but assert that "most American leaders" were well aware of that fact even as they ordered the initial intervention and subsequent escalation. [16] And still others reject the so-called "quagmire myth," declaring instead that the U. S. intervention in, and conduct of, the war in Indochina was a logical consequence of the "stalemate machine" that was—and remains—the U. S. decision-making system. [17]

Whatever their individual appeal or analytical validity, all of these explanations (as well as their numerous variants) have one thing in common. Each assumes that the U. S. intervention and eventual failure in Vietnam can be attributed, in whole or in part, to some of the fundamental attributes of the American political system itself. [18] It would surely be unwarranted to assign too much of the responsibility for the U. S. defeat in that war to the American political process. Still, the existence of significant political constraints cannot be denied. Understanding what those constraints are and how they affect the intervention process may well help us understand what we can, or at least cannot, hope to accomplish by exercising our military option abroad.

AN OVERVIEW

It is immediately apparent, of course, that whatever political constraints inhere in the American political system do not have to apply equally to all forms of conflict. In many respects, as I have suggested earlier, they appear to have the greatest potential significance during what can properly be termed a "Presidential war." This is not necessarily a conflict waged by the executive in the face of vociferous opposition from the American people and their representatives in the Congress, nor does it imply the use of any and all weapons in the U.S. arsenal. It is rather a war undertaken at Presidential initiative, usually without prior approval of Congress, and without either a formal declaration of war or a direct attack upon the United States. Congress and the public are rarely involved in the decision process. [19] It is a classic "limited" or "small" war, probably--but not necessarily--fought without recourse to tactical nuclear weapons. It is also a conflict whose conduct requires this country to come to terms with the trade-off between Presidential accountability and operational effectiveness so characteristic of the classic "democratic dilemma."[20]

There are, broadly speaking, four potential political constraints on Presidential war that I will address in this paper, reflecting the basic sources of support or opposition with which the President must deal. Two are governmental: one is the Presidency itself; the other encompasses the checks that the Congress can impose on the waging of a Presidential war. Two other potential constraints are nongovernmental: they are public opinion and the media. All four are closely related, although they can be considered separately for analytical purposes. [21]

In addition, each of these constraints can be operative (albeit with differing degrees of success) at any or all of three stages in a war. The first stage is the decision to initiate such a war. This conventionally receives the most attention. But the second and third stages—that is, the conduct and the termination of such a conflict—also merit close attention. There is, after all, no sound reason to assume that those constraints having the greatest impact on the initiation of an intervention will necessarily have the same degree of influence on the way in which it is conducted or terminated. This is particularly true with respect to the final stage of a Presidential war if that conflict must be terminated without achieving at least some of the principal objectives for which the war was fought in the first place. [22]

This paper will address the actual and potential effects of these political constraints on the three stages of a Presidential war. It will conclude with an appraisal of their combined effect on the waging of Presidential war in the future. This is by no means a definitive study of the subject. Other factors could certainly be taken into account, and the potential constraints examined here could be dealt with at much greater length. What follows should therefore be seen as a preliminary assessment of one part of the larger question of Presidential war, as well as a prospectus for later research on the subject.

GOVERNMENTAL CONSTRAINTS

Shared powers are seldom exercised well or balanced success-fully. Many of the questions raised concerning the legitimacy, feasi-bility, or desirability of Presidential war have a common origin. That origin is the Constitutional ambiguity concerning the extent of the Executive's authority to exercise the war power independently of Congress, and the degree to which the Congress can properly restrain the Executive's use of that power. In many ways, the constitutionally mandated separation of powers and system of checks and balances were intended to promote that ambiguity. This was done to ensure that no single branch or officer of the Federal government would acquire uncontested control of public policy, particularly in the area of what we would now call "national security policy. "[23]

The presumed need to provide Constitutional checks on the making and waging of war (the so-called "war power") was therefore of special concern to the framers of the Constitution. [24] Even as staunch an advocate of Presidential prerogatives as Alexander Hamilton noted (without necessarily approving) the limitations placed on the Executive's war powers. [25] Over the years, however, custom, convention, the courts, and Congressional default facilitated a signif-icant increase in the scope of the President's competence in foreign affairs in general, and his exercise of the war power in particular. [26] On at least two important occasions after World War II, Congressional joint resolutions gave the President virtual carte blanche to employ the U. S. armed forces as he deemed necessary. These were the well-known "Formosa Straits" and "Tonkin Gulf" resolutions of 1955 and 1964, respectively. [27] To some, this development simply reflected the political reality that the "Constitutional law of foreign rela-tions . . . must begin with the President, "[28] and with that precedence went the de facto possession of the war power as well. But to others, it reflected the growth of an "Imperial Presidency" in which, as Paul Schratz has neatly put it, "The 'dog of war' which Thomas Jefferson thought had been tightly leashed to the legislature somehow had shifted into the executive kennel. "[29]

As the Vietnam War progressed, of course, significant changes seemed to be taking place. Congress appeared to be assuming, or at least trying to assume, a greater role in the foreign policy process. The object of these changes was to inhibit, if not overcome, Presi-dential dominance of the "high ground" in foreign affairs and espe-cially the Presidential exercise of the war power. [30] The extent to which these changes have actually weakened the President's hold on the war power is, however, far from clear. There are internal constraints in the Presidency itself on the waging of Presidential war, as well as those that Congress may possess or acquire. What those specific constraints are, how much they reflect a fundamental shift in the relationship between the Presidency and the Congress, and the probable future course of that relationship will be examined in the following sections.

PRESIDENTIAL RESTRAINTS

When Charles Burton Marshall remarked that "Presidential primacy inheres in the American constitutional order,"[31] he summarized an often challenged yet enduring feature of the Chief Executive in this country. This is certainly the case with respect to the direction of foreign policy. Indeed, the effective direction of foreign policy in any country requires precisely the concentration of power, information, and expertise that can only be located in the executive branch of the government.[32] What is true with respect to the conduct of foreign policy in general applies even more to the exercise of the war power. Certainly, the resources available to the President give him the potential to administer a policy-making apparatus capable of responding to international developments quickly and effectively, even if that entails use of the armed forces.[33]

Unfortunately, that potential is often not realized. It assumes that the President will be a strong executive with a comprehensive understanding of foreign affairs, a combination that appears all too seldom on the U.S. political scene. It also assumes that the President will have a reasonable degree of control over the relevant bureaucracies. This, again, is--to be charitable--rarely the case. In fact, the complexity of the bureaucracy that has grown up about the President frequently results in the presentation of what are essentially compromise policies. Henry Kissinger, himself no mean practitioner of the bureaucratic politics game, concluded on one occasion that the elaborate and fragmented nature of the American policy-making process often dictated that the President, once he had made a decision, should announce it publicly in order to settle the "internal debate" within the government.[34] Kissinger's experience in government undoubtedly confirmed his earlier judgment on the nature and the role of the bureaucracy. It is also likely that his experience would lead him to take a less sanguine view of the ability of Presidential public pronouncements to end the internal bureaucratic debate and insure compliance with the President's decision.

These vagaries of bureaucratic politics within the executive branch, whatever their actual extent, serve to confuse rather than constrain the waging of Presidential war. They are also partially subject to manipulation and control by the President. Presidents seem to enjoy a fair degree of success in their efforts to garner support at the higher levels of their Administrations for the initiation of a policy they are determined to undertake, even though its implementation may run afoul of the bureaucracy. In fact, internal opposition to Presidential policies has been described as a "herculean task for senior officials and bureaucrats."[35] Especially recalcitrant appointees are even, in some circumstances, replaced by individuals more closely attuned to the President's personality or political philosophy, or--less drastically--they can be transferred to other positions where they can do less damage if their outright dismissal is not politically feasible. In short, while bureaucratic opposition certainly cannot be ignored by the President, it can usually be managed, at least in the opening stages of a commitment. Later, of course, bureaucratic obstructionism can become an extremely serious obstacle to the successful conduct and, in some circumstances, termination of a Presidential war.

Two other factors have the potential to exercise even greater constraints on the waging of Presidential war. One is the character of the President. The other is the consideration of Presidential tenure.

The first factor is in certain respects the more important. James David Barber, a prominent scholar of the Presidency, has argued strongly that the way to understand how a President is likely to act in office is to "look to [his] character first."[36] Obviously, not all Presidents are alike. The way a President interprets the justifiability or the necessity of an intervention will have a crucial effect on his decision. The judgments he makes are also highly subjective in a number of respects, reflecting his personality, operational code, individual and political style, and perceptions of domestic and international politics.[37] Other things being equal, an activist President with a strong sense of moral superiority and an inclination to "worst-case" the actions and intentions of a potential adversary would probably be more inclined to use military force than would a President who differed on any or all of these points. A strong, committed President would not be inclined to exercise restraint in the conduct of a war, or to end it without achieving at least some of the objectives for which the war was being fought.

It is sobering to recognize that the type of President least likely to initiate a Presidential war is as little likely to wield executive power effectively. To be sure, any President would probably be reluctant to commit U.S. forces to another protracted limited war, with all the political dangers such a step would entail. Yet such self-restraint can never be considered certain, even on the part of the most passive and self-deprecating President. There is something

"imperial" about the American Presidency that may incline even weak
and vacillating Presidents to act as if they were strong and decisive.
Kenneth W. Thompson's assertion that "The moral burdens . . .
placed on the executive and the temptation to hubris are overwhelming"[38] is very much on the mark. The fact that this temptation
at least partially reflects the Presidential dominance of the war
power and is nurtured by the continuation of the war power in the hands
of the executive[39] underscores the magnitude of the problem.

The significance of Presidential character is reinforced and
extended by the nature of Presidential tenure, including the ever-
present threat of what Kenneth N. Waltz has termed "electoral punishment."[40] It should be immediately apparent that a President who
hopes to implement any policy successfully needs to maintain a base
of political support for that policy sufficient to neutralize the potential opposition to it. It is no exaggeration to say with Milton J.
Rosenberg that the

> broad approval by the majority of a national public of
> the visible policies of its leaders, or at least assent
> to those policies, would seem to be a sine qua non
> for the successful execution of policy and for the
> maintenance of governing power itself. [41]

The fact that a President is responsible to a nationwide electorate is far from being an unmixed blessing. The support of that
electorate may help sustain Presidential policies in the face of actual
or potential opposition from a more parochially-oriented Congress.
This is especially likely if the President and the Congressional
majority are from the same party and if the President was elected by
a comfortable margin. The characterization of the President as a
"national spokesman" clearly reflects the Presidential belief "that
it is easier to carry the country . . . than to rely upon the Congress."[42] But it is also clear that the opposition of that electorate,
or at least the President's perception of its growing opposition, will
eventually inhibit Presidential action and undermine whatever Congressional support existed for the Administration's policy in the first
place. [43] Avoiding such an eventuality obviously ranks very high on
any President's list of priorities, no matter what issue is involved.

The consequences of electoral rejection, as well as Presidential anticipation of the electorate's reaction to his policies, brings
us to the heart of the matter of Presidential tenure as a potential constraint on the waging of Presidential war. There are, as Stanley
Hoffmann has pointed out, two principal weaknesses in the American

system of Presidential tenure that bear on the subject at hand. These are what he called the "first/fourth year syndrome" and the election campaign itself. [44]

The first of these weaknesses is simply a manifestation of the difficulties that usually attend the first and fourth years of a President's initial term of office. During the first year, even the most sophisticated and informed individual is required to gain a detailed personal knowledge of the national security process while simultaneously attempting to build a team of competent and compatible advisors in the field. The fact that some Presidents are neither sophisticated nor informed on these issues simply compounds the problem. In the fourth year of the first term, a President is either trying for his own re-election or for the election of a successor from his own party. In both instances, the decision-making process becomes more difficult.

The second handicap associated with the problem of Presidential tenure is the election campaign itself. The political realities with which any President must deal on a day-to-day basis do not encourage adventurism overseas in any but the most extraordinary circumstances. National security questions can rarely, be considered in isolation from the entirety of an Administration's program. The usual Presidential inclination to avoid taking steps that might result in the failure of his Administration's broad political program is greatly strengthened in election years. [45] Correctly or not, as Morton Halperin has observed,

> . . . Presidents and potential Presidents themselves
> see a closer link between stands on foreign policy
> issues and the outcome of Presidential elections
> (than analysts seem to find). [46]

This places an incumbent in something of a dilemma if a crisis that raises the possibility of military action appears on the political horizon. On the one hand, there is a strong temptation for most Presidents to temporize and refrain from carrying the proverbial "big stick" of armed intervention in too overt a fashion. This is partly due to a proper recognition of the uncertainties attending virtually any decision to resort to force. But it is also because peacemakers generally enjoy a reasonably good press in the United States. Certain advantages can accrue on election day to a President who can remind the electorate that he has kept the country out of war. Yet on the other hand, a President cannot afford to create an impression of weakness or indecisiveness, or to be vulnerable to charges by the political opposition that he is an "appeaser." Strong Presidents who are "winners" (in all senses) are admired, and there is at least a short-term electoral payoff for an incumbent who is seen acting vigorously in defense of U. S. interests. [47]

Resolving this dilemma is clearly no easy task. On the one hand, a President may do little or nothing before the election in the hope that any ensuing difficulties will be minor and therefore preferable to the political consequences of an inappropriately strong action on his part. This has the effect of at least deferring decisive action until after an incumbent's personal political future has been decided at the polls. On the other hand, the President may be inclined to react strongly (and perhaps unnecessarily so) to a minor aggravation rather than risk alienating part of the electorate by his inaction, if the situation in question deteriorates significantly before election day. Further, even an incumbent who refused to commit U. S. forces to battle before an election might be equally predisposed to take the opposite stand after that election. Once committed, however, disengagement or withdrawal is extremely difficult in the absence of clear-cut indicators of success. A President who intervenes militarily must either win (however that might be defined in a given situation), or accept the political and electoral costs of failure, even if it is only a failure to make peace on politically acceptable terms.

Precisely what stance a President will assume in a given instance depends on a number of factors, including his character, the nature of his constituency, and his own appraisal of the situation. One particularly striking example of the difficulties with which an incumbent must deal is provided by the experience of Lyndon Johnson. It is unfortunate, in retrospect, that his first year in office--certainly a crucial year in the entire Vietnam decision process--was also a "fourth" year. That is, during his initial year Johnson was compelled simultaneously to become acquainted with the Presidency, campaign for his own election, and deal with the extraordinarily demanding situation developing in Southeast Asia. [48]

Johnson's response to that situation provides a near-classic illustration of the sequential adoption of all the alternatives open to an incumbent President faced with a demanding foreign policy decision. During the course of the 1964 campaign, Johnson adopted a relatively "peaceful" posture. He was the "dove" in the 1964 election, a fact later overlooked by many of his more vociferous critics, and continually asserted that he was not prepared to send U. S. soldiers to fight a war that ought to be fought by "Asian boys." The deliberately ambiguous character of his election campaign was matched by his response to the Tonkin Gulf incident in August 1964. The talionic air strikes on North Vietnamese installations were the least that Johnson—if he hoped to remain in office and not be castigated as an "appeaser"—could do in response to reported attacks on American warships in international waters. The Tonkin Gulf Resolution, passed unanimously in the House and with only two dissenting votes in the Senate, provided a basis for that action without committing U. S. forces to more extensive operations.

These measures were fully in keeping with the temporizing inclination of a President experiencing the combined weight of the "first/fourth year syndrome. " They effectively postponed a final determination of what the United States ought to do in Indochina, since either a precipitous withdrawal or a massive intervention would have presented grave political difficulties before the election. But merely postponing a decision does not always mean that it can be avoided altogether. Some problems simply do not disappear of their own volition, or with only a marginal commitment to resolve them. Vietnam was such a problem. Johnson's escalation of the U. S. military commitment to South Vietnam after his successful election campaign did not necessarily mean that his views on the proper American response had changed. It could easily be argued that he was then acting just as he would have earlier, had there been sufficient provocation and had the election campaign not been underway. Whatever interpretation one chooses, however, one thing is clear. Once the intervention was well along in 1965, Johnson's subsequent inability either to win the war or to make an acceptable peace had disastrous political consequences. Even discounting what happened to the country, Johnson's own experience, like that of Truman before him, underscores the political consequences of Presidential failure in a Presidential war.

CONGRESSIONAL CHECKS

Internal restraints on the Executive's use of the war power are obviously a weak reed on which to base a system of political constraints. Others must be found. The principal governmental constraint outside the Presidency itself clearly lies in Congress. All agree that the Congressional role in foreign affairs has changed in recent years. In fact, Congress is more assertive for a variety of reasons, not least of which is its concern over the use of the war power by the President in the Indochina conflict. Whether that assertiveness has been, or can be, translated into a greater constraint on the Presidential exercise of the war power is still the subject of much debate.

Congressional checks, old and new, on the waging of Presidential war fall into two categories. [49] The first comprises constraints on the initiation of hostilities by the President. One is the Constitutional requirement that the Senate ratify all treaties. This helps define the commitments in whose name intervention can be undertaken. Another constraint is the Congressional power to declare war, or—as in the case of the Formosa Straits and Tonkin Gulf resolutions of 1955 and 1964, respectively—to otherwise authorize the use of the armed forces by the President. A Congressional refusal either to declare war or to endorse the commitment of U. S. forces to battle—even the passage of a resolution enjoining the President not to intervene in a particular situation—could constrain Presidential initiatives in this matter.

The second category of Congressional constraints includes those measures by which Congress can affect the conduct and the termination of a conflict already underway. An important measure here, and perhaps the one with the greatest practical significance, is the Congressional control of appropriations--the "power of the purse." Wars, like all other acts of policy, require continual funding. A Congressional refusal to authorize funds for an intervention, a prohibition against the transfer of funds from other budget categories, or the specification of restrictions on the use of funds allocated for defense can all affect the way a war is waged and even force its termination. [50] Second, the Congress can withdraw authority given earlier for the use of the armed forces, as was eventually done with the Tonkin Gulf Resolution. Third, it can enact legislation or pass a resolution aimed at terminating the U. S. role in a given conflict. An example of such an action is the Mansfield Amendment to the Military Procurement Authorization Act of 1972, regarding U. S. involvement in Indochina.

A number of constraints in both categories were incorporated in the War Powers Act of 1973. This legislation has been described by Professor Norman J. Ornstein, a noted authority on the Congress, as "an enormously symbolic act"[51] that expressed Congressional disenchantment with the Presidential conduct of the Vietnam War at the same time as it seemingly codified the constitutional separation of the war powers themselves. This legislation defined the circumstances in which the President could use the armed forces, when and how Congressional oversight would come into play, and the President's responsibility to consult whenever possible with Congress concerning the initiation of hostilities. It also defined the terms under which an intervention could be continued and specified conditions that would require the President to end such intervention.

The fact that Congress is generally more assertive in foreign affairs and has now added the War Powers Act to its legislative arsenal does not imply Congressional domination of the Executive in these areas. It simply reflects the potential ability of Congress to constrain Presidential adventurism abroad. [52]

What is sometimes overlooked, however, is the fact that there have been a number of significant changes inside the Congress that reduce its ability to translate that potential into political reality. There has been a sharp decline in party discipline in recent years, a development indicative of both the abilities and the styles of Congressional leadership, as well as the amenability (or its lack) among Congressional members toward that leadership. Also, both the Senate and the House of Representatives have become more decentralized. This partly reflects the decline in party discipline (and contributes to it as well), and partly the growing importance of subcommittees in the Congressional system. This decade has also seen a marked increase in "single-issue" politics and politicians, something that mirrors the absence of a foreign policy consensus and inhibits the articulation of a new consensus. [53]

The conslusion to be drawn is that the ideological tendency of the Congress may be a less important constraint on the President than the lack of both a Congressional consensus and effective party discipline. Certainly, the ability of the Congressional leadership to "deliver the vote" and the willingness of the membership to "stop politics at the water's edge" are more problematical now than in the pre-Vietnam era. The debate over the Panama Canal Treaties provided ample proof of that. This makes it more difficult for the President to mobilize Congressional support for his exercise of the war power, even if his party also dominates both houses of Congress. But what is less commonly understood is that these same changes also inhibit the ability of Congress to oppose the President--that is, to constrain the waging of Presidential war--except in the event of a flagrant abuse of executive authority.

In addition to these changes within the Congress, which reduce its ability to check the President, there is also reason to doubt the effectiveness of some of the important (if somewhat nominal) constitutional and statutory constraints on Presidential war. It is clear that, as James MacGregor Burns succinctly put it, "The power of Congress to make a declaration of war has become hardly more than a formality."[54] Indeed, it is probably an anachronism, an ox-cart relic in the age of supersonic aircraft and intercontinental ballistic missiles. Nor is the War Powers Act necessarily more potent, even discounting some reservations about its constitutionality or the extent to which it actually inhibits the waging of Presidential war.[55] The War Powers Act may well have some effect on the conduct and the termination of an intervention, but such statutory constraints on the President's ability to initiate a conflict do not seem particularly compelling. Awareness of Congressional unwillingness to support an intervention may make a President reluctant to initiate an intervention that, if unsuccessful, would be blamed solely on himself and his Administration.[56] But it seems that the War Powers Act itself, in the words of Norman C. Thomas, "does little of an operational nature to strengthen Presidential accountability"[57] and thereby limit the President's ability to exercise the war power independently of Congress.

THE FUTURE OF CONGRESSIONAL CHECKS

There is little doubt that Congressional support for protracted Presidential wars, if not for all such interventions, is both essential for their success and a potential constraint on the President's use of the war power. A President can override or ignore the Congress in some circumstances, the War Powers Act notwithstanding, as President Ford's handling of the Mayaguez incident in 1975 demonstrated. Whether any President would do so in most other situations that raise the prospect of intervention is, however, open to question. Certainly any President who continued to wage war after the Congress had explicitly directed him to cease operations in accordance with the provisions of the War Powers Act would be courting political disaster. Even Presidents who have sent troops abroad after receiving the express endorsement of Congress, but attempted to maintain that commitment after Congressional enthusiasm had waned, incurred politica losses for their transgressions. [58]

At the same time, it seems that Congress has little direct ability to prevent the President from initiating an intervention if he is determined to do so. A President often has opportunity to manipulate information and events sufficiently to gain support for an initial intervention, or at least to neutralize opposition to it. The Tonkin Gulf in dent, in which it was subsequently claimed that the Congress acted hastily "on the basis of . . . incomplete information"[59] may be a cas in point. Once the intervention is underway, however, the dynamics the situation will probably determine the Congressional response. This is because the Congressional membership is politically sensitiv to the costs of war and changes in the degree of public support for it. If the United States appears to be winning at a reasonable cost, Congress is unlikely to invoke the War Powers Act, regardless of the degree of Presidential compliance with its provision. [61] But if the United States seems to be losing, or if the human and material costs of the intervention become too high, then the War Powers Act will probably be invoked. This could be ignored by a President only at his grave political peril.

Finally, to return to Paul Shratz's metaphor, the decision to unleash the "dog of war" is likely to remain in the Presidential "kennel," claims of greater Congressional assertiveness notwithstan ing. [62] The future relationship between the President and the Congres certainly subject to change. [63] But even now there are indications tha the Congress is becoming more willing to grant the President a freer hand in foreign affairs than might have been anticipated at the time the War Powers Act was voted into law over a Presidential veto. [64] This is not the era of Vietnam and Watergate, of course, and there is now a different person in the White House. Yet the changing Congressional attitude may also be due to a growing awareness that only the President can respond effectively to international challenges within the parameters of the existing constitutional order. [65] The only question is whether such behavior on the part of the President will permit the present constitutional order to remain in effect, or if--as one scholar of the Presidency has concluded--it may eventually result in "a return to the imperial presidency, perhaps with a vengeance, in the face of a future crisis."[66]

NONGOVERNMENTAL RESTRAINTS

To examine nongovernmental constraints on Presidential war requires a rather broad definition of "political" constraints. The two nongovernmental factors to be discussed here—public opinion and the media—cannot directly constrain the waging of Presidential war. Obviously, though, policy is never made in a political vacuum. Both the President and the Congress are aware of, and sensitive to, the opinion of the electorate. For their part, the media act in a dual capacity. They provide a medium of communication among the President, the Congress, and the public, and they constitute a particularly effective (if not very cohesive) set of interest groups with the ability to influence opinions and, eventually, policy. Thus, both public opinion and the media can at least exercise an indirect political constraint on Presidential war.

THE PUBLIC RESPONSE

No democratic politician, President or otherwise, can readily dismiss public opinion out of hand. "More formidable in many respects than treaty commitments," it has been observed, "are the constraints imposed on policy makers by national and international moods, attitudes, and opinions."[67] Each of these merits attention.

A distinction is conventionally made between issue-specific opinions, which can change rapidly over time, and those presumably more stable attributes that have their origin in a nation's political culture. [68] An enduring concern of most practitioners and analysts of U. S. foreign policy is whether there exists an American "character" that influences the formulation and conduct of foreign policy in a general sense. The classic statement affirming this position is the so-called "mood theory" of U. S. foreign policy, formulated over thirty years ago by Gabriel Almond. [69] Many characteristics were said to be part of the American "mood," the most important of which were instability and a tendency to alternate rapidly between extremes. From Almond's perspective, then, a given policy could be sustained only so long as it managed to be successful. If challenged, Americans preferred to marshall everything at their disposal to overwhelm the opposition. If that failed, disillusionment and withdrawal followed. [70]

Despite some pointed criticism in recent years, [71] Almond's "mood theory" retains considerable intuitive appeal. The basis for this enduring appeal becomes readily apparent when one considers the overall response of the American people to international challenges in recent years. It is hard to escape the conclusion that American political culture, unlike that of certain other countries, does not encourage Americans to endure protracted adversity. The political will of at least part of the American leadership may be more durable than the "cost-tolerance"[72] of the public at large, but the distinction is often hard to draw. Americans simply do not take well to calls for self-sacrifice when an unambiguous threat to their personal well-being or national survival cannot readily be discerned. Some demands can be met and some prices paid, but the justification for that effort must be incontrovertible, and the objectives for which the effort is being made must be attainable in short order. Americans also have a tendency to respond erratically to crises, with uncertain consequences for the implementation of effective policies to deal with them. As Herman Kahn has written:

> Both of the American biases--the unwillingness to initiate the use of moderate levels of force for limited objectives and the too great willingness, once we are committed, to use extravagant and uncontrolled force-- are potentially dangerous and should be guarded against. [73]

It is clear that to speak of general tendencies in American political culture can be misleading. Doing so risks overlooking differences that can, and often do, exist within the body politic on a wide range of issues. There are a number of ways in which one can differentiate among "publics." Discounting the apathetic and ineffectual elements of society, however, two broad categories can be identified: an "attentive minority" or elite public, and the so-called mass public comprising the remainder of the population. [74]

The elite public is essentially composed of better-educated persons in the professions who tend to be knowledgeable about foreign affairs and active participants in the foreign policy process (formal or informal) to the greatest extent possible. Their numbers are variously estimated at from one to 30 percent of the potential electorate with the average expertise and competence of its membership varying

inversely with its size. The influence this group exerts on foreign po-
icy is disproportionately great relative to its numbers. Its views can
be of particular importance with respect to the resolution of specific
issues between election years. [75] In general, a President contem-
plating intervention abroad during those years would be principally
concerned with the attitude of this group toward his action, at least at
the beginning.

This situation is reversed during an election year, and particularly in a Presidential election year. At that time, the opinion of the
mass public carries more weight than is usually the case. [76] This
does not mean that a President would ignore the views of the elite
public on such an issue, but the weight of numbers is not with them.

Certainly, it is fully in keeping with democratic tradition for
the Chief Executive to defer to the wishes of the electorate, even if
that tradition often receives little more than lip service in the world of
practical politics. To the extent that it occurs in the realm of foreign
affairs, however, it is profoundly disturbing. The basic characteristics of the mass public are generally considered ignorance, disin-
terest, and unpredictability. Those comprising the mass public tend
to see foreign affairs in only the vaguest terms. They may hold very
strong opinions on specific issues, but the level of information on
which those opinions are based is often remarkably low. A recent survey conducted by CBS News and the New York Times, for example,
found that only 23 percent of the respondents knew which nations were
involved in the SALT-II negoiations. An additional 24 percent selected
countries other than the United States and the Soviet Union, and an
astonishing majority of 53 percent simply had no idea! [77]

In addition, those in the mass public frequently appear to feel
uncomfortable in the province of world politics, if only because such
politics are of little immediate relevance to their lives. Sensing, perhaps, their remoteness from, and ignorance of, most international
matters, the majority of the electorate are usually willing to defer to
the judgment of their elected officials, at least initially, although their
acceptance of assurances from those officials comes less readily now
than formerly. If aroused from this seeming passivity, however, the
mass public is far more likely to respond emotionally than rationally
to the turn of events. It is here that the "moodiness" noted by Almond
applies with particular force. The obstacles this poses to those
charged with the effective conduct of any policy, much less an armed
intervention overseas, are such that at least one respected political
scientist has suggested that the passivity of the mass public actually
"introduces a factor of stability into the policy-making process." [78]

However, the greatest handicap encumbering the mass public is
probably the fact that a time lag often exists between executive decisions and the formation of collective opinion on particular issues.

In many instances, the mass public simply finds itself obliged to respond to the results of a foreign policy decision, instead of partici-pating in the policy process that led to it. President Kennedy's author-ization of the Bay of Pigs operation (1961) and his confrontation with the Soviet Union during the Cuban Missile Crisis (1962), President Johnson's decision to send U.S. forces into the Dominican Republic (1965), President Nixon's Cambodian "incursion" (1970), and President Ford's conduct of the Mayaguez rescue operation (1975) exemplify the mass public's difficulties in this regard. [79]

There is, of course, one situation in which this time lag does not usually apply: the conduct of a protracted Presidential war. The mass public may have little or no impact on the decision to initiate such a conflict, particularly between elections. But the situation presents the mass public with an opportunity to make its considerable weight felt when it comes to the way that war is being conducted, as well as the need to end it. Not surprisingly, this is precisely what happened during the limited wars in Korea and Vietnam. It could reasonably be expected to occur in the future.

Given these considerations, it is important to understand how the weight of mass public opinion can make itself felt during a Presi-dential war. It has been suggested that the attitude of the mass public toward such a war passes through five principal stages. [80] The initial intervention first produces a "rally around the flag" response in which Presidential popularity increases, sometimes significantly. [81] Next, there appears a "permissive majority" content to allow the President to conduct the war as he sees fit. It he is unable to bring the conflict to a successful conclusion in a fairly short time, however, a pro-nounced pro-escalation sentiment takes form in which the mass public endorses the use of even greater levels of force than the President may be inclined to employ. It is, in short, a clear case of "if fight, then win." The Presidential rejection or the failure of the escalation strat-egy, in turn, leads to a growing sense of disillusionment or "disaffec-tion." This undermines the effectiveness of the armed forces, weakens the political base of the incumbent President, and mandates the withdrawal of U.S. forces and the eventual cessation of U.S. participation in the war. [82] The ultimate end of the fighting gives rise to a sense of grim relief and a "never again" attitude reflecting a belief that the war should never have been waged in the first place. In the case of the war in Vietnam, this was compounded by a strong desire to forget about Vietnam and the war altogether. [83]

The consequences remain with us today and help define the parameters within which a decision to intervene would have to be made For now, it appears that the American public at large has recovered surprisingly well from the divisiveness that attended the Vietnam War There is a mood of "cautious internationalism," in light of which a

more assertive U. S. role in world affairs seems increasingly important. The need to secure sufficient energy resources and arms control rank high on the public's list of preferred U. S. policy goals. But
63 percent of those surveyed in a poll conducted in late 1978 believed
that "containing communism" was also very important. [84]

The source of this reassertion of more traditional U. S. goals
and interests is depressingly straightforward. There is a growing
public concern about the security of the U. S. position in the world,
reinforced by apprehension about the continuing growth in Soviet power
and influence. Surveys taken in November 1978 found that 43 percent of
the respondents believed that the United States is now playing a less important role in world affairs than it did a decade ago. Fifty-eight percent of those surveyed asserted that the United States was less
respected abroad than it had been ten years earlier. And 56 percent
concluded that this country's power and influence had been falling
behind that of the Soviet Union's in recent years. [85] This opinion was
reinforced by the growing belief that the United States was becoming
militarily weaker than the USSR, as depicted in Figure 8.1.

However, the fact that there is a greater public concern about
the U. S. position and a growing desire for a more active role in foreign affairs may be somewhat misleading. It does not necessarily
mean that the Vietnam War has been wholly forgotten, or that armed
U. S. intervention abroad is now endorsed by a majority of the American people. [86] To be sure, support for higher levels of defense spending is greater now than at any time since 1960, as Figure 8.2 illustrates. But the same group of respondents were also more willing to
cut defense spending than to reduce federal aid to education or funds
allocated to federal health programs[87]--an indication, perhaps, of
the internal inconsistency so common in mass public opinion.

As for intervention itself, there are some indications that support is growing for the selective use of U. S. armed forces overseas,
as the findings presented in Figure 8.3 demonstrate. John Mueller
has recently suggested that there may even be as much support
now for intervention on behalf of an important ally subjected
to external attack as there was before the Vietnam War. [88] But such
findings hardly constitute a blanket endorsement of interventionist
strategy. There is in too many instances a surprising disparity
between the political-military importance of certain U. S. commitments or interests and the absolute levels of support for armed intervention in defense of them. It does appear that a majority (58 percent)
of those surveyed in late 1978 would endorse the use of U. S. troops if
the Panamanian government closed the Panama Canal to U. S. shipping,
although that may have been an artifact of the debate that had recently
taken place on the Panama Canal treaties. But only 42 percent of the
respondents wanted the United States to intervene if the Soviet Union

FIGURE 8.1

Perceived Decline of United States Military Power[a]

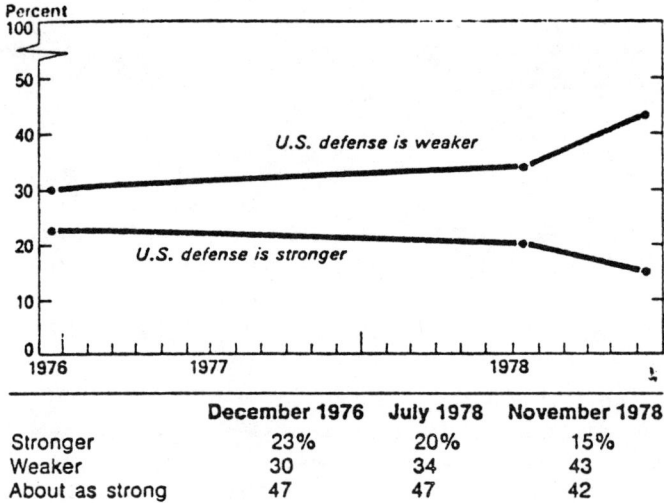

	December 1976	July 1978	November 1978
Stronger	23%	20%	15%
Weaker	30	34	43
About as strong	47	47	42

[a]Data reflect responses to: In general, do you feel the military defense system of the United States is stronger than that of the Russians, weaker, or about as strong as the Russian military defense system?
SOURCE: Public Opinion (January/February 1979), p. 29, based on surveys by Louis Harris and Associates. The last poll was taken on 24-27 November 1978.

invaded Japan—our principal Asian ally. And only 21 percent wanted the United States to provide South Korea with armed assistance in the event of a communist invasion. The lack of domestic support for military action against aggressors has an adverse affect on the ability of military units to carry out assigned missions. Soldiers in the 8th Army may well question their purpose in Korea. [89]
        Much of this lack of support undoubtedly reflects a popular unwillingness to see this country become involved in another land war in Asia, with all its associated costs. Perhaps the best that can be said is that the American people do not like the notion of using limited

FIGURE 8. 2

Trends in Support of Increased Defense Spending[a]

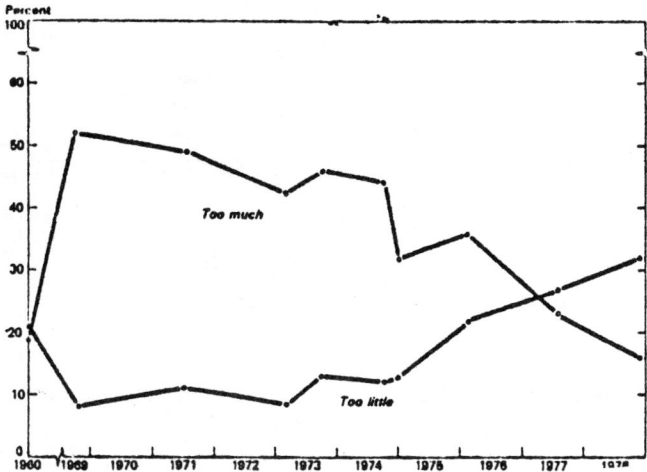

	1960	1969	1971	Feb. 1973	Sept. 1973	Sept. 1974	Dec. 1974	1976	1977	1978
Too much	18%	52%	49%	42%	46%	44%	32%	36%	23%	16%
About right	45	31	31	40	30	32	47	32	40	45
Too little	21	8	11	8	13	12	13	22	27	32

[a] Data represent responses to two slightly different questions. Those for December 1974 and November 1978 were to: Do you think that we should expand our spending on national defense, keep it about the same, or cut back?

All other responses were to: There is much discussion as to the amount of money the government in Washington should spend for national defense and military purposes. How do you feel about this? Do you think we are spending too little, too much, or about the right amount?

SOURCE: Public Opinion (March/May 1979), p. 25. Survey of December 1974 was by Louis Harris and Associates for the Chicago Council on Foreign Relations. All others were by the American Institute on Public Opinion (Gallup).

FIGURE 8. 3

Trends in Support for American Military Intervention[a]

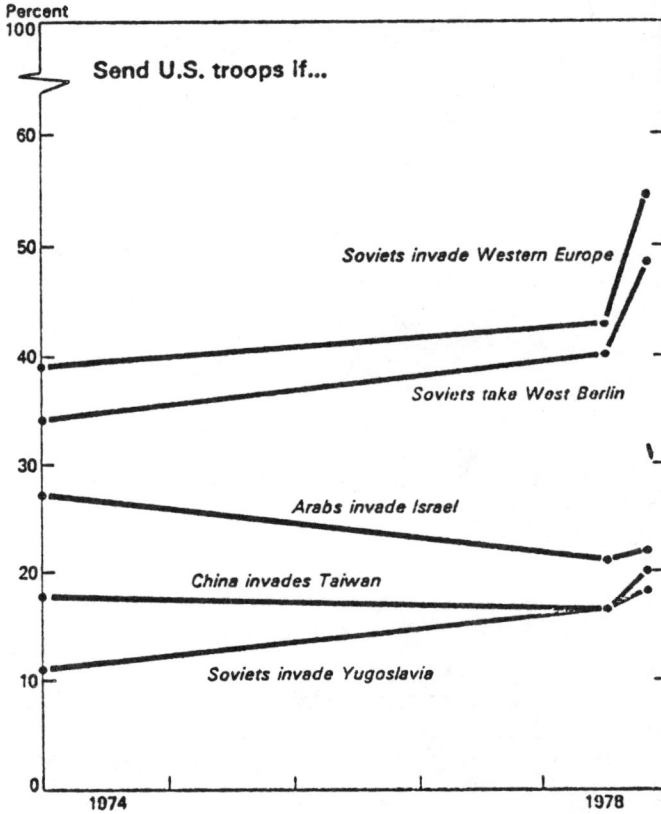

Percent

Send U.S. troops If...

Soviets invade Western Europe

Soviets take West Berlin

Arabs invade Israel

China invades Taiwan

Soviets invade Yugoslavia

1074   1978

[a] Question wording differs slightly in some instances.
SOURCE: Public Opinion (March/May 1979), p. 26.

military force for limited political ends, no matter how attractive that concept may be to strategic planners. They do not appreciate the need for restraints on the use of the U. S. military once it is committed to battle. They do not like protracted conflicts that seem to lack clearly defined and readily attainable objectives. They do not, most emphatically, like to lose, and their discontent will be reflected on the battlefield and in the voting booth alike. [90]

It certainly seems fair to say that the public in general still looks to the President for leadership. Whether it actually finds that leadership, or is predisposed to accept whatever leadership is proffered, is another matter. A crisis would most likely produce at least a temporary consensus within which the President could act for a limited time. But public skepticism is greater now than at the beginning of the Vietnam War, and this skepticism might constrain the conduct (if not the initiation) of a Presidential war. [91] This is not because such a war would necessarily be considered immoral, ex post facto judgments on Vietnam notwithstanding. For most Americans, a just war is a successful war, and moral outrage at home generally follows rather than precedes military failure abroad. The simple fact is that public support for a Presidential war will fall as the war lengthens and the costs of the war increase. When that support has declined sufficiently, either the President will move to end U. S. involvement or the electorate will move to end the tenure of that particular Administration. [92]

THE MEDIA AS AN INTERESTED PARTY

Last, but certainly not least, it is essential that we consider the role of the media as a constraint on the waging of Presidential war. [93]

The media as a whole function in a dual capacity. First, they transmit information to official and unofficial elements in the policy process, and serve as a vehicle by which the government can make known its decisions (and the rationale for them) in an effort to build public support. This is important to the President, who often relies on direct appeal to the public for support that might not be readily forthcoming from Congress. [94] Also, the media can serve as a vehicle for the expression of public support for a given policy, or public opposition to it.

In many respects, the second function of the media is the more important and controversial. The media function as interested parties, whose members can act much like members of other interest groups. Such groups are conventionally seen as intermediaries that provide a selective linkage between the government and the public. They can exert influence directly on individuals in the government, or indirectly by focusing on the constituents of those individuals whose views they wish to shape. The extent to which interest groups in general are able to influence public opinion and shape government policy even on crucial foreign policy decisions is far from clear.[95]

Much less uncertainty exists with respect to the potential impact of the media as an interest group. Unlike some interest groups, the media disseminate messages in a way that is difficult for the public to wholly ignore. Certainly the media do not comprise a unified entity directed from a single center, nor do their different components affect all segments of the political system equally. Political or partisan preferences aside, the so-called "mass prestige press" helps shape more selective public opinion and elite attitudes, whereas the electronic media—especially television—are particularly influential among the mass public.[96] It does not appear that television news is less informative than sensational, and that its precise impact on the opinions of its viewers (like those of a newspaper on its readers) varies widely. Yet it is also apparent that the media in general, and television in particular, can mold public opinion and help "set the public agenda"[97] if conditions are right.

Three principal factors can influence the role the media play in this process. One is the relationship between the media and the President. The media, broadly speaking, can be an advocate of Presidential policies, a relatively disinterested neutral (that is, an "honest broker" of information), or a Presidential adversary. It has been suggested that "stability . . . [may be] the norm in the presidential relationship with the press,"[98] if only because such a relationship can be mutually advantageous. President Kennedy's relationship with the media is a case in point. At present, however, it is also clear that the relationship between the media and the President (as well as other members of the government) is far from cordial. Much of the personal antagonism that characterized that relationship during the Nixon era has happily abated. But what has emerged is not the foreign affairs "partnership" that once existed. It may not even be an exaggeration to speak of an emerging rivalry between what some informed sources consider the two most powerful American institutions: the Presidency and an "imperial media."[99]

A second factor is the philosophical or ideological predisposition of those in influential positions within the media. There are, as Richard Hofstetter has written, three types of bias: lying, distortion, and value assertion.[100] The last is of greatest importance here, even assuming the possibility of deliberate distortion in the presentation of a controversial subject (e. g., U. S. military intervention in the Third World.) The views of those who present the news shape the news.[101] The fact that what is variously called "advocacy journalism" or "new journalism" is somewhat in vogue among many of the younger member of the media is indicative of the growth of this third form of bias. That one of the values asserted in some instances is a form of antimilitary sentiment common to college-educated liberals of the last decade and earlier both reflects and exacerbates the tension between the national security concerns of the Presidency and the preferences of part of the media. [102] This increases the likelihood that the media as a whole would be neither neutral nor supportive of the President in the event of military intervention abroad.

The third factor that can influence media presentation of its message is the nature of the issue or event being covered. Some issues simply do not lend themselves to balanced coverage. If, for example, information cannot be obtained from one of the parties to a dispute, news coverage will necessarily be incomplete, and opinions may well be ill-founded. Certain issues or events also touch more emotional chords than do others. This makes it difficult for even an honest person to deal with the subject in an even-handed manner. Vietnam, it appears, was--or became--such an issue. Another Presidential war would likely be the same.

All these factors affect the impact the media could have on the public attitude toward a Presidential war. First, it can create or reinforce pro-intervention sentiment by directing attention to the war in a manner that is both affirmative and politically compelling. In some instances, the very reporting of an incident can create a sense of public outrage that may overwhelm opposition to intervention within the government or the elite public. The sinking of the USS Maine in 1898 and the reported attacks on American destroyers of North Vietnam in 1964 crystallized public (and, therefore, Congressional) support for intervention. In this capacity, then, the media incite intervention, not constraint.

Second, the media may consciously attempt to inform rather than persuade the public. It may essentially abstain from passing editorial judgment on an intervention pending further developments. In fact, on most issues, coverage in both the electronic media and the press does tend to avoid an advocacy position. Even as emotionally charged an issue as the Vietnam War was frequently presented in a predominantly neutral format, although both editorial positions and the selection of material sometimes departed from that position of neutrality. [103] Such a stance would not mobilize support behind the waging of a Presidential war, but neither would it discourage such support.

Third, and finally, the media can attempt to undermine support for intervention and can serve as a vehicle for expressing opposition to it. This can be done by structuring the news and weighting editorials so as to stimulate criticism about the effectiveness of the government, the legitimacy of this country's basic institutions, and its participation in a particular conflict. This would, in all probability, lead to a decline in support for the continuation of the commitment, which would in turn inhibit the effective prosecution of the war, increase the likelihood of failure, and provide added impetus for the premature termination of the U. S. intervention on whatever terms might be obtained.

Vietnam once again provides an illustration of both the changing role of the media and its impact on public opinion and the conduct of the war. In the early years of the U. S. intervention (e. g. , during the Kennedy Administration), the media were largely supportive. By the mid-1960s, as the U. S. role increased, the situation began to change. This change continued until the early 1970s, by which time the opinions presented in the media had become neutral and in some cases overwhelmingly hostile toward the U. S. intervention. The media sometimes distorted crucial events to put the United States and the South Vietnamese in an unfavorable light. The coverage of the Tet offensive of 1968 exemplifies this distortion. On other occasions, the media were simply unable to see what was happening in the opponent's camp, and ended up "distorting by default" by presenting only one side of the picture. Extensive criticism of basic American institutions also increased the sense of political disaffection felt by many people. Such criticism does not seem to have been made in a systematic manner, but the effect was considerable. [104] This pattern would likely be repeated in the event of another Presidential war.

The combined significance of these considerations does not augur well for the support of the media in a future Presidential war. In fact, a "free press" (broadly defined) is a liability in any war, Presidential or otherwise. We are unlikely to fight other democracies, and dictatorships of any political coloration do not feel obligated to give their own or any other people access to conflicting or controversial information. On the contrary, they sometimes rely on the free press of their opponent—if, that is, two dictatorships are not fighting one another—to carry their message to their opponent's electorate, while remaining relatively free of countervailing pressure. [105] The net effect is that the U. S. electorate receives a one-sided, and therefore biased, view of an intervention in which U. S. forces are involved. Ironically, even objectivity on the part of the U. S. media could be a liability in such a conflict. Presidential wars require public support, and a media that does not actively work to sustain that support implicitly lays the groundwork for public disillusionment and political failure.

WAGING PRESIDENTIAL WAR: A NET ASSESSMENT
OF POLITICAL CONSTRAINTS

Three principal conslusions emerge from this study. One is
that the political constraints on military intervention are considerable,
and make it extremely difficult for the United States to contemplate
waging a Presidential war. Part of the difficulty inheres in this country's political system. "The American Constitution," as former
Senator J. William Fulbright observed, was never meant to operate
in a condition of permanent warfare and crisis."[106] Much the same
can be said for politics in general in this country. Yet that condition
is very nearly what a Presidential war in the modern world entails.
When it comes to waging Presidential war, our constitutional order
checks more than it balances. It inhibits the timely and effective conduct of an intervention when it functions smoothly, and undermines
that effort when it does not. The political interaction of the Presidency, the Congress, public opinion, and the media combine to exacerbate the dilemma. [107]

Second, it must be recognized that Presidential wars remain
possible despite these obstacles. The political constraints on Presidential war that exist outside the Constitution are certainly more
likely to operate in the future than they have in the past: Vietnam demonstrated how effective they could be. But the only practical constraints on the <u>initiation</u> of a Presidential war are the character and
the perceived political self-interest of the President himself. A
President convinced that it is right and possible for this country to
police the world will be inclined to intervene more readily than one
who is not. Even an activist President may be restrained by uncertainties during the initial year in office, if only to gain time for
stronger measures later, although over-reaction on his part is also
possible. During the fourth year of the first term, temporizing and
selective response are the rule. In all cases, however, a President
must approach an election with either peace or victory in his hands—or
at least in sight. There are considerable political costs in failure to
make that case persuasively. Nevertheless, one point cannot be
overemphasized: <u>A President can intervene anywhere if he chooses
to do so, and is willing to risk paying the political price if he fails.</u>

Third, these political constraints outside the Presidency have
their greatest impact on the <u>conduct</u> and the <u>termination</u> stages of a
Presidential war, especially if it has not resulted in a clearly identifiable and generally acknowledged success. Direct Presidential

appeals to the public via the electronic media, if forceful and carefully planned, may produce a temporary consensus in support of an intervention. That consensus, however, will be short-lived in the absence of measurable success. Once a President implicitly concedes failure by negotiating for a settlement when the initial objectives have not been achieved, the process of disengagement--once begun--becomes irreversible. Congress, public opinion, and the media implicitly combine to force an end to the U. S. role in the war, even if that means abandoning the interests and the allies in whose name the intervention was made.

In sum, it seems that Hans Morgenthau was only half right when he suggested that a more judicious appraisal of means and ends would permit the United States to "intervene less and succeed more."[108] We may well intervene less in the future, although a growing awareness of the increasing precariousness of our position in the world may bury the memory of the Vietnam War once and for all. But this analysis of the political constraints on Presidential war also suggests that success in such an endeavor will be extremely elusive even under the best of circumstances. The precise parameters of successful interventions will be explored in a subsequent study.[109]

NOTES

1. See, for example, the remark by Robert W. Tucker in Nation or Empire? The Debate Over American Foreign Policy (Baltimore: Johns Hopkins University Press, 1971), p. 17.

2. W. Scott Thompson and Donald L. Frizzell, eds. , The Lessons of Vietnam (New York: Crane, Russak, 1977); and Alan Ned Sabrosky, "An Imperial Recessional: The 'Domino Theory' Revisited," Intercollegiate Review, 11/2 (Winter/Spring 1976).

3. For concise summaries of the basic characteristics of the postwar foreign policy consensus, see Howard Bliss and M. Glen Johnson, Beyond the Water's Edge: America's Foreign Policies (Philadelphia: Lippincott, 1975), esp. pp. 6-7; and Graham T. Allison, "Cool It: The Foreign Policy of Young America," Foreign Policy, 1 (Winter 1970/71): 150-52.

4. James A. Nathan and James K. Oliver, United States Foreign Policy and World Order (Boston: Little, Brown, 1976), pp. 488 and 518; and Arthur M. Schlesinger Jr. , The Imperial Presidency (Boston: Houghton, Mifflin, 1973), esp. Chs. 3, 6-9.

5. J. William Fulbright, The Crippled Giant: American Foreign Policy and its Domestic Consequences (New York: Vintage Books, 1972), pp. 181ff. refer to the Indochina conflict in these terms. See also Richard Holbrooke, "Presidents, Bureaucrats, and Something In

Between," in The Vietnam Legacy, ed. Anthony Lake (New York: New York University Press, 1976).

6. Nathan and Oliver, United States Foreign Policy, p. 522; and John E. Mueller, War, Presidents and Public Opinion (New York: John Wiley and Sons, 1973), pp. 53-56.

7. Alastair Buchan, "The Indochina War and World Politics," Foreign Affairs, 53/4 (July 1975), and Earl C. Ravenal, "Consequences of the End Game in Indochina," Foreign Affairs, 53/4 (July 1975) address this point. But others caution against overstating the extent to which that consensus actually has eroded, at least as it is usually defined. See Bayliss Manning, "Goals, Ideology and Foreign Policy," Foreign Affairs, 54/2 (January 1976), esp. pp. 271-72; and Leslie Gelb, "Dissenting on Consensus," in Anthony Lake, ed., The Vietnam Legacy (New York: New York University Press, 1976), p. 107.

8. James Chace, "Is A Foreign Policy Consensus Possible?" Foreign Affairs, 57/1 (Fall 1978), p. 9; and Kenneth Thompson, "New Reflections on Ethics and Foreign Policy: The Problem of Human Rights," Journal of Politics, 40/4 (November 1978), esp. 988.

9. Chace, "Foreign Policy Consensus," p. 16.

10. Alan Ned Sabrosky, "America and the Asian Power Game," Sea Power (February 1979). Paul Schratz's comment to the effect that Americans see war as "a contest of logistics rather than of politics" is uncomfortably close to the mark. See his "National Decision Making and Military Intervention," in The Limits of Military Intervention ed. Ellen P. Stern (Beverly Hills: Sage, 1977), p. 347.

11. Doris A Graber, "Intervention Policies of the Carter Administration: Political and Military Dimensions," in Defense Policy of the Presidency: Carter's First Years ed. Sam C. Sarkesian (Boulder, Col.: Westview Press, 1979), pp. 226-27. Some have suggested that the United States is still in the midst of one of its cyclical periods of quasi-disengagement from interventionist policies. For recent discussions of such arguments, see Irving Kristol, "Consensus and Dissent in U.S. Foreign Policy," in Legacy of Vietnam ed. Anthony Lake (New York: New York University Press, 1976), p. 81; and Laurence I. Radway, "Domestic Attitudes as Constraints on American Foreign Policy," in America in an Interdependent World, ed. David A. Baldwin (Hanover, N.H.: University Press of New England, 1976), p. 296.

12. For discussions of the conditions under which interventions may occur, see Herbert K. Tillema, Appeal to Force: American Military Intervention in the Era of Containment (New York: Thomas Y. Crowell, 1973); James L. Payne, The American Threat: The Fear of War as an Instrument of Foreign Policy (Chicago: Markham, 1970); Barry M. Blechman and Stephen S. Kaplan, Force Without War: U.S. Armed Forces as a Political Instrument (Washington, D.C.:

Brookings, 1978); Graham Allison, Ernest May, and Adam Jarmolinsky, "Limits to Intervention," Foreign Affairs, 48/2 (January 1970); Robert Tucker, "Oil: The Issue of American Intervention," Commentary (January 1975) and "Further Reflections on Oil and Force," Commentary (March 1975); Roland A. Paul, "Toward a Theory of Intervention," Orbis, 16/1 (Spring 1972); and Frederic S. Pearson, "Foreign Military Interventions and Domestic Disputes," International Studies Quarterly, 18/3 (September 1974).

13. Graber, "Intervention Policies," p. 203 and pp. 206-207.

14. See, for example, Alexander L. George, David K. Hall and William R. Simons, The Limits of Coercive Diplomacy (Boston: Little, Brown, 1971), p. 223; William V. O'Brien, "Guidelines for Limited War," Military Review (February 1979), p. 66; and Bruce Russett and Miroslav Nincic, "American Opinion on the Use of Military Force Abroad," Political Science Quarterly, 91/3 (Fall 1976), p. 431.

15. Arthur M. Schlesinger, Jr. The Bitter Heritage: Vietnam and American Democracy, 1941-1966, rev. ed. (New York: Fawcett World, 1968), p. 47.

16. Leslie Gelb, "Vietnam: The System Worked," Foreign Policy 3 (Summer 1971): 140.

17. Daniel Ellsberg, Papers on the War (New York: Simon and Schuster, 1972), chapter on "The Quagmire Myth and the Stalemate Machine."

18. Tillema, Appeal to Force, pp. 30-33; Ravenal, "Consequences," pp. 657-58; Leslie Gelb and Richard K. Betts, Irony of Vietnam (Washington: Brookings, 1978), p. 2; and Sabrosky, "Imperial Recessional," pp. 86-89.

19. This definition seems implicit in the War Powers Act of 1973 itself. See W. Taylor Reveley III, "The Power to Make War," in The Constitution and the Conduct of Foreign Policy, eds. Francis O. Wilcox and Richard A. Frank (New York: Praeger, 1976), p. 114; and the discussion of "Congressional Checks on Presidential War" in this chapter.

20. John Spanier and Eric M. Uslaner, How American Foreign Policy Is Made, 2nd ed. (New York: HRW/Praeger, 1978).

21. Nicholas deB. Katzenbach, "Foreign Policy, Public Opinion, and Secrecy," Foreign Affairs, 52/1 (October 1973): 2; Gelb and Betts Irony of Vietnam, p. 25.

22. One of the few discussions of all three aspects of this issue appears in Reveley, "Power to Make War," pp. 103-109. War initiation is discussed in Merlo J. Pusey, The Way We Go To War (Boston: Houghton Mifflin, 1969). For the domestic consequences of war-termination, see Fred Ikle, Every War Must End (New York: Columbia University Press, 1971), Chs. 4-5.

23. Louis Henkin, Foreign Affairs and the Constitution (New York: W. W. Norton, 1972), esp. pp. 31-35 and 89-123; Spanier and Uslaner, How American Foreign Policy Is Made, pp. 3-7; and Lee H. Hamilton and Michael H. Van Dusen, "Making the Separation of Powers Work," Foreign Affairs, 57/1 (Fall 1978): 27ff.

24. For a brief and informative discussion, see Pusey, Way We Go To War, Ch. 4.

25. Alexander Hamilton, "Federalist No. 69," in The Federalist Papers, ed. Clinton Rossiter (New York: New American Library, 1961), pp. 417-18.

26. See, for instance, Gene E. Rainey, Patterns of American Foreign Policy (Boston: Allyn and Bacon, 1975), who notes that "In each of the four foreign policy arenas . . . Congress (was) a junior partner; the role of the Supreme Court was to legitimize the President's expansion of power or to step aside" (p. 220).

27. For discussions of the origins of this resolution, see Jacob K. Javits with Don Kellermann, Who Makes War: The President Versus Congress (New York: William Morrow, 1973), Chs. 17-18; and Pusey, Way We Go To War, Chs. 7-8. It is worth mentioning that President Johnson's decision to commit troops to Vietnam would have been legal even under the War Powers Act of 1973. Congress did explicitly grant the necessary authority in 1964 and reaffirmed it in subsequent appropriations, as Section 5(b) of the War Powers Act requires.

28. Henkin, Foreign Affairs, p. 35.

29. Schratz, "National Decision Making," p. 359. See also Schlesinger, Imperial Presidency. Some criticism of the "imperial presidency" was at least partially partisan in character. Some who disliked a Republican imperium had not been disturbed by a Democratic imperium in Camelot.

30. Richard Burt, "Test of Arms: On Foreign Policy, Count Congress In-Emphatically," New York Times (May 14, 1978); Daniel Yankelovich, "Farewell to President Knows Best," Foreign Affairs, Special Edition of America and the World—1978 (1979), pp. 670-72; and Radway, "Domestic Attitudes," pp. 312-13.

31. Charles Burton Marshall, The Exercise of Sovereignty (Baltimore: Johns Hopkins University Press, 1965), p. 76.

32. Spanier and Uslaner, How American Foreign Policy Is Made, p. 1. The President is clearly seen (as of 1978) to be the most important actor in the foreign policy process, especially by the elite public.

33. Richard M. Pious, The American Presidency (New York: Basic Books, 1979), p. 388; Norman L. Hill, The New Democracy in Foreign Policy Making (Lincoln: University of Nebraska Press, 1970), p. 3; Ellis Briggs, Anatomy of Diplomacy (New York: David McKay,

1968), p. 14; Marshall, Exercise of Sovereignty, p. 83; and Kenneth W. Thompson, The Moral Issue in Statecraft (Baton Rouge: Louisiana State University Press, 1966), p. 214. This is not without its costs, however, including the executive's tendency to bypass the Congress in some instances by relying on executive agreements that do not require Congressional approval. See James McCormick, "Foreign Policy By Executive Fiat," Foreign Policy, 28 (Fall 1977).

34. Henry Kissinger, American Foreign Policy: Three Essays (New York: Norton, 1966), pp. 18-19, 22-23, 43.

35. Gelb and Betts, Irony of Vietnam, p. 365. See also pp. 286-94, and Richard E Neustadt's Presidential Power: The Politics of Leadership (New York: John Wiley, 1960), esp. pp. 18-19.

36. James David Barber. The Presidential Character, 2nd ed. (Englewood Cliffs, N.J. Prentice-Hall, 1977), p. 445.

37. Barber, Presidential Character, pp. 210-11. See also Defense Policy and the Presidency: Carter's First Years, ed. Sam C. Sarkesian (Boulder, Col.: Westview Press, 1979), p. 10; Tillema, Appeal to Force, pp. 33-36, 117-27; and Ole R. Holsti, "The Belief System and National Images: A Case Study," Journal of Conflict Resolution, 6/3 (September 1962).

38. Kenneth W. Thompson, "American Foreign Policy: Values Renewed or Discovered," Orbis, 20/1 (Spring 1976): 127.

39. Pusey, Why We Go To War, p. 167.

40. For a general discussion of the threat of electoral rejection, see Kenneth N. Waltz, "Electoral Punishment and Foreign Policy Crises," in Domestic Sources of Foreign Policy, ed. James Rosenau (New York: Free Press, 1967).

41. Milton J. Rosenberg, "Images in Relation to the Public Process: American Public Opinion in Cold War Issues," in International Behavior: A Social-Psychological Analysis, ed. Herbert C. Kelman (New York: Holt, Rinehart and Winston, 1965), p. 279. See also James Rosenau, ed., Domestic Sources of Foreign Policy (New York: Free Press, 1967), p. 4; Kissinger, American Foreign Policy, p. 14; Richard W. Cottam, Competitive Interference and Twentieth Century Diplomacy (Pittsburgh: University of Pittsburgh Press, 1967), p. 105; George, et. al., Coercive Diplomacy, pp. 223ff.

42. Pusey, Why We Go To War, p. 167.

43. Spanier and Uslaner, How American Foreign Policy Is Made p. 5; George, et. al., Coercive Diplomacy, p. 223; Brian Crozier, Masters of Power (London: Eyre and Spottiswoode, 1969), pp. 146, 326-27; Lester W. Milbraith, "Interest Groups and Foreign Policy," in Domestic Sources of Foreign Policy, ed. James Rosenau (New York Free Press, 1967), p. 236; George C. Edwards III, "Presidential Electoral Performance as a Source of Presidential Power," American Journal of Political Science, 22/1 (February 1978): 167; Neustadt,

Presidential Power, Ch. 5; and James L. Sundquist, "Congress and the President: Enemies or Partners?" in Congress Reconsidered, eds. Lawrence C. Dodd and Bruce L. Oppenheimer (New York: Praeger, 1977), p. 241. One recent study, however, found that intervention had the best prospects for success with either very popular or very unpopular Presidents in office! See Blechman and Kaplan, Force Without War, pp. 119-23.

44. Stanley Hoffmann, Gulliver's Troubles or the Setting of American Foreign Policy (New York: McGraw Hill, 1968), pp. 229-33.

45. Ellsberg, Papers on the War, pp. 100-101, 103-106, 119-20, 126-27 and 130-31. See also Gelb, "Vietnam," esp. pp. 141-43; and Gelb and Betts, Irony of Vietnam, pp. 291ff.

46. Morton H. Halperin, Bureaucratic Politics and Foreign Policy (Washington: Brookings, 1974), p. 67.

47. Halperin, Bureaucratic Politics, pp. 67-68. Presidential popularity tends to increase, at least for a short time, immediately following strong Presidential actions in foreign affairs. See Robert B. Smith, "Disaffection, Delegitimation, and Consequences: Aggregate Trends for World War II, Korea and Vietnam," in Public Opinion and the Military Establishment, ed. Charles C. Moskos, Jr. (Beverly Hills: Sage, 1971), pp. 225-28.

48. Seyom Brown, The Faces of Power (New York: Columbia University Press, 1968), p. 328.

49. For general studies of the Congressional role in foreign policy process, see James A. Robinson, Congress and Foreign Policy-Making, rev. ed. (Homewood, Illinois: The Dorsey Press, 1967), esp. Chs. 1 and 6; Henkin, Foreign Affairs, esp. Chs. 3 and 4; and Robert A. Dahl's classic Congress and Foreign Policy (New York: Harcourt, Brace and World, 1950). Other commentaries on the more assertive role assumed by the Congress in recent years are Robert E. DiClerico, The American President (Englewood Cliffs, N.J.: Prentice-Hall, 1979), esp. pp. 52-56; Hamilton and Van Dusen, "Separation of Powers"; and Alton Frye, "Congress: The Virtues of Its Vices," Foreign Policy, 3 (Summer 1971).

50. The "power of the purse" actually has little practical effect on the President's ability to initiate an intervention. The witholding of sufficient funds to make a President incapable of initiating a war against the wishes of the Congress would also make the President incapable of waging war at the behest of Congress.

51. Norman J. Ornstein, "The Emerging Role of the Congress in the Foreign Policy Process," lecture presented at the United States Military Academy, West Point, N.Y., May 1, 1979. For a good summary of the War Powers Act, see Reveley, "Power to Make War," pp. 113-22.

52. Hamilton and Van Dusen, "Separation of Powers," p. 21; Frye, "Congress," pp. 110-15.

53. Albert R. Hunt, "The Newcomers' Impact on Congress," Wall Street Journal (March 6, 1978); Norman J. Ornstein, Robert L. Peabody, and David W. Rhode, "The Changing Senate: From the 1950s to the 1970s," in Congress Reconsidered, eds. Lawrence C. Dodd and Bruce I. Oppenheimer (New York: Praeger, 1977), esp. p. 18; Adam Clymer, "Congress's O'Neill and Byrd: Two Leaders, Two Stykes," New York Times (July 7, 1978); DiClerico, American President, p. 56; and Burt, "Count Congress In."

54. James MacGregor Burns, Presidential Government (Boston: Houghton Mifflin, 1965), p. 209. See also Pious, American Presidency, p. 373.

55. It has been suggested, for instance, that the War Powers Act "changed the Constitution from reading that war cannot be waged without the consent of Congress to the president can wage war until Congress stops him." See Spanier and Uslaner, How American Foreign Policy Is Made, p. 47.

56. Pious, American Presidency, pp. 403-404; Reveley, "Power to Make War," pp. 122-25.

57. Norman C. Thomas, "Presidential Accountability Since Watergate," Presidential Studies Quarterly, 8/4 (Fall 1978): 420.

58. Russett and Nincic, "American Opinion," p. 431; Kristol, "Consensus and Dissent," p. 84.

59. Fulbright, Crippled Giant, pp. 187-88. A cynic might argue that a Congress so easily fooled, and so easily stampeded, is hardly a Congress capable of exercising responsible oversight of the foreign policy process.

60. Paul Burstein and William Freudenburg, "Changing Public Policy: The Impact of Public Opinion, Antiwar Demonstrations, and War Costs on Senate Voting on Vietnam War Motions," American Journal of Sociology, 84/1 (July 1978): 110, 116.

61. As one critic of Presidential war-initiation conceded, "If the war (in Vietnam) had gone well, it is quite probable that no great question would have been raised about how we got into it." Pusey, Why We Go To War, p. 10.

62. Schratz, "National Decision Making," p. 359.

63. See the discussions in Harvey G. Zeidenstein, "The Reassertion of Congressional Power: New Curbs on the President," Political Science Quarterly, 93/3 (Fall 1978): esp. 393; and Frank R. Bax, "The Legislative-Executive Relationship in Foreign Policy: New Partnership or New Competition?" Orbis, 20/4 (Winter 1977).

64. John W. Finney, "War Powers Pendulum Swings Back--A Little," New York Times (April 8, 1979).

65. Thomas, "Presidential Accountability," p. 432.

66. Thomas, "Presidential Accountability," pp. 432ff.

67. Graber, "Intervention Policies," p. 209. See also Richard O. Gillick, "Public Opinion in a Time of Troubles," in New Dynamics in National Strategy: The Paradox of Power (New York: Thomas Y. Crowell, 1975), esp. p. 24.

68. For studies of this subject, see, for example, Gabriel Almond, The American People and Foreign Policy (New York: Praeger, 1950); James Rosenau, Public Opinion and Foreign Policy (New York: Random House, 1961); Bernard C. Cohen, The Public's Impact on Foreign Policy (Boston: Little, Brown, 1973). A study focusing more directly on the subject of this paper is John E. Mueller, War, Presidents and Public Opinion (New York: John Wiley and Sons, 1973).

69. Almond, American People and Foreign Policy, esp. Chs. 3-6. The basic dichotomies of mood identified by Almond were: withdrawal-intervention, mood-simplification (over-and under-reaction), optimism-pessimism, tolerance-intolerance, idealism-cynicism, and superiority-inferiority (pp. 54-65).

70. Yankelovich, "Farewell," p. 689.

71. For a dissenting view that characterizes American public opinion as having a "strong and stable permissive mood toward international involvements," see William R. Caspary, "The 'Mood Theory': A Study of Public Opinion and Foreign Policy," American Political Science Review, 64/2 (June 1970).

72. For a discussion of the implications of the concept of "cost-tolerance" (the ability to endure losses in pursuit of an objective), see Steven Rosen and Walter Jones, The Logic of International Relations (Cambridge, Mass.: Winthrop Publishers, 1974), pp. 148-49.

73. Herman Kahn, Thinking About The Unthinkable (New York: Horizon Press, 1962), p. 78.

74. For discussions of the various "publics" and their composition, see Rainey, Patterns, pp. 84ff; Rosenau, Public Opinion, Ch. 4; and Ralph B. Levering, The Public and American Foreign Policy, 1918-1978 (New York: William Morrow, 1978), Ch. 1.

75. Levering, The Public and American Foreign Policy, p. 152; Robert E. Lane and David O. Sears, Public Opinion (Englewood Cliffs, N.J.: Prentice-Hall, 1964), p. 3; Alfred O. Hero, Americans in World Affairs (Boston: World Peace Foundation, 1959), p. 6; Michael H. Armacost, The Foreign Relations of the United States (Belmont, Cal.: Dickinson, 1969), p. 123; and Cottam, Competitive Interference, p. 26.

76. Levering, The Public and American Foreign Policy, p. 152.

77. Public Opinion (March/May 1979), p. 27.

244 / NONNUCLEAR CONFLICTS

78. Rosenau, Public Opinion, pp. 36-37. For discussions of the attitudes of the "general" or "mass" public and their implications for the conduct of foreign policy, see, for example, Lane and Sears, Public Opinion, esp. Ch. 6; Rita James Simon, Public Opinion in America: 1936-1970 (Chicago: Markham, 1974), p. 122; Burns W. Roper, "The Limits of Public Support," Annals of the American Academy of Political and Social Science, 442 (March 1979); Angus Campbell, Philip E. Converse, Warren E. Miller, and Donald E. Stokes, The American Voter (New York: John Wiley and Sons, 1960), esp. pp. 280-82ff; Hill, New Democracy, pp. 22,39-40, 53; Cottam, Competitive Interference, p. 229; Hero, Americans in World Affairs, p. 13; Alfred O. Hero, Mass Media and World Affairs (Boston: World Peace Foundation, 1959), p. 22; Armacost, Foreign Relations, p. 123; and Dahl, Congress, p. 73.

79. For discussions of the concept of a "time lag" in this context, see Betty H. Zisk, "The Grand Rules of Policy-Making," in Issues of American Public Policy, ed. John H. Bunzel (Englewood Cliffs, N.J.: Prentice-Hall, 1964), p. 4; Warren E. Miller, "Voting and Foreign Policy," Domestic Sources of Foreign Policy, ed. James Rosenau (New York: Free Press, 1967), p. 217; Rosenberg, "Images," p. 284; and Spanier and Uslaner, How American Foreign Policy Is Made, p. 93.

80. William L. Lunch and Peter W. Sperlich, "American Public Opinion and the War in Vietnam," Western Political Quarterly, 32/1 (Spring 1979): esp. 29-32. See also the opinion pools reported in Mueller, War, Presidents and Public Opinion, esp. Chs. 3,4 and 6. The Lunch/Sperlich study applied explicitly to Vietnam, although the pattern paralleled that of the Korean War in several respects.

81. Smith, "Disaffection," pp. 226-29.

82. This phenomenon is described in Smith, "Disaffection," pp. 22-129, and Mueller, War, Presidents and Public Opinion, Ch. 9. The impact of public disaffection on the armed forces, and the consequences thereof for the conduct of the war, are described in David Cortright, Soldiers in Revolt (Garden City, N.Y.: Anchor Press, 1975) and William L. Hauser, America's Army in Crisis (Baltimore: Johns Hopkins University Press, 1973), esp. Chs. 6-8.

83. John E. Reilly, "The American Mood: A Foreign Policy of Self-Interest," Foreign Policy, 34 (Spring 1979), found that almost three-quarters of the respondents agreed that "the Vietnam war was more than a mistake, it was fundamentally wrong and immoral."

84. Yankelovich, "Farewell," p. 674; John E. Mueller, "Changes in American Public Attitudes Toward International Involvement," in The Limits of Military Intervention, ed. Ellen P. Stern (Beverly Hills: Sage, 1977), p. 341; William Watts and Lloyd A. Free

"Nationalism, Not Isolationism," Foreign Policy, No. 24 (Fall 1976); Simon, American Public Opinion, p. 84; Daniel Yankelovich, "Cautious Internationalism," Public Opinion (March/April 1978); and "Opinion Roundup," Public Opinion (March/May 1979): 24.

85. Public Opinion (January/February 1979): 29; and Public Opinion (March/May 1979): 22.

86. Reilly, "American Mood," pp. 74, 76, 80-81; and Radway, "Domestic Attitudes," p. 300.

87. Public Opinion (January/February 1979): 29.

88. Meuller, "Changes in American Public Attitudes," pp. 331-37.

89. Public Opinion (March/May 1979): 26. See also Radway, "Domestic Attitudes," p. 313; Russett and Nincic, "American Opinion."

90. Interestingly enough, this disaffection does not extend to the conduct of "total" wars (e. g. , World War II)--perhaps because the United States won. See Mueller, "Changes in American Public Attitudes," pp. 328-29, and Smith, "Disaffection," pp. 221-29.

91. Kristol, "Consensus and Dissent," p. 84. See also Spanier and Uslaner, How American Foreign Policy Is Made, p. 93, and Lunch and Sperlich, "American Public Opinion."

92. See Michael Handel, "The Study of War Termination," The Journal of Strategic Studies, 1/1 (May 1978): esp. 63.

93. For general discussions of the role of the media in the foreign policy process, see Rosenau, Public Opinion, Ch. 6; and Bernard C. Cohen, The Press and Foreign Policy (Princeton, N. J.: Princeton University Press, 1963), Ch. 8.

94. Michael Baruch Grossman and Francis E. Rourke, "The Media and the Presidency: An Exchange Analysis," Political Science Quarterly, 91/3 (Fall 1976): esp. 467.

95. Robert H. Trice, "Foreign Policy Interest Groups, Mass Public Opinion and the Arab-Israeli Dispute," Western Political Quarterly, 31/2 (June 1978); and David B. Truman, The Governmental Process (New York: Knopf, 1971), Ch. 8.

96. Robert S. Frank, Message Dimensions of Television News (Lexington, Mass.: D. C. Heath/Lexington Books, 1973); and Ernest W. Lefever, "The Prestige Press, Foreign Policy, and American Survival," Orbis, 20/1 (Spring 1976).

97. See, for example, Thomas E. Patterson and Robert D. McClure, The Unseeing Eye: The Myth of Television Power in National Politics (New York: G. P. Putnam's Sons, 1976).

98. Grossman and Rourke, "Media and the Presidency," p. 468.

99. Grossman and Rourke, "Media and the Presidency," p. 470; Max M. Kampelman, "The Power of the Press: A Problem for our Democracy," Policy Review, 6 (Fall 1978); and Charles R. D'Amoto,

"The Press and National Security," in Civil-Military Relations, ed. Charles L. Cochran (New York: Free Press, 1974).

100. C. Richard Hofstetter, Bias in the News: Network Television Coverage of the 1972 Election Campaign (Columbus: Ohio State University Press, 1976), pp. 4-11.

101. Cohen, Public's Impact on Foreign Policy, pp. 108-109; Hofstetter, Bias in the News, p. 9.

102. Kampelman, "Power of the Press," pp. 17-20; William H. Lewis, "The Cloning of the American Press," The Washington Quarterly, 2/2 (Spring 1978); and William Schneider, "Public Opinion: The Beginning of Ideology," Foreign Policy, 17 (Winter 1974-75): 108. But Robert S. Frank did not find "(liberal) bias existing uniformly across all message dimensions" (italics in original). See Message Dimensions, p. 73.

103. Arthur H. Miller, Edie N. Goldenberg, and Lutz Erbring, "Type-Set Politics: Impact of Newspapers on Public Confidence," American Political Science Review, 73/1 (March 1979): 69; and Hofstetter, Bias in the News, pp. 85-89, 106-108.

104. Hofstetter, Bias in the News, pp. 172-74; Miller, Goldenberg, and Erbring, "Type-Set Politics," pp. 69 and 80; Michael J. Robinson, "Public Affairs Television and the Growth of Political Malaise: The Case of 'The Selling of the Pentagon'," American Political Science Review, 70/2 (June 1976); Richard A. Pride and Barbara Richards, "Denigration of Authority? Television News Coverage of the Student Movement," Journal of Politics, 36/3 (August 1974); Gelb and Betts, Irony of Vietnam, p. 291; Peter Braestrup, Big Story: How the American Press and Television Reported and Interpreted the Crisis of Tet-1968 in Vietnam and Washington (Boulder, Col.: Westview Press, 1977); and Ernest W. Lefever, TV and National Defense: An Analysis of CBS News, 1972-73 (Boston: Institute for American Strategy Press, 1974).

105. Handel, "War Termination," p. 63; Gelb and Betts, Irony of Vietnam, p. 334.

106. Fulbright, Crippled Giant, p. 177.

107. As in the case of the Vietnam War, "The presidents, Congress, public opinion and the press all both reinforced the stakes against losing and introduced constraints against winning." Gelb and Betts, Irony of Vietnam, p. 25. See also Yankelovich, "Farewell," p. 691.

108. Hans J. Morgenthau, A New Foreign Policy for the United States (New York: Praeger, 1969), pp. 128-29.

109. Alan Ned Sabrosky, Presidential War: The Politics of Military Intervention (in preparation).

4
THE INTERNATIONAL
ENVIRONMENT

This part examines the nonnuclear capability and posture of major European powers, the Soviet Union, China, and Japan. Additionally, it provides an interesting and insightful assessment of alternative doctrines for the conduct of nonnuclear war in Europe. Germany, France, and Great Britain have responded to the post-World War II period in different ways. While Great Britain and West Germany have retreated from a major power posture of the pre-World War II period, France appears to be trying to re-establish some semblance of such a status, at least in the area of nonnuclear capability. West Germany has been the most cautious in this regard, as is to be expected because of its past history. Yet it has undertaken limited "quick strike" operations. Until recently, Great Britain was more concerned with its economic situation than military outreach. Yet both France and Great Britain have been involved in a series of nonnuclear conflicts (low-intensity operations) over the past two decades. The spread of conventional as well as nuclear weaponry will make this an increasingly difficult prospect in the future, particularly if there is involvement by the Soviet Union. The Suez incident seemed to prove this point. There is no denying, however, that energy sources are of vital interest to European powers and prompt concern for some capability to intervene in nonnuclear situations.

One of the most pressing concerns for Western Europe is a conventional response to the possibility of an invasion by Soviet and Warsaw Pact forces. Exploring a German and a French view, the chapter points out the possibilities of political as well as conventional response (deep defense) to such an invasion, combined with a nuclear threat against Soviet and Warsaw Pact political systems. Examining these perspectives, the chapter provides new dimensions to the concept of deterrence. Yet it suggests that the United States as well as its Western allies have little understanding of the role that conventional forces play in Soviet foreign and defense policy. Discussing the changing role of such forces, the chapter notes the shift of Soviet perspectives, which were Western-oriented and focused on Europe. Under the present Soviet leadership, the policy rests on a concept of Hold-Contain-Explore. Thus, conventional forces are used to pursue a policy of holding and stabilizing relations with the West, containing the Chinese threat, and exploring ways to exploit non-European areas. Indeed, the chapter observes that the Soviet Union is assuming an expansionist and imperial role in world affairs, while the United States and the West appear to be retreating from such a role. Finally, Soviet conventional forces perform a variety of political-military roles, including consolidation of Party hegemony and nation building.

The chapter concludes with an examination of China and Japan. While both nations have sought independence and autonomy in international affairs, they differ regarding their military capabilities and military posture. The Peoples Liberation Army has served as an instrument to achieve poser for the Chinese Communist Party, to protect contiguous areas, and secure the Chinese border. It has maintained a close relationship with the Party and has become involved in many political-military functions within China. One of the major concerns is the protection and security of its border with the Soviet Union. The Chinese military power remains primarily conventional, although its nuclear weaponry is improving quantitatively and qualitatively. The Japanese military remains conventional and limited in its capability, although there is significant internal discussion about the role of the Self Defense Forces. Japan's conventional forces are not in a posture to move outside the homeland. Their primary role is defense. Many observers feel, however, that they are hardly capable of succeeding against a determined enemy. In the final analysis, the Japanese military has little influence outside the homeland. Its nonmilitary instruments are by far the most important instruments of policy. Without any appreciable military force or credibility, the Japanese seem to have maximized the effectiveness of their nonmilitary instruments. Yet both China and Japan recognize that conventional military capability is necessary for long-range impact in Asia.

9
THE CONFLICT WITHOUT: EUROPEAN POWERS AND NONNUCLEAR CONFLICT OUTSIDE EUROPE
Catherine McArdle Kelleher

Any assessment of the present capabilities of the major Europea powers for nonnuclear conflict outside Europe must begin with the fundamental ambiguities of national power in a nuclear age. By any objective standard, each of these states--Britain, France, and Germany--ranks as a major power with a broad resource base, signif icant diplomatic and military capabilities, and a critical stake in the maintenance of the existing international order. Viewed broadly, however, only France now actively pursues the political and military goals that were the hallmarks of a prewar major power. These, at a minimum, included the search for (1) a global "reach"; (2) the capacit for swift, decisive, independent intervention in third party disputes; (3) recognition, at home and by others, of a hierarchy of "legitimate" economic and political interests in critical regions outside Europe; and (4) exploitation of targets of opportunity at times of international tension, negotiation, or crisis. Neither Germany nor Britain now pursues such goals or has allowed their principal ally, the United States, to impose these upon them for at least the last decade. More-over, even France has been unable or unwilling to develop the capa-bilities required for effective deterrence and defense outside Europe on the scale pursued in the interwar period.

Acknowledgement is made of the assistance of Robert Beattie, Micha Boyd, and Jeffrey Sanborn in the preparation of the data base used i the preparation of this paper, and the earliest version presented at t International Studies Association Meeting in Toronto, March 1979; a for the critical comments by Edward Kolodziej and Alden Mullins.

The underlying causes are familar and reflect the basic transformation of the postwar international system. For much of the recent
past, only the superpowers have functioned as global actors, able and
willing to attempt worldwide influence and extended nonnuclear
engagement. Both voluntarily and involuntarily, the European states
have pursued a more limited role--Britain and France, at the end of
empire; Germany, after crushing military defeat and occupation. The
principal responsibility for the active defense of Western global interests was to be held by the United States--whatever European doubts,
frustrations over coordination, or ambitions (particularly in France)
for greater direct influence. The European states evolved military
strategies and capabilities that were primarily European-centered,
nuclear-based, and linked (however grudgingly) to a broad Western
consensus on the nature of both the primary Soviet threat and the
requirements of nuclear and nonnuclear defense. More important, each
assigned at least equal importance to stimulating and defending the
national economic base and promoting domestic prosperity. Some of
the reasons were external: the perception, for example, of the ever-
increasing significance of "low politics" and the influence to be gained
by them. Most were domestic, principally the recognition of new,
national welfare "thresholds" that could be lowered only at great political peril and in the face of direct threat to the national integrity. [1]

Yet each of these three states has always possessed sufficient
military capability to have major impact on nonnuclear conflicts
outside the European arena. For Germany and Britain, it is now
largely potential capacity--a function of a broad mobilization base or
of the high levels of military manpower and material now maintained
for NATO purposes. Presently, limited French capabilities are
expandable, given time, resources, and domestic support.

Change in the base conditions of postwar European foreign policy
might activate a shift in national extra-European strategies, whether
it be a significant decrease in U.S. capacity to maintain tolerable
power balances in critical regions (the Middle East, Africa), the
persistence of new threats to economic security (e.g., energy
supplies), or the long-discussed emergence of a European political-
military directorate. The possibility of such changes in the foreseeable future--at least, during the next decade--appear very small:
the domestic and international costs involved are almost certainly
beyond the grasp of existing European political coalitions. But neither
this force potential nor the continuing utility of military force as
national hedge against an uncertain future in Europe or outside it
can be ignored.

Our brief review of European "external capabilities" has three
components: (1) an overview of the postcolonialist evolution of present
extra-European policies and doctrines; (2) a specification of the

conditions for and constraints upon change; and (3) a sketch of critical scenarios for the 1980s. The scope must of necessity be suggestive rather than exhaustive, but the intention is to stimulate comparisons for the international system of the 1980s and the 1990s.

MIDDLE POWERS AND THE USE OF FORCE

We must first ask, however, what are the uses of military force for European powers in a nuclear era? For such states, the usual wisdom has held the exercise of force more broadly, the acquisition of military capability to be of relatively limited direct utility compared to that garnered in earlier eras. The nuclear revolution has imposed both technological and political constraints on European abilities to ensure even minimum levels of national security and to pursue conquest or coercion. The preeminence of the superpowers and the continuation of at least military bipolarity has established even more fundamental limits. Without the acceptance, if not support, of either the United States or the Soviet Union, no European middle power is willing to risk the retaliation which independent large-scale military action outside Europe might provoke. This, it is argued, is as true for nuclear weapons states as it is for those that remain nonnuclear. Middle power military capability, then, has only political uses--the indication of status, the entry fee for alliance with a superpower, the symbol of interest and concern, but not military commitment.

At the most general level, this analysis appears compelling. It reflects the special conditions of postwar East-West stalemate in Europe and the special shape of resulting Atlantic military cooperation. But this broad formulation builds on several critical assumptions that are open to question on both theoretical and practical grounds. [2]

Obviously, middle powers and especially the major European states have used force throughout the postwar period (see Tables 4.1 and 4.2, 4.4 and 4.7 below). [3] Without question, their targets have not been the superpowers, close superpower allies, or even states of essentially the same power rank. The mode of use has also not been large-scale conventional operations of long duration or those resulting in widespread loss of life or destruction, at least to themselves. In part, this reflects the nature and evolution of the decolonization process, the major context in which these states have used force. But the European powers have also used their capability outside Europe for quite traditional ends--to deter threats or compel preferred behavior by hostile states, to support or induce preferable or tolerable political and military outcomes. And their rates of success, while not those of earlier periods of European dominance, have been substantial, particularly if decolonization conflicts are disregarded.

The critical point is that, like the superpowers themselves, the European states have most frequently employed lower levels of violence. Their capabilities have been used to deter, to demonstrate commitment and willingness to engage, to pursue limited objectives and shape limited changes. In the majority of postwar incidents, their use has been reactive or defensive--attempts to stablize existing regimes or restore the status quo ante against the challenges of nationalism, ideological insurgency, or recurring participation crisis. Economic and domestic political restrictions have perhaps left these states less able or willing than they were in the past to use force to exploit targets of opportunity. But in many instances, they have seized the initiative--to show the flag, to exert direct and indirect pressure, to cap or preempt a potential threat.

Moreover, the European middle powers have shown considerable skill in exploiting the political resources which flowed (outside the colonial context) from the simple possession of deployments to show presence, to exhibit to both foes and their own publics their involvement and preparedness against future contingencies. Shifts in capability, modernization of forces and equipment, exploitation of visits, exercises, tendering of emergency or civic assistance--all have symbolized technical prowess and potential performance. Perhaps of greatest short-range significance have been those functions that now seem the surrogates for direct military activity or deployment--grants and equipments, training missions and technical advisors, personal and institutional linkages. [4]

As discussed in greater detail below, the key factors restraining their exercise of force have been economic and political constraints at home. Of almost equal importance, however, has been the posture of the United States. In positive terms, it has been the willingness of the United States, particularly in the 1960s, to act as "world policeman" in the name of the West as a whole. After Korea, the involvement of the European states was often sought and encouraged by Washington but not made a central requirement of alliance. Participation in NATO, and particularly in the Central Front, was deemed their primary direct military contribution. Viewed negatively, the major contextual factor has been the unwillingness of the United States to impede the global decolonization process or to upset the informal regional balances it had ordered (increasingly with Soviet toleration) in Western interest. Any direct European action--military or economic--that sought influence outside these bounds was to be discouraged, if not directly opposed.

HISTORICAL OVERVIEW

A historical overview of the 1960s and early 1970s must distinguish between the three major European states--Britain, France, and
Germany--in terms of changes along two fundamental dimensions:
(1) postwar international involvement; and (2) postwar political and
economic strength. In both cases, the implicit standard of measurement is the position of the emerging superpowers, the United States
and the Soviet Union.

Postwar International Involvement

Britain and France: The most salient characteristic of postwar
European foreign policy is the greatly reduced scope of international
involvement--political, military, and, at least for the first decade or
so, economic. For Britain and France, the most obvious and dramatic
decreases came through the loss of empire and influence in the face of
new nationalisms, and through the precipitous decline in their domestic
economies. The national experiences were different in detail, with the
French both suffering greater direct losses (in Indochina and Algeria)
and retaining eventually a greater number of dependencies or integral
ties (the former French Community, Northern Africa). The broad
pattern, though, was the same: (1) losses of symbolic as well as
physical bases for continuing exercise of influence and power projection; (2) repeated demonstration of apparent military inadequacy,
if not incapacity, across a spectrum of deterrence and defense efforts;
and (3) growing disenchantment at home with the force requirements,
the economic costs, and even the political trappings of graceful retreat
from past imperial commitments.

Perhaps a more traumatic decrease in capability for both countries was that resulting from Suez in 1956. [5] The direct costs were, of
course, far lower than those of Algeria or even Aden. But the loss of
international stature and the demonstration of basic dependence on
superpower wishes were perceived as far more costly, both inside and
outside the national arena. Suez was not just the result of an inadequate
"quick strike" or of an underestimation of the chips held by a resolute
national liberation movement. More basic was the obvious failure to
perceive the limits placed on the use of military force from above. To
be successful, European military intervention--direct or indirect,
using surrogate or national forces--was to be carried out with, not
against, the United States, with Washington secure in its nuclear preeminence, its dominance of European defense requirements, and its
control of European economic destinies. And to confront the Soviet

Union directly over a client state was not only to court a disaster but probably to lose U. S. support as well.

Britain and France drew quite different lessons for future international involvement from this general context. For Britain, Suez was the beginning of fifteen years of "agonizing reappraisal" of its international political and military role. [6] The foundations were laid by Macmillan in 1957: they led to reinstitution of the closest possible alliance with the United States within NATO and throughout the world; the shift primarily to a strategic nuclear emphasis; the reduction of conventional forces both in Europe and overseas; and eventually a quickened pace in decolonization in response to the "wind of change."

The subsequent pattern of reduction and retreat, however, was gradual and marked by continuing employment of force outside Europe (Table 9.1). Under continuing U. S. and senior Commonwealth pressure, Britain continued to perform order-maintaining functions (albeit at lower levels) in its four areas of traditional involvement-- the Far East, the Indian Ocean and the Persian Gulf, the Middle East, and Southern Africa. There were a number of painful and protracted failures--the continuing conflicts on Cyprus, the bloodied withdrawal from Aden, and the self-induced immobilism over Rhodesia. But these were more than matched by British successes in policing or stabilization missions, involved demonstrations, or limited use of forces--Jordan in 1958, Kuwait in 1961, the East African mutinies of 1964, and defense of Malaysia against the Indonesian confrontation of 1963 to 1967. All were supported, directly or indirectly, by U. S. policies and military and economic capabilities, under the "special relationship."

It was not until the middle 1960s, however, that the decisive reappraisal decisions were reached--in the framework of bitter 1966-68 debate about British withdrawal from east of Suez. [7] Continuing British commitments were challenged on two levels: (1) the increasing political vulnerability of the traditional chain of strategic bases in the Near and Far East; (2) the intolerable burden of maintaining even minimal force deployments or credible air and naval intervention capabilities in the face of acute domestic economic crisis. In direct military terms, the era of global engagement as the U. S. junior partner with major deployable, if not deployed, forces for non-nuclear functions outside Europe was at an end. The shift to an exclusively European orientation was a necessity, in terms not only of economic structures but also of the realignment of basic British foreign policy (e. g., the entry into the Community) and of the primary threat to British national security.

TABLE 9.1

Use of Force: 1957–70,
Britain

Year	Country	Action
1957–59	Cyprus	Control of civil crisis
1958	Libya	Stabilization of regime
1958	Jordan	Stabilization of regime
1958	Lebanon	Stabilization of regime
1958	Iceland	Conflict over fishing rights
1960	Congo	Intervention in civil crisis
1961	Kuwait	Defense against Iraq
1961–63	British Guiana	Border dispute with Surinam and Venezuela, civil unrest
1962	Brunei	Control of civil crisis, Indonesian assault
1962	Aden	Defense against Egyptian Invasion
1963–67	Malaysia	Indonesian confrontation
1963–66	Bahamas	Defense against Cuban subversion
1963	Swaziland	Civil unrest
1963–67	Cyprus	Civil crisis, U. N. Force support
1964	Kenya Uganda Tanganyka Zanzibar Zambia	Quelling of civil unrest and East African mutinies
1964–65	British Guiana	Civil insurgency
1964–67	Aden	South Yemen independence conflict with Egypt and insurgents
1966	Rhodesia	Beira channel patrol
1966	Mauritius	Civil insurgency
1969	Anguilla	Constitutional crisis

N. B. Obvious colonial conflicts omitted.
Source: Compiled by the author.

By the end of the 1960s, therefore, the limits of British policy were clear and broadly accepted:

1. no use of force in or outside Europe, without the sanction and support of the United States;
2. no use of force that was not proportionate to, or in deterrence of direct threat to the British homeland;
3. primary reliance outside Europe on methods and strategies of influence that did not involve direct military power (e.g., economic aid, financial manipulation) or direct use of force (e.g., military training, arms sales, limited demonstrations of force);
4. primary reliance on the United States above the lowest conflict levels.

France, and particularly General deGaulle after 1958, drew somewhat different implications for France's future international role.[8] The key was the now-familiar policy of grandeur, the search for a French role proportionate (though not equal) in influence to that of the superpowers. A policy of autonomous national nuclear power under a U.S. nuclear umbrella that could not be folded against France would eventually produce the greatest degree of influence, both in Europe and outside it. The areas of major French interest--North Africa, Francophone Africa, the Mediterranean, the Middle East-- would remain within the French circle of influence because of France's global standing, its active membership in the nuclear club. The pre-servation of French influence would be easiest within the type of global foreign policy directorate deGaulle proposed in 1958 to the United States and Britain; but it would still be pursued in the face of minimal U.S. opposition or toleration.

The search for influence outside Europe primarily involved diplomatic, not military, instruments. Once the nightmare of Algeria was ended, deGaulle began an ambitious two-pronged strategy toward the Third World. The first was a posture of opposition to superpower, particularly U.S., hegemony and intervention in the Third World. With rhetoric, focused economic and military assistance, and flying Presidential visits, Gaullist France was prepared to support neu-tralist positions vis-a-vis the superpowers. It attempted to pose a rhetorical alternative, without direct national confrontation, to U.S. policies (except perhaps on Vietnam) and to demonstrate a willingness to make common cause, according to circumstance, with any regime-- Third World, Soviet, or Chinese. It was a balancing act requiring the greatest flexibility and skill: in the period before the crisis of 1968, deGaulle indeed scored a number of symbolic and personal victories. But there were unquestionably a larger number of diplomatic defeats (e.g. Latin America, Canada, Cambodia, the 1967 Arab-Israeli dilemma).

DeGaulle's strategy, however, also placed considerable emphasis on both the maintenance of an overseas presence and the demonstration of French willingness to use that force to defend its interests and its friends (Table 9.2). In all but the most limited demonstrations of force or deterrence attempts, the principal instrument was not to be regular French forces, scarred by Algeria and the several coup attempts, and which would drain scarce resources needed for the initial phases of the nuclear programs. Rather, special elite forces would be used from within the professional military—those trained within the Gendarmerie, the traditional French Legion. With respect to former Community members in Africa and the mini-territories France still retained in the Indian Ocean and the Pacific, these forces could be regionally deployed and used primarily for quick, decisive interventions (e.g. Gabon). Some might also be assigned longer low-level missions given adequate supplies and a relatively friendly general environment (e.g., the protracted war in Chad). But all would operate in direct response to French interests in regional balances, not those of the broader Western coalition from which France had now overtly withdrawn.

In effect, most of the uses of French military force outside Europe during the 1960s were virtually indistinguishable from the domestic policing functions of a colonial power. Most were in Black Africa and in the poorest and weakest of the former colonies. Most involved exercises in regime support through limited demonstrations of force or continued campaigns of limited engagements against dissident troops or rebel groups. Only a few were directed at external enemies or the client states of the superpowers. And in several instances, France was unable to prevent its clients from seeking additional or substitute "indirect" assistance from the Soviet Union--in the form of economic aid or military shipments.

Thus, by the end of the 1960s, the lines of French policy were generally these:

1) no use of force in direct opposition to direct U.S. or Soviet presence;
2) no use of force not proportionate to the direct threat to established French overseas interests or the national homeland; and
3) reliance on a mixed strategy of direct military presence and control in important dependent regions, "indirect" military capability (training, arms sales, demonstrations of force) elsewhere, rhetorical support for anti-superpower actions, symbolism of military strength (establishment of credibility in terms of military

TABLE 9.2

Use of Force: 1957-70,
France

Year	Country	Action
1960-64	Cameroon	Regime support
1961-63	Tunisia	Conflict over Bizerte Naval Base
1963	Brazil	Fishing dispute
1963	Congo Brazzaville	Regime support
1964	Gabon	Regime support
1965	Martinique	Civil crisis
1965-67	Chad	Regime support
1966-67	Somalia	Conflict over boundaries and insurgency in territory of Afars and Issas
1967	Guadaloupe	Civil unrest
1967	Central African Republic	Regime support
1968-78	Chad	Regime support

Note: Exclusively colonial conflicts with Algeria, Cameroons,
      Morocco, and Tunisia have been excluded.
Source: Compiled by the author.

capability and national resolve).

Germany: Germany's pattern of postwar international involvement throws these developments into even sharper relief. For at
least the first two decades after defeat, German international activity
outside Europe was at an imperceptible level and largely conducted in
direct coordination with, if not at the urgent request of, the United
States. German colonies had disappeared after World War I; Bonn's
attempts at postwar reinstitution and rehabilitation involved only
secondarily states other than the major belligerents in World War II.
Perhaps the only exceptions involved German relations with Israel
and German attempts to deny legitimacy to the GDR, both clearly
symbolic acts.

During this period there were massive constraints, domestic and international, on the acquisition of independent German military power. [9] Bonn's involvement even in the European strategy of the West was subject to strict external control through alliance integration and a major U. S. presence, not to mention shrill challenges from the East. A role outside Europe was explicitly rejected by the allies for Germany and by the Germans themselves, acutely conscious of their own political and diplomatic vulnerability and of their own unresolved past. President Johnson's attempts to secure German involvement in Vietnam in the late 1960s met with direct resistance in Germany and considerable amazement elsewhere. Germany's fundamental dependence on the United States for its own security notwithstanding, German involvement of this type was simply unthinkable.

Basically, then, the German policy was

1. no use of force or even nominal military pressure outside the integrated Central Front; and
2. reluctant use of military-related influence strategies--training, assistance, weapons transfer or trans-shipment—only when all other instruments had been tried, and at the explicit request of the United States.

Postwar Political and Economic Strength

The details of the postwar decline in European political and economic strength are so well-known as to require only a brief sketch here. The broad concusions to be drawn are three. First, despite the high growth period of the 1960s, the economic stature of Britain and France declined both absolutely and relative to that of both the United States and West Germany. The causes were and still are complex and in many senses not totally amenable to national solutions. Most observers argued that France had a better chance than Britain (even with North Sea oil) to stabilize at its present level, but both states were increasingly seen as "falling behind."

Second, a significant component in this decline during the 1950s and early 1960s was the loss of assured national access to traditional overseas investments, markets, and resources. Both Britain and France were able to reverse this trend during the late 1960s, through vigorous diplomatic efforts (the stability of the pro-British Persian Gulf states and the Malaysian balance). Both states, however, remained more the beneficiary than the manager of critical economic patterns in major overseas areas--a position that presumably will not change in the foreseeable future. Germany's overseas economic dependence was far more limited in scope and, because of the broader domestic economic base, was far more insulated against short-run perturbations, political crises, or even regime changes.

Third, all three states experienced marked increases in perceived international economic vulnerability during the 1960s and the early 1970s. The principal causes were (1) successful U. S. export of Vietnam-related inflation; (2) continuing (and sometimes intervening) dispute between the United States and the major European states over monetary and fiscal coordination; and (3) adverse impacts, primary and secondary, of the 1973 oil crisis and its political aftermath.

The cumulative impact of these developments was the continuing European paradox: increased external economic weakness and vulnerability (and thus, increased dependence on Western coordination) at a time when national capabilities to influence extra-European events and prospects for concerted Atlantic or European action were at postwar lows. Each of the three states drew up quite distinct national strategies both to deal with direct consequences and to hedge against future developments outside Europe that would leave them even more exposed.

The British, hardest hit because of their declining domestic economy, retreated perhaps the farthest toward a Eurocentric or even a "little England" solution. While all public expenditures underwent major reduction, the most substantial cuts were in categories concerning overseas commitments and expenditures.[10] By 1962, Britain had replaced its major imperial commitments with Commonwealth links. By the end of 1975, it had divested itself of all but the smallest mini-territories (e.g., the Falklands, Hong Kong, Bermuda,) and the least onerous Commonwealth pledges (e. g., the Five Power agreement in defense of Singapore). Public monies were spent overseas either on transitional assistance or to promote development toward eventual autonomous status. All future planning, including that on the utilization of North Sea oil profit, was oriented toward maintaining the existing level of domestic prosperity in terms of economic growth and broad social welfare.

In many respects, therefore, Britain returned to an earlier strategy: reliance on private commercial organizations and quasi-governmental agencies to pursue and defend basic British extra-European interests. Beyond the activities of oil companies and other multinationals, Britain apparently relied to an increasing degree on its long-standing financial links, and its position as arms supplier (not always officially) and traditional training center for both newer Commonwealth and non-Commonwealth states. However, no objective measure of the scope or the impact of these activities exists, nor was the degree of governmental steering or control made totally explicit.

The French government, first under Pompidou and then under Giscard, pursued a more ambitious strategy of domestic and international economic growth.[11] Domestic programs posited simultaneous efforts toward greater domestic welfare (e. g. , social capital investment, employment stimulation, draw-down of inefficient industries) and rigorous efforts to control inflation and lagging growth rates. Success was gradual, and, under Giscard, perceived as heavily dependent on intra-European, especially Franco-German, coordination. The external strategy, on the other hand, was posited on independent French efforts in areas of greatest risk to French economic security-- the Mediterranean and the Arab oil producers. French goals in these areas required a combination of greater economic involvement (investment, assistance, and technology transfer) and "indirect" military capability (training, arms transfer, and arms sales) as well as vigorous diplomatic efforts to establish Paris as both the Arabs' friend and the "interlocuter" for the West.

German policies involved the most extensive international orientation and the most ambitious efforts to secure and maintain global economic influence. Particularly under Chancellors Brandt and Schmidt, the key was expansion outward from a vigorous, controlled, noninflationary domestic base--the real Modell Deutschland. Moreover, successive German governments took steps to exploit their economic base both to gain new areas of influence and to reduce their political vulnerability. Such steps were made possible primarily by Germany's increasing role as Europe's banker, but also by progressively more skillful German manipulation of foreign trade, governmental development assistance, and her position as the third-ranking power in the Western economic system. Military aid programs were kept low-key, although there were several significant efforts in Black Africa.

The consequences of these economic strategies for national defense efforts were, however, quite similar. For no one of these states was a major increase in either military expenditure or military manpower deemed a necessary or appropriate policy. As Table 9. 3 demonstrates, the trends in both areas were downward or relatively flat. Moreover, the share of defense expenditure as a proportion of either state budgets or of overall GNP declined measurably.

TABLE 9.3

European Military Expenditures and Personnel, 1960-77

	1960	1967	1970	1974	1977
Indices of Military Expenditures in constant prices (1970 = 100)					
Britain	100.6	109.3	100	115.4	139.4
France	85.7	102.3	100	108.1	120.7
Germany	70.2	102.6	100	124.2	123.8
Numbers of Military Personnel (in thousands)					
Britain	520	417	373	345	330
France	781	500	506	503	503
Germany	270	452	466	490	489

Source: I. I. S. S. The Military Balance 1978-1979

PRESENT DOCTRINE AND CAPABILITIES

France

Of the three states, France is clearly the most ambitious and the most explicit in its planning for nonnuclear capabilities for use outside Europe. In part, this is the result of continuing French commitments, particularly within the former French community (Tables 4.4, 4.5, and 4.6). But in largest measure, it is a function of the explicit reorganization of French military doctrine and capabilities being attempted by the Giscard government.

The keynote of the Giscard program is an overall increase in France's capability to influence an increasingly complex international environment. [12] Giscard has reaffirmed the continuing need for an independent modernized force de frappe, for French "autonomy of decision" over questions of national existence. But, in the face of heated debate even within his own coalition, the President and military leaders close to him have stressed the pressing dictates of conventional force improvement and increase. Strengthened conventional forces would (1) increase the credibility of the nuclear deterrent by vitiating "all or nothing" choices; (2) allow for a more active French role in European defense, including the possible protection of the "extended sanctuary" of West Germany; and (3) allow limited, timely support for the defense of wide-ranging French interests outside Europe, hopefully without compromising the deterrent or France's European obligations.

The particular extra-European interests to be defended have been defined in a number of somewhat ambiguous and occasionally contradictory statements by French leaders. One clear arena is Francophone Africa--both because of France's "historic links" and because of the "expanding economic interests" France has with many of the other new states there. France has tendered military assistance and direct support to the former French community states since the early 1960s (Tables 9.4 and 9.5). The Giscard program thus builds on the French post-colonial strategy of "deployed forces"--the maintenance at key points of small numbers of regular and special forces that can be used for demonstrations, limited rapid interventions, or even protracted limited operations. Thus, what is new is only the reaffirmation of French determination to remain in place, the renewed emphasis on technical and equipment assistance, and the relative relaxation of earlier French strictures on relations with and assistance from other Western states (Table 9.6).

TABLE 9. 4

Use of Force: 1971-79,
France

Year	Country	Action
1973-78	Chad	Regime support
1976	Djibouti	Defense against Somali intervention
1977-79	Mauritania	Regime support, over Western Sahara
1977	Zaire (Shaba I)	Airlift of Moroccan troops for regime support
1978	Zaire (Shaba II)	Legion used for regime support
1978	Lebanon	Participation in UNFIL (UN force in Lebanon)

Source: Compiled by the author.

French participation in the Zaire interventions marks a new turn in French involvement. Shaba II in particular underlined the willingness for integration with U. S. transport/support groups and the pressures for Moroccan cooperation, as well as the direct use of French Legionnaires. The enthusiastic French domestic reaction has also not been a liability. A precisely similar set of circumstances is unlikely to recur, but the potential for limited, direct French interventions outside the former Community states now seems established. And the demonstration of France's inflexibility--its willingness to cooperate with the United States and to act in the name of broader Western interests--marks a definite policy shift.

Giscard's definition of critical areas seemingly places the Middle East, particularly the Eastern Mediterranean, in the second rank of concern. In this he is continuing the Pompidou efforts to consolidate French influence with "traditional friends" (e. g. , Syria), to develop France's position as the intermediary between Western Europe and the Arab world, and to set some limits to superpower preeminence and pre-emption. The measure of French success is not yet clear.

TABLE 9.5

Overseas Deployments: France

	1966[1]	1978[2, 3]
I Total Forces	522,500	
II Army Overseas		
Algeria	3 rgts	
Africa	3 rgts	
Senagal		1,000
Ivory Coast		400
Gabon		450
Chad		1,500
Niger		200
Djibouti	3 bn	4,000
Lebanon		
UNIFIL		1,244
Overseas		
Commands		
Caribbean		1 bn
New Caledonia	1 bn	1 bn
Polynesia	1 bn	1 bn
Contract	3,000	3,000
Totals overseas	15,000	19,000
III Navy Overseas		
Indian Ocean		
And Pacific Command	not available	9 freighters
		1 tender
		transport/support
Africa	not available	5 coastal escorts
IV Air Force Overseas		
Algeria	400	400
Senegal		500
		transport/support
Overseas		36 helicopters
Commands		15 transport
		12 combat aircraft

Note: bn = batallion rgt = regiment
Sources: [1] I. I. S. S. The Military Balance 1966-67
[2] I. I. S. S. The Military Balance 1978-79
[3] Dupuy, T. N. The Almanac of World Military Power, 1974

TABLE 9.6

French Military Assistance (Africa), 1960-78

Country	Type of[1] Agreements	Direct Assistance[2]	Training Aid[2]	Bases[1,2]
Algeria	D		yes	
Benin	C		no	
Cameroon	B	$7 million annually (until 1973)	yes	
Central African Republic (Empire)	A		yes	
Chad	C	$1.2 million annually	yes	yes
Congo (Brasaville)	C	equipment	no	
Dahomey		$10 million subsidy	yes	
Afars and Issas (Djibouti)	A/B	equipment stocks future pledges	yes	yes
Gabon	A	$.8 million annually	yes	yes
Ivory Coast	A	equipment aid	yes	yes
Malagasy Republic	B	$12.5 mil. annually (until 1973)	yes	yes
Mauritania	D	$1.2 million (until 1966) equipment	yes	
Morocco		$? (until 1966)	yes	
Niger	A		yes	
Senegal	B	(since 1974)	yes	yes
Togo	C		yes	no
Upper Volta	A	initial $43 mil.	yes	no
Zaire	D	assistance	yes	no

Key to Defense Agreements:

A. Treaties of defense and military cooperation providing for technical and equipment assistance, training, basing rights, internal security aid, transfer and overflight rights

B. Military cooperation agreement

C. Agreement on technical military cooperation

D. Training, equipment assistance

Sources: [1]I. I. S. S. The Military Balance 1978-1979

[2]Dupuy, T. N. et al. , The Almanac of World Military Power, 1974

Did, for example, Giscard's 1978 offer of a French force to stabilize the situation in Lebanon provoke only more "imperialist" memories among the Arab states, or was it recognized as a legitimate expression of continuing French concern? Has French participation in the trouble-ridden UNFIL (Lebanon) alleviated anxieties, exacerbated them, or had basically no effect?

A third geographic area of French interest is unquestionably the Indian Ocean-Persian Gulf arena. Since the early 1970s, the French have maintained a considerable naval presence in the region, accounting at several points for a greater number of "ship days" than either the United States or the Soviet Union. French capability is unquestionably vulnerable--both to the availability of basing (Djibouti and the Diego Suarez base in the Malagasy Republic) and the somewhat aging French long distance navy (the strains, for example, of attempting a regular rotation of a French carrier from the Mediterranean to the Indian Ocean). But it is an effort Giscard is publicly committed to continue and, despite Gaullist opposition, one for which he, at least, has been willing to sacrifice a faster-paced modernization of French strategic nuclear forces.

A more general class of interests to be defended are what the Giscard government has defined as "vital components of French economic security." The argument of the 1976 White Paper, the first postwar document to specify these interests, focused on two issues: (1) French dependence on access to energy resources, raw materials, and foreign markets; and (2) new French obligations for the defense of the 200-nautical-mile economic zone ordained in 1976 under Law of the Sea agreements around not only France, but its scattered small islands in the Pacific and in the Caribbean. [13] Both are sources of new vulnerability--targets for threats which may or may not "bring France to its knees," but where the limited application of disruptive force could have enormous consequences for French stature and overseas credibility.

The broad French response to these concerns formed the basis of the 1976 loi de programmation for 1977-82, [14] which emphasizes conventional capability and the decoupling of nuclear forces from extra-European capability "except under extreme circumstances." The basic requirements of a new naval strategy have been most clearly stated: (1) the need to maintain a naval presence in both the Mediterranean and in the Indian Ocean; (2) the need to deploy swiftly in the face of impending crisis (e.g., the 1976 deployment of warships to the Red Sea at the time of Djibouti's independence); and (3) the need to develop small, fast naval forces capable of limited combat actions, a holding defense against interruption of the sea lanes, and military support functions. Larger operations will probably involve allied cooperation (e. g. , recent French cooperation in NATO naval exercises) because of French limitations and anticipated convergence of Western interests.

In implementing both this force reorganization and the broader extra-European strategy, the Giscard government faces formidable and perhaps insurmountable obstacles. The most obvious are the economic constraints. The past three defense budgets have seen substantial slippage in naval allocations, absolutely essential to maintain the naval profile at 1976 levels (Figures 9. 1 and 9. 2).[15] The demands for domestic economic prosperity, the unresolved problems of unemployment, and the impact of continuing inflation on force acquisition--all insure a continuing gap between programmatic reach and grasp.

More fundamental is the adamant opposition both on the political level and within the French military establishment to major emphasis on French extra-European commitments and capabilities: particularly on the left, this stems in part from ideological objections to a new French imperialism or Giscard's edging backward to an "Atlantic France."[16] But the problem is viewed primarily as one of opportunity cost--the impossibility in an era of slowing economic growth and constrained economic resources of maintaining both a modern nuclear force and a major conventional capability for global influence, if not direct intervention. As yet, there has been no major forced choice. But any significant economic downturn or French intervention that leads to a protracted engagement of any scale may well precipitate a debate over France's extra-European role. In the present French political line-up, it is by no means certain that the Giscard position will prevail.

Britain and Germany

Neither Britain nor Germany has developed as systematic or as explicit a policy on the use of nonnuclear forces outside Europe. Most of Britain's "economic security" aims seem equally applicable to her current economic situation; few of the "traditional links" would seem applicable. For both countries, however, public discussion of such aims or strategies seems unthinkable, and, for very different reasons, each faces major domestic constraints even on the eventual design, let alone implementation, of specifically designated capabilities. Both, however, possess considerable deployment flexibility in terms of their general nonnuclear forces now depolyed in Europe (Table 9. 7).

Britain: The British posture is the clearest, an outgrowth not only of the finality of the withdrawal from east of Suez, but also of the outcome of recent defense debates, both within the military structure

FIGURE 9.1

Number of Ships: France

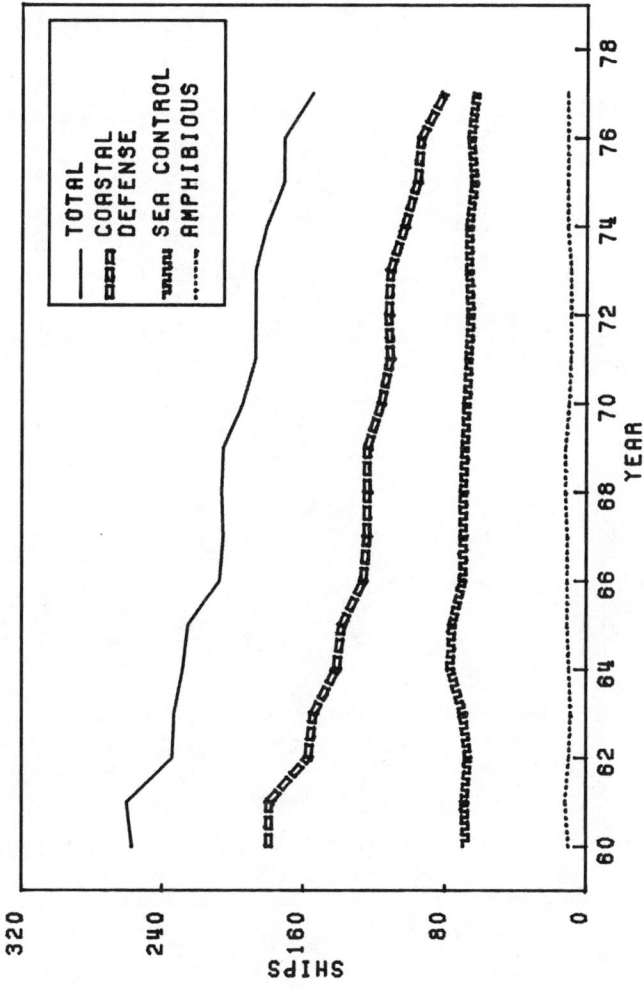

Source: Constructed by the author.

FIGURE 9.2

Average Age Per Ship: France

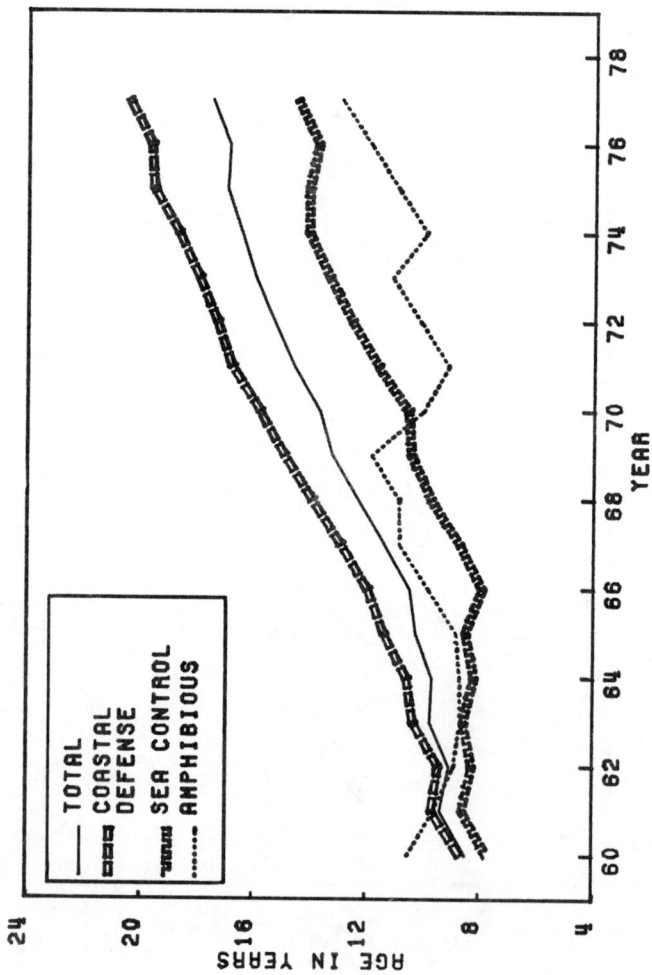

Source: Constructed by the author.

TABLE 9.7

European-Based Forces Potentially Deployable
Outside of Europe, 1978-79

	LONG-RANGE (1500+ miles)	MID-RANGE (1500 Miles)	GROUND TRANS-PORTABLE
United Kingdom	1 CDO bde 3 paratroop bn 1 SAS rgt 1 ASW/CDO carrier 2 helo cruiser 2 assault ships 4 Royal Marines (7500) 5 sqd Vulcan 2 sqd tankers VC 10 transports	inf bn-regular 3 sqd light transport 20 Cl30s	10 armed rgt 9 armed recon rgt
France	4 DC 8 F 6 sqd Mirage 33 3 sqd KC 135 F 1 para div 1 airmobile div 2 light aircraft carrier 2 LDS 2 supply ships ? DC-6s	2 inf div 1 alpine div 45 c-160s 60 Noralas	3 mech div (CRS capability) (Gendarmerie capability)
Federal Republic of Germany	1 para/cdo bde Frontier Police grp	inf bn-regular 10 LST 50 Noralas 12 C 130s 100 + C47 + C160	1 armed div 1 armed bde

Note: rgt = regiment
      bn = batallion
      bde = brigade
      cdo = commando
      helo = helicopter

Source: I.I.S.S., The Military Balance 1978-1979

and in public. The expenditure constraints and double-digit inflation of the 1970s have led to three successive defense reviews that provided for even more geographic contraction (to the Central Front essentially), command reorganization, divisional reductions, and stretch-out, if not cuts, of supply, transport, and logistics functions. [17] Many commentators have agreed with Government assessments that there is very little left to cut, and certainly no margin for the assessments that there is very little left to cut, and certainly no margin for the assumption of new responsibilities within Europe, let alone outside it. Indeed, one Labour Executive study concluded in 1977 that it might soon be a question of choosing between major military functions for the 1980s—an independent air arm, a refitted SSBN force, even a "gray water" navy, and a British Army on the Rhine. In terms of current structures and rates of men/material expenditures, only two might be "supportable."

Clearly, such prognoses are too extreme. Neither Britain nor any European middle power is "too fat" or "too poor" to maintain existing capabilities given even a moderate level of economic growth and popular support. Moreover, even the post-east-of-Suez drawdown has left Britain with significant deployable forces. Of the non-American NATO navies, the British force unquestionably has the "longest reach" (Figures 9.3 and 9.4). [18] It maintains a larger number of sea control vessels (albeit some of advanced age) as well as those suited by tonnage, fueling requirements, and hardware to perform presence missions, and demonstrate direct and indirect military support. Its bases are sharply reduced in number, but alternatives in the close Commonwealth states and in other relatively friendly nations are both possible and currently in commercial use.

The more fundamental questions for Britain appear to be the scope and areas of use that would be politically acceptable, both domestically and among its present client states. Present deployments are clearly at minimal levels (Tables 9.7a and 9.7b). Recent exercises in the use of force have been very limited in scope and largely restricted to points of little political significance or controversy. (Table 9.8). The latest phase in the Cod War with Iceland was perhaps something of an exception, but it was generally considered irrelevant, and wasteful. On the other hand, any major new independent British attempt at direct support or intervention--say in Southern Africa or the Persian Gulf--would appear to be unacceptable and to risk major opposition and intolerable political and economic costs. The present deployment of forces and available transport and support capabilities rule out any rapid actions without substantial allied (i.e., U.S.) approval, support, and cooperation. And without a major shift in the present international environment, any extended operation would almost certainly elicit a domestic political veto, however tough-minde

FIGURE 9.3

Number of Ships: Britain

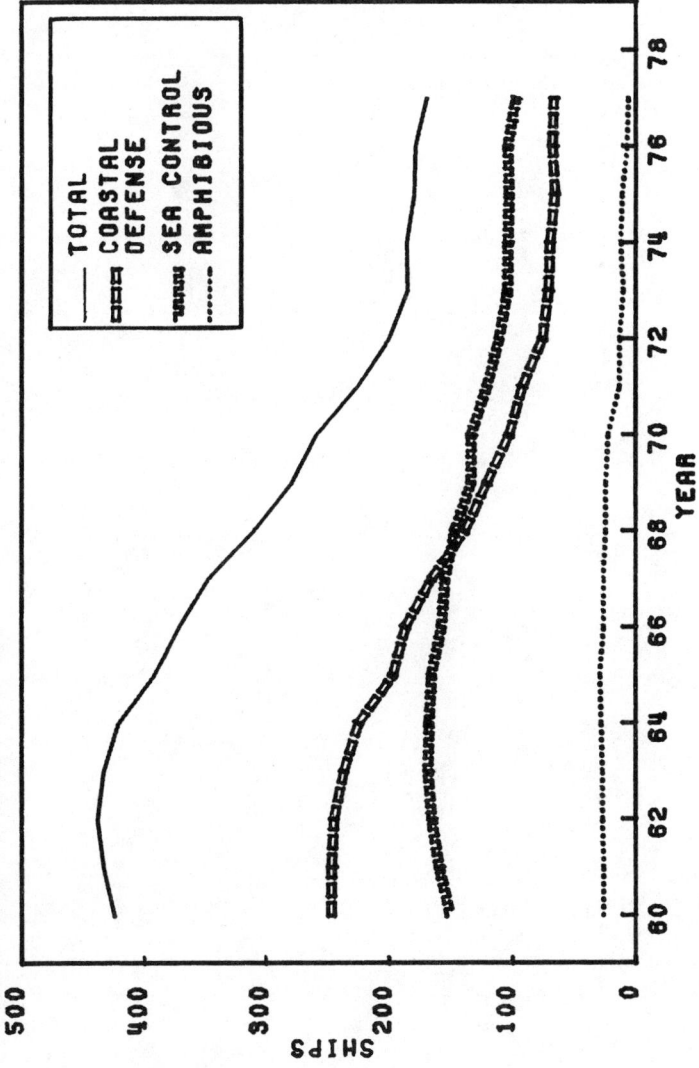

Source: Constructed by the author.

FIGURE 9.4

Average Age Per Ship: Britain

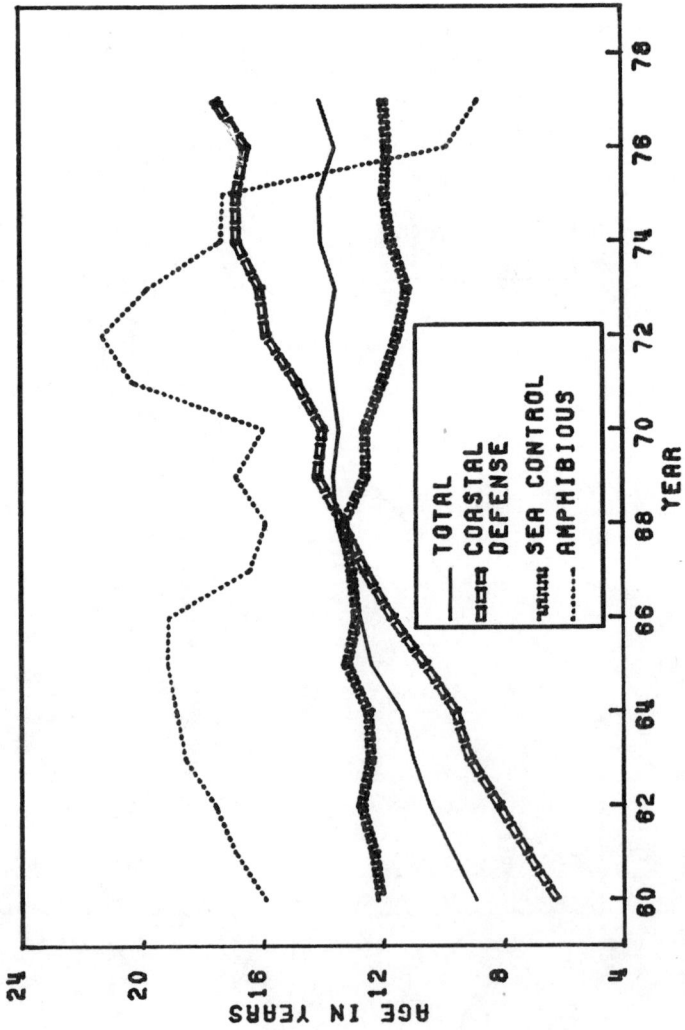

Source: Constructed by the author.

TABLE 9. 7a

Overseas Deployments : Britain (Army and Navy)

	1966[1]	1978[2]
I Total Forces	437,600	313,253
II Army		
Gibraltar		1 inf bn/support forces
Cyprus		
Base Forces	2+ bn	1+ inf bn, 1 recon sqn
		1 helicopter flight
UN Forces	1,000 men	1 inf bn, 1 recon sqn
		1 helicopter flight,
		Support Forces
Aden and The		
Persian Gulf	7 bn	Loan Personnel
Hong Kong	4 bn	1 British bn
	Support Units	3 Gurka bns, Support Units
Malaysia and	9 bn	
Singapore		
Borneo	2 British bns	
	6 Gurka bns	
Brunei		1 Gurka bn (contract)
Malacca	1 inf bn	
	(Commonwealth	
	Brigade)	
Belize	Colonial Forces	1+ inf bn, 1 recon sqn
		1 helo flt, support units
Others	Libya, Malta	
	Swaziland	
III Navy		
Belize	No	1 Frigate, Support
Malta	Specific	1 Commando Group
	Information	(through 1979)
Falkand	Available	1 Marine Detachment
Islands		
Hong Kong		5 Patrol Craft
Far East		1 Helicopter Cruiser
(Group		Frigates
Deployment)		

Note: bn = battalion   grp = group   recon = reconnaisance
          flt = fleet   helo = helicopter   sqn = squadron
Sources: [1] I.I.S.S. The Military Balance 1966-1967
              [2] I.I.S.S. The Military Balance 1978-1979

TABLE 9.7b

Overseas Deployments: Britain
(Air Force and Totals)

	1966	1978
IV Air Force		
Aden	1+ sqn	
Belize	Colonial Forces	2 sqns
Cyprus	1 Fighter sqn	2 sqns
	1 strike wing	
Gibraltar	1 recon grp	Aircraft
Hong Kong		1+ helo sqns
Malta	1 recon grp	2 sqns (through 1979)
Far East	1 V Bomber Det	
	other gnd attack,	
	recon, and fighter	
	aircraft	
V Total		
Men Deployed Outside Europe	136,000[1]	60,000[2]
VI Total		
Costs Outside Europe	£190 millions[3] out of £2,172 defense expenditures (£= $2.80)	£92 millions[4] out of £7,212 defense expenditures (£= $1.80)

Sources: [1] C.J. Bartlett, The Long Retreat, Ch. VI
[2] Great Britain, Statement on Defense Estimates 1978
[3] I.I.S.S. The Military Balance 1966–1967
[4] I.I.S.S. The Military Balance 1978–1979

the posture of Thatcher Conservatives.

Germany: Viewed broadly, the German posture on extra-European involvement remains that of the 1960s: Germany maintains no interests or intentions worth the political or economic costs of direct action. The Federal Republic has capabilities that could unquestionably be deployed over an extended period. It has insisted on maintaining

TABLE 9. 8

Use of Force: 1971-79
Britain

Year	Country	Action
1972	Guatemale	Defense of British Honduras
1972-73	Iceland	Cod War I
1974	Cyprus	Greek-Turkish crisis
1975	Guatemale	Defense of Belize
1975-76	Iceland	Cod War II
1976	Argentina	Falkland Islands dispute
1977	Guatemale	Defense of Belize
1977	Bermuda	Response to civil unrest

a sea control mission within the loose NATO naval structure (Figures
9. 5 and 9. 6) and has at times contemplated the development of a
longer naval reach. Moreover, the dramatic rescue of hijacked pas-
sengers at Mogadishu demonstrated both a limited rapid response capability and the determination to protect basic national commitments,
at least to German citizens. In a crisis, without too much stretching,
extra-European deployment of German contributions to NATO's
mobile task forces might also be possible.

But, even more than for Britain, the issue is the limits of
political acceptability, domestic and international. It is difficult to
imagine the circumstances under which allied agreement for a German
initiative, even within an allied force, would be forthcoming. It is
even more difficult to imagine what would prompt agreement on the
part of the present or any foreseeable German government. The
dramatic political costs to be borne within Europe as well as outside
it, the domestic outcry, the range of nonmilitary instruments available to an economically strong Germany—all make consideration of
direct military involvement outside Europe appear virtually impossible.

What might be expected is a gradual expansion of indirect
German involvement—through larger training and equipment assistance programs (or sales). The rationale would have far less to do
with economic factors--the lowering of unit production costs or the
offsetting or resource constraints--than have the French and British
decisions. Rather the aim would be demonstration of German interest

FIGURE 9.5

Number of Ships: West Germany

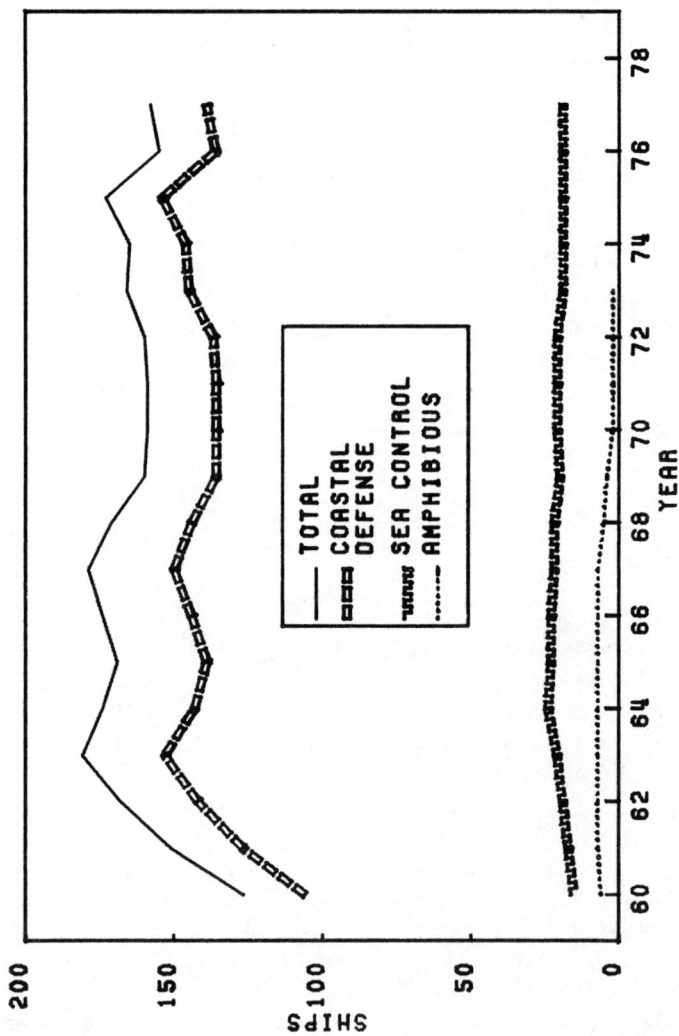

Source: Constructed by the author.

FIGURE 9.6

Average Age Per Ship: West Germany

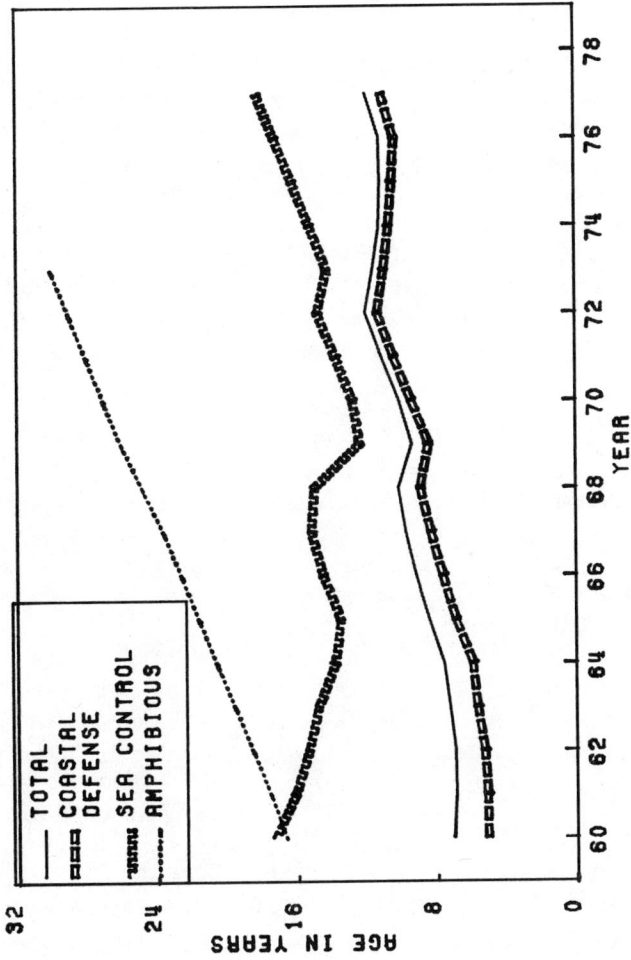

Source: Constructed by the author.

and potential for political purposes. This would, however, undercut German efforts within Europe to stimulate arms production cooperation and to insist on a NATO-wide two-way street. And in some respects, it would face the convictions of German business that larger military production is of relatively little interest when compared to other more profitable domestic and international economic activities.[19]

FUTURE PERSPECTIVES

The question remains: Under what circumstances might there be an increase (or decrease) in the use of force by the major European powers in conflicts outside Europe? Our analysis suggests a number of possibilities, but four base conditions clearly emerge as most salient. These would be major changes in (1) the present domestic political and economic context of European policies; (2) the level of congruence between U.S. and European interests outside Europe; (3) the technological and production requirements of European military capability; and (4) European perceptions of external threat.

Factors that would produce changes of the first type are perhaps the most difficult to predict. In the present international environment, there seems little popular or elite support for an expansion of extra-European military involvement. Whatever the decline in optimism about detente, few are willing to consider significant military expansion even to meet European defense requirements. Domestic economic needs are the first priority and the cycle of rising expectations and frustration with governmental performance in improving the quality of individual life leaves little room for considerations of influence attempts outside the European or perhaps the national realm.

What might precipitate change is a series of clear external threats, particularly to resource flows of critical significance to everyday existence. Protracted interruption of energy supplies would constitute a base case; other types of resource-related threats are more difficult to conceive. A second set of contingencies might be those involving systematic attacks on normal commerce and communication, individual and national. Extensive extra-European support of terrorism against European targets or continuing piracy and blockage would probably stimulate domestic support for a vigorous national response and a twentieth century version of gunboat diplomacy.

But other responses are more likely. First steps would almost certainly include a full range of diplomatic moves. Moreover, both Britain and Germany have consistently preferred economic payoffs, direct and indirect, to the use of military means against low-level blackmail or obstruction. At a somewhat higher level of threat, there would be pressure to explore an alliance response rather than national action--one that would involve at least the United States, if not other major European actors.

This would clearly be the preferred option in the event of widespread Soviet or Soviet-backed disruptions of critical regional balances. Again, primary importance would be attached to the Middle East and the assurance of oil supplies. For Britain and France, local balances in Africa would seem significant secondary concerns. France clearly has the highest stakes under its current foreign policy; British interests are probably largely symbolic. Only one highly improbable event might stimulate major British debate and demands for action: clear Soviet backing for a direct invasion of or racial civil war in South Africa.

A change in the degree of convergence between American and European interests in global and regional balances would be a second critical factor. A number of Europeans on both the Left and the Right already see a steady erosion of the Atlantic consensus on questions of European defense, as well as energy policy, fiscal coordination, and future economic growth. A direct threat to European energy supplies that did not engender an appropriate U. S. response might well precipitate an alliance crisis—though not necessarily national or European action. Similarly a degree of U. S. -Soviet agreement that was seen to disregard or penalize European interests, military or economic, would produce debate and further attenuation of alliance ties.

The most likely replacement, however, would be a series of bilateral European agreements establishing cooperative and consultative arrangements. Past experience apparently indicates that these would not, in the short run, stimulate emergence of a European instance (inter-nation or supra-nation) with both the legitimacy and the capability to demonstrate and defend overseas stakes and preferences.

A final set of changes to be considered is new weapons technologies and production arrangements. Over the past several years, numerous analyses have emphasized the new opportunities for more efficient, less costly military accuracy, and firepower of conventional weaponry. European states, among others, will presumably be able to acquire a "longer reach" and more rapid response capabilities at far less cost, in terms of both military expenditures and personnel requirements. While the principal advantages would be within the European arena, these improvements could be applied to extra-European missions as well.

Such developments, however, would involve as many constraints as opportunities. First, lower costs may as easily lead to lower levels of effort in the absence of political support and direct threat or incentive. The cost of alternative diplomatic and political responses will almost certainly be still lower, without a simultaneous change in the international environment. More basically, past experience with other "wonder weapons" suggests the need for considerable skepticism about short-range and long-range consequences of new weaponry. These advantages will be as available to non-European states who can afford advanced weaponry as to European states. And the type of technology involved--especially that of cruise missiles--will in a very short time be within the grasp of the majority of states.

NOTES

1. For a more detailed examination of this theme see Catherine Kelleher, William Domke, and Richard Eichenberg, "Guns, Butter and Growth: The European Experience 1920-70," prepared for the 1978 Uppsala Conference of the International Sociological Association (Ann Arbor: mimeo), to be published in revised form in the Zeitschrift fuer Soziologie, January 1980.

2. Compare the discussion with the thought-provoking analysis of Barry M. Blechman and Stephen S. Kaplan for the superpowers in Force Without War (Washington: The Brookings Institution, 1978), especially Chs. 1-4. Other relevant literature includes James F. Cable, Gunboat Diplomacy (London: Praeger, 1971); Alexander L. George, et. al., The Limits of Coercive Diplomacy (Boston: Little, Brown, 1971); Alexander L. George and Richard Smoke, Deterrence in American Foreign Policy (New York: Columbia University Press, 1974); and Oran Young, The Politics of Force (Princeton University Press, 1968).

3. One source quotes a British government contention that between 1950 and 1966, Britain alone used force in 85 politico-military intervention incidents (22 of which were "major"); Geoffrey and Alan Williams, Crisis in European Defense (London: Charles Knight, 1974), Ch. X. A recent Soviet military encyclopedia indeed condemned Britain as the "most aggressive" Western state and cited 21 cases of direct British aggression from 1945 to 1973 (the U.S. total was 17). (Quoted in The London Times, June 16, 1976). See also the dispute data in Robert L. Butterworth, Managing Interstate Conflict 1945-1974 (Pittsburgh: UCIS, University of Pittsburgh, 1976), and that collected by Richard Stoll and Michael Champion in 1978-79 for the Correlates of War Project, University of Michigan.

4. Compare here the broad conclusions reached by the several contributors to Cynthia A. Cannizzo, ed., Arms Transfers and International Security (New York: Pergamon Press, 1979); by Anne Hessing Cahn, et. al., Controlling Future Arms Trade (New York: McGraw-Hill, 1977); and Edward A. Kolodziej in his forthcoming work on French arms trade.

5. The literature on Suez seems endless. One of the best sources is still Antony Nutting's No End of a Lesson (London: Constable, 1967).

6. See here C. J. Bartlett, The Long Retreat (London: Macmillan, 1972); Neville Brown, Arms Without Empire (London: Penguin, 1967); Andrew Pierre, Nuclear Politics (London: Oxford University Press, 1972); and Richard Rosecrance, Defense of the Realm (New York: Columbia University Press, 1968).

7. See Philip Darby, British Defense Policy East of Suez 1947-1968 (London: Oxford University Press, 1973).

8. See here Wilfred I. Kohl, French Nuclear Diplomacy (Princeton: Princeton University Press, 1971); and Edward A. Kolodziej, French International Policy Under DeGaulle and Pompidou (Ithaca: Cornell University Press, 1974).

9. See Catherine M. Kelleher, Germany and the Politics of Nuclear Weapons (New York: Columbia University Press, 1975).

10. Compare here the somewhat different views of David Greenwood set forth in his "Constraints and Choices in the Transformation of British Defense Effort since 1945," British Journal of International Studies, 2 (1976); and in "Defense and National Priorities since 1945" in British Defence Policy in a Changing World, ed. John Baylis (London: Croom Helm, 1977).

11. See here the formulations of Kolidziej, op. cit., and Edward L. Morse, Foreign Policy and Interdependence in Gaullist France (Princeton: Princeton University Press, 1973).

12. See here the papers on recent French stragegy prepared by D. Bruce Marshall (South Carolina), Stephen S. Roberts (Center for Naval Analysis), and David Yost (UCLA-Munich) for the SOMS Conference on Comparative Military Policy, Kiawah Island, November 1978, to be published in a forthcoming volume by James Roherty.

13. Ambassade de France, Press and Information Service, New York, 1977.

14. Rapport sur la programmation des defenses militaires. . . , Paris, Services du Premier Ministre, 1976.

15. See Catherine M. Kelleher, Alden F. Mullins, and Richard C. Eichenberg, The Structure of European Navies (Ann Arbor, June 1979, mimeo) to be published in the Proceedings of the Conference on European Navies, Royal Netherlands Naval College (Den Helder: forthcoming).

16. See, for example, Central Committee, French Communist Party, L'imperialisme francais aujord'hui (Paris: Editions sociales, 1977); Tom Nairn, ed., Atlantic Europe? The Radical View (Amsterdam: Transnational Institute, 1976); and Jean Klein, "La gauche francaise et les problemes de defense," SOMS-Kiawah papers, 1978.

17. See John Baylis, op. cit., James Bellini and Geoffrey Pattie, A New World Role for the Medium Power (London: Royal United Services Institute, 1977), and the Labour Executive study chaired by Ian Mikado, published as Sense about Defence (London: Transport House, 1978).

18. See Kelleher, Mullins and Eichenberg, op. cit.

19. See the essay by Michael Dillon on German arms sales in Cannizzo, op. cit. and the contrasting views of Ulrich Albrecht, Politik und Waffengeschaefte (Munich: Carl Hanser, 1972) and the various reports of the Kaldor-Robinson project at the University of Sussex. The official German White Paper of 1971-1972 took the later position: "The German economy cannot afford to forego the benefits deriving from such defense projects . . . especially since national development of weapons and equipment, as well as collaboration in international armament projects, are dependent on a high technological standard." (Bonn: Ministry of Defense, 1972).

10

NEW DIMENSIONS OF STRATEGIC THOUGHT IN WESTERN EUROPE
Georg Bluhm

With the strategic nuclear forces now in place on each
side, it is almost certain that neither nation could survive as a viable society after an all-out nuclear exchange. . . . This nuclear balance means that both
sides are now effectively constrained to the use of nonnuclear force in nearly every conceivable situation in
which force may be needed. [1]

The recovery and reconstruction of Western and Central Europe
after World War II and the following industrial expansion, have resulted in an unprecedented and possibly unparalleled concentration of
people, industries, and services, which has immediate effects on the
conditions for defensive military operations. This is particularly true
with respect to the Federal Republic of Germany. The conditions in
the Low Countries are quite similar, and in Eastern France somewhat
better. About 61 million people live in West Germany on about 96,000
square miles. The population density is about 640 persons per square
mile. The North-South extension is 600 miles, East-West only 100-
250. (The concentration of people, industries, and services in the
United States is comparable in a stretch of land ranging from Ports-
mouth, New Hampshire, to Norfolk, Virginia, and reaching up to
150 miles inland. In an area of 72,300 square miles live about 42.6
million people, i.e., a density of 593 persons per square mile).

In view of their high degree of industrialization and the
density of their population and the consequent vulnerability of all their state machinery, the NATO countries
of western Euripe are hardly in a position to incur territorial losses without jeopardizing their existence.

This is particularly true of the Federal Republic of
Germany, situated along the dividing line between NATO
and the Warsaw Pact in the centre of the field of political tension.

Here, the great concentration of population and
economic potential is marked by 24 areas of density, in
which 45 per cent of the population and even 55 per cent
of those gainfully employed live and work--in fact in an
area comprising only 7 per cent of federal territory.
These areas of density are expanding still farther and
accrete along the main traffic arteries to form urban-
ized corridors . . . [2]

Concerning the consequences for defense strategy, the official West
German position is as follows:

The industrial structure of our country and the extremely unfavourable ratio between its north-to-south
and east-to-west dimensions do not admit of any losses
of territory. About 30 percent of the population and 25
per cent of the industrial capacity are located in a 100
kilometres wide zone west of the Federal Republic's
border with the Warsaw Pact states.

Hence it is obvious that the security of the Federal Republic of Germany must be based primarily on
effective deterrence. Should deterrence fail to dissuade
an enemy from attacking, the effectiveness of the military strategic principle of Forward Defence will be of
vital importance to our country. [3]

The most vulnerable components of West Germany's infrastructure are the railroad system and especially the general energy supply.
The railroads are totally electrified: thus the system's operation
depends on the working of the electric power supply and of a few
dozen transformer stations. A large part of the electric power
supply--which also brings natural gas and oil through the distribution network into homes and factories--is generated in nuclear
power plants. The official planning expects that in 1985, 45 nuclear
plants will be in operation in West Germany, with a total of over
45,000 megawatts output. The vulnerability of these installations to
military attack, and the dangers resulting from any damage, are
obvious.

The Western European allies, because of this vulnerability,
tended throughout NATO's history to emphasize deterrence over
defense. The European rejection of the Kennedy Administration's

"fire-break" ideas was motivated by the need to preserve the deterrent effect in keeping the escalation risk for the enemy incaluculable. It was the superiority of the United States, and indirectly of NATO, on all levels of nuclear armament that denied to the opponent the chance to "win" with his inevitable superiority in conventional forces. The opponent was to be deterred from attacking by NATO's likely recourse to nuclear weapons for tactical use if defense with conventional means failed.

Credible deterrence, however, rests in no small measure on the perceived military capability of NATO forces to defend Europe. As stated by former U. S. Defense Secretary James Schlesinger,

> Deterrence is not a substitute for defense; defense capa-
> bilities representing the potential for effective counter-
> action, are the essential condition of deterrence. This
> simple truth becomes especially evident in a crisis,
> when forces designed only for 'deterrence' are increas-
> ingly found to be lacking in credibility both to opponents
> and to their potential users.

> Deterrence, in other words, is not something free-
> floating that exists independently of a credibile, imple-
> mentable threat. It requires the most careful structur-
> ing of forces that is fully consistent with an agreed–upon
> strategic concept. By contrast with the 1950s when the
> great nuclear superiority of the United States concealed
> any basic deficiencies in strategic analysis and force
> structure, it is now evident that deterrence does not
> simply derive from a pile of nuclear weapons--a pile
> which one anticipates, at least, will frighten one's
> opponents as much as the people it is designed to
> protect. [4]

Stragegic parity and the superiority of the Soviet bloc's conven-tional forces have considerably diminished the credibility of NATO's deterrence posture. This problem has led to new efforts in strategic analysis in some West European countries. It is the purpose here to discuss these new concepts and analyze them with respect to their impact on the defense of Europe. While such concepts are developed in the context of nuclear technology, they are primarily focused on nonnuclear posture, albeit there is some consideration of tactical nuclear weapons.

THE GERMAN MILITARY POSTURE

The West German Research "Institute fur Internationale Politik und Sicherheit--Stiftung Wissenschaft und Politik" (Science and Policy Foundation) published in a study in 1974, "On Problems of a Defense Option for Central Europe in the Nineteen Eighties."[5] The Institute had been established in the early sixties as the German Federal government's major resource for policy analysis and for decision preparation in foreign policy and defense matters.

Having analyzed the security situation in Central Europe, the study concluded:

(a) It is still not possible to exclude the contingency that the Federal Republic of Germany must defend itself against military attack or against threats of military force.

(b) "Under current conditions defense of Central Europe is not possible with exclusive use of conventional military means, nor would total nuclear war be of any use for the Federal Republic. Both alternatives, therefore, must be excluded from the formulation of defense options" (10).[6] In another context the study states:

> The current (1974) situation of the defense concept and
> its internally and publicly asserted official military
> mission demands the preservation and, in case of an
> aggression, the restoration of security and integrity
> of NATO territory. This mission can be accomplished
> with the existing forces only against a limited attack
> which would not exceed a specific intensity; that accom-
> plishment is not possible, however, against limited
> attack of greater intensity, nor against a large scale
> conventional aggression by the Warsaw Pact. (22)

This view obviously contradicts, or severely qualifies, the American view that a nonnuclear defense of Western Europe is possible.

(c) Defense must be conceived in terms of limited war. This limitation follows not from the oppenent's lack of capability but from the characteristics of the strategic nuclear weapons (unacceptable nuclear damage). Thus, the limitation of war becomes a task of strategy. As long as nuclear deterrence is kept effective on the "strategic" level, it will be possible with appropriate means on the tactical level (i. e. , in the European theater) to impose a choice of limitation upon a rationally acting adversary (11).

(d) Technological innovations can make West Germany's problems of credible defense options less difficult. New weapon technologies, in complementary coordination can solve the specific defense task of West Germany. "That specific defense task of the Federal

Republic is to deny the enemy success, in limited war through combat, and in total war through deterrence, and to prevent--this is crucial-- that the enemy pursues success at the border line (between limited and total war), in other words . . . that he undercuts 'deterrence'" (12).

Constraints on Force Expansion

West Germany rejects the idea of enhancing conventional combat capabilities of NATO—and especially German—forces in order to match the conventional Warsaw Pact forces. Although there is a clear interest on the part of West Germany to avoid any situation that would necessitate early escalation, it would be against her interest if the perception or impression arose that "the function of the risk of nuclear escalation in Central Europe could be replaced by conventional defense." Moreover, the massive enlargement of the German forces needed to better match the Pact's capabilities would require an enormous increase of defense expenditures. This is inconsistent with the established social and financial policies of Western Europe. Nor is such a policy compatible with basic requirements of detente and its instrumentary agenda, especially the MBFR project.

Response to Armor Assault

The most dangerous contingency for the Federal Republic and NATO, the "Blitzkrieg" seizure of West Germany, would require rapid advances of massive armored forces. To begin such attacks, the enemy must for short periods form massed concentrations. These offer the defender chances to paralyze and subsequently eliminate those concentrations. The NATO-deployed weapon systems make it possible that "for the first time since in the 'materiel battles' of the first World War operative movement was paralyzed, defense has become again the 'essentially stronger kind of combat'" (42). However

it would not be sufficient just to paralyze the attacker. Rather the mass concentrations for attack have to be destroyed so that the attacker must recognize that the option of continuing the attack offers no prospect. This task requires concentrations of firepower which are engaged on very short order and at places not previously known . . . In the specific situation of Central Europe, presumably only the engagement of minimized nuclear weapons with precision guided means of delivery will have that military effect. (43)

The most logical approach (for flexible, timely
engagement) would be to exempt the minimized nuclear
weapons from the realm of the actual nuclear doctrines,
and to include them in the conventional doctrine. If, for
complex reasons, such "exemption" proves not feasible,
the problem is to define within the general concept of
nuclear escalation one first, clearly limited level of
nuclear weapon action which in contrast to other "first
steps" would be militarily fully effective, and nevertheless as free of the risk of uncontrolled escalation as it
is possibly conceivable . . . This would lift the commen-
cement of the actual nuclear escalation to a higher, and
therefore more credible level. (47)

On the operative side, rules of engagement and procedures of
operation would have to be redefined. Generally the minimized nuclear weapons should be ready for instant action in case of attack.
Accordingly, "limits of tolerance" should be defined and adopted by
the allied governments in peace time. SACEUR should be given
"pre-conditions" for engagement of minimized nuclear weapons. Political control would be retained through a veto arrangement that
would--on grounds of a policy decision--intercept the contingent
action (48).

Compared with the concepts of engagement of larger nuclear
weapons, defense with minimized nuclear weapons appears feasible
and credible.

The proposed tactics insure more than any hitherto
accepted concept of defense the observation of . . .
'constraints' without . . . being inferior from the very
beginning and . . . forced inevitably later into massive
tactical or even strategic nuclear engagement. . . . It
is crucial to combine the incalculable risk of deterrence
with a calculable risk of defense in such a way that the
political and the military decision makers of the potential aggressor are convinced that the stakes don't
warrant this risk. (52)

The authors of this tactical concept propose to name it "Limited
Response"--instead of the rather unhandy term "contingently reflex
defense" (in literal translation). The term shall indicate "the self-
imposed limitation of the means, the reflex character of this defense,
and the fact that here a peculiar line of tolerance is defined" (15).

Similarly there is great interest in the German Federal government in the deployment of enhanced radiation ("neutron") weapons, replacing older tactical nuclear weapons with much greater destructive effects. Their very restricted collateral damage capacity would make their engagement discriminating. The greater credibility of action that results from those properties enhances deterrence. "These weapons would not make that decision (of any President to engage nuclear weapons) any easier. But by enhancing deterrence, they could make it less likely that the President would have to face such a decision. "[7]

TACTICAL ALTERNATIVES:
A FRENCH VIEW

The views of this study are challenged by Guy Brossollett, a French Army officer. In his work, "Essay sur la non-bataille," Brossollett states, "To engage the enemy in battle with the same weapons and tactics he uses only with obviously much less of them, seems to be imprudent, to say the least. "[8]

A Critique of Prevailing Concepts

Brossollet's essay sets out with a critical assessment of the French armed forces' capability to fulfill their mission. France's forces are organized along functional lines: strategic nuclear forces, territorial defense forces, intervention forces (airborne) and the "field army"—"corps de bataille." He concentrates on the latter, the field army, which in 1973 consisted of five armored or mechanized divisions with 170,000 men and 800 medium tanks, and of the tactical airforce (FATAC) with 300 aircraft and 100 to 150 tactical nuclear weapons expected for the early 1980s (9).[9] In the 1973 budget, this component was allocated 7.312 million francs, about 21 percent of the military appropriations (216). The mission of this field army is to put up such a resistance that the enemy either abstains from attack or must attack with such force "that in his own judgement as well as in the French and in the whole world's opinion would justify a nuclear tactical strike" (112). In any case, the field army is to fight the battle to gain time for the French government's strategic decision-making process. "The decision on engagement of tactical nuclear weapons against an enemy who could not be stopped by other means puts the government in the position to demonstrate and to warn him that he will make the engagement of the strategic nuclear weapons inevitable" (112).

Brossollet's criticism of this concept is based on several key considerations. First, the battle concept is rather obsolete, because the opposing forces are not in balance. "The disproportion between our field army and the potential enemy's army is so ostensible that no illusions about the outcome of the battle are permissible . . ." (120). Second, although the tank continues to have an important tactical role, it is no longer the central weapon, nor—because of budgetary limits—could it be. The tactical airforce and the anti-aircraft units are, due to lack of funds, inadequate for the task of supporting the armored forces in battle, which in turn reduces the battle effectiveness of the tanks (124). Third, the engagement of tactical nuclear weapons will inevitably trigger the enemy's counterstrike. The deterring effect this is supposed to produce because of "the incalculable consequences" of nuclear exchanges might not work. "If one side possesses five to ten thousand war heads, and the other side just one hundred, the outcome of the battle is a priori settled" (127). The dilemma of the tactics of the field army, an army which is conceived and intended for tactical nuclear warfare, consists in these choices: "To engage the field army without nuclear action? That would mean to deny its specific characteristics. To engage it with nuclear action? That would escalate the conflict automatically to a level of violence which might still be avoided. Not to engage the field army? That would leave the initiative for the outcome (of the conflict) to the enemy" (130).

With regard to the military structures, Brossollet raises these objections: first, the structure of today's field army (in 5 armor/mechanized divisions) is caused by deference to history. "In an essay published in 1935 . . . de Gaulle proposed the build-up of six mechanized divisions. We have five now, the sixth one we had to give up for financial reasons" (132). When after the Algerian war the army reorganized, for lack of imagination the traditional structures were retained. Second, the modern complexity of leading large units, divisions, and corps in battle exceed the capacities of even genial military leaders, especially since all Western strategic foresight concedes the initiative for attack to the enemy. Third, communications between units in combat and the army leader are slow, unreliable, and cumbersome (133-38). Fourth, the traditional structure of the field army requires an almost impossible logistic capability. "One single division of our field army consumes every day in combat a supply of 1,000 to 2,000 (metric) tons of fuel, ammunition, food, etc., that requires 200 to 400 5-ton trucks." These must operate under the enemy's omnipresent tactical airforce, on clogged roads and from most likely nonexisting depots and storages (139).

The effectiveness of the weapons and equipment of the field army's large units are also questionable, particularly in light of continuing technological development. Artillery in the form of the traditional field cannon has become rather obsolete, at least in combat against enemy tank assaults. "In order to 'incapacitate' i. e. not 'destroy', an enemy tank company (about 10 tanks), which would normally operate on an area of about 300 to 400 meters by 500 meters, about 800 rounds of 155-mm ammunition is needed, i. e. the load of ten 5-ton trucks (139)." (Brossollet does not address other modes of the field artillery's action.) For fire support of tank assaults, Brossollet believes mortars would do a better job (143). The tank, though still an important and indispensable weapon, can no longer play its former salient role. It has become very vulnerable. As Brossollet states, "50% of the tanks lost in the 1973 Arab-Israeli war were destroyed with light weight remotely-guided projectiles (144)." The flexibility of the tactical neclear weapons of the Pluton types (10 or 25 KT yield) is severely limited. At a distance at which enemy tank forces can be reliably located, tactical nuclear weapons are too close (less than 3- or 4-km) to their own units. At greater distances, the accuracy of locating enemy units diminishes. In any case, the use of tactical nuclear weapons requires an alert period for friendly troops of one to two hours. In this time, the enemy may be able to move his units. Even under constant tracking of the enemy, the elimination of a tank battalion (i. e., destruction of 40-50 percent of it) would require three Pluton missiles at 25 KT. Thus Brossollet does not regard the cost-effect ratio of the Pluton system as satisfactory. On the other hand, delivery of nuclear weapons through the tactical airforce against moving targets is technically very difficult and also severely restricted.

The Module Concept

As a tactical alternative to the concept of the "field army," Brossollet develops a defense concept "which uses different methods, modes of combat and weapons than the enemy" (158). The alternative defense concept is based on "modules" of different specifications that have an "autonomous fighting capability," will be deployed in great depth, will engage in decentralized single actions, and will fit in a coherent, coordinating tactical system (158-59).

Three types of modules are proposed: local ground units, airborne helicopter-destroyer units, and heavy tank modules. The Local Ground Unit would consist of about 15 men, divided in five groups: three anti-tank groups, each armed with a wire-guided anti-tank projectile system (Milan), or one recoilless (high velocity) 106-mm cannon, with several rounds of the respective ammunition, and a set of anti-tank mines and "off-route" anti-tank mines; one mortar group with an 81-mm mortar and about 20 pieces of ammunition; and one command group; officer, driver, and radio operator. In addition, each group would have a light machinegun, a rifle with telescope, and anti-infantry mines, and a jeep with trailer.

Local Ground Units (LGU): Light Modules

Each Local Ground Unit would have a specific combat area (about 2.5 kilometer radius) and a combat assignment (e. g. , a minimum goal of destruction of three enemy vehicles: tanks, APCs, or reconnaissance vehicles, or the incapacitation of ten men in case of enemy infantry attack). The local ground unit would be thoroughly familiar with the terrain; it would have full discretion about the details of the accomplishment of the combat assignment. Once the assignment had been accomplished, the unit would be regarded as "spent. " The men could then decide either to withdraw and re-unite with their own forces or go underground. If the local ground units were engaged in action only one time, the supply, and thus the logistic, problems would be minimal. The indispensable basic supply would be rendered by support elements, one for each four or five local ground units, consisting of one or two officers for the LGUs' coordination, of a group of pioneers (for building obstacles), mechanics, radio operator, a medical orderly, drivers, and several trucks for supplies. This cluster, combining and coordinating four or five local ground units with the support unit, is the "Light Module," the updated form of the traditional company. The next higher level, the batallion, would have operative control over an area of 400 to 500 square kilometers (160-65).

Destroyer Units: Medium Modules

The airborne destroyer unit consists of two attack helicopters and one reconnaissance helicopter. The attack helicopter is armed with HOT missiles, anti-tank wire-guided projectiles with a range up to 4,000 meters with great accuracy. The success of tank-destroying helicopters had been proven in combat, in the last phase of the Vietnam War. In deliberately conservative assessment, Brossollet assumes a loss ratio between tank and helicopter of 5:1. Twenty units of three helicopters form one airmobile destroyer module, which also contains a command and support element (operative guidance and control, communications, supplies, maintenance, engineers) and anti-aircraft defense units. The three helicopter units could fly two to three engagements per day. They would fight best if left to their own search-and-destroy initiative, "like the pirates of old" (165-68).

Tank Regiments: Heavy Modules

The third component of Brossollet's tactical disposition is the "heavy module." This would be an upgraded version of currently (1974) existing tank regiments: 54 tanks, one infantry company (mechanized), supply and maintenance units complemented with anti-aircraft weapons (SAMs of the Roland type, a French-German system) and 120-mm mortars for fire support. These heavy modules, or autonomous tank regiments, would be capable of rapid reactions and flexible operation because they are no longer integrated in the rigid structures of the Field Army. Their specific task would be to attack enemy concentrations where they locally overwhelm (saturate) the local ground units, and withstand the helicopter assaults. These fighting forces, in all three components, are linked with each other and the theater command through communication units.

Deep-Territory Defense

For the "non-battle" or deep-territory defense, Brossollet proposes a deployment that would cover the eastern and north-eastern border of France, from Basel to Dunkerque, a distance of about 500 kilometers, in a depth of 120 kilometers. The defense force covering those 60,000 square kilometers would be deployed in depth, throughout the area, with a slightly greater density in the south-western part of the Federal Republic and in Alsace. The size of the force needed to create the "mesh" of such dimensions would be 2,500 Local Ground Units; a fleet of 200 Airmobile Destroyer Units with 600 helicopters organized in ten Airmobile Destroyer Modules, each with 60 aircraft; and 20 Heavy Modules, i. e., fully self-sustaining tank regiments, each consisting of 54 tanks (AMX 30), 26 APCs (AMX), etc.

The combat task of the LGUs would be to observe, report, and fight. It would also involve slowing down the enemy's advance and forcing him to engage his reserves. The Airmobile Destroyer Units and Heavy Modules would already have taken position in their bases during the stage of heightened tension.

"Even when the enemy was stopped in the meshes of the large net, and when he was seriously harassed by the helicopters, he could still keep his units intact and despite his losses he could keep up the threat. To bring this coherence to collapse (and to eliminate this threat), is the task of the tank units . . ." (177). The disposition, which includes predetermined areas reserved for the armored units' operation, would be determined to a large extent by the specific properties of the terrain.

The enemy approaching the French, or in case of integrated or coordinated West European defense, the much deeper and more numerous allied, deep-defense disposition, may choose to jump over it with airborne assaults. The territorial defense forces and the airborne intervention force are intended to counter this tactic. The enemy may try to breach, to break through, the 120 kilometers deep-defense deployment. Of an original strength of thirty to forty divisions, ten to twenty enemy divisions may survive the conquest of West Germany. Brossollet, accordingly, assumes a Soviet attack in the strength of about ten divisions, its first echelon about four or five divisions. If a breakthrough is attempted over a width of 200 kilometers, it will run into 1,000 light and 15 heavy modules; the same operation over a width of 50 kilometers would engage only 250 light and 12 heavy modules. On the basis of the assumed destruction capability, the enemy would loose between 2,000 and 2,500 tanks of the first echelon's 3,000 in a 50 kilometer wide attack. That loss would no longer permit those five divisions to perform as operative, coherent units. If the enemy attacks with his infantry ahead of his tanks, the 50 kilometer wide breach would cost the loss of more than 10,000 men, i.e., 35 battalions, equalling all the infantry of four Soviet mechanized divisions. In either case, "the first invasion echelon would be destroyed even without engaging a single tactical nuclear weapon." In no way would the units of the traditional field army be capable of achieving such results (181-86).

If the enemy presses on with his attack despite such losses, recourse to tactical nuclear weapons shall signify to him that the last level is reached before France with her limited strategic nuclear forces will extract the price for her defeat. Thus, the role of the tactical nuclear force is changed by Brossollet. It is fully separated from the initial ground combat in which substantial parts of the attacking enemy tank and infantry forces are being destroyed in the module mesh. Because its new role is to warn of and to "signify" the imminence of strategic escalation, Brossollet renames this component of the French defense "force de signification" (191-96). The French strategic nuclear forces, currently consists of 64 SLBM in four nuclear powered submarines (the fifth is under construction), 18 IRBM, and 33 Mirage IV supersonic bombers. [10] Even if one-half to two-thirds of this force were destroyed before they went into action, 40 to 60 major targets in the Soviet Union would have to be sacrificed for the conquest of France. In Brossollet's view, this should dissuade the enemy from an all-out attack.

A NEW POLITICAL-MILITARY STRATEGY:
A GERMAN VIEW

A work of considerable complexity has been presented by Dr.
Horst Afheldt of the Max Planck Institute in Starnberg, Germany. [11]
His study offers a comprehensive theory of peace based on the premise
that the current military balance appears to be the only realistic basis
for international stability. No concept for disarmament, according to
Afheldt, has provided credible strategy, security, or assured peace.
Afheldt critically analyzes the Western and especially American
current (or recent) strategic doctrines, and elaborates propositions
designed to make short and medium-range strategic plans compatible
with long-range protection of world peace.

Afheldt suggests a combination of tactical-strategic options combined with political and psychological factors to deter and respond to
Soviet attack. These options include nonnuclear means, tactical nuclear weapons, and strategic nuclear weapons, which are to be integrated with political and psychological warfare to exploit the apparent
political, economic, and military vulnerabilities of the Soviet Union.
The adoption of such strategies will in themselves create an effective
deterrent, according to Afheldt.

Revised Module Concept

Afheldt proposes the adoption of Brossollet's tank assault absorbing "mesh" strategy, but would use only the "light modules," that
is, the infantry component. The airborne and the "heavy" tank
modules are rejected. The sole purpose of such forces would be to
prevent a fast Soviet fait accompli, in order to make possible a U. S.
decision to counteract the Soviet aggression. [12] These single-method
tactics will admittedly not be able to prevent occupation of the Federal
Republic after the enemy has suffered heavy conventional losses.

There are serious weaknesses with Afheldt's tactical proposal.
Any army with only a single-method capability would be unable to
adopt to the attacker's tactical changes. Moreover, the single method
capability severely limits the flexibility and effectiveness of the defender. Limiting any opportunity to exploit tactically the enemy's potential blunders and failures is in itself a serious tactical error. The
concept of holding until the allies, particularly the United States, are
able to respond with tactical nuclear weapons is also fraught with difficulties. It does not seem plausible that the Soviet forces and those
of the Warsaw Pact would necessarily withdraw under threat of nuclear
attack. In light of the Soviet nuclear and retaliatory posture, it does
not seem probable that such a threat by NATO would achieve its
purposes.

Strategic Considerations

Elaborating his thesis, Afheldt argues that

> The addressee of the engagement of strategic weapons--
> and of the threat thereof--in the concept of deterrence is
> the enemy government. This implies: 1) The deterring
> effect results from the threat of such disadvantages
> which are--in the view of the enemy government--in-
> tolerable. 2) Intolerable for that government are not
> necessarily just high casualty rates among the civilian
> population. Rather, nothing is more intolerable for a
> government than the termination of its own—or a com-
> patible successor government's—authority and rule. [13]

If "deterrence fails," Afheldt suggests that, if deterrence fails,
a strategy that destroys the enemy government's rule is more effective
than any variation of the Mutual Assured Destruction concepts. An opti-
mal strategy would "disolve the population's obedience" to the enemy
government. He develops a few related scenarios for such "counter-
government" tactics. The threat to destroy one or several specified
cities with ICBMs is announced in advance and repeated hourly over
radio and satellite-TV. On the other hand, safety is promised for the
region of the enemy's capital. The intention behind this threat is to
cause panic that should result in the flight of millions of people to the
capital region. If panic and flight do not begin, the destruction of only
a single city will most likely cause that effect. If the Soviet government tries to keep the population under control through its expanded
evacuation, shelter, and other civil defense programs, the threat
could be altered: "If you, the inhabitants of X continue to obey authorities' evacuation orders we shall destroy your evacuated city. If you
don't obey, we shall save her." The military ability to carry out
such a selective and purely political use of strategic nuclear arms
would, of course, be applicable only in crises.

The demand for restoring the status quo ante in a Berlin crisis,
or in a crisis over Cuba, or about virtually anything of importance,
could be accompanied by such a threat. The political exchange might
be as follows: "Unless you restore the status quo ante, we shall chase
your population to Moscow." The enemy's reply could be: "Then we
chase your population to Washington." Or the reply could be different.
Whatever it might be, a new dialogue—a new attempt to solve the
crisis through negotiations—would have begun. A deterrence system c
such capabilities and direction stabilized the diplomatic, nonviolent
crisis management against the escalation into (and of) the use of
force. [14]

His aversion for engagement of nuclear weapons, strategic as well as tactical, led Afheldt to propose unfeasible tactics such as the deep-territory defense of West Germany through "techno-commandos," a watered-down variation of the much more complex tactics Brossollet proposed. It seems striking, however, that Afheldt does not venture any thoughts on the potential of a strategy that would engage commandos to "counter-government warfare," i.e., in actions designed to terminate an enemy government's rule by creating conditions conducive to destroying the population's obedience. If that could be done with nonnuclear though not traditional means, it would appear preferable to a version of "counter-government" strategy based on the threat with, or a selective engagement of, strategic nuclear weapons. One possible reason for Afheldt's lack of attention to this kind of approach is his apparent belief that the defender's strategic and operative goals must remain limited by the status quo ante bellum border line.

POLICY ALTERNATIVES

The premises of most strategic thought concerning the confrontation between NATO and the Eastern bloc seem to be irrefutable. The existing demographic, social, and economic conditions in Central Europe make deterrence the foremost concern of the alliance.

In the past, deterrence was achieved through the threat of escalation into the tactical and strategic levels if conventional defenses were inadequate. Since nuclear parity has been established, the intended deterring effect has lost credibility. This has decisive effects on the strategic importance of the subnuclear level of confrontation and warfare.

If the enemy can win the campaign on the subnuclear level, it is hard to see how this outcome could be changed by escalating the war to the levels of nuclear exchange. On these levels, parity denies victory to both sides. The presumed deterring effect on the enemy of imminent escalation to the horrors of nuclear exchange is neutralized by their correct assessment that the same effect must also deter NATO as long as all act rationally. (In case they do not, the probable consequences might quickly force them to.) For rationally acting opponents, nuclear deterrence is neutralized by nuclear counter-deterrence.

It may be that acceptance of defeat in a subnuclear campaign is preferable to escalation of the war to limited or all-out nuclear exchange that would far exceed the damage and costs of the subnuclear defeat. The costs of nuclear conflict in loss of life, in devastation, and in social and economic ruin would likely outweigh the costs of the enemy's original demands, if these were limited. If no countervailing strategic concepts were available, the anticipation of such a prospect could erode a country's allegiance to the alliance.

As the deterring credibility of NATO's tactical and strategic nuclear arsenals erodes against the Warsaw Pact's conventional superiority, the vital interest of the West European allies in preventing war through successful deterrence must be secured with military postures and strategies that can be regarded as capable of defeating the Pact's subnuclear forces in the European theater without recourse to nuclear weapons. The Warsaw Pact's superiority in conventional weapons cannot be matched through a mere increase of NATO's conventional forces. In the context of Western Europe, such an increased conventional armament would be politically and militarily undesirable, financially unrealistic, and incongruous with MBFR endeavors, the desirable corollary of detente. Moreover, in terms of military manpower, this could be futile because the Soviet Union could outrace any numerical increase of the NATO forces.

The task given to NATO's strategic planning of the subnuclear level is to find ways to balance the opponent's superiority in conventional force. Brossollet's view about the imprudence of fighting an enemy with the same weapons and methods he uses is particularly relevant. On the one hand, NATO forces must tackle the advancing attacker's fronts and spearheads—possibly in a mesh-like deep-territory anti-tank combat as Brossollet proposes. (West Germany is reported to have transformed part of her reserves—500,000 men—into small anti-tank commandos that would operate in their familiar home area in a deep-territory defense, apparently analogous to Guy Brossollet's concepts.)[15] On the other hand, they must be capable of exploiting and utilizing with all necessary force the enemy's limits, weaknesses, and vulnerabilities.

Although the subnuclear forces of the Soviet Union in Central Europe, i.e., those that would be engaged in an attack without preceding reinforcement, are formidable (20 divisions in East Germany, two in Poland, five in Czechoslovakia, four in Hungary, totaling 31, of which 16 are armored divisions), major losses of this force would be a serious strategic setback. This amounts to one-third of all Soviet class A and class B divisions, and probably to more than half of the class A divisions. [16]

The Soviet Union's ability to replenish losses of her Western forces are limited because of Moscow's second conflict dyad, the precarious relationship with China. (The consideration of the NATO-Soviet strategic relationship as a solitaire conflict dyad, i.e., without regard to the overall strategic situation of the Soviet Union, constitutes a grave systemic and methodological error in contemporary discussion.) Because a Soviet military operation against Western Europe or West Germany alone, would if successful enhance the Soviet power base enormously, it could not fail to alarm China. An alarmed China must necessarily alert the whole mutually interacting military system of the Soviet-Chinese conflict dyad, which will tightly restrict the Soviet ability to reinforce and replenish losses in the Western theater. Most significant is the restriction in regard to the tactical air force. Of the 7,400 Soviet combat aircraft, 2,700 are assigned to the strategic defense of the Soviet homeland, 2,400 are on the Chinese front, and 2,300 are in the European theater. [17] Replenishing losses in a European war could be made only at the expense of the strategic air defense forces of the homeland ("PVO Strany"). (However, if the United States fails to replace the increasingly obsolete B-52 system with the B-1, those forces reciprocal to the strategic air defense force of the Soviet homeland will shrink, and more Soviet aircraft could be earmarked for transfer from PVO Strany to the tactical air forces against China and Western Europe.)

The strategic task for NATO in nonnuclear war in Europe is two fold. First, it must devise a military capability and doctrine to take advantage of the Soviet's limited reinforcement capability. Second, NATO must develop political-military strategy that can exploit the Soviet Union's critical weaknesses in East Central Europe and its military vulnerabilities.

The political and strategic weakness of the Soviet Union's position in East Central Europe results from the fact that any attack against NATO members would have to start from satellite territory, 600 to 800 kelometers west of the Soviet borders. Therefore, the Soviet government would need the consent and cooperation of the governments of East Germany, Poland, Czechoslovakia, and Hungary. Although the compliance of these governments with Soviet politicies and expectations are matters of record, the prospective implications of a war might make them particularly difficult for the Soviets. Evidence of the government's lack of support from the population, at least in the case of Poland and East Germany, seems irrefutable. Thus those governments have compelling reasons for preserving the peace.

In peace, political resistance is the exception, because the average individual knows that his dissent and acts of resistance would not change the political realities in the slightest. For most people, accommodation is standard behavior in totalitarian conditions. But war could change that attitude for many. Its dynamics make the regime's breakdown conceivable. Thus the individual's actions and commitments could be perceived as making sense and as "making the difference."

The psychological and attitudinal behavior of people under dictatorial rule differs, then, in response to external factors, including the normalcy of peace and the unpredictability of war situations. If a specific Western military capability could effectively assist, supply, join in fighting, and bring success to popular uprisings, then the governments of East Germany, Poland, Czechoslovakia, and Hungary would have irresistible cause to deny consent to and participate in a Soviet attack against NATO members. (The denial of that consent and participation by any one of those governments might foil such aggressive designs, because the absence of the military units from a refusing country would bring the Pact's attack deployment into disarray.)

It seems probable that NATO countries, if they would acquire a military capability for "counter-government" operation in East Central Europe, could deter those governments from cooperation with a Soviet attack in Western Europe. In Afheldt's view, "No damage is more unacceptable for a government than the termination of its rule" through the "dissolution of the people's obedience". The obvious military pattern for this counter-government strategy would be autonomously operating commandos and commando-"modules" quite similar to Brossollet's basic ground units in the deep-territory, anti-tank defense concept.

If a war in Central Europe occurred, triggered by an assault of the massive Soviet and Warsaw Pact tank and mechanized divisions, the obvious political weaknesses in the satellite countries would demand vigorous exploitation requiring appropriate military means.

A third dimension of a military strategy designed to defeat a Soviet and Warsaw Pact assault in Central Europe would be directed against the manifold military vulnerabilities of the attacking forces. Let us briefly consider the dependence of the 70 Soviet and Pact divisions, which are fully armored and have formidable artillery components, on a steady supply of fuel, ammunition, and other essentials. (As mentioned earlier, Brossollet estimates a French division's daily supply needs at 1,000 to 2,000 metric tons. Although Soviet devisions seem to be trained to live from occupied territory and people, each division's daily fuel and ammunition needs remain staggering. They are estimated at about 1,000 tons or more.) NATO forces have to develop the capability to cut the enemy's supplies in the rear by destroying his logistic system: storages, railroad junctions and yards, airfields, and hauling facilities. While the enemy's front is being tackled and bogged down in the Western anti-tank defenses, his offensive could be paralyzed by grand-scale destruction of its vital supplies. The means to accomplish this tactical goal, without the engagement of nuclear weapons, are airborne and air assault operations.

(A special case for airlifted attacks against the enemy's logistic facilities, though not necessarily one that would be essential in the war's initial phase, is the destruction of the eight railroad junctions in East Prussia and Eastern Poland in which all rail traffic converges Konigsberg, Allenstein/Olsztyn, Lyck/Elk, Bialystok, Czeremcza,

Brzest-Litowsk-Terespol, Lublin, Przemysl; or of the some 16 railroad yards for the change from broad to standard gauge along the Soviet-Polish border.)

Strategic analyses and models should be developed that incorporate a multidimensional deterrence capability, including political varibles. In the context of this design, deterrence would be effective in a tactical, a strategic, and two political dimensions.

With only minor changes in the deployment of forces in Central Europe, NATO might achieve the capability to defeat an attack of the Western deployment of the Soviet forces, and possibly even eliminate it, without use or first use of nuclear weapons. This military prospect should be an effective deterrent in itself.

The strategic implications a defeat in a sub-nuclear war in Europe would have on the Soviet-Chinese conflict would pose a second complex of military-strategic deterrence.

The possibility that a defeat of a conventional attack in Central Europe could lead to, or be accompanied by, a breakdown of the political domination over East Central Europe could not fail to have a deterring political effect on the Soviet government.

The same prospect would probably make it likely that the East German, Polish, Czechoslovakian, and Hungarian governments would resist, and refuse to cooperate with, any Soviet plans of aggression in Europe, as long as the NATO countries' policies do not pose a threat to them.

This last point has a vitally important implication for the policy of the member governments of NATO. If the alliance, anticipating a Soviet-Warsaw Pact attack in Central Europe, plans and prepares strategies and capabilities that rely on "counter-government" warfare to fully exploit political weaknesses in those communist-governed countries, then NATO governments, including the United States, must abstain unconditionally from all policies, actions, statements, and messages in peacetime that would appear to interfere with the internal political weaknesses and deficiencies of the communist countries. Actions which contain a potential—and in the context of this thesis an implied—strategic threat, have no place in the conduct of diplomacy. (Because of the logic of the sovereignty principle, the concern for Human Rights can be pursued in intergovernmental relations only through discreet channels, anyway.)

The strategic hypothesis presented here differs from those discussed earlier as well as from NATO's publicly stated doctrines. The military capability advocated here could appear to some observers as "provocative" or "threatening," presumably in the sense that NATO, if it possessed such a capability, could decide to use it for aggression.

This view disregards several important aspects. Two of the three main components of this posture are mostly effective in defensive combat. The deep-territory anti-tank defense, analogous to Brossollet's concept, would cast large parts of NATO armies in roles that, because of the specific armament and training, cannot easily be changed to forward mobility in an offensive. Also, the expected effect of air-lifted assaults against the vital logistic system of the attacking enemy tank masses, designed to immobilize their advances, could not be achieved in support of their own offensive on the ground. The enemy's supply lines would be much shorter and therefore more easily defended. The storage areas and all vital logistic targets would be saturated with defending troops, who would have many more supply alternatives in their own territory than they would have in offensive advance in enemy (i. e., NATO) territory.

Finally, if NATO armies were structured and equipped for a strategic conduct as advocated in this hypothesis, they would lack the thrust for an offensive against an opponent with the current strength of the Warsaw Pact in Central Europe.

Nothing in this strategic posture and capability would make a Central European war more tolerable for West Germany, the Low Countries and Denmark, or any other Western European country. The guarantee for NATO's abstention from any military initiative, "provocation," and threat, lies in the geographic vulnerability of West Germany and the other Western European countries in any kind of modern warfare. The unprotected populations are hostages for the political and military restraint of the governments, so the enormity of prospective losses even in a limited war in Central Europe imposes the same restraint on the governments of the NATO countries.

Under the conditions that exist in Central and Western Europe, the avoidance both of war and of surrender to the opponent's demands remains a paramount interest. Yet no other alternative to deterrence seems possible. And as we have frequently noted, deterrence depends on the credibility of the implicit threat. The current search for new reliable methods of deterrence has become necessary because of the implicit logic of "parity" on the various levels of the nuclear stand-off. The threat of escalation in the face of imminent defeat on a lower level of hostilities is no longer credible, and therefore does not reliably deter. The resulting gap in deterrence can be filled if NATO acquires a credible capability to defeat a potential massive Soviet and Warsaw Pact assault without recourse to nuclear weapons. In other words, NATO must develop a plausible capability to "win" a sub-nuclear war in Europe. "Deterrence" in such a concept would result from the assessment of several credible strategic and political implications, threatening "unacceptable damages" and tactical defeat to a Soviet attack in Central Europe.

NOTES

1. David Packard, "Perceptions of the Military Balance", Conference Paper; Amsterdam 1973, p. 5.

2. White Paper 1975/76, The Security of the Federal Republic of Germany and the Development of the Federal Armed Forces (Bonn 1976, #46).

3. Ibid. #155.

4. James Schlesinger, Department of Defense, Annual Report, 1976/77, I/II (Henceforth cited: Report 1976/77), Washington, D. C.

5. SWP 0 S2023 Z, Fo. Pl. II 2a/74; Mai 1974, Hans Breithaupt, Dieter Kalix, J. A. Graf Kielmannsegg, Peter Stratman Zur Problematik einer Verteidigungsoption fur Mittleeuropa in den achtziger Jahren (Henceforth cited: SWP).

6. This quotation and all of the following that refer to the SWP are not identified individually. The page references are included in the body of the text.

7. The Times, London, July 14, 1977, p. 5, quoting an NSC memorandum that was made public the previous day.

8. Guy Brossollet, "Essay sur la non-bataille" (Editions Belin, Paris 1975). The texts thereof quoted in this chapter are taken from the German edition "Das Ende der Schlact", published in Spannocchi/Brossollet: Verteidigung ohne Schlacht; Munchen, Carl Hanser Verlag, 1976. Page references of quotes follow the German edition, p. 158.

9. This quote and all of the following that refer to Brossollet's essay are not identified individually. The page references are included in the body of the text.

10. The International Institute for Stragegic Studies, The Military Balance, 1978/1979, London, p. 101.

11. Horst Afheldt: Verteidigung und Frieden— Politik mit militarischen Mitteln; Munchen, Carl Hanser Verlag, 1976. (Defense and Peace— Conduct of Politics with Military Means)

12. Ibid. , p. 231, "Result #62"

13. Ibid. , p. 64. See also the following: Edmund O. Stillman "Civilian Sanctuary and Target Avoidance Policy in Thermo-Nuclear War" in Annals of the American Academy of Political and Social Sciences, 392, 1970: 116-32. Bruce M. Russett, "Counter-Combattant Deterrence—A Proposal" in Survival, 1974, pp. 135-40.

14. Afheldt, p. 79, referring to a work edited by Johan Holst and Uwe Nerlich, Beyond Nuclear Deterrence—New Aims, New Arms (New York: Crane Russack, 1977).

15. Edgar O'Ballance "Is Weapon Development Still Possible?" Military Review, 63/11, November 1978: 6.

16. The Military Balance 1978/79: 9, 10, 111-12.

17. Retsae H. Miller, "Air Superiority at the Treetops," _Military Review,_ March, 1979, pp. 2-9.

11

SOVIET AND AMERICAN APPROACHES TO THE ROLES OF CONVENTIONAL FORCES IN INTERNATIONAL POLITICS
Roman Kolkowicz

Europeans seem better able to understand what until recently escaped many U. S. analysts and strategists: the massive strategic-nuclear deterrent forces of both superpowers have lost much of their political and diplomatic-psychological influence. The less glamorous, conventional, general purpose, theatre forces have regained political utility, diplomatic instrumentality, and vital military roles. While U. S. deterrence strategists, intelligence specialists, and military leaders remained under the spell of the elegant deterrence scenerios and paradigms, the Soviets were steadfastly developing a powerful, modern conventional military force, without neglecting the strategic deterrent. It is only very recently that U. S. expert and public communities have become aware of the disturbing facts of Soviet military activism and probing via proxies, "combat brigades," naval movements, and massive military aid in areas of great strategic, political, and economic importance. These concerns are, in part, assuaged by orchestrated Soviet campaigns of peaceful coexistence, detente, arms control, SALT, and summitry; by deliberate Soviet accommodation and reasonableness in dealing with U. S. Presidents, Secretaries of State, Senators, or journalitst; by their dogged adherence to the presidential formulations of "negotiations and not confrontations." The Soviets have been helping us to see what we wanted to see anyway, the quintessential U. S. military strategy and weaponry: strategic nuclear deterrent forces, intercontinental missiles and warheads poised on the brink of destruction and held back by the curious restraining notion of Mutual Assured Destruction, MAD. The Soviets preferred to rivet our attention to the central stage of East-West interaction and confrontation, the Europe-centered, NATO-Warsaw

Pact axis, rather than stimulate excessive Western interests in the more obscure and poorly understood regions of Africa, Persian Gulf, Middle East, and Asia.

The purposes and roles of the conventional forces in Soviet foreign and defense policies remain poorly understood in the United States. There is an increasing unease and uncertainty about the meaning of large and growing Soviet armies and about the intent behind them. We shall attempt to deal with the several aspects of this complex problem as follows: first, we present a brief historical description of the evolution of Soviet policy and doctrine regarding the role of conventional forces; then we examine some reasons for Western difficulties in properly understanding Soviet approaches to the role and uses of strategic and conventional forces; next we discuss the changing nature of international politics and the varying perceptions of and adaptation to these changes in the Soviet Union and the United States; and finally, we assess current and future roles and utilities of conventional forces within the framework of Soviet foreign and defense policy.

BACKGROUND

The role and mission of conventional forces in the Soviet Union have undergone several changes since World War II. During the post-war period until the death of Stalin, Soviet military policy was marked by a basic reliance on massive conventional forces deployed in an active defense posture, with a narrow continental mission. This policy derived from Stalin's "Permanent and Temporary Principles of Warfare" that were based on his experiences during the Great Patriotic War. Although modern military weapons and technology were being introduced in the post-war period into the military establishment, Stalin forced his strategic analysts and planners to "look back" to the successful Russo-German war and draw theoretical and practical lessons of warfare from it. As one Soviet military analyst suggested, "Stalin did not consider the atomic bomb to be a radically different weapon"[1] and he therefore continued to view problems of war and uses of force in the nuclear context in the light of his past experiences. [2] Stalin's sterile principles of warfare, his resistance to innovation in strategic doctrine and policy, his fiat on the need to study the past rather than the future—all these impediments had to be removed before a necessary and orderly transformation was to take place in military affairs.

In the decade after Stalin's death, Soviet military policy underwent far-reaching evaluations and innovations. Military technology and weaponry were modernized, the massive conventional forces were

gradually reduced by more than half, and strategic doctrine and policy were sharply modified. Sometime in 1959, Khrushchev and the
Communist Party Presidium decided to shift Soviet strategic doctrine
from its previous rather ambivalent position to one firmly grounded
on a policy of nuclear deterrence. (The formal promulgation of this
new policy was made in January 1960). The reasoning underlying the
new strategic doctrine and the policies resulting from it were based on
the belief of Khrushchev and other Party leaders that a war with the
United States was highly unlikely, on the rising needs of the Soviet
economic domestic sector, and on the decreasing utility and burden-
some cost of large standing conventional forces. The new strategic
policy provided for a sharp reduction of Soviet conventional "theatre"
forces, a significant upgrading of the roles, missions and resources
of the newly formed strategic missile forces, and a shift of the
burden for the conventional theatre forces to the Warsaw Pact forces
which remained firmly under Soviet control. [3]

This new strategic doctrine and policy reflected Khrushchev's
views that a future war, no matter how initiated, would rapidly become an all-out nuclear exchange. Soviet policy thus called for reliable strategic deterrent capabilities and only minimal conventional
forces. An underlying premise of the new strategic doctrine was
Khrushchev's belief that nuclear war had become politically useless,
since there would be no victors and damage would be so devastating
that organized society would cease to exist. He arrived at that position
gradually, having maintained in 1954 that in the event of a nuclear war
the "imperialists will choke on it and it will end up in a catastrophe for
the imperialist world."[4] In 1955, he still subscribed to the view that
"we cannot be intimidated by fables that in the event of a new world war
civilization will perish."[5] In 1956, he began to hedge, saying that
"war is not fatalistically inevitable"[6] and two years later he reversed
himself, asserting that "a future war would cause immeasurable harm
to all mankind."[7]

Having dismissed the idea of the political utility of nuclear warfare, Khrushchev also rejected the idea of limited local and limited
nuclear warfare, since according to his new strategic doctrine, these
would rapidly become major nuclear wars: "Should such limited wars
break out, they could rapidly grow into a world war."[8] For ideological and tactical reasons he retained the formulas about the "wars of
national liberation" as being "just" and meriting the support of the
Soviet government. It is rather unlikely that he actually contemplated
direct involvement of Soviet forces on behalf of such "just" wars,
given the rather inadequate size and quality of his conventional forces.

Having brought the Soviet Union out of the Stalinist isolation and
inertia, Khrushchev launched an activist foreign policy carried out by
means of a vigorous diplomatic campaign and nuclear blackmail (in the

form of exploitation of overstated strategic capabilities for political gains), and by committing Soviet policy and prestige to situations that were risky and from which he had to extricate himself under Western pressure, or because the West called his bluff. He also accelerated the erosive forces within the Communist bloc through his de-Stalinization campaign, simplistic economic solutions and crash programs, and his dangerous external military and political gambles. The results were destructive: the West tested the credibility of his nuclear blackmail diplomacy and clearly showed the world the hollowness of Soviet militancy; within the bloc, China turned from an ally into an enemy and other satellites challenged the Soviet lead; domestically, his sweeping reforms confused planners, and alienated powerful bureaucracies and most of the military. Khrushchev was easily ousted from power in October 1964.

The new regime of Brezhnev and Kosygin confronted the problems brought on by their "harebrained" predecessor, including the credibility of Soviet military policy and its international political prestige and influence. To the new regime, the proper answer to Khrushchev's bombast, irresponsible claims, erratic political behavior, and confusing and demoralizing "shturmovshchina" seemed to be sobriety, pragmatism, and the establishment of credibility through the attainment of conspicuous capabilities to match declaratory policy and policy objectives. Brezhnev struck this note of prudence and restraint by asserting that "we are striving to make our diplomacy vigorous and active, and at the same time we exhibit flexibility and caution."[9] The new policy was to be one of "opposing aggressive imperialist circles without allowing ourselves any sabre-rattling or irresponsible talk."[10]

The new regime, however, faced some immediate bleak prospects at home, in the bloc, and in the international arena. The United States represented a virtually unchallengeable military, political, and economic giant, while the Soviet Union, in the aftermath of the Cuban missile fiasco, seemed to have been reduced to a secondary power. Soviet relations with China were at a nadir; Soviet commitments undertaken by Khrushchev became a burden to Soviet economy; and the expected gains in Soviet political influence failed to materialize. Internally, the Party leaders faced a restless and demoralized set of bureaucracies, while in Eastern Europe the forces of nationalism and polycentrism were eroding Soviet influence and control. Above all, Soviet military power was shown to have been quite inferior to that of the United States.

The new Politburo leadership appears to have launched a thorough reassessment of the traditional pattern of Soviet foreign and defense policies. The center of gravity and the main direction of Soviet political and military policy since World War II was Western-oriented, focused on Europe. Throughout much of the post-war peri

Soviet leaders had remained preoccupied with the central political-military axis of East-West confrontation, while the Third World played a peripheral and minor role, and China remained an ally. Thus, the bulk of Soviet military deployments, their strategic doctrine and policies, and their political activism had focused largely on NATO and the United States.

The new Soviet leadership appears to have assessed this traditional pattern of policies and priorities, and undoubtedly found it to be in the long run unproductive: a high-cost, high-risk, low-pay-off policy. The new alignment of forces in the international arena and their corollary changes seemed to have persuaded the Brezhnev leadership to modify and realign the direction of Soviet foreign and military policies.

The emerging new Soviet military and foreign policy direction under the Brezhnev regime may therefore be characterized as one of Hold-Contain-Explore: hold, stabilize and normalize Soviet political, economic, and military relations with the West, thus gaining a larger measure of freedom and resources to deal with; and contain the mounting pressures and challenges from Communist China, while simultaneously continuing to explore and exploit the areas south of Russia for promising targets of opportunity.

This new Soviet policy design is reflected in a number of their political, economic, military, and diplomatic initiatives since the mid-1960s. The Soviets have strongly supported detente, arguing for a relaxation of tensions and peaceful coexistence with Europe and the United States; they supported strategic arms limitations talks, European Security proposals, and general normalization of relations between Eastern and Western Europe; they espoused the principle of active cultural and scientific exchanges between East and West; they even relaxed their traditional emigration and travel laws and practices; they reduced the anti-Western militant rhetoric and embarked on dramatic summitry meetings in Washington, Moscow, and elsewhere. While these initiaitves were to serve specific purposes, there is little doubt that they were also intended to stabilize, normalize, and de-ideologize their relationship with the West; and to hold and stabilize their western flank, while strengthening their eastern flank facing China and their southern flank in the areas of Middle East, Persian Gulf, and Africa. The Soviets have therefore shifted the traditional axis of confrontation from Europe and the West into the less contentious yet strategically and economically vital areas south of the USSR.

Since the Soviet objectives in the three major areas of interest differ, so do their tactics and strategies. They seem to prefer stability in Europe in their relations with the United States and, for different reasons, with China. On the other hand, they prefer selective and controlled instability in regions more vulnerable to their current expansionist objectives. The successful pursuit of these objectives depends to an overwhelming extent on conventional and nonstrategic forces. While the Soviets therefore pursue negotiations on the limitation of strategic arms, they insist on retaining freedom to maintain, deploy, and expand their nonstrategic forces.

The changes in Soviet foreign policy directions brought about corollary changes in their strategic doctrine and policy. By the late 1960s and early 1970s, Soviet strategic policy began to shift from the earlier positions. As the Soviets began to acquire substantial nuclear capabilities, moving into strategic parity with the United States and therefore gaining a great measure of security, they began to modify the stark Khrushchevite finite-deterrence, neo-massive retaliation doctrines of the preceding decade. The latter view had been clearly stated by the then Minister of Defense, Marshal Malinovskii:

> A future world war . . . will be a decisive armed clash
> of the opposed social systems . . . it will inevitably be
> thermonuclear, a war in which the main means of de-
> struction will be the nuclear weapon, and the basic
> means of its delivery to the target, the rocket . . . War
> might arise without the traditional clearly threatening
> period, by surprise, as a result of the mass use of
> long-range rockets armed with powerful nuclear war-
> heads. [11]

The official Soviet doctrine of 1960 was set out by Khrushchev:

> Our state has at its disposal powerful rocket equipment.
> The military air force and navy have lost their pre-
> vious importance . . . In the navy the submarine fleet
> assumes great importance while surface ships can no
> longer play the part they once did . . . In our times the
> defense potential of the country is determined not by the
> numbers of our soldiers under arms and the number of
> persons in naval uniform . . . but by the total firepower
> and the means of delivery available. [12]

After Khrushchev's ouster, various Soviet strategists began to modify this doctrinal orthodoxy. In 1965, the fourth edition of the authoritative Marxism-Leninism on War and the Army stated that while "our military doctrine gives the main role in defeating the aggressor to the nuclear rocket weapon . . . it does not deny the important significance of other kinds of weapons and means of fighting."[13] Several years later, in the fifth edition of the same volume, a qualification was added to the end of the above sentence stressing ". . . and the possibility in certain circumstances of conducting combat actions without the use of the nuclear weapon."[14]

The growing importance of nonstrategic, conventional forces and weapons was reflected in the public writings of authoritative Soviet analysts. Communist of the Armed Forces stated that under modern conditions "the role of conventional means and the traditional services of the armed forces are greatly increased." The author then stressed that it therefore "becomes necessary to train troops for various kinds of warfare." Indicating that his views are not without opposition among the Soviet strategic community, the author suggests that while his view may be "interpreted as a negation of the contemporary revolution in military affairs . . . one cannot agree with this opinion." He then proceeds to lecture his more obtuse colleagues on the basic proposition regarding the stability of nuclear deterrence and the corresponding greater utility of forces and weapons below the nuclear and strategic threshold: "The point is, that the new possibilities of waging armed struggle have arisen not in spite of, but because of, the nuclear missile weapons."[15]

The various roles of conventional forces were expanded in the 1970s, including now their external, projective, and expansionistic functions:

> Greater importance is being attached to Soviet military presence in various regions throughout the world, reinforced by an adequate level of strategic mobility of its armed forces . . . In those cases wherein support must be furnished to those nations fighting for their freedom and independence against forces of international reaction and imperialist interventions, the Soviet Union may require mobile and well-trained and well-equipped forces . . . Expanding the scale of Soviet military presence and military assistance furnished by other socialist states is being viewed today as a very important factor in international relations.[16]

This projective and interventionist role of the conventional forces was spelled out by Admiral Gorshkov, the "father" of the modern Soviet navy, who argued that "demonstrative actions of the fleet in many cases make it possible to achieve political goals without resorting to armed conflict by just indicating pressure by their potential might and the threat of initiating military actions."[17] He also lectured his listeners on the fact that:

The neutral waters of the world ocean permit accomplishing the transfer and concentration of forces of the fleet without breaking the positions of international law, without giving the opposing side formal ground for protests or other forms of counteractions. [18]

CONTEMPORARY ROLES AND MISSIONS OF SOVIET CONVENTIONAL FORCES

The Soviet Union is assuming an expansionist, imperial role in world affairs. Although Soviet policy and tactics remain cautious, prudent, and generally nonprovocative, they nevertheless maintain constant, unrelenting pressure upon areas of assumed vulnerability and potential payoff. The cutting edge of this expanding and pressing juggernaut is not the nuclear shield of deterrence, but the more flexible conventional sword. The Soviets seem to have understood that massive nuclear weaponry is vital for the primary purpose of deterring other nuclear powers; however, they seem also to have understood that the political, diplomatic, and psychological utility of these strategic weapons would decrease as they became more massive, more terrible, more politically and militarily inert. Conventional forces are eminently suitable to Soviet thinking, traditions, ideological and political objectives. Conventional forces serve many purposes and objectives of the Party and the State.

Internal Purposes

The Soviet Union contains what is probably the most entrenched, powerful, and largest military establishment in the world. This vast military system claims the highest priority in national planning, allocations, and resources; it absorbs a vast proportion of the GNP, skilled manpower, scientific and technological personnel and facilities. Representatives of the military participate in the most important decisions of the state and Party, and have virtual veto-power over certain policy processes that might affect military interests. [19]

The Soviet Union is presently ruled by a coalition of aging Party bureaucrats, who have come to rely more and more on the military for maintenance of Party hegemony at home, for policing the restless alliance partners, and for projecting Soviet influence abroad. It is not ideological elan, revolutionary fervor, economic and technological vitality, or political strength that serves as the primary source of

Soviet expansion and penetration in the Third World. These objectives are accomplished, instead, through military aid, military personnel, and military equipment and weaponry.

The conservative and aging Party leadership depend upon the military to help them retain power and to serve the vast and diverse nation as a "school for communism" seeking to Russify and pacify the restless anti-Moscow and anti-Communits nationalities. The Party relies on the military to maintain a vast network of paramilitary organizations that create a nation-in-arms effect and attitude in the populace. As the erosion of bloc-coherence is compounded by pressures from nationalities and aggravated by rising consumer demands that threaten Party hegemony, the military appears to the Party leadership to be a staunch, reliable source of order, of tradition and nationalism. The military has, indeed, remained over the years the very loyal, supportive, reliable, conservative, and nationalistic bulwark of several regimes. [20]

These vital internal and alliance-wide functions are performed primarily by the conventional forces, the infantry, armor, artillery, communications, tactical aviation troops, and the large network of schools and camps, rather than those of the more sophisticated, remote, outward-oriented strategic-nuclear forces of the Strategic Missile Forces, Strategic Aviation, and Nuclear Submarine Fleet.

Soviet military leaders are clearly aware of their vital and powerful position in Soviet politics. They play low-key institutional and bureaucratic politics, accumulating vast amounts of weapons and technology, and biding their time. The cutting edge of their military probes abroad are the conventional forces.

Alliance Purposes

The Soviet Union has two kinds of alliance problems that are absent from the Western alliance system: the most powerful former ally of Russia became the most formidable foe and challenger in Asia, necessitating a vast amount of manpower, military technology, and military defensive infrastructure at great cost; and the Soviet Union insists on maintaining a large military force in several countries of Eastern Europe for purposes that include the assurance of alliance loyalty. In effect, a large part of Soviet military forces are tied up in defending its borders from Chinese pressures and maintaining Warsaw Pact coherence and loyalty. The role of conventional forces, particularly in Eastern Europe, is vital to that Soviet mission, both as a quasi-police force, as a core and cadre force for the Warsaw Pact conventional military establishments. and as a potential spearhead of a conventional attack against NATO.

External Purposes

Soviet strategic doctrine and policy since the ouster of Khrushchev have generally rejected the stark U. S. concept of deterrence by punishment that effectively gave the protagonists a singular either/or option (either peace or nuclear incineration). The Soviets argued that neither total peace nor total nuclear war was the most probable outcome of U. S. -Soviet interaction or conflict of interests. Instead, the Soviets maintained that conflicts, hostilities, and wars were very likely to occur in various parts of the world, particularly in the Third World, and that Soviet involvement by conventional means in such developments was not to be excluded. Moreover, Soviet strategists maintained that, in the event of a nuclear war, conventional forces were to play a vital though not primary role.

Strategic Supportive Role of Conventional Forces. A recent Brookings study of the Soviet Military Buildup asserted that

> ground forces dominate the Soviet defense establishment.
> From 1964 to 1976 Soviet ground forces expanded from
> 140 divisions to 170, an increase of 21%, and were ex-
> tensively redeployed. The largest increase took place
> in the Far East, where approximately 29 divisions have
> been sent since 1964. The number of Soviet divisions in
> Eastern Europe was increased from 26 to 31. [21]

The vital role of conventional forces is also emphasized in a recent study of Soviet Theatre Nuclear Offensive:

> The ground forces are the key to the Soviet offense, nu-
> clear and non-nuclear; and to defeat the Soviet Strategy,
> one must first destroy their ground forces offensive con-
> cept . . . The key attributes of the Soviet offensive con-
> cept . . . are surprise, attack from the march, and
> rapid exploitation. The three elements critical to the
> success of their concept are the troops (tanks and mo-
> torized infantry), mobility, and command and control. [22]

The role of armor in the context of nuclear war is widely and repeatedly stressed by Soviet writers, who maintain that "tanks are better able to withstand the effects of nuclear weapons, possess a high cross-country ability and speed of movement off-roads, and are capable of accomplishing rapid maneuvers and delivering an attack to a great depth. "[23] Expressing a similar viewpoint, Marshal Sokolovskii states,

"In the theater of ground operations, offensive operations will develop along fronts, in the course of which
strategic tasks will be accomplished. This will be a
theater offensive following nuclear strikes by strategic
means which will play the decisive role in the defeat of
the enemy. Following the retaliatory nuclear strikes,
airborne landings may be launched in great depth, and,
depending upon radiological conditions, the ground
forces formations which are still intact will initiate a
rapid advance with the support of the air force, in order
to complete the destruction of the surviving armed
forces of the enemy."[24]

Quasi-Revolutionary, Political, and Military Roles Abroad. A
fervent hope and policy objective of U.S. diplomats and political leaders in recent years has been to establish a common set of interests
and responsibilities for both superpowers, to domesticate, as it
were, the Red Bear, the modern heirs of the Bolsheviks. The accom-
odational line of U.S. policy toward the Soviet Union was to bring
about "linkage" whereby Detente, Disarmament/Arms Control, and
Deterrence were to "mellow" and "modernize" the Soviets, who were
assumed by the Western strategists to be "rational" and therefore
aware of the stark either/or alternatives to deterrence.

The Soviets once again surprised and disappointed the Western
strategists. Soviet leaders succumbed to their traditional dualist
roles, whereby they adopted the gospel of Detente, SALT, and Stable
Deterrence, while simultaneously pursuing the quasi-revolutionary,
expansionist, destabilizing business-as-usual. Moreover, the Soviets
seem to be surprised by the naivete, obtuseness, or perficy of the
Western strategists, diplomats, and politicians:

It would be utopian to assume that peaceful coexistence
between countries with different social systems could
at once rule out any armed clashes. So long as imperialism and armed adventurism exist, they will inevitably, if only by virtue of their own momentum, unleash
armed action against the liberation movement of oppressed classes and peoples . . . That is why all the
talk about an end of the "era of wars" and the arrival
of an "era of universal peace" is premature and dangerous. [25]

The CPSU Central Committee in its Theses of December 1969 force-
fully reiterated the Soviet position: "Peaceful coexistance has nothing

in common with class peace and does not even cast the slightest doubt upon the oppressed peoples' sacred right to use all means, including armed struggle, in the cause of their liberation. "[26]

The Soviet government's main paper, Izvestiia, maintains that while

"wars can and must be banned as a means for resolving
international disputes" between the superpowers and
their alliances, "we must not 'ban' civil or national
liberation wars, we must not 'ban' uprisings, and we
by no means must 'ban' revolutionary mass movements
aimed at changing the political and social status quo. "[27]

The primary task of the Soviet military in recent years, especially of their conventional, nonnuclear forces, has been linked with the revolutionary movements in the Third World: its aim is to play a decisive role in supporting these national liberation, anti-imperialist regimes and forces against Western encroachments. The chief ideological spokesman for the military, General of the Army Yepishev, claims that

The defense of the socialist countries is closely bound
up with all-round assistance to national liberation movements, progressive regimes and young states fighting to
free themselves from the imperialist strangle-hold. The
function of each socialist army in defending its own country and the socialist community as a whole thus objectively merges with the liberation struggle of the international working class, with the national liberation
movement of the entire progressive mankind. [28]

The role of the Soviet conventional forces is seen by the Soviets as a central and vital factor in supporting anti-Western movements and regimes, as a protector of anti-Western fledgling regimes against "exported counterrevolution" and as the primary influence-building factor in the Third World. These objectives the Soviets seek to accomplish by means of intensified port visits, showing the flag, and influence-building measures; by means of proxy-support, arms assistance, and training and education programs; by the manning of key defensive technological sectors of indigenous armies in the Third World, and other means. General Yepishev maintains that

The Soviet Union's ability to give assistance to the
working people waging revolutionary liberation struggles
and the volume of this assistance have become greater

still in the present conditions. This manifests itself, above all, in deterrence of the militarist elements of the imperialist states, prevention of the export of counterrevolution by the imperialists, and in the provision of certain instances of the armies of the developing countries with weapons and training of military specialists for them. [29]

PROBLEMS OF PERCEPTION: PERSISTENCE OF DOCTRINAL ORTHODOXIES

To the Western analyst, Soviet strategic scholars behave like scholastics, rigidly adhering to absolutist dogmas premised on timeless doctrines with universal applicability across political, geographic, and ideological boundaries. "The laws of strategy are objective and apply inexorably and to the same degree to all belligerents."[29] To Western deterrence theorists, the public formulations of Soviet strategic concepts and theory would appear peculiarly simplistic, anecdotal, tautological, and "soft" as compared with their own deductive theories, which seem to them tightly reasoned and logically impeccable.

> One of the problems of military strategy is the study of the laws of armed combat by means of theoretical analysis of military experience on a strategic scale, giving due considerations to the state of military art. One of the main missions for strategy is to study the conditions and nature of future war and to develop the methods and forms of its conduct. [30]

Western deterrence theorists might argue that Soviet strategic theory and doctrine are excessively politicized and subordinated to the values, interests, and whims of political elites:

> In defining the essential nature of war, Marxism-Leninism proceeds from the proposition that war is not an aim in itself, but rather a tool of policy. In his remarks on Clausewitz' book Vom Kriege (On War), V. I. Lenin stressed that "politics is the guiding force, and war is only the tool, not vice versa. Consequently it remains only to subordinate the military point of view to the political." The relationship of war as a tool of politics

determines the relationship of military strategy to politics and makes the former completely dependent upon the latter. [31]

Western strategists and experts become quite exasperated with the primitive and "unsophisticated" aspects of Soviet strategic doctrine and policy:

> This theme of automaticity of global nuclear war seems calculated not only to reinforce the credibility of Soviet nuclear retaliation, but also to discourage the United States and its allies from entertaining the idea that ground rules of some sort might be adapted for limiting the destructiveness of a war, should one occur. Nowhere in this book (Soviet Military Strategy by Marshal Sokolovsky), as in most Soviet military literature as well, are there to be found signs of serious professional interests in concepts like controlled response and restrained nuclear targeting, which have been widely discussed in the West. [32]

Of course, Western exasperation with Soviet ways is reciprocated: Soviet military and political experts dismiss Western strategic theory as pretentious, unscientific scribbling:

> The idea of introducing rules and games and artificial restrictions by agreement seems illusory and untenable. It is difficult ot visualize that a nuclear war, if unleashed could be kept within the framework of rules and would not develop into an all-out war. In fact, such proposals are a demagogic trick designed to reassure the public opinion. [33]

Serious Soviet strategic writers, as well as the Party hacks, are in agreement that a fundamental flaw in Western deterrence theories is their detachment from the political and social context within which they are to operate, and the excessive determinism of numbers and technological imperatives that drive deterrence theory and practice. The authoritative Sokolovsky volume states:

> It is quite evident that such views are the consequence of metaphysical and anti-scientific approach to a social phenomenon such as war and are the result of idealization of the new weapons. It is well-known that the essential nature of war as a continuation of politics does

not change with changing technology and armament. The
imperialist ideologists require contrary conclusions to
justify their preparations for a new war . . . in their
opinion, it is not the civil but rather the military organization which, with science, has taken over the
leadership. [34]

This sort of reasoning continues to be dismissed in the West as
ritualistic formulations of little or no relevance to serious study of
strategy. The occasional critical question about the "questionable
character of many of the premises and assumptions upon which deterrence theory has been based"[35] seems not to have substantially affected the basic faith in the body of deterrence theory and dogma.

It is clear, however, that there are several fundamental disparities and asymmetries in Soviet and U. S. approaches to strategy,
foreign policy, and the uses of force in the pursuit of national interests and policy objectives. The main reason for the persistence of
these conceptual, perceptual, and doctrinal disparities lies in the
dogmatic nature of the two strategic belief systems, and in the historical, cultural, and political conditions of the two countries. We are
dealing here with two orthodoxies that are by their natures mutually
exclusive: each claims a monopoly on scientific truth.

The fundamental divergence and disparity between the two belief
systems and strategies for action are readily seen in this brief schematic listing of their different approaches to the formulation of strategy and theory, and to the uses of force in support of foreign policy.

Strategic Theories and Doctrines

United States	Soviet Union
Unitary Theory	Dualistic Theory
Universal Applicability	Particularistic Applicability
Deductive Approach	Inductive/Deductive Approach
Normative Compellence	Selective Relevance
Ahistorical Context	Historical Relevance
Apolitical Context	Political Relevance/Context

Deterrence theory is a uniquely American construct, shaped
historical, political, institutional, and idiosyncratic influences and
circumstances in the postwar period. A recent critical study of deterrence stated that:

> Deterrence was conceived in its modern sense when it
> became possible to threaten vast damage and pain while
> leaving opposing forces intact. [36]
>
> The atomic bomb that ended World War II and the
> bipolar system that emerged out of it set the stage for
> the emergence of contemporary deterrence theory: the
> former made deterrence necessary and the latter made
> it possible. [37]
>
> Two major historical factors shaping the develop-
> ment of deterrence theory have been the locus of the
> most salient threat to the United States and, somewhat
> related, analysts' and policy makers' image of the rel-
> evant conflict. Until recently, by far the most salient
> threat has been strategic. [38]

The problem with deterrence is that it tends to "reinforce policy
makers' tendency to rely too heavily on deterrence strategy and deterrent threats in lieu of the more flexible instruments of inter-nation
influence associated with classical diplomacy."[39] By the mid 1950s,
"the U.S. reliance on deterrence threats and alliance commitments as
the primary tool of foreign policy vis-a-vis the Soviet Union had become a rigidified response to almost any perceived communist en-
croachment anywhere in the world."[40]

A fundamental flaw of deterrence was that it became "theoretically most-developed and practically best-applied to acute bi-polar
conflict where great values are at stake, and where the potential for
great violence is high."[41] Thus the American ur-model of war and
strategy envisions a direct confrontation between the superpowers and
their respective alliance along a central axis in Europe that crosses
NATO/Warsaw Pact territories. This is further characterized by
clearly delineated rules of the game, properly deployed capabilities,
and communications and signalling characteristics so dear to the
hearts of pure deterrence strategists. This was to be a bipolar
either/or type of confrontation, which by the very nature of its
terrible and terrifying consequences would mitigate against a suicidal
initiation of hostilities and thus validate and legitimize the logical,
theoretical, and political content of deterrence.

This might be called a Cowboy Strategy, reflecting U.S. preferences, styles, and values: a High Noon, Shoot-Out-On-Main-Street
strategy with a despised adversary. It also reflects a set of very
practical concerns and preferences, since this ur-scenario is premised on American advantage and Soviet disadvantage.

The Soviets, however, have not complied with U.S. deterrence
theories, preferences, or fantasies. Instead of confronting us directly
and frontally in the European NATO/Warsaw Pact theatre, the Soviets

have chosen to probe, feign, and challenge the United States and its
allies in areas remote from Europe and largely by the use of
allies and proxies. Soviet military and political behavior reflect what
may be called a Comissar Strategy, which is essentially nonconfronta-
tional, or more properly, confrontation-avoidance under low control
conditions. It is a strategy that is secretive, manipulative, deceptive,
theoretically inelegant, and methodologically unsophisticated. It is a
strategy of negotiations and confrontations, one that rejects the stark
U. S. deterrence alternatives of either/or (either peace and stability
or the prospects of nuclear incineration) in favor of a kind of neither/
nor deliberativeness (accepting neither the imperative of perfect peace
nor the alternative of nuclear mutual suicide as its cost.) The Soviets
appear to approach the problems of strategy as a highly politicized
means-ends process, rather than as the American ends-means teleo-
logy of Armageddon-avoidance.

Ultimately, deterrence strategy is one that is logically and politically suitable to a conservative, status-quo and balance-of-power
state with vital international economic interests; a power possessing
strategic superiority, whose traditional values favor minimal direct
involvement in remote areas; a power that historically relies primarily on technological and economic solutions for the implementation
of its foreign policy by military means. It is a strategy eminently
suitable for dealing with a troublesome but weaker adversary, for
launching terrible threats in order to appeal to the bully's sense of
survival.

Soviet strategy is one suitable to a quasi-revolutionary, expansionist power, one interested in changing the international system and
status quo; it is suitable to a power that has emerged on the international scene as a strategic inferior, that has traditionally relied on
brute force of mass armies motivated by primarily defensive continental strategies, with coastal defensive navies; a country that has
had little experience with massive projection of its forces beyond the
Eurasian mass. It is a strategy of a country with global and universal
ideological and political interests and claims, but one that is not in a
hurry, believing that history and time are on its side. Deterrence may
therefore have been a most logical and suitable strategic theory and
policy for the United States during the period of its ascendance in
international affairs, when it enjoyed strategic superiority and a
supportive public whose internal values were in harmony with its external goals, and when it confronted a Soviet Union whose leadership
was divided, and whose armed forces were inadequate and inferior to
those of the West. However, times have changed: the Soviet Union
has become at least as militarily powerful as the United States and
has moved from its previous continental, defensive military policy
and strategy into the direction of a global superpower. Soviet strategic
doctrine and policy in the post-war period have shown themselves to be

more flexible and adaptable than those of the West. While the United States remained largely committed to deterrence strategy and some of its variations, [42] despite the profound changes in international and regional politics, the Soviets have shown a lively interest in experimenting with strategic formulations in an effort to fit strategy to policy and to the changing political and technological circumstances. At present, Soviet strategy consists of a deterrent strategic nuclear shield for the primary purpose of deterring and thus neutralizing the threat from the West, and of a flexible and powerful strategy of engagement in the vulnerable and vital areas of the Third World by means of a conventional force sword.

CONCLUSIONS

There is a fundamental disparity in Soviet and U. S. approaches to the role and utility of military forces in the nuclear context. The U. S. approach has largely been conditioned by the initial monopoly of atomic/strategic weapons, by the two- to three-decade long strategic superiority vis-a-vis the Soviet Union, and by the parallel confrontation with the Soviets across political and ideological boundaries. Being primarily a status quo, stable power with complex international interests and commitments, the United States pursued a foreign and strategic policy that logically reflected these interests. That policy is one of balance, stability, and equilibrium: essentially a linear, monistic, unitary policy of deterrence by punishment, which envisages a single either/or alternative to the protagonists—war avoidance or nuclear annihilation, behave or else.

The Soviets pursued a different line of analysis that resulted in disparate strategic doctrines and policies as well as dissimilar foreign policy objectives and strategies. These may be characterized as inherently dualistic, pursuing simultaneously formal policies of stability and balance while at the same time advancing policies of disruption of international order, fomenting destabilizing and revolutionary conditions, and generally seeking substantial changes in the status quo. Soviet military policy therefore sought to build large strategic nuclear forces for purposes of deterrence and supported policies of detente and arms control. At the same time, the Soviets continued to maintain and modernize their conventional forces in support of their secondary policies and objectives.

Soviet conventional forces perform many functions of great importance to the Soviet state and the Communist Party: internal functions of integration and consolidation of Party hegemony, "nation building," and maintenance of vigilance and levels of military preparedness against internal and external foes; alliance functions, including policing of unreliable allies, containment of dangerous former allies who have turned enemy, support of indigenous regimes that may be unpopular, and containment of indigenous regimes that may seek excessive autonomy from Moscow's influence; external military-political functions, including support for strategic forces in their deterrent deployments, or, in case of nuclear or conventional war, support for revolutionary or pro-Moscow regimes in the Third World by various means and exploring various targets of opportunity for purposes of expansion and exploitation by Moscow.

In the final analysis, as long as Soviet leaders claim to be at the head of a world revolutionary movement, whose historical and ideological duty it is to resist imperialism and support Marxism-Leninism in its various forms, they need to retain and maintain a flexible military arm, a quasi-revolutionary vanguard. A rigid adherence to a passive, deterrence-only strategy would have created a fortress-Russia effect, abdicating Moscow's claims to global roles, and would have reduced and negated the political vitality and military activism that is presently enjoyed by the Soviet military and Party leaders.

NOTES

1. Col. I. Korotkov, "The Development of Soviet Military Theory in Postwar Years," in Voenno-Istoricheskii Zhurnal, 4 (April 1964).

2. See R. L. Garthoff, Soviet Strategy in the Nuclear Age, (Praeger: New York, 1958); and H. S. Dinerstein, War and the Soviet Union (Praeger: New York, 1959).

3. See R. Kolkowicz, The Soviet Military and the Communist Party (Princeton: Princeton University Press, 1967) Ch. V.

4. Pravda, June 13, 1954.

5. Pravda, March 27, 1955.

6. TASS, February 14, 1956.

7. Radio Budapest, April 3, 1958.

8. Pravda, January 9, 1960.

9. L. Brezhnev, Pravda, September 30, 1965.

10. Kommunist, editorial, August 1965.

11. Bditel'no Stoyat Na Strazhe Mira, Moscow Voenizdat, 1962, pp. 24-27.

12. N. S. Khrushchev, O Vnezhnei Politike Sovietskogo Soiuza, 1960gl, Gospolitizdat, Moscow, 1961, Vol. 1.

13. N. Sushko and S. A. Tyushkevich, eds. Marksism-Leninism O Voinye i Armii, 4th ed., Voenizdat, Moscow, 1965, p. 244.

14. Harriet F. Scott and William F. Scott, The Armed Forces of the USSR, (Boulder, Col.: Westview Press, 1979), p. 54.

15. Lt. Col. V. M. Bondarenko, Kommunist Vooruzhennykh Sil, December 1968.

16. V. M. Kulish, ed. Voennaya Sila i Mezhdunarodnoe Otnoshenia, 1972, cited in H. F. Scott and William F. Scott, op. cit., p. 57.

17. Admiral S. G. Gorshkov, Morskaya Moshch Gosudarstva, Voenizdat, Moscow, 1976, p. 403.

18. Ibid., This is a long way from the Khrushchevite assertions of the early 1960s, which were then accompanied by veiled threats to the disbelievers, who were called "supporters of traditions, who do not want to recognize the changed roles of the various branches and arms of the armed forces, while dogmatically expounding the well-known thesis . . . about their harmonious development." Thus "adherence to past experience is inevitably accompanied by an overappreciation and fetishism of former models, especially if they led to victory."
Also, in Kommunist Vooruzhennykh Sil, 11, 1961: 52-53.

19. R. Kolkowicz, The Soviet Military and the Communist Party.

20. R. Kolkowicz, "Future of Civil-Military Relations in Socialist Countries: The Soviet Union," presented in Santa Barbara, May 1979.

21. Barry Blechman, et. al., The Soviet Military Buildup and U.S. Defense Spending (Washington: The Brookings Institution, 1977), p. 9.

22. Joseph D. Douglass, Jr., The Soviet Theater Nuclear Offensive (U.S. Air Force, 1976), pp. 102-3.

23. V. Ye. Savkin, The Basic Principles of Operational Art and Tactics (Moscow: Voenizdat, 1972), p. 195.

24. Marshal of the Soviet Union, V. D. Sokolovskii, ed. Voennaia Strategiia, rev. ed. (Moscow: Voenizdat, 1962), p. 372.

25. Gen. P. Zhilin, "The Military Aspect of Detente," International Affairs, Moscow, 12, 1972: p. 25.
It is instructive to notice how Soviet thinking regarding conventional forces has changed since the days of Khrushchev, who in one of his last public announcements prior to his ouster stated:

When I went out into the training field and saw the tanks attacking and how the antitank artillery hit these tanks, I became ill. After all, we are spending a lot of money to build tanks. And if—God forbid, as they say—a war breaks out, these tanks will burn before they reach the line indicated by the command.
(Pravda, September 22, 1964)

26. Pravda, December 23, 1969.

27. Izvestiia, September 11, 1973.

28. A. A. Yepishev, Some Aspects of Party-Political Work in the Soviet Armed Forces (Moscow), 1975.

29. Marshal V. D. Sokolovskii, Soviet Military Strategy, (Rand edition), p. 90.

30. Ibid.

31. Ibid.

32. The American Editors' Introduction (by H. S. Dinerstein, Leon Goure, and Thomas W. Wolfe) to Sokolovskii volume, pp. 44-45.

33. G. A. Arbatove, Problemy Mira i Sotsialisma, 2, (February 1974): 46.

34. Sokolovskii, p. 99.

35. Alexander L. George and Richard Smoke, Deterrence in American Foreign Policy (New York: Columbia University Press, 1974), p. 2.

36. Ibid. p. 21.

37. Ibid. p. 20.

38. Ibid. p. 47

39. Ibid. p. 2

40. Ibid. p. 7.

41. Ibid. p. 38

42. Ibid. passim.

12

CHINA AND JAPAN
James H. Buck

Since 1945, China has shifted from a major ally of the United States in World War II, to enemy during the Korean War, and now to a tentative friend. In those three decades and more, China has, with great difficulty, established a measure of internal unity, apparently worked its way through the loss of Mao's leadership, secured the allegiance of its people, effectively isolated the Republic of China (Taiwan) from any pretensions to alternate government status, and secured universal recognition as a vital force in global politics.

During the same period, Japan has changed from unyielding enemy to an ally whose relations with the United States form a "cornerstone of world stability and progress." Japan has developed an enormously productive economy supported by a working democratic system with strong public support.

With hugely differing social, political, and economic systems, China and Japan followed varied courses of development after World War II. Each was influenced importantly by its "patron state" until about 1960. China gained from Soviet economic, technical, and military assistance. Japan benefited from occupation reforms and security guarantees introduced by the United States.

For the past two decades, however, each nation has sought greater independence and autonomy in international affairs, while continuing broadly to build on the bases established in the 1950s. Both Japan and China seek to protect their interests by helping to decide important matters within the international community.

This paper deals with the conventional military power of China and Japan, which is essential to this participation. Of course, other nations' perceptions of these conventional military forces are influenced by various "nuclear equations" and the variety of triangles and other geometric forms used to give a short-hand description of the interests, actual and potential alliances, or counterbalancing political configurations in East Asia. But this paper is not about them. Writing last summer, Senator Edward Kennedy opined that for the first time in this century, China, Japan, and the United States enjoy good relations with each other, and for the first time in a half-century, we do not have to choose between China and Japan in our Far East relations. [1] Be that as it may, this paper does not speculate on how these new relationships may develop. It does treat China and Japan separately and in the following topical order: postwar development of forces, decision making for military matters, crisis areas/threat perception, policy perspectives, force posture, and future prospects—a summary assessment of the capacity of each power to affect the nonnuclear international environment.

CHINA: HISTORICAL OVERVIEW

China's military forces trace their origin to the mid-1920s, when they were organized as the military instrument of the Chinese Communist Party (CCP). For the next two decades they operated as a revolutionary guerrilla army, attacking and defending against the Chinese Nationalist forces and the Japanese. After the defeat of Japan in 1945, the communist forces expanded their capability to fight conventional land warfare during the Chinese Civil War and brought military victory to the party in 1949.

The People's Liberation Army (PLA)—so designated to commemorate its role in the political liberation of the Chinese people—soon gained valuable experience in the successful conduct of large-scale conventional military operations against modern and well-trained UN forces during the Korean War (1950-53). This experience taught the PLA leadership that much of Mao's doctrine for a "people's war," while appropriate to the Civil War, did not apply to a war fought outside China against modern forces that used close air support, massive firepower, and infantry-armor-artillery teams. [2] With Soviet assistance in the 1950s, the PLA became a relatively modern and professional force. But the transformation to professional military forces brings forth professional interests that may conflict with those of the political leadership.

In overly simple terms, Chinese military doctrine has evolved from the tension between alternate military purposes: to prepare to fight a "people's war" or to prepare to fight a modern conventional and nuclear war. The PLA was strongly influenced by two decades of experience in guerrilla and conventional mass infantry operations against the Chinese Nationalists and Japan within China's borders. During those years, Mao's doctrine was fixed on "people's war," with emphasis on "fish swimming in the friendly sea," and tactics summarized as "when the enemy advances, we retreat; when the enemy halts, we harass; when the enemy seeks to avoid battle, we attack; when the enemy seeks to retreat, we pursue." Soviet aid to China during the Korean War was followed by equipment modernization assistance estimated to be worth two billion U. S. dollars by mid-1957. Soviet advisors were influential in modernizing the PLA until the late fifties. [3]

Modernization meant that PLA officers became increasingly aware of the complexities of modern military operations. This awareness cast doubt on the value of the pre-1949 experience. A long-standing disagreement over the proper role and mission of the PLA is highlighted by the dismissal of one defense minister, P'eng Teh-huai, in 1959 and the attempted coup d'etat by Lin Piao in 1971. [4] But the contention was not simply between political versus professional orientation toward military problems in the PLA, or of the proletarian versus the bourgeois line, or of reds versus experts, or of the older generation versus the newer generation among PLA officers. [5]

According to Harding, this dichotomy is misleading because the options of people's war and professionalization are not mutually exclusive. He suggests that it is most accurate to speak of competition among people's war, modern ground forces, and strategic forces. This is because China has had to satisfy three criteria regarding its military concerns: (1) the deterrence or repulsion of external threats, (2) the maintenance of a strategic posture at lowest cost, and (3) simultaneous execution of the extensive PLA domestic responsibilities of internal security, socialist construction (civilian economic projects and agricultural production), and training for government and party cadres. Each criterion is, in turn, related to a different military posture and force structure. At the same time, threats to China's security have changed over time. In the fifties, the major concern was U. S. naval and air invasions. In the sixties, there was the fear of preemptive action by the Soviet Union against China's nuclear capabilities and the escalation of conflict in Vietnam. For the last ten years, the major threat has been a border war with the Soviet Union. [6]

On balance, the PLA seems to have adapted to changing political and military requirements with more or less timely compromises between the proponents of people's war and professionalization, while continuing to develop an appropriate strategic posture.

DECISION MAKING FOR DEFENSE POLICY

In theory, broad national policy formulation in China is guided by the Chinese Communist Party (CCP), which demands obedience from all sectors of the society, including the state organs and the PLA

The 300 or so member Central Committee (CC) of the Party carries out directives of the National Party Congress and is responsible for the operation of the state apparatus. The PLA, a tri-service force consisting of ground, naval, and air forces, carries out its missions in line with directives from the CC. The genuine locus of decision making is the Politburo of the CC, a small group ranging in membership from 11 in 1949 to a current high of 27. The Politburo, as well as its smaller Standing Committee (four to nine members), is empowered by the Party Constitution to exercise the functions and powers of the CC when it is not in plenary session. Theoretically, the Politburo is the formal organization that permits coordination of national policy by the leaders who represent China's most powerful political constituencies. Furthermore, these party leaders often hold important posts in China's major political organs and the PLA. Currently, Hua Kuo-feng is Chairman of the Central Committee and also "commands the armed forces of the PRC" (Article 15, 1978 PRC Constitution). Teng Hsiao-p'ing serves concurrently as Vice-Chairman of the CC, Prime Minister of the PRC, Chief of Staff of the PLA, and Vice-Chairman of the Military Commission of the Party.

Of course, this central leadership group concentrated in the Politburo is not a single-minded actor; rather it is the focus for the compromise of competing demands on China's resources. It is the usual locus of decision making, but on some important issues, the circle of participation has been widened; at other times, important decisions have been made elsewhere by some ad hoc bodies and then approved pro forma by the Politburo or its Standing Committee. [7]

Nor is the PLA a unitary political actor. In the 1950s the PLA acted more or less like a pressure group that lobbied the CCP leadership to protect and enhance its corporate interests. In the 1960s, under the leadership of Lin Piao, the PLA turned away from the rather more "professional" pursuits of his predecessor P'eng Teh-huai and turned to the task of assuring party dominance of the PLA. The principle of collective leadership at all command levels was reinstated to enhance the role of political officers. Strong efforts were made to demonstrate the common interests and identity of the PLA members and the people by stressing agricultural and industrial projects and nonmilitary public works.

After 1963, the PLA became, according to Professor Chang, the "object of national emulation and rivaled the party in prestige and political/ideological correctness." In the early stages of the Cultural Revolution in 1966, the PLA was a "veto group" directly participating in settling conflicts at the highest political level. After January 1967, the PLA intervened directly and massively to replace civilian party/government officials in most provinces with a form of direct military rule. As Professor Chang states, the PLA did not gain political power

by a premeditated coup; rather it was through circumstances not of
its own making. The Party lost control and Mao appealed to the army
to bring order out of chaos to save the state and the revolution. When
the Cultural Revolution was terminated, the PLA did not "return to
the barracks." The Ninth Party Congress (April 1969) legitimized
the army's position "in control of nearly every aspect of life in
China,"[8] and named Lin Piao as Mao's successor.

Mao let the genie out of the bottle, with unexpected results that
were political and ideological anathema to him. Mao soon took the
initiative to weaken Lin. A variety of policy differences[9] were involved, but Mao was determined to restore Party supremacy and to
put the PLA in its place. As Mao wrote in 1938, "The Party commands the gun, and the gun must never be allowed to command the
Party." Since Lin's death in the abortive coup d'etat in September
1971 and the subsequent purge/reassignment of Lin's supporters in
the PLA and in the party, this dictum has been followed. Party supremacy was clearly formalized in the Tenth Party Congress (August
1973) when PLA representation in the CC was severely diluted. Mao
seems to have succeeded in controlling the PLA leadership factions by
use of the operational method of "divide and rule, check and balance,"
although that approach may be dysfunctional in the long run,[10] given
the fact that Mao's successors, Hua and Teng, lack the soaring stature
of Mao. Nevertheless, to date, the PLA appears to be a stable force
uninterested in reasserting political power to the extent it did under
Lin's leadership.

While China's defense policy and military posture have been
subjects for decision making at the highest level, it is true that the
top leadership of the PLA, as a component of that decision making
group, should be seen as the aggregate of officers who have individual differences in values, viewpoints, and goals.[11] Whitson has
sought the sources of these differences by analysis of formal and informal groupings of 700 key leaders in the PLA. The formal groupings consisted, prior to the Cultural Revolution, of six major career
channels, usually mutually exclusive: (1) local forces (militia and
public security); (2) ground forces; (3) General Political Department;
(4) General Rear Services Department; (5) navy; and (6) air force.
The informal groupings cut across career lines and confuse the definition of collective interest. These are military generations, field
armies, military regions, the central elite, and personal relationships.

Whitson's analysis highlights the complexities of making analytic
judgments or predictive statements about the origins and precise content of broad military or national security decisions. Generational
differences are probably perceptible in most armies. Certainly, the
U. S. platoon leader of World War II and the platoon leader of the

Vietnam War could be expected to have differing views of the role of the military in society, or say, the most effective tactics for application of military power. On the other hand, the field army experience of PLA officers has no counterpart in the U. S. or postwar Japanese experience. The five field armies that won the Civil War in 1949 had developed independently over the previous two decades. When the armies were replaced by military regions in 1954, the institutional loyalty to the army was reinforced by geographic regional loyalty—at least until the Cultural Revolution. Over these many years, most of the top leadership had served only in one army and one region, with the result that strong regional political loyalties developed, even to the point that Whitson could argue that each region ought to be viewed as a unitary purposive actor. On the other hand, different military regions have historically had different interests among themselves, and also with the center. These differences are strengthened by stable PLA region leadership connected firmly to its allies among the central PLA region leadership in Peking. Yet the central leadership must be under strong pressure to view regional demands in terms of national requirements. By such factors, military policy decision-making analysis is complicated to a degree not encountered in armed forces of Western industrialized nations.

The PLA ground forces (which make up about 80–85 percent of the PLA strength of 4,325,000 personnel) are the dominant service. The senior leadership of the navy and air force had their early careers in the ground forces because of the rather recent development of these two arms. However, the ground force outlook has been inward toward the missions of internal control and preparation for defense against external ground threats and to fight a "people's war," and the navy and air force perspectives have been outward. If the ground forces have favored decentralization and a ground defense strategy oriented to separate military regions, the other two forces favor centralization of control, the acquisition of technologically advanced equipment with accompanying tactics for its use, and the projection of power into the nearby region beyond China's borders. [12] The variant outlooks influence not only broad matters of force posture; they also affect, and are affected by, economic decisions relating to development of steel, automotive, electronics, and shipbuilding industries, and the political aspects of economic and military decision making.

Undoubtedly, the PLA will continue to have interservice rivalry and intraservice conflicts. At the same time, one may expect the PLA as a whole to have a strong common corporate interest in getting larger resource allocations, maintaining an influential role in the political system and to close ranks when threatened. [13] Since 1954, only the PLA has an unbroken record of institutional viability. [14]

In short, decision making on military matters is not solely a function for the party nor for the PLA, nor is it properly viewed as the outcome of Party-PLA disputes. Each probably has a fairly wide spectrum of opinion on major issues. Decisions most likely result from complex coalitions that have both military and party representation.

The next section outlines some decisions to use conventional military force.

CRISIS AREA/THREAT PERCEPTION

If there are significant lacunae in our knowledge of the specific content and process of national security policy formulation in China, the results of the process are observable. Most observers would probably agree that China's actions have been successful, reached on pragmatic grounds, but overlaid with ideological justification.

Earlier mention was made of three major threats perceived by the PRC: U. S. air or naval invasion in the fifties; preemptive Soviet strike against the PRC nuclear establishment in the sixties; and border war to the north since the late sixties. Crisis areas, that is, situations seen to be threats dangerous enough to cause the PRC to use military power, are reviewed here to provide the raw material for this very rough categorization of the purposes for which the PLA has been employed, as well as some general basis for future use in cases where the threat is still seen to exist.

The PLA has been used in a variety of roles in line with its constitutional mission, which has changed little since its founding in 1954. The mission assigned to the PLA in the 1978 PRC Constitution is this:

> The Chinese PLA is the workers' and peasants' own armed force led by the CCP; it is the pillar of the dictorship of the proletariat. The State devotes major efforts to the revolutionization and modernization of the Chinese PLA, strengthens the building of the militia, and adopts a system under which our armed forces are a combination of the field armies, the regional forces, and the militia.
>
> The fundamental task of the armed forces of the PRC is: to safeguard the socialist revolution and socialist construction, to defend the sovereignty, territorial integrity and security of the state, and to guard against subversion and aggression by social-imperialism, imperialism, and their lackeys.

The actual military activity of the PLA needs to be described somewhat differently. It can be divided into three categories: (1) internal actions; (2) actions to support neighboring communist states; and (3) conflict over boundaries. [15]

The major internal actions include the extension of CCP power to the borders of China proper during and after the Civil War of 1946-49, and the suppression and elimination of internal Chinese Nationalist resistance to the CCP. PLA troops moved into Tibet in 1950 to reestablish control there, and were again used in 1959 to suppress, with violence, Tibetan resistance to PRC control and to drive the Dalai Lama and 85,000 Tibetans over the Himalayas into exile.

In the CCP view, the Civil War against the Chinese Nationalists was only suspended temporarily with the flight of the Republic of China (ROC) government to Taiwan. The military actions with the ROC, especially the offshore island "crises" of 1954 and 1958, were clearly regarded as internal matters. The PRC just as clearly regarded U.S. actions in the summer of 1950 as intervention in the Civil War. With U.S. abdication of any role in the defense of Taiwan as of December 31, 1979, the "intervention" will formally, as well as actually, end. Whether the PRC regards its relationship with the ROC today to be one of "civil war" is hard to say. In any event, Peking refused to disavow publicly the use of force in extending its de facto political control to Taiwan, and "The reunification of the motherland is the sacred mission history has handed to our generation."[16] Peking no longer speaks of "liberation" of Taiwan.

The second category of PRC military action is to support the contiguous communist states of North Korea and North Vietnam. In the fall of 1950 (at the same time it was extending military control into Tibet), the PLA began its massive intervention to save North Korea from defeat and occupation by UN forces. Hundreds of thousands of PLA troops fought in Korea from 1950 to mid-1953, when an armistice took effect. PLA withdrawal from Korea was completed in 1958. The Korean intervention was the most important use of military force in PRC history. Primarily defensive in origin, it occurred in territory clearly outside China's borders, was not marked by an extension of political control, and ended, for the most part, with a return to the status quo ante bellum, except that the UN Command and U.S. forces have remained in the Republic of Korea for the past 29 years.

With regard to support of North Vietnam, the PRC deployed up to 50,000 troops on Vietnamese territory from 1965 to 1968, during the latter part of which it was estimated that more than a million PLA personnel within China were assigned to political and economic activities during the Cultural Revolution. [17] As with the Korean case, the

PLA simultaneously carried out large-scale domestic missions as well as out-of-country operations of some magnitude. However, the PLA employment role in Vietnam was quite different from that in Korea. The Chinese troops were "presumably requested by Hanoi to relieve Vietnamese forces for combat in the South and to serve as a deterrent to an American invasion of North Vietnam."[18] Apparently, PLA activity was restricted to construction tasks and to air defense. In both the Korean and Vietnamese cases, military power was projected beyond China's borders for what the PRC considered defensive purposes, was withdrawn when no longer useful, and did not result in expansion of China's territory or extension of direct political control outside its borders.

The third category is border conflicts. There is a great deal of terra irredenta in several directions from China—a set of claims made by successive Manchu, Nationalist, and Communist governments. The PRC has used military force in two "border conflicts"—with India and the Soviet Union. Armed conflict occurred in areas where the relative legal merits of the disputants' claims were not clear, so one may argue that the PLA did not operate beyond its borders. At the same time, both conflicts occurred after other serious issues had arisen; in neither case does it seem that PRC sought solely, or primarily, formal recognition by the antagonist of Chinese sovereignty over particular pieces of territory per se.

After India gave assistance and sanctuary to Tibetans in 1959, Sino-Indian relations deteriorated rapidly. China established new outposts in Ladakh in 1960 near the western edge of their common border, and India countered with a "forward policy" to block a possible Chinese advance.[19] By the summer of 1962, Nehru claimed that India had outflanked the Chinese posts and gained the military initiative. Hostilities erupted (reports differ as to which side began the fight) on October 20, 1962, at both ends of the Sino-Indian border—in Ladakh and in the Northeast Frontier Area (NEFA). Within a few days, PLA units advanced deeply in the NEFA and occupied all the land the PRC claimed in Ladakh. Nehru called these moves a "major invasion" and claimed that the fate of Asia and the world was at stake. India was powerless to repel or eject the PLA. Having demonstrated the strategic vulnerability of India and having gained world recognition of its military superiority along the Sino-Indian border, the PLA withdrew in the next several weeks, leaving a chastened India acutely aware of the PRC's willingness to use force as needed.

China's border dispute with the Soviet Union has centered on navigation rights along the border rivers—the Amur and the Ussuri—and sovereignty over very restricted patches of territory—Bear Island at the confluence of the two rivers near Khabarovsk, and Chenpao/Damansky Island about 100 miles up the Ussuri. Peking's assertion of its rights in these areas is seen as "crucial to China's whole relationship to the Soviet Union and therefore to its standing in the world" and not as an exaggerated concern for inconsequential pieces of land. [20] The border question is a long-standing issue, but it became the focus for the comprehensive Sino-Soviet rivalry and contention in the winter of 1969 when the USSR sought to keep the Chinese off the frozen surface of the rivers. The PRC chose to fight for Chenpao Island in March 1969 and did so successfully. Negotiations for a more or less permanent settlement occur sporadically. But tension remains high. The platoon-sized penetration into Chinese territory by KGB troops on May 9, 1978, was quickly withdrawn and Moscow apologized, but other incidents are possible until a comprehensive settlement of the current impasse is attained. [21]

A rather novel show of force by up to 100 Chinese fishing boats, over half of which were armed, was carried out by the PRC in late April 1978 near the Senkaku (Tiao-yü-tái) Islands northeast of Taiwan. [22] The islands are claimed by both China and Japan, but the question of sovereignty over the Senkakus had earlier been ignored in Sino-Japanese negotiations for diplomatic recognition in 1972 and in the then ongoing negotiations for the Treaty of Peace and Friendship eventually signed on August 12, 1978. Treaty opponents in Japan forced the government, in March, to raise the Senkaku issue and to restate that Japan owned the Senkakus. Thereupon the PLA naval forces, almost certainly with Politburo approval, sent a flotilla of armed fishing vessels to sail around the Senkakus displaying signs claiming the islands as Chinese territory. Faced with a strong Japanese reaction, Chinese officials soon insisted the incident was "accidental" and "not ordered by the PRC." Japan took no military steps to match those of China, but reasserted its sovereignty by regular overflights and seemingly forced Peking to accept Japan's position on the Senkakus if it wanted the Treaty.

As in the case with disputed territory along the Soviet border, the territory per se seems less important than other considerations. China was willing to risk the success of negotiations for an important treaty with Japan by use of military force, perhaps to remind its neighbors that China's claims in other parts of Asia are to be taken seriously. China reiterated on December 26, 1978 its claims to sovereignty over the Spratly and Paracel Islands, and to Pratas Reef and Macclesfield Bank, an act that once again raises territorial disputes with Vietnam, the Philippines, and Malaysia. [23]

POLICY PERSPECTIVES

Of the nine members of the Standing Committee of the Politburo four years ago, all but one has died or been purged. A new top leadership has emerged and apparently consolidated its control. Yet, one cannot say whether it is stable.

The successors to Mao's power have legitimized their control through the 11th National Party Congress (August 1977) and the promulgation of a new PRC Constitution (March 1978). Among the Politburo's 27 full members (average age 68) there is a heavy emphasis on senior military officers (ten), veteran technocrats (five) and party leaders who were purged during the Cultural Revolution (four).[24]

For domestic policy, the new coalition has sought policy legitimacy by re-publication of Mao's older works,[25] and seeks to carry out Chou En-lai's "four modernizations"—agriculture, industry, defense, and science and technology. New departures in foreign policy, such as establishment of diplomatic relations with Japan and the United States, should be viewed in the authoritative framework of the "Three Worlds Thesis" attributed to Mao, and also associated with Chou.[26]

The basic source for the PRC view of the world is "Chairman Mao's Theory of the Differentiation of the Three Worlds Is a Major Contribution to Marxism-Leninism."[27] In Mao's view:

> the United States and the Soviet Union form the first world. Japan, Europe and Canada, the middle section, belong to the second world. We are the third world. The third world has a huge population. With the exception of Japan, Asia belongs to the third world. The whole of Africa belongs to the third world, and Latin America too.[28]

China belongs to the third world—the "main force combatting imperialism, colonialism and hegemonism"—and faces a long struggle against imperialist superpowers.[29]

Mao always believed that the second world could be united in the struggle against the "two hegemonist parties." It is argued that such a development is even more likely today, because Europe and Japan are freeing themselves from U.S. domination and East European peoples wage increasing struggles against the Soviets. Furthermore, European countries face the grave threat of invasion and annexation from the Soviet social-imperialists,[30] and hence, ought to strengthen resistance to the USSR.

The two "hegemonist powers"—the United States and the Soviet Union—are the first world. In the Chinese view, both are imperialist superpowers who control the economy and politics of many countries, export arms in huge quantities, subvert other governments, station troops on foreign soil, and send mercenaries out to fight.[31] In the past few years, however, the analysis continues, the United States has lost strength compared to the Soviet Union, has overreached itself, and "all it can do at present is to protect its vested interests and go over to the defensive in its overall strategies."[32] Therefore, the Soviet Union is "undoubtedly" more dangerous than the United States as a source of world war, and will inevitably adopt an offensive strategy.

Chinese perception of the Soviet threat dominates its foreign policy concerns, which are in turn dominated by the PRC position in Asia. In Asia, the PRC declares:

> Soviet strategy is to put down a strategic cordon around the continent, stretching from the Mediterranean, the Red Sea, the Indian Ocean and up to Haishenwei (Vladivostok), and using the 'Cuba of Asia,' Viet Nam, as its hatchetman, seize the whole of Indochina to dominate Southeast Asia and South Asia and so edge the United States out of the continent.[33]

To counter this Soviet "strategic design," as well as to provide security against employment of Soviet military forces in China's northern border, it is imperative that China proceed with the four modernizations. The recent demarches with Japan and United States affirm China's technological backwardness and openly recognize the need to use the economic and technological know-how of the second world and the United States. There is no other place to learn, save the Soviet Union. Anxious about its northern border, Chinese leaders advise NATO to become stronger, and they support second world nations against the USSR to tie down Soviet forces in Europe. China needs to modernize its conventional armed forces and "Hua Kuo-feng's backers in the army have shifted their defensive planning from Mao's 'people's war' to a more conventional defense."[34] Here again, the acceptable sources of supply are the second world and, in time, perhaps, the United States. For the long term, the PRC seeks to promote unity among the third world, whose united strength can overcome Soviet hegemonism.

The PRC sees Vietnam's "war of aggression" against Kampuchea (Cambodia) as a prerequisite to the extension of its "aggressive forces" to Thailand, Malaysia, and Burma and the achievement of its goal of regional hegemony. Vietnam, then, is a willing Soviet pawn in its own strategic deployment for hegemony over Southeast Asia and the Pacific.[35]

Sino-Vietnamese tension increased markedly during 1978. China exerted pressure on Vietnam either to create a diversion to lessen Vietnamese actions in Kampuchea or to warn that further action would provoke a Chinese attack. These measures failed, and apparently a decision was made in late 1978 that China would attack Vietnam. In remarks made in the United States, in Japan, and in Peking, Teng Hsiao-p'ing said that China felt she must "punish" Vietnam.[36] The PLA moved across the Vietnamese border on February 17, 1979 in a "defensive counterattack." The PRC action seemed to have been planned with caution, executed with vigor, and probably conveyed the message that further moves toward Vietnamese-Soviet hegemony in Southeast Asia would be resisted. PLA troops began their withdrawal in mid-March, and negotiations began in Hanoi in mid-April, 1979.

FORCE POSTURE/CAPABILITIES

The PLA's operational theater nuclear force, capable of reaching much of Asia and the Soviet Union, is the inevitable backdrop for a brief summary of the PLA conventional forces.[37] Fission and fusion weapons may number several hundred and could be delivered by tactical fighter aircraft and by TU-16 medium-range bombers with a radius of 2,000 miles. Thirty to 40 each of medium and intermediate range ballistic missiles, with ranges up to 1750 miles, are deployed.

PLA ground force strength reportedly increased during 1977 by 375,000 personnel to a strength of 3,625,000 in 1978, but the number of divisions remained stable. The Army has 11 armored, 121 infantry and three airborne divisions classified as Main Force units available for nationwide deployment under the operational control of the Military Affairs Committee, as well as 70 infantry divisions classified as Local Force units that are assigned regional defense missions. The major shift in force deployment initiated in 1969 has resulted in the deployment of about 40 percent of the PLA opposite the estimated one-quarter of all Soviet forces positioned along the common border.[38] There have been no indications of substantial mechanization or motorization of the infantry; the main emphasis is on upgrading of infantry division armor regiments and independent tank regiments, expanding river crossing capabilities, and increasing artillery firepower. The majority of the PLA main force units are deployed in the vicinity of expected wartime positions and are close to full strength in personnel and equipment.[39] War reserves of supplies, ammunition, and POL are dispersed throughout the PRC. Mobility has been improved by doubling the number of trucks, but the road net is similar to that of the United States a half century ago. A major conflict would severely test the PLA logistical system.[40]

The Chinese Air Force, including navy fighters integrated into the system, has some 5,000 combat airplanes, most of which are a generation behind those of the USSR and major Western powers. About 4,000 of the aircraft are assigned air defense missions, supplemented by about 100 SAMs and over 10,000 AA guns. The air defense system is capable of a limited defense of key urban and industrial areas.[41]

Naval forces include 23 major surface combat ships (destroyers and frigates) and several hundred smaller vessels. These are deployed in three fleets: North Sea Fleet (300 vessels); East Sea Fleet (450 vessels); and South Sea Fleet (300 vessels). Like the ground and air forces, the PLA navy is a defensive force. It is capable of projecting naval power into the nearby seas at a low level for short periods of time, as during the occupation of islands in the South China Sea.

The PLA has not developed a capability to project a significant military force much beyond its immediate borders. Its overall force posture is deterrent and defensive. About 75 Main Force divisions are deployed at some distance from the Soviet border (25 divisions in Manchuria, 30 in the Peking Military Region [MR], nine in the Lanchou MR, and 11 in the Sinkiang MR).[42] Faced with a full-scale invasion by conventional forces from the north, the most probable strategy would be for Main Force units in conjunction with the Air Force to try to disrupt and defeat the attacking force. If this attempt were unsuccessful, the Main Force units would withdraw while Regional Forces conducted guerrilla warfare in concert with the Armed Militia and the Main Force units prepared for a counter-offensive. If this strategy failed, China would try to "lure the enemy deep and engage in the protracted defense characteristic of 'people's war.' "[43]

FUTURE PROSPECTS

China's capacity to use its conventional military forces to influence developments in Asia depends on its demonstrated will to use that force in the past (a topic treated above), and on others' perceptions of whether it might be used in the future. This is the basis for its deterrent effect. How such deterrence might be used depends on the nature of China's weapons and its force structure and deployment, which have earlier been described as defensive. Whether or not the PLA strength is adequate to its purposes is a subjective judgment of the Chinese leadership. One might argue that the leadership is uncomfortable with current military capabilities and that this is one important reason behind China's drive to modernize and the rather remarkable diplomatic successes with Japan and the United States. These actions seem designed to enhance China's national security by increasing internal power and ameliorating the international environment.

The Soviet Union is likely to remain China's most hostile and dangerous neighbor. China has a considerable capacity to deter politically and to defend, with conventional forces, against the Soviet Union. If forced to defend itself, China would have the advantages of geographic and population mass, and of interior and shorter lines of communication within friendly territory. The PLA is relatively weak in armor, deficient in mobility, and would face difficult logistical problems—all of which may be corrected in time, but which presently inhibit military action outside its borders.

Vietnam is currently China's number two enemy. The PLA demonstrated, in early 1979, its capability for limited ground operations into, and withdrawal from, Vietnamese territory. Whether China will be satisfied with the results of the punitive expedition is arguable. Further Chinese military operations against Vietnam might occur if the current Peking-Hanoi negotiations are inconclusive, or if Vietnamese policies toward Cambodia, Laos, or perhaps Thailand, pose an intolerable threat to China's interest.

Taiwan is a third area in which the PLA might be employed. China is actively seeking Taiwan's "reunification" within publicly stated time frames that envision certain goals to be achieved within a year, a ten year period, and finally goals to be achieved by the turn of the century. China has not disavowed the use of force in bringing Taiwan under Peking's control. The PLA is probably incapable of an invasion of Taiwan, but limited military action against the Pescadores or the offshore islands might be undertaken to encourage a more rapid reunification if other means fail.

Conventional forces may also be used to defend or to reassert China's claims to sovereignty over islands claimed by Vietnam, Malaysia, the Philippines, or Japan.

JAPAN: HISTORICAL OVERVIEW

In late August 1945, allied armies entered Japan. It remained an occupied enemy nation under effective U.S. control until sovereign was restored in 1952. The Occupation authorities dismantled the Imperial Army and Navy, destroyed its weapons, halted industrial production related to war, obliterated all traces of militarism in the schools and media, and prevented military and civilian ultra-nationalists from holding any public office. Japan's military establishment was thoroughly discredited by the Occupation, and most Japanese accepted the result with tacit approval.

The demilitarization of Japan was formalized in the 1947 Consituation, which contained the following unique provision (Art. 9):

> Aspiring sincerely to an international peace based on justice and order, the Japanese people forever renounce war as a sovereign right of the nation and the threat or use of force as a means of settling international disputes.
>
> In order to accomplish the aim of the preceding paragraph, land, sea, and air forces, as well as other war potential, will never be maintained. The right of belligerency of the state will not be recognized.

In the same year, Japanese leaders proposed that Japan depend on the United States for defense against external aggression (until the UN could handle it) and that a national police force be organized to prevent civil insurrection. Both overtures were ignored.[44] Three years later, in July 1950, General MacArthur ordered Japan to organize the paramilitary National Police Reserve (NPR), despite the apparent constitutional prohibition of armed forces. The 75,000-man NPR was to assure Japan's internal security and to replace U.S. Army Occupation forces moved to Korea to repel North Korean aggression. During the negotiation, in early 1951, for the Security Treaty between Japan and the United States, Special Ambassador John Foster Dulles urged conversion of the NPR to a 350,000-man army capable of defending Japan against invasion by a rather large-scale conventional force, such as that of the Soviet Union. Despite the war in Korea, Japan's Premier Yoshida held to the view that the proper role of Japan's forces was the maintenance of internal security. So Japan refused, in 1951, to rearm to the scale urged by the United States. In fact, Japan's military forces are smaller today than Dulles had recommended so many years ago. The result was the compromise 1951 Security Treaty, which "was not a mutual agreement and which satisfied neither side." It did provide for stationing U.S. forces in Japan, itself a de facto guarantee of Japan's external security.[45]

In the spring of 1952, the Peace Treaty and the Security Treaty came into effect. The NPR was reorganized into the 110,000 man National Safety Force with ground and sea components. In 1954, the Defense Agency Establishment Law and the Self-Defense Forces Law created the present tri-service Self-Defense Forces (SDF) and explicitly charged the SDF to defend Japan against <u>direct and indirect aggression,</u> and when necessary to maintain public order. The SDF was authorized 150,000 personnel. The United States, which had 260,000 troops in Japan at the time the Peace Treaty took effect, withdrew all combat units from the main islands by 1957. Currently, the United States has about 48,000 combat and support troops in Japan (including Okinawa), and the SDF numbers about 240,000.

SDF force development has been carried out for the past 25 years in accordance with the "Basic Policies for National Defense" (1957) and a series of "Buildup Plans." According to the former,

> The objective of national defense is to prevent direct and indirect aggression, and once invaded, to repel such aggression, thereby preserving the independence and peace of Japan founded upon democratic principles.
>
> To achieve this objective, the government of Japan hereby establishes the following principles:
>
> 1. To support the activities of the United Nations, and promote international cooperation, thereby contributing to the realization of world peace.
>
> 2. To stabilize the public welfare and enhance the people's love for country, thereby establishing the sound basis essential to Japan's security.
>
> 3. To develop progressively the effective defense capabilities necessary for self-defense, with due regard to the nation's resources and the prevailing domestic situation.
>
> 4. To deal with external aggression on the basis of the Japan-U.S. security agreements, pending more effective functioning of the United Nations in future deterring and repelling such aggression. [46]

Listed in preferred priority, the first two principles (objectives) of national defense policy are nonmilitary in nature—the promotion of world peace through international cooperation, and the achievement of domestic stability with heightened recognition among the public of the need to protect the peace and independence of Japan. The military policies involve gradual development of defense power and reliance on security arrangements with the United States.

The constitutional renunciation of war as a sovereign right, the self-denial of war potential, and forfeiture of the right of belligerency do not, in any legal sense, constitute an objection to Japan's right as an independent nation to provide for its own defense against aggression a right embodied in Article 51 of the UN Charter. Japanese government policy prohibits the dispatch of armed personnel abroad for armed action, prohibits any role in a collective security system (including the UN) that would require Japan to take action against aggression aimed at allied nations, and strictly limits the SDF military power to self-defense requirements, to those minimum capabilities required to cope with armed aggression.[47]

Force development has been carried out by a succession of "Buildup Plans" which are summarized in Table 12.1 (Defense Capability Development). Over the two decades covered by these plans, authorized personnel increases have been minimal.

	SDF			
	Ground	Maritime	Air	Total
First Plan (1958-60)	180,000	34,000	41,586	255,586
Fourth Plan (1972-76)	180,000	37,000	48,000	265,000

In all essentials, the magnitude and composition of the SDF were set 20 years ago. Personnel strength has remained stable, increasing by less than 5 percent. Each buildup plan set modest goals for manpower and equipment modernization, seeking qualitative improvement in air and sea defense operations in addition to enhancing ground force mobility and combat effectiveness.

Defense costs have risen in proportion to increases in Japan's GNP and, since 1970, have ranged from .79 percent to .90 percent of the GNP. As a percentage of the national budget, costs decreased 7 percent (1972) to 5.5 percent (1978). For the past decade, defense expenditures have compounded annually, at rates from 21.4 percent to 10 percent,[48] reaching a total of $10.5 billion for the fiscal year beginning April 1, 1979. Japan's rank among world military forces is about seventh in defense expenditures and about nineteenth in number of personnel.[49]

The fourth principle of Japan's basic defense policy is to deal with external aggression on the basis of the Japan-U.S. Security Treaty of 1952 (revised in 1960), which is susceptible to termination by either signatory with one year's notice. Article 5 of the Treaty declares that

> Each party recognizes that an armed attack against either party in the territories under the administration of Japan would be dangerous to its own peace and safety and declares that it would act to meet the common danger in accord with its constitutional provisions and processes.

Under this arrangement, the Japan Defense Agency believes armed aggression by another nation against Japan "would lead to a direct confrontation with the enormous military potential of the U.S.,

TABLE 12.1

Defense Capability Development

Item (FY)	1st Buildup Plan (1958–1960)	2nd Buildup Plan (1962–1966)	3rd Buildup Plan (1967–1971)	4th Buildup Plan (1972–1976)
Self-defense official quota	170,000 men	171,500 men	179,000 men	180,000 men
GSDF				
Units deployed regionally in peacetime	6 divisions 3 composite brigades	12 divisions —	12 divisions —	12 divisions 1 composite brigade
Basic Units — Mobile Operation Units	1 mechanized combined brigade 1 tank regiment 1 artillery brigade 1 airborne brigade 1 training brigade	1 mechanized division 1 tank regiment 1 artillery brigade 1 airborne brigade 1 training brigade	1 mechanized division 1 tank regiment 1 artillery brigade 1 airborne brigade 1 training brigade 1 helicopter brigade	1 mechanized division 1 tank brigade 1 artillery brigade 1 airborne brigade 1 training brigade 1 helicopter brigade
Low-Altitude Ground-to-Air Missile Units	—	2 anti-aircraft artillery battalions	4 anti-aircraft artillery groups (another group being prepared)	8 anti-aircraft artillery groups
MSDF				
Basic Units — Anti-Submarine Surface-Ship Units (for mobile operation)	3 escort flotillas	3 escort flotillas	4 escort flotillas	4 escort flotillas
Anti-Submarine Surface-Ship Units (Regional District Units)	5 divisions	5 divisions	10 divisions	10 divisions
Submarine Units	—	2 divisions	4 divisions	6 divisions
Minesweeping Units	1 flotilla	2 flotillas	2 flotillas	2 flotillas
Land-based Anti-Submarine Aircraft Units	9 squadrons	15 squadrons	14 squadrons	16 squadrons

Major equip-ment	Anti-Submarine Surface Ships	57 ships	59 ships	59 ships	61 ships
	Submarines	2 submarines	7 submarines	12 submarines	14 submarines
	Operational Aircraft	(Apx. 220 aircraft)	(Apx. 230 aircraft)	(Apx. 240 aircraft)	Apx. 210 aircraft (Apx. 300 aircraft)
ASDF Basic Units	Aircraft Control and Warning Units	24 groups	24 groups	24 groups	28 groups
	Interceptor Units	12 squadrons	15 squadrons	10 squadrons	10 squadrons
	Support Fighter Units	—	4 squadrons	4 squadrons	3 squadrons
	Air Reconnaissance Units	—	1 squadron	1 squadron	1 squadron
	Air Transport Units	2 squadrons	3 squadrons	3 squadrons	3 squadrons
	Early Warning Units	—	—	—	—
	High-Altitude Ground-to-Air Missile Units	—	2 groups	4 groups	5 groups (another group being prepared)
Major Operational Aircraft equip-ment		(Apx. 1,130 aircraft)	(Apx. 1,100 aircraft)	(Apx. 940 aircraft)	Apx. 490 aircraft (Apx. 900 aircraft)

Note: Parenthesized numbers of operational aircraft denote total number of aircraft including trainers. The number of units from the first to third buildup plans are as of the end of each plan period.

Source: Defense Agency, *Defense of Japan, 1978*, Tokyo, 1978, p. 66.

resulting in substantial sacrifice, a consequence which actively deters aggression against Japan."[50]

In summary, Japan's SDF was organized by order of the Occupation authorities to provide a national force for internal security. Having regained its sovereignty in 1952, Japan was tied to the United States by the MST (as part of the price for a Peace Treaty) and has since relied fundamentally on that treaty for its security against external aggression. Force development has been gradual and thoroughly planned in accord with the 1957 Basic Defense Policies for qualitative improvement in capabilities, with little change in personnel strength.

DECISION MAKING FOR DEFENSE POLICY

From Japan's emergence into world politics in the 1870s until 1945, Japan's military men were major decision-making figures. General rank officers served as Premier for much of the three decades from the initiation of constitutional government in 1890 until after World War I. Army and Navy ministers (active duty officers) had direct access to the Emperor, and they excluded civil officials from vital military policy formulation. In the 1930s, the military were able to interfere in and often to control broad areas of both domestic and international policy formulation.[51]

Fundamental reforms in Japan's polity were specifically designed by the Occupation to make sure that militaristic leaders could never again lead Japan astray. One result is that Japan has become a unitary parliamentary democracy. Sovereignty lies in the people and is exercised through their elected representatives in the Diet, the bicameral national legislature. Civilian control of military policy formulation and of the SDF's execution of its mission is assured by several constitutional and institutional restraints.

The Prime Minister sets the tone for all policy and is ultimately responsible for military policy. He must be a civilian and a member of the Lower House of the Diet. He possesses the power of "command and control" (shikikantokuken) of the SDF. The all-civilian National Defense Council assists him in this role (the NDC prepared the 1957 Basic Defense Policies), and its actions must be ratified by the Cabinet. Major defense measures are probably decided by a small informal group of men that includes the Foreign Minister, the Finance Minister, and possibly the Minister of International Trade and Industry and the Director-General of the Japan Defense Agency (JDA).[52]

The Director-General of the JDA, who must be a civilian and ranks one level below cabinet minister, is not a powerful political force. Thirty-five men have held the post since 1950, for an average term of nine to ten months. He is assisted by two vice-ministers who are civilians. All bureau chiefs of the JDA are civilians, usually recruited from government ministries. The input of uniformed military men into defense decision making is minimal but increasingly important.

Under the parliamentary system, Japan's defense policy is the defense policy of the Liberal Democratic Party (LDP), which has been the governing party since its inception in 1955. As majority party, the LDP members of the Lower House select the Prime Minister. The LDP provides Cabinet ministers and the chairman of all Diet committees. It also decides what bills become law. Nearly all bills originate in a ministry, and when presented to the Diet they reflect consensus among LDP leaders, bureaucrats in the concerned ministries and the responsible Diet committees. To date, there are no Diet committees charged with defense policy, so defense bills are not studied by a specific committee. Nevertheless, defense policy matters (and the defense budget) are well-ventilated publicly and the LDP gets what it wants in these matters.

However, the LDP should not be viewed as a solid political entity with one uniform perspective on defense policy; rather, it is a congeries of factions that pursue factional interests within limits fixed by the prime requirement to stay in power as a party. All LDP Dietmen support the SDF and the Japan-U.S. MST; at the same time, there are intra-party disagreements about the size, missions, and force structure most appropriate for Japan's military forces.

Defense policy in Japan is not a bipartisan matter. A general polarization is more or less characteristic of all Japanese politics, with the LDP versus a disunited opposition of socialists, communists, and others. Until quite recently, the polarization of views concerning the SDF and the MST has been especially pronounced,[53] but the LDP monopoly on power has limited the opposition role to criticism, delay, and obstruction.

A couple of examples show how such activity can influence defense decision making. The Security Treaty Crisis of May-June 1960 occurred when the LDP decided to revise and renew the MST for ten years. The opposition debated the draft revision for 100 days, filibustered it until the hour the Diet session had legally to end, and finally locked the Speaker of the House in his office. About 500 police were called to the Diet building and freed the speaker. He called the House to order, voted to extend the Diet session with only eight minutes left, reopened the new Diet session, and approved the Treaty without debate and with only LDP members present. All opposition Dietmen were absent.[54] In the next few weeks, hundreds of thousands of people joined in mass street demonstrations, 5.5 million communications workers conducted a work stoppage, and 13 million

people signed petitions demanding the Premier's resignation, dissolution of the Diet, and the undoing of the Security Treaty. The Premier
was forced from office by LDP faction leaders and President Eisenhower cancelled his visit to sign the Treaty, but the LDP policy on
defense (reliance on the MST) held. Nevertheless, the opposition's
criticism and public outcry promoted caution in defense matters.

Diet debate can also affect defense policy. In 1969, for example,
in debating whether the F-4 was a defensive or offensive airplane,
the point was made that its bomb racks and range made it offensive;
therefore, the ASDF removed the racks, and a few years later the
in-flight refueling equipment was removed. No one could then argue
that the F-4 mission was other than defensive.[55]

In short, Japan's defense policy is not the result of a broad
national consensus: it is the policy of the governing LDP. But a trend
toward wider acceptance of that policy is apparent. To encourage
further public debate and understanding of the necessity for national
defense, the JDA issued White Papers on Defense in 1970, 1976, 1977,
and 1978. These moves for greater public support have been facilitated by the return of the Ryukyu Islands to Japanese control, the
U.S. withdrawal from Vietnam, China's open approval of the Japan-
U.S. Security Treaty, and softening of the views of some opposition
parties.

THREAT PERCEPTION/POLICY PERSPECTIVES

Unlike China, Japan has not felt threatened to such an extent
that it has used military force. There has been, over the years, a
feeling that the Japan-U.S. security ties could endanger Japan's
security, that Japan would be drawn unwillingly into U.S. wars in
Korea, Vietnam, or with China. But these anxieties have receded.

The current JDA analysis sees the basic theme of the international military structure as the forward deployment of U.S. military
forces against Soviet troop concentrations in the European and Far
Eastern theaters, with the U.S. and Soviet nuclear capabilities sup-
plying mutual deterrence as the background. The improvement of
Soviet military capabilities since the 1960s, however, leads the JDA
to conclude that "Both in Europe and the Far East, the strength of
Soviet forces now surpasses that of the United States, and the safety
of U.S. sea and air lanes is now being jeopardized."[56]

In East Asia, the Soviet Union seeks advantage by expanding
and modernizing its conventional forces, increasing its territorial
air defense capabilities, and modernizing its tactical air force[57]
while the Soviet Navy routinely deploys in the East and South China
Seas, the Philippine Sea, the South Pacific, the Indian Ocean, and

waters adjacent to the U.S. West Coast.[58] The United States keeps a
deterrent posture based on navy and air forces to deny dominance of
Northeast Asia to any single power.[59] In East Asia, the JDA identifies two areas of "high tension" with a "confrontation atmosphere":
the Sino-Soviet border (discussed above) and the Korean peninsula.[60]
Northeast Asia has sufficient equilibrium, based on the relative
power of China, the Soviet Union, and the United States, to reduce
the probability of hostilities reaching a critical state, but the North
Korea-Republic of Korea tension is the major cause of anxiety, highlighted by the U.S. policy to withdraw ground combat forces from the
ROK. At the same time, "Japanese defense policy has been predicated on the assumption that the present situation" in Korea will not
change basically.[61]

If Japan perceives any military threat at all, it is the Soviet
Union. Japanese attitudes toward the USSR are deeply affected by
the Soviet attack on Japan in August 1945 in violation of the Soviet-
Japanese Neutrality Pact (1941); by Soviet treatment of, and failure
to repatriate, thousands of Japanese prisoners-of-war; by continuing
harassment of Japanese fishermen; by occupation of four of the Kurile
Islands that Japan claims, and by Soviet displays of military power.

Beginning in May 1978, the Soviets have increased their troop
strength on Kunashiri and Etorofu Islands (in the Kurile Archipelago)
from 1,500 to between five and six thousand men, constructed a
3,500 meter runway, and are building facilities to secure the passage
of its fleet into the Pacific and to try to control the Sea of Ohkotsk. A
Japanese spokesman said the Russian occupation of the Japanese
islands was "illegal" and "intolerable."[62]

Japan is made aware of Soviet power by Soviet naval exercises
of Japan's Pacific coast, by the yearly transit of 200 Soviet warships
through straits near Japan, and by the 200 Soviet military aircraft
that annually approach Japan to test its air defenses and, at times,
violate Japan's airspace.[63]

It is probably true that Japan senses no direct military threat
to its security. It is also likely that "Korea is the key to the power
balance of Asia," as one eminent Japanese scholar has suggested.[64]
Japan is vitally concerned with Korea. Arguing that Japan's preeminent interest lies in preserving peace, Nathan White reasons that even
limited hostilities in Korea would pose difficult policy choices for
Japan.[65] If the United States chose to support the ROK, any Japanese
support of U.S. military operations in Korea could endanger its relations with China or the USSR; and the damage to these relations would
increase in proportion to U.S.-ROK military success. If Japan did
not cooperate with the United States, the "cornerstone" of all Japan-
U.S. relations—the MST—would crumble. On the other hand, if the
United States did not support the ROK in case of war, Japan would

have to reevaluate immediately the worth of the MST and simultaneously face a situation in Korea that it could not influence in any significant way.

For these reasons, Japan's perspective on defense policy must be rooted in the maintenance of peace and stability in Asia, the guarantees of the Japan-U.S. Security Treaty, and the "strong hope"[66] that the United States will continue its commitment to the security of the ROK.

FORCE POSTURE/CAPABILITIES

The SDF force posture and capabilities are limited by several factors. In addition to the doubts of some about the constitutionality of the forces and the fact that the defense policy has not derived from a national consensus, Japan has no mobilization plan, no civil defense system, and no state-of-emergency law. Furthermore, the SDF is an all-volunteer civil service force, which has no military law or court system. The SDF is denied any offensive mission. Government policy on nuclear weapons is firm: no possession, no manufacture, and no entry of nuclear weapons into Japanese territory.

With the end of the Fourth Buildup Plan in 1976, Japan adopted the "National Defense Program Outline."[67] The program outline embodies "an entirely new theoretical concept, not seen in any of the previous defense programs" and calls it the "Standard Defense Force Concept."[68] It seeks to replace specific objectives over fixed time frames with fundamental guidelines for the basic management and operation of the SDF.

This concept approaches defense capability in three ways: as a functional (force posture) capability, as a quantitative capability, and as a qualitative capability.

The required force postures (functional capabilities) are six in number: (1) surveillance posture—to conduct warning and surveillance missions within Japan's territory and in nearby air and sea space, and to collect intelligence; (2) indirect aggression posture—to handle externally supported, intense domestic insurgency; (3) direct aggression posture—to repel limited and small-scale aggression, in principle without outside assistance; or to continue effective resistance until U.S. help arrives; (4) command, communications, and logistic support posture; (5) education and training posture; and (6) disaster relief posture.

The quantity of defense capability set by the Program Outline is roughly that contained in Table 5.1 above. The Maritime SDF is short two submarines and ten tactical aircraft. The air SDF lacks an Early

Warning squadron, while the ground SDF will reorganize the Seventh Division into a tank division in 1980.[69]

The third aspect, the qualitative capability, will assure highest effectiveness for functional and quantitative aspects. Japan must gain parity with the technical standards of other nations—parity with the potential scale of threat. Otherwise, the "possession of a defense structure is meaningless."[70]

Ground defense against land invasions of Japanese territory is the primary mission of the ground SDF. Probably, the GSDF has a very limited ability to deal with a moderate-sized conventional invasion for any sustained period. The GSDF plans to improve its fire-power, mobility, and antitank and anti-aircraft defenses. Currently, it is at 86 percent of authorized strength. About one-third of its divisions are deployed in Hokkaido, with the remainder spread throughout Japan.

Defending Japan against seaborne invasions and securing the safety of maritime transport in the peripheral waters around Japan are the primary missions of the maritime SDF. To develop further its high priority anti-submarine warfare (ASW) capability, Japan will purchase and/or co-produce perhaps 50 ASW p-3C aircraft from the United States and acquire additional surface components for ASW. There is no way that Japan can guarantee the safety of its seaborne commerce by military means, but it will try to improve its capability by cooperation with others and will reportedly extend the operational limits of its own forces from 200 miles to about 500 miles for air patrols and to about 1,000 miles for surface patrols.[71]

Japan's air defense is complicated by the long and narrow configuration of the islands. The Air SDF is responsible for the air defense of Japan and for attacking and defeating invading sea or airborne forces. Major ASDF goals include the replacement of the F-4EJ with ten squadrons of the F-15 (the world's premier fighter-interceptor) over the next few years and development of three squadrons equipped with the Japan-built F-1, an all-weather, ECM-equipped ground support aircraft. Mobile three-dimensional radar units will be introduced to improve the AD capability.[72]

If the SDF is to execute its defensive missions, each of the three services must be operationally effective. It is equally important that the national leadership be able to coordinate SDF activities effectively by transmitting operational directives through a system of command, control, and communications (C^3). A national defense microwave system is now under construction to provide secure, flexible, and survivable communications for the SDF,[73] the lack of which inhibits SDF responsiveness.

A major institutional limitation on SDF responsiveness is the legal requirement that the Prime Minister alone may order SDF forces into defensive military operations: the SDF cannot act on its own even in the case of a surprise invasion. This problem was highlighted when former Chairman of the Joint Staff Council General Hiroomi Kurisu was forced to resign for telling a group of newsmen that the SDF might be forced to take "supralegal" action in just such a case.[74] Nevertheless, his remarks have resulted in initiation of a formal JDA study of the problem.

Japan's force posture and capabilities cannot be summarized without reference to the indispensable component of Japan's security— the Japan-U.S. security system. Japan's basic defense policies rest on the assumption that the system will work effectively. This means that smooth operational coordination between the SDF and U.S. forces is of critical importance. In July 1976, the Joint Subcommittee for Defense Cooperation (which advises the Japan-U.S. Consultative Committee) was established to deal with the enormously complex problem of joint operations, which include logistics, intelligence operations, and C^3.[75] The first formal guidelines for Japan-U.S. joint action were announced late last fall. The SDF is to engage in defensive operations while U.S. forces will undertake offensive operations to repel "aggressor forces." A team of military experts from both countries will continue to study the entire spectrum of operational coordination, as well as the joint use of existing or new facilities and joint military exercises.[76]

The militarily important "postures" by which Japan's defense capabilities are approached in the National Defense Program Outline are the surveillance posture; direct aggression posture, and command, communications, and logistics posture. Japan recognizes that it is seriously deficient in all three; however, current plans and actions can probably remedy most deficiencies in time. In the interim, the capacity for self-defense is limited. Japan continues to depend ultimately on the United States for its defense.

THE FUTURE

This section deals with some ideas and attitudes omitted from the section on perspectives because of their relatively inchoate character and because they are not yet policy.

A debate of some consequence is now taking place in Japan. Outspoken questioning of the assumptions undergirding Japan's defense policy has its origins in the announcement of the Nixon Doctrine and the U.S. withdrawal from Vietnam. It gained momentum from the planned withdrawal of U.S. ground combat units from Korea, the subsequent U.S. reemphasis on Europe and the Middle East, and the withdrawal of recognition of the Republic of China. Six years ago a Japanese analyst questioned whether any U.S. President would dare risk American lives in a crisis involving Japan and whether the United States had lost its moralistic commitment to contain communist expansion.[77] Others have argued that it is not possible for Japan to depend decisively on the United States for any length of time in the new multi-polar world.[78] The contrary case is that while it may be unreasonable for one nation (Japan) to depend on one other nation (United States) for peace, it may also be dangerous to rely on a regional balance of power for the simple reason that local balances do not have real autonomy; and this is true of northeast Asia. It is also true that U.S.-Japanese security arrangements are based on a community of interests, such as a stable international order, preservation of peace in northeast Asia, economic cooperation, and the values associated with representative democratic government and peaceful interstate relations among nations.[79]

For the past several months, this "debate" has covered several topics, most of which relate to the "defects" in the SDF law and the extent to which Japan ought to improve its ability to fight coordinated defensive operations. If there is a long-term trend, it is toward world-standard equipment, increased defense budgets, and greater autonomy and assertiveness in military matters coupled with independence and firmness in foreign policy—all backed up by better public understanding and stronger support.

With regard to the latter, one observer sees a "press campaign in favor of rearmament orchestrated by the JDA."[80] General Kurisu's warning about the defects in the C^3 system and his resignation were followed in a few weeks by a quite remarkable event—a meeting of the chiefs of staffs of the Air, Ground, and Maritime SDFs with members of the opposition Democratic Socialist Party. All three uniformed-officers recommended legislation to clarify actions to be taken in an emergency, a position at variance with that of the civilian JDA representative who attended.[81] The government position is that the current law is appropriate, but some powerful LDP leaders think otherwise; so this issue is alive.[82]

Defense expenditures will continue to increase. From 1960 to 1970, defense costs rose 362 percent. In the ten years 1970–79, the defense budget has nearly quadrupled (up 367 percent) to reach about $10.5 billion. For the past 15 years, these expenditures have been less than 1 percent of GNP. Now Masamichi Inoki, former President of the National Defense College, has called for defense expenditures equal to 2 percent of the GNP[83] and military commentator Hideo Sekino suggests that expenditures be raised .2 percent of GNP yearly until the total reaches 2 or 3 percent.[84] World-standard weapons systems are expensive: Japan will spend $2.3 billion for F-15s and $1.7 billion for ASW aircraft. In the past, higher defense expenditures have not been accompanied by personnel strength increases.

In the international area, Japan may see some utility in the SDF to encourage settlement of conflicting territorial claims over the Senkaku Islands (claimed by China and the Republic of China), Takeshima (claimed by the ROK), and the "Northern Islands" (claimed by the USSR). With regard to the Senkakus, Japan has apparently got tacit acceptance of its sovereignty by Peking, and plans to build a civilian heliport there. [85] Sovereignty over Takeshima Island has been disputed by Japan and the ROK since the end of World War II. Last year Japan decided to use patrol boats and helicopters to protect Japanese fishing boats outside Korea's claimed 12-mile territorial seas. [86] By far the most serious territorial dispute is over the "Northern Islands," the Kurile Islands closest to Japan—Etorofu, Kunashiri, Shikotan, and the Habomai group. Japan recently demanded that the Soviet Union withdraw troops and military facilities on the islands. The Soviet Union flatly rejected the demand, repeating its position that no territorial problems exist between the two nations, and that the Soviet military buildup is a domestic affair of the Soviet Union. [87]

The success of Japan's defense policy depends on the future evolution of the complicated and sometimes dangerous bilateral relationships of the nations of East Asia with each other and with the United States and the Soviet Union. It also depends importantly on internal developments in Japan. It just may be that domestic politics is approaching the point where a suprapartisan foreign policy could take root for the first time since World War II. The crucial factor is the changed attitudes of the various political parties toward defense issues, especially the MST, which has been the most debated foreign policy issue since 1952. [88] If a broad national consensus does emerge over the next several years, the domestic underpinnings for defense policy will be markedly strengthened.

On balance, it is unlikely that the SDF will be used in military operations in any situation short of defense of Japanese territory. At the same time, the SDF will continue to acquire the most modern equipment available and seek the capacity to defend Japan without external help, while relying on the United States for deterrence and for offensive military action if Japan is attacked.

NOTES

1. Edward M. Kennedy, "US Must: Improve Peking, Moscow Ties," Boston Globe, July 28, 1978, p. 17.

2. William W. Whitson, The Chinese High Command: A History of Communist Politics 1927-71 (New York: Praeger, 1973), pp. 524-25.

3. Ellis Joffe, Party and Army: Professionalism and Political Control in the Chinese Officer Corps, 1949-1964, East Asian Research Center, Harvard University, 1965, pp. 40-41.

4. See Harry Harding, "The Evolution of Chinese Military Policy," in Comparative Defense Policy, eds. Frank B. Horton III, Anthony Rogerson, and Edward L. Warner III (Baltimore: Johns Hopkins University Press, 1974), pp. 216-32.

5. Ibid., pp. 217-18.

6. Ibid., pp. 219-22.

7. Parris H. Chang, "Mao Tse-tung and his Generals: Some Observations on Military Intervention and Chinese Politics," in Comparative Defense Policy, p. 126.

8. Ibid., pp. 121-23.

9. Y. M. Kau and P. M. Perolle, "The Politics of Lin Piao's Abortive Coup," Asian Survey, 14/6 (June 1974): 572.

10. Chang, op. cit., p. 125.

11. This summary is based on William W. Whitson, "Organizational Perspectives and Decision-making in the Chinese Communist High Command," Comparative Defense Policy, p. 25.

12. Whitson, op. cit., pp. 37-37, and Chang, op. cit., p. 125.

13. Chang, ibid.

14. Whitson, op. cit., p. 37.

15. Peter Van Ness, "Is China an Expansionist Power?" Comparative Defense Policy, p. 524.

16. National People's Congress Standing Committee, "Message to Compatriots in Taiwan" (January 1, 1979), Beijing Review, 1 (January 5, 1979): 17.

17. Harding, op. cit., p. 227, quoting William Dorill, et al., China in the Wake of the Cultural Revolution, RAC-R-81 (McLean, Va.: Research Analysis Corporation, September 1969), p. 23.

18. Van Ness, op. cit., p. 525.

19. This portion is based on Lorne J. Kavic, "The Himalayan Conflict, 1962," Comparative Defense Policy, pp. 547-56.

20. Neville Maxwell, "Why the Russians Lifted the Blockade at Bear Island," Foreign Affairs, 57/1 (Fall 1978): 141.

21. Ibid., p. 145.

22. See Daniel Tretiak, "The Sino-Japanese Treaty of 1978: The Senkaku Incident Prelude," Asian Survey, 18/12 (December 1978): 1235-49.

23. V. G. Kulkarni, "Oil Islands heat up Vietnam-China diplomatic front," Christian Science Monitor, January 3, 1978, p. 1.

24. The International Institute for Strategic Studies, Strategic Survey 1977 (London, 1978), p. 80.

25. For example, see Mao Tse-tung, "On the Ten Major Relationships April 25, 1946," Peking Review, 1 (January 1, 1977): 10-25. This formulation of Mao's views is "an important guarantee for the political stability of society" was given some prominence in the Communique of the Third Planning Session of the 11th Central Committee of the Communist Party of China. Peking Review, 52 (December 29, 1978): 11.

26. Chalmers Johnson, "The New Thrust in China's Foreign Policy," Foreign Affairs, 57/1 (Fall 1978): 128.

27. Editorial Department of Renmin Ribao, "Chairman Mao's Theory of the Differentiation of the Three Worlds as a Major Contribution to Marxism-Leninism," Peking Review, 45 (November 4, 1977): 10-41. The Three Worlds Thesis is treated in somewhat different contexts in Richard F. Starr, "The Bear Versus the Dragon in the Third World," Policy Review (Winter 1979): 93-105; and in Shirin Tahir-Kehli, "Chinese Objectives in South Asia: 'Anti-Hegemony' vs. Collective Security," Asian Survey, 18/10 (October 1978): 996-1012.

28. Peking Review, 45 (November 4, 1977): 11.

29. Ibid., pp. 24, 28.

30. Ibid., p. 32.

31. Ibid., p. 21.

32. Ibid., p. 22.

33. "Social-Imperialist Strategy in Asia," Beijing Review, 3 (January 19, 1979).

34. Johnson, op. cit., p. 129.

35. "Soviet and Vietnamese Hegemonists' True Colors," Peking Review, 51 (December 22, 1978): 16-18.

36. The International Institute for Strategic Studies, Strategic Survey 1978 (London, 1979), pp. 79-80.

37. See The International Institute for Strategic Studies, The Military Balance 1978-79 (London, 1978), pp. 55-57.

38. General George S. Brown, U.S. Military Posture for FY 1979, Statement to the Congress, January 20, 1978, p. 56.

39. Ibid., p. 70.

40. Ibid., p. 94.

41. Military Balance 1978-79, p. 57.

42. Defense Agency, Defense of Japan, 1978, Tokyo, 1978, p. 41.

43. Harding, op. cit., p. 231.

44. Ikuhito Hata, "Japan Under the Occupation," Japan Interpreter, Tokyo, 10/3-4 (Winter 1976): 375.

45. Martin E. Weinstein, "The Evolution of the Japan Self-Defense Forces," in The Modern Japanese Military System, ed. James H. Buck (Beverly Hills and London: Sage, 1975), p. 43.

46. Defense of Japan, 1978, p. 55.

47. Ibid., pp. 55-58.

48. Defense of Japan, 1978, p. 209.

49. The Military Balance 1978-1979, pp. 88-91.

50. Defense of Japan, 1978, p. 60.

51. James H. Buck, "Civilian Control of the Military in Japan," in Civilian Control of the Military, ed. Claude E. Welch, Jr. (Albany: SUNY Press, 1976), pp. 149-86.

52. Gaston J. Sigur, "Power, Politics, and Defense," The Modern Japanese Military System, pp. 188-89.

53. See Defense of Japan, 1978, pp. 180-81, for statements of the Komeito Party, the Democratic Socialist Party, the New Liberal Club, and the United Social Democratic Party which show increasing acceptance and support for the SDF and the MST, albeit with qualifications.

54. Theodore McNelly, Politics and Government in Japan, 2d edition (Boston: Houghton Mifflin, 1972), p. 221.

55. Defense of Japan, 1978, pp. 130-31.

56. Ibid., pp. 12-13.

57. Ibid., p. 16.

58. Admiral Maurice F. Wiesner, "The U.S. Posture in Asia and the Pacific: The View from CINCPAC," Strategic Review (Summer 1978): 44.

59. Defense of Japan, 1978, pp. 12-13.

60. Ibid., p. 16.

61. Ibid., p. 49.

62. "Soviets Maintaining North Isles Troops," Japan Times Weekly (JTW), February 3, 1979, p. 2; "Tokyo Charges Soviet Builds Bases on 2 Islands Near Northern Japan," New York Times, January 31, 1979.

63. Defense of Japan, 1978, pp. 34-35.

64. Kosaka Masataka, "Detente and East Asia," Discussion Paper No. 50, California Seminar on Arms Control and Foreign Policy (Santa Monica, Calif., September 1975), p. 13.

65. See Nathan White, "Japan's Security Interests in Korea," Asian Survey (April 1976): 299-318.

66. Defense of Japan, 1978, p. 49.

67. See ibid., pp. 63-80, 83-106, 199-206, on which this summary is based.

68. Ibid., p. 68.

69. Masanori Tabata, "Impressive Review Marks New Era in History of GSDF's 7th Division," JTW, February 10, 1979, p. 7.

70. Defense of Japan, 1978, p. 77.

71. Michael Pillsbury, "A Japanese Card?" Foreign Policy, 33 (Winter 1978-79): 5.

72. Defense of Japan, 1978, pp. 101-2.

73. Ibid., pp. 103-4.

74. "Joint Staff Council Head Ousted for Remarks in Defense Policy," JTW, August 5, 1978, p. 1.

75. See James H. Buck, "Japan: The Problem of Shared Responsibility," in Foreign Policy and U.S. National Security, ed. William W. Whitson (New York: Praeger, 1976), pp. 166-78.

76. "Japan, U.S. Approve New Action Guidelines," JTW, December 2, 1978, p. 2.

77. See Kimio Murdoka, Japanese Security and the United States, International Institute for Strategic Studies (IISS), Adelphi Paper 95, London, February 1973.

78. See Kiichi Saeki, "Japan's Security in a Multipolar World," East Asia and the World System Part II: The Regional Powers, IISS, Adelphi Paper 92, London, November 1972.

79. Kosaka, op. cit., pp. 6-7.

80. Henry Scott-Stokes, "It's All Right to Talk Defense Again in Japan," New York Times Magazine, February 11, 1979, p. 70.

81. Kiyoaki Murata, "'Self-Defense' for SDF—Top Brass Rejects Invocation of Penal Code Provision," JTW, September 9, 1978, p. 3.

82. Takuya Kubo (Secretary-General, NDC), "Defense Furor Shouldn't Lead to Big SDF Budget," JTW, November 18, 1978, p. 5.

83. Scott-Stokes, op. cit., p. 20.

84. Hideo Sekino, "Defense Agency Seems to Work Backward," JTW, December 16, 1978, p. 4.

85. Bradley K. Martin, "Japanese to build heliport in islands claimed by China," Baltimore Sun, January 18, 1979, p. 2.

86. "Japan Will Begin Patrolling Waters Off Takeshima Island," JTW, May 20, 1978, p. 1.

87. "Soviets Snub Japan's Protest in N. Isles Bases," JTW, February 10, 1979, p. 1.

88. Kei Wakaizumi, "Consensus in Japan," Foreign Policy, 27 (Summer 1977): 166-68.

5
NONNUCLEAR CONFLICT

The final chapter examines broad political and psychological factors regarding the motivations, risks, costs, and implications of military intervention in nonnuclear conflicts. Aimed primarily at the U.S. political system, the chapter notes the "subjectivity" of the factors that go into decisions regarding military intervention. Examining such concepts as commitment, involvement, power, national interests, and credibility, the chapter observes that the frequency of nonnuclear wars will not decrease. Moreover they are likely to occur in areas of the world where the United States has an aversion to intervene militarily. No superpower can avoid some kind of involvement. Thus, American leadership must be prepared to consider the nature of the U.S. response. This requires the ability to integrate a variety of subjective factors in order to identify the intensity and form of involvement. Adequate military capability and political resolve are essential in carrying out such a policy. Finally, all of these must be congruent with the U.S. value system. In the final analysis, the world view of the leader and the manner and intensity with which he can commit the American people to a particular course of action is crucial to the success of military policy to deal with nonnuclear conflict. The burden of such success rests with the leadership and relates to the earlier discussions of Presidential wars. This chapter touches upon a variety of issues raised by preceding chapters regarding military capability and posture, political will, perceptions of the potential enemy, relationships with allies, and, most importantly, perception of the domestic political environment, and character and style of leadership.

13

NONNUCLEAR CONFLICT: PERSPECTIVES FOR SUPERPOWER SECURITY POLICY

William Whitson

What do leaders mean by "nonnuclear conflict"? Will it continue to happen on the way to future resolution of vital international issues? Will the superpowers participate in such conflicts? Are there objective criteria by which U.S. policymakers may design an "appropriate" involvement? What perspectives might best insure an American sense of security in a political environment of pervasive nonnuclear conflict that threatens nuclear apocalypse?

At best, answers to these questions provide only a frail intellectual cloak for outlining the diverse forms of ego conflict in the international body politic. Nevertheless, this essay will use the flow of ideas imbedded in those answers to suggest another way for U.S. policymakers—and citizens—to define and deal with the problem of nonnuclear conflict, or more specifically low-intensity conflict.*

The term "nonnuclear conflict" normally means a "limited" war, that is, the use of limited military force to resolve a conflict. Much has been written about those limits of time, space, and resources that define such wars. In U.S. strategic parlance, the "half-war contingency" is explicitly concerned with nonnuclear—particularly low-intensity—conflicts, inasmuch as a major war would invoke the full panoply of resources available to both sides. Whether measured in terms of time, space, or resources, the precise point at which a limited war becomes a full-scale war is unclear—and probably unimportant.

---

*In this context, nonnuclear conflict and low-intensity conflict are intended to be used almost synonymously, although nonnuclear conflict suggests a broader view, extending beyond a counterinsurgency involvement (see Chapter 1).

What is important is commitment. The emotional investment of a people and their leaders, their commitment to certain values and institutions, and their determination to support that commitment—even "irrationally"—with all necessary resources distinguish a major war from a limited war. "Rational" decisions are possible when less-than-total commitments are involved; rationality becomes increasingly elusive as the commitment deepens. There would thus appear to be a case for applying the rationality of cost-returns calculus to limited conflict precisely because "limits" have been applied to the situation. But a cost-returns calculus implies "rational" and possibly "objective" criteria by which to measure limits, costs, and returns.

Before returning to those criteria, however, we may address the question of the future likelihood of nonnuclear conflict. There can be no doubt about the continuing use of military force for the attempted resolution of conflict in the international arena. Many factors support what must appear to be an obvious characteristic of international relations, namely, that military violence, along with economic and political pressure, will not disappear from the international scene in the near future. Indeed we will propose that the frequency of limited war is likely to increase in the last decades of the twentieth century.

More pressing, then, is the issue of superpower participation in such conflict. At risk of begging the question, it seems clear that superpowers will continue to be involved in all such conflicts! The operative word is "involvement." Thanks to the pervasive spread of superpower political and economic communications across the world, no conflict in the 1980s will be totally insulated from superpower presence, direct or indirect. The issue, therefore, for superpower policymakers is one of degree. How active should superpowers be in any given crisis? What mix of resources is most appropriate?

According to the traditional paradigm, the answers to those questions appear to be imbedded in the notion of cost returns mentioned above. Since rationality is presumed to be associated with a limited war, certain ground rules or objective criteria must be available for calculating the importance of an issue, its preferred outcome, and appropriate resources needed to move the issue toward that outcome. Indeed, many computer and notional models of the international arena and models of political-military dynamics presume a mathematical calculus for estimating "how much is enough."

Unfortunately, as this essay will discuss in greater detail below, such an assumption of objectivity is invalid. There are no objective measures of "power," of "national interests" (whether assessed in terms of freedom, security, way of life, or economic prosperity), of threats to such interests, or of effectiveness of countervailing power projection. Whether or not a superpower should raise the ante in a low-intensity conflict must be determined by vision and judgment on the part of its leaders. The importance of the issue, the preferred outcome, and the optimum mix of resources for favorable issue resolution are all judgments based on the perceptions of leaders, that is, on subjective criteria. Indeed, without a need for such judgments, computers could answer all of those questions and leaders could take a permanent vacation.

CRITERIA: COSTS, LIMITS, AND RETURNS

Four different but related judgments about the situation are worth our attention:

1. Perceptions of the structure and process of the power system within which the conflict is taking place;
2. Perceptions of the appropriate role for a superpower in the situation, given self-image of role on the larger stage;
3. Perceptions of the most important components of that system on which alternative outcomes of the conflict may have impact (power distribution; institutional process; institutional power structure; credibility of one or more of the major actors; sense of security of a major actor);
4. Perceptions of the utility and effectiveness of material and psychological resources available for application to the conflict.

If rationality according to objective criteria must remain a fiction in any calculus of power in a nonnuclear conflict, and if nonnuclear conflicts are likely to continue to attract superpower involvement and even confrontation, what perspective may best arm U.S. leaders to handle such conflicts with balance? To answer this question is to focus on the state of mind of leaders when they come to grips with such conflicts.

Leaders' perceptions must be profoundly influenced by an underlying belief system, the angle of vision, the unwritten mind-set with which a leader or group of leaders begins an assessment of a nonnuclear conflict. If the leader starts from a premise of fear, whether for personal or professional reasons, he will perceive the political power system as a rigid structure of alienation, separation, and adversarial confrontation employing material power, and he will see no outcome from which all participants could gain. He will therefore see his own role and status to be under some form of challenge, and he will probably apply excessive resources to the situation in hopes of gaining a quick, favorable decision. Such mind-set is reinforced by a sense of urgency. If the leader believes that "time is running out," all fears become exaggerated, and perceptions of crisis become even more unbalanced.

Conversely, if a leader's central perspective is one of inner security, his approach to national security policy will reflect that sense of peace with himself. He will be more likely to perceive the international system as pluralistic, a flow of "power" that is essentially psychological and spiritual rather than material and structural; he will be much more interested in the impact of a crisis on relationships, values, and the human condition than on power structures and credible images; he will seek outcomes from which all actors might gain and will thus cast his role in terms of mediation and healing. He will, therefore, be less likely to overinvest resources in the situation, because he will define power in nonmaterial terms. These perspectives will be reinforced if he is persuaded that time is an ally. So perceived, time reinforces a sense of balance and the promise of appropriate involvement.

From this latter perspective leaders are most likely to communicate to the domestic and international press and their readership a sense of vision and rationality instead of the political myopia and emotional hysteria typically associated with "crisis management." Therefore, perhaps the single most important shift in state of mind required to "center" an approach to a nonnuclear conflict is the shift of sense of time from enemy to ally. Such a shift will not accomplish a miraculous metamorphosis of fear into inner peace in a leadership. But "buying time" is a psychological goal toward which bureaucratic energies should be directed, even while resources are being applied to issue resolution.

However, there is a more important dimension to a leader's mind-set, a dimension on which this essay will end. A leader cherishes a private conviction about the nature of man. He believes—or does not believe—that mankind is deeply joined in spirit, and separated only in ego. A leader's approach to all conflict will be profoundly influenced by his choice among these two alternatives.

PROSPECTS FOR NONNUCLEAR CONFLICT

The international community of states faces the prospect of nonnuclear conflict with increasing frequency and increasing geographic recurrence in the 1980s. Among the prime contributors are systemic complexity, prospects for unusually rapid change in values and goals, and frustrated popular aspirations for a better life. These encourage the search for greater local control of political destiny, and the availability of weapons of violence.

The international political system has added more than 100 new member states since 1945. There is no reason to believe that that number will decrease in the 1980s. Indeed, the likelihood of an increase in the number of groups who claim sovereign specialness is high. Ireland, the Basques in Spain, border regions in various European states, new states in Africa, minorities in the USSR and the Peoples' Republic, Quebec, and even certain groups in the United States clamor for autonomy, if not separation, from the mother country.

With each new member added to the nation–state system, multiple energies are evoked to express the domestic and foreign aspirations of the populace. Faith in ego–centered nationalism offers an answer that promises collective fulfillment via proclamation of statehood and official separation from a larger political unit. But a new state must soon encounter the harsh realities of power exercised by multinational corporations and multilateral associations. With the ongoing proliferation of actors on the world stage, collisions over traditional boundaries and new sovereign jurisdictions, supplemented by conflicting claims to clean air, clean water, and natural resources, must add fuel to an increasingly complex system of _human_ energy transfer.

Increasingly, "sovereignty" is a meaningless memory of past symbols and values in the current context of complex global communications among MNC's, regional and multilateral organizations, and the state system. Put simply, people who believe that a better life can be achieved by seizing control over their own political fortunes must soon find frustration in their interdependence among many other states and organizations. That frustration with an increasingly complex political system is reinforced by burgeoning domestic and foreign expenditure of political energy for almost no noteworthy return to the private claimant on political stability. Frustrations will probably be reinforced by the declining productivity of the international economic system. The growing economic interdependence of the global economy seems to produce rather than resolve conflict, while also failing to satisfy a worldwide demand for more and better goods and services. Popular aspirations for a better life tend to define "better" in terms of economic criteria: housing, food, and clothing. Political independence, no matter how ephemeral the definition, cannot guarantee material well–being if the global economy fails to grow. In a context of anticipated resource shortages and psychological fear of deprivation by Southern hemisphere resource countries against Northern hemisphere manufacturing countries, global economic growth in the 1980s may fail to keep pace with the rising expectations of people who refuse to accept the "rationality" of the traditional international political and economic system.

A growing outrage at the inequities of distribution practiced by the economic system will likely find expression in wars for political control that pit the relatively rich against the relatively poor, both within and between states. Whether they are driven by fear of loss (of gasoline, of income, of "way of life," of material security) or fear of exploitation (by others, by leaders, by foreigners), the sense of alienation engendered by that fear may be expected to promote both civil war and international war with increasing frequency.

The attraction of war as a "solution" to a mood of economic and political deprivation after 1980 will be reinforced by the unprecedented availability of conventional weapons. By any measure, the per capita expenditure on and distribution of weapons is now at an all-time high. But because the world's nuclear powers are so fearful of the consequences of an uncontrolled nuclear war, a ceiling seems to have been imposed on acceptable levels of violence. Thus low-intensity conflict must become the only rational option for leaders to whom military violence may offer the only solution to an unbearable situation.

THE ROLE OF SUPERPOWERS

For leaders and planners in the Soviet Union and the United States, the question of superpower participation in any nonnuclear conflict will be a central issue for impassioned debate. If superpower "involvement" is defined narrowly in terms of military participation, the debate will center on the role, costs, and likely returns of different kinds of military force. If involvement is defined more inclusively, the debate will center on a reexamination of a superpower's role in the global structure and process of governance.

The narrow definition of "involvement" presumes that only military instruments need be examined, because the other components of power and the role of the superpowers are givens, largely beyond sensible exploration. Such an approach will be attractive because it avoids the psychological and political costs of self-examination; it assumes that the only ingredient required to resolve the conflict is more (or less) force; and it lends itself to quantification, delighting trade-off analysts, budgeteers, force planners, and other people who convert concepts into programs and resource commitments. We will discuss the shortcomings of this approach in greater detail below; however, its principal weakness is that it starts from a premise of fear and an unwarranted faith in physical forms of power for resolving conflict. Historical evidence suggests that massive additions of external military energy to a civil war do not promise a favorable resolution and can backfire against the donor's own political and economic system. Americans used military power unsuccessfully in Vietnam in the 1960s. They used other forms of power successfully in Nicaragua and the Middle East in the 1970s. Maybe they were maturing in their understanding of the limited utility of their own military power.

The broader definition of involvement presumes that all countries, including the superpowers, are already involved in any and all situations of conflict because there is a spiritual and moral bonding that joins all people in their common agonies and joys. From that perspective, any low-intensity conflict would demand instant and continuous thought on the part of superpower planners. These views would become part of the review process in which a state reexamined its moral and material commitment to other obligations. Such a review, whether or not so labeled, is a review of the self-image of superpower role on the world stage.

This essay is based on the broader definition of superpower involvement in nonnuclear conflict. It thus assumes that leaders really have no option about being involved; instead, their question is one of intensity and form. Based on their current perception of their role in the world, what form of power applied by the superpower promises an outcome to the situation that will express and confirm the prevailing sense of role? Any other outcome (denying or substantially altering that role) would force a full-scale review of the superpower's collective sense of Self and the commitment of its people to their own world view.

CRITERIA FOR RATIONAL INVOLVEMENT

Rational U.S. participation in nonnuclear conflict must therefore require a holistic assessment of the conflict in terms of at least four criteria:

1. the existing system of power and how it operates;
2. the role of the United States in the system;
3. the most important potential impact of issue outcome on the prevailing system and the U.S. role; and
4. the utility of available resources and institutional channels for influencing the emergence of the preferred outcome.

Before exploring these criteria in turn, it is important to observe that none of them is objectively measurable. We are dealing with competing American perceptions of those criteria. Objectively, there is no such thing as the international system of power, the role of the United States, the most dangerous versus the most desirable outcome, and the best mix of resources for fostering a preferred outcome.

Indeed, the most glaring shortcoming of macrogovernment is

its persistent inability to arrive at a holistic assessment of those criteria. Institutional fragmentation into competing bureaucracies fosters alienation instead of integration and seriously impedes a unified perception by leadership of any remote conflict or an issue over which a conflict might emerge.

An American leader's perception of an issue is deeply influenced by his prior perception of the international political system and its apparent operational mode. If he sees the system as an adversarial system in which Soviet and American power are in fundamental confrontation for short-term advantage and long-term survival, every issue must be related to that zero-sum perspective. There is no possibility of more than a temporary, tactical compromise between these two great adversaries and every issue involves the risk of loss to one or the other. All other relationships are subordinated to the superpower bilateral relationship, which rests on a past and a promised future of fear.

From such a perspective, it logically follows that the proper role for the United States is one of leadership of allies in the accumulation of more resources, especially weapons, with which to defend against the Soviets. The leadership role may evoke different images, but a host of burdens and obligations must clearly be borne by the United States in all international forums and conflicts. The image of "leader" and the credibility of that image become the foci of policy initiatives over and over.

Indeed, the most important component of that perception of the system and of the U.S. role that may be damaged by an issue is the credibility of the American image of leadership. The literature of the 1950s and 1960s is filled with public statements that rationalize U.S. involvement in Korea, Vietnam, and a hundred other low-intensity conflicts because a failure to be involved would damage U.S. credibility. "Self-respect" in the eyes of the international community—and especially America's allies and adversaries—became a salient factor in defining "rational interest" and in determining U.S. commitment of resources to situations. Without so much concern for the collective American ego, those same situations might have demanded a lower U.S. profile and a less profligate expenditure of lives and material.

Other components of the system and the perceived American role may appear to be threatened by any nonnuclear conflict in a perceived "reality" of bipolar superpower confrontation. Because survival is presumed to be at stake in that "game," power tends to be measured in physical terms, especially in military and material units of measure. The global distribution of "power" can therefore be quantified with long lists of weapons comparisons and tonnages of steel, oil, and other industrial production indices. These possessions become the symbols for measuring who is ahead. Indeed, just as leaders may believe they <u>are</u> their personal possessions (three cars? a large house? the best of <u>everything</u>?), so they must believe that the power of the United States is a physical fact, not an idea or a state of mind.

From such a definition of power, a leader must perceive any low-intensity conflict as a potential addition to or deduction from the physical totality of U.S. power—a loss or a gain. Should a loss be indicated, U.S. credibility will obviously decline among allies and adversaries, the confidence of the American people in their leader will be undermined, the leader's sense of security will be threatened, and he will begin to wonder if the "American way of life" is in jeopardy! Surely any situation that might cost him his job must be a threat to <u>his</u> way of life and, by inference, that of all other Americans. By such reasoning can a situation become overinflated.

The bipolar, adversarial "model" has the additional tendency to excite a sense of urgency among leaders. There is a pace to the bipolar adversarial relationship that discourages patience and caution. Action now, explanations later tend to reinforce the mood of crisis management that easily infects a confrontationist leadership. Time is always "running out."

In such a mood of urgency, a leadership evaluates its resources in terms of their operational readiness. Readily available physical power is presumed to be most effective for intervening in a conflict situation. To insure that such power may be brought to bear, a complex system of bases and troop deployments must be maintained together with agreements to permit American transfer of such "power" through an ally's jurisdiction. Since conflicts are increasingly perceived as demanding quick resolution, resources must be in place, pre-positioned for a rapid response to any contingency.

Since time is of the essence, according to this perspective, military resources should be tailored to the weather and geographic conditions of the most likely conflict situations. However, it is an irony of the current world scene that U.S. nonnuclear military resources have been tailored primarily for a conflict in Europe, where a low-intensity conflict is much less likely than in other tense situations for which available U.S. material is <u>not</u> very appropriate.

But even if U.S. weapons were being tailored for intervention in the most likely situations, the experience of the United States and other former colonial powers does not encourage leaders to believe that modern military force is likely to have a predictably favorable effect on a civil war. The outcome of such a war is dependent on internal political and social forces, not external military power. Local international wars may be influenced by third country troops (e.g., Cubans in Africa), but such a deployment of U.S. troops is very unlikely if the current mood of the American people prevails. In brief, conventional U.S. military intervention abroad would seem to promise diminishing returns to American leaders and rising risks of domestic political criticism because most nonnuclear conflicts pose no direct threat to the United States.

Many of the foregoing ideas have been challenged by rising costs of weapons (and all other forms of material power), and problems posed by prevailing U.S. military doctrine (skewed to accent the European geographic scenario and massed conventional reinforcement by tactical nuclear firepower). Also, the deepening erosion of the foregoing perspective of the bipolar global system, the U.S. leadership role, and utility of military instruments of power for conflict resolution in the 1970s has encouraged the emergence of an alternative view of system, role, alternative outcomes, and resource utility. As yet not fully developed, this alternative world view perceives a system much more diffused in terms of power and influence. While the U.S.-Soviet relationship remains central to any appreciation of regional and local conflict, the structure and distribution of power is more complex than the simple bipolar model discussed earlier. Within a context of diffused power among regional systems, the importance of any nonnuclear conflict situation becomes very difficult to assess. Many issues may have only marginal relevance to the superpower relationship; short-term and long-term impact of the conflict on various U.S. interests cannot easily be measured as gain or loss; and a requirement for innovation and creativity in foreign policy tends to replace the older rituals of fear.

Within the wider boundaries of this newer paradigm for viewing the world political system, the U.S. role is not so easily defined. But "leadership" is not always a comfortable label. "Partnership" will often seem a more appropriate term because it implies the image of an uncle rather than a father, a companion and guide rather than a leader. American leaders with this perception of the world system may feel more comfortable in a mediating role, seeking to foster a spiritual and emotional healing of nonnuclear conflicts instead of a hard institutional resolution that relies on traditional procedure.

The efforts of the Carter Administration to heal the Middle East conflict involved some of the elements of such a role. But it was clear that the Administration was still engaged in and was substantially confused by the superpower bilateral game, a game that also confused the principal actors in the Middle East. Their confusion notwithstanding, Carter Administration planners clearly sought to realign global U.S. military power and U.S. commitments to reflect more accurately the pluralism and diversity of power in post-Vietnam international affairs. Negotiations on Panama, troops in Korea, bases in the Philippines, commitments to Taiwan, NATO standardization,

Soviet troops in Cuba, and a host of other issues reflected a search for a new role for the United States and a new set of symbols by which to measure power.

Such a search for new symbols and new measures of effectiveness for assessing the new U.S. role in an emerging international system has not been without costs. It has been very threatening to traditionalists accustomed to more rigid structures of power and ritualistic procedures for resolving conflict. Judgments about the loss of American will, lack of vision, indecisiveness, and even hypocrisy and ad hoc opportunism have inevitably accompanied Carter Administration efforts to bridge the Cold War and a new era as yet ill-defined. American doubts about a leadership role have found echoes among foreign leaders, fearful about the decline of American capacity or caring. Indeed, the very process of experimentation with new perceptions and a new role has undermined the older image of leadership without providing a clear image of the new American role.

If that new image lacks clarity either at home or abroad, any low-intensity conflict cannot easily be assessed in terms of its possible impact on either the changing global system or the American role. However, if American leaders clearly stated their intention to foster a new era of shared regional solutions to intra-regional problems, only marginally influenced by U.S. military resource commitments but substantially supported by mediating efforts and economic incentives (technology, trade and aid, New International Economic Order measures), a different image of the United States could emerge. However, until such clarity of vision and purpose have been articulated, confusion will continue to characterize any assessment of the importance and the boundaries of a nonnuclear conflict.

In part, such confusion must reflect a shifting definition of power, no longer neatly quantified along military and industrial lines. "Power" defined in psychological terms encourages, indeed requires, a more flexible approach to the definition and resolution of any conflict situation. It finally demands that leaders search deeply for the spiritual and moral significance of such an event and the means for resolving it in a way that considers the interests of all participants. From such a perspective, U.S. mediators would seek an "all win" formula instead of a win-loss formula.

Another dimension of the new paradigm is that of time urgency. If the global system and the U.S. role cannot easily be labelled or measured but require more deliberate judgments including questions about the significance of each event for the spiritual growth and confidence of people everywhere, then urgent resolution of a crisis becomes absurd since the situation need not assume crisis proportions, at least from the perspective of U.S. leaders.

By accepting a conflict situation as a problem essentially for local and regional resolution, perhaps marginally influenced by U.S. mediating efforts; by communicating that perspective to the American people; and by seeking an innovative outcome whereby everyone gains, American leadership might become less concerned with "security" and more interested in understanding how to bring U.S. influence to bear for harmony. Such efforts might not always succeed, but they would reassure Americans weary of false crises and crisis management, American pretensions to a global policeman role, and American misperceptions of threats to American security.

From the perspective of this paradigm, leaders would evaluate available resources with less concern about their immediate operational readiness and more interest in their capacity to mitigate the emotional investment of local adversaries. How can we Americans help them redefine their problem? How can we help them buy time in which to cool down tempers (American leaders' tempers included)? How can we employ the prestige of our leaders, the wit and humor of our people, and the vision and love of both to "intervene" for a concept of shared equity, not continuing conflict?

Such questions, addressed in an atmosphere of at least muted hysteria and modulated crisis, might evoke from the American people innovative contributions to which the leadership would have no access in the time-urgent circumstances of crisis management. There might also be a greater chance for holistic solutions to a holistic conflict, instead of the traditional tendency to apply military power to a perceived military crisis, economic power to an economic crisis, and so forth.

A major obstacle to such an approach to the assessment of and participation in a low-intensity conflict is the prevailing style of the U.S. national security policy community. The crisis, short view atmosphere within that community offers little hope for member perception of the long view outside. The problem is not simply bureaucratic procedure; it has to do with the state of mind in which planning proceeds.

PERSPECTIVE FOR LEADERSHIP

The state of mind with which an American leader approaches his assessment of a nonnuclear conflict—or any crisis, for that matter is not primarily a function of the crisis but a product of the leader's perception of himself as a human being. If he believes that the nature of man is physiological, that man is an object, a collection of atoms fundamentally subservient to the universal laws of Newtonian physics and therefore predictable in behavior within broad rules for large numbers, such a statistical view of man must govern a leader's perception of a political situation and options for resolving it. In its extreme form this view supposes that a computer model, which is the scientific climax of the Newtonian illusion, can digest all "relevant" factors in a battlefield or strategic situation and print out the optimum cybernetic solution.

The fundamental assumption is that humans are captives of patterned rituals of behavior. Having learned these rituals in countless repetitions of thought and action, humans may choose among only a finite number of options that must fit into alternative "logic trees." A sophisticated computer can handle those alternatives with ease. Therefore, the human role in a political situation is tantamount to playing out a script that a computer could easily write.

For the leader with such a perspective on himself and mankind, the chief task would seem to be stuffing a computer with enough information to provide an "objective" assessment of the situation. Since only the computer, stripped of the frailties of "human error," can dispassionately portray the "input-output" dynamics of a situation, the leader can quickly determine the focus for additional "input" that would most efficiently alter the "output" in his favor. In effect, his lack of confidence in himself and his misplaced confidence in "modern technology" as a substitute for his own judgment would encourage the leader to define and respond to a situation involving human relationships as if a software program could provide the best measure of "reality."

In the intelligence field, the foregoing logic has argued for the collection of information about the distribution of things around the earth's surface. Because "power" is physical, those things are symbols of power; human relationships hinge on the possession of things and the perception of dominance by those states with the most things. Therefore, any information on human relationships is much less reliable than "objective" data about observable things! Indeed, in the United States, some people boast that more than 90 percent of intelligence is collected by non-human means.

In the strategic field and policy planning, the foregoing logic argues for reliance primarily on physical things applied to a situation to alter its outcome. "Weapons," whether military, financial, food, technological, or sheer numbers of people are seen as decisive instruments for altering the structural distribution of the same things—and thus altering political relationships.

There is another way. If a leader believes that man is not primarily a physiological entity, if he perceives the human condition in spiritual terms that transcend the self-imposed, ego-oriented interpretations of a situation and illuminate that situation as an opportunity for the extension of help, then older patterns of political behavior need not be prisons governed by universal laws of large numbers.

This is not the place to dissect the evolution of the Middle East situation. But the courageous behavior of the leaders of Egypt and Israel in 1978 stunned the world of political theorists and realists. They were stunned because those leaders dared to extend love in a context of ancient enmity and fear. With enormous patience and vision, they applied a different kind of "resource" to their relationship and watched their own peoples respond in kind. The American role was not always clarifying, consistent, or even supportive. But a nontraditional perspective in the Carter Administration refused to accent the superpower relationship as the central means for defining the situation. Instead, the American effort to mediate, to bring a spirit of sharing to two old adversaries, unquestionably contributed to the profound shift in mood while exacting major costs from all participating leaders in terms of political risk.

That crisis has taught contemporary leaders that the political courage to perceive and treat a nonnuclear conflict situation with love and compassion instead of fear far exceeds the courage required to send troops, money, weapons, and things into the crisis. It requires no courage to call upon patriots to sacrifice blood and treasure lest the nation's "security" be undermined. Such pleas often reflect a belief that security is a matter of boundaries and sovereignty.

Security is nothing more—or less—than a state of mind. Vietnam should have taught U.S. leaders that billions of dollars worth of men, equipment, and explosives do not necessarily bring "victory." The shift in relationships between China and the United States did not follow a major favorable shift in resource distribution, especially in defense terms. Indeed, after 1953 the presence of sophisticated weapons of war in the Northeast Asian arena increased dramatically. What changed among Chinese and U.S. policymakers was their state of mind and their willingness to forget the past.

Yet the past is hard to forget. Perhaps the most important element of a leader's state of mind while reviewing a nonnuclear conflict situation is fear of appearing ridiculous in "the eyes of history." If he is determined to insure continuity of trends from the past, he makes himself a captive of the past and automatically denies himself innovative options. Of those innovations, the most crucial may be a different mind set, a different way of defining "now" without worrying about "then."

Slavish adherence to "the done thing" (usually so defined by the experienced professional) requires a careful review of the past not only associated with a situation but also expressed in the American style of doing things. If "American honor" is defined so that the ritual of American style or the credibility of American image must not be challenged, then the chances for an innovative approach will be reduced substantially. Yet the political leader may have to pay the ultimate price (the rejection by the electorate) if he dares to ignore old rituals and older stereotypes, still unchanged in the popular mind, about the destiny of the United States and its role in the world. Such rituals and stereotypes, defined and understood in terms of form rather than spirit, become an expression of the American collective ego, in competition with which the American collective spirit requires true leadership, not merely government management.

Yet it is precisely the need for leadership that now underscores the possibility of an alternative U.S. approach to a world in which nonnuclear conflict may proliferate. The vision of a different role, a better way, and, fundamentally, a different conception of mankind could radically change the design and employment of both American physical and metaphysical resources for the salvation rather than the destruction of spaceship earth. Such a vision is clearly not dominant today in the context of fear that permeates governance around the world. Whether or not such vision can be articulated and applied in time may become the central issue for American leadership in the critical period, 1980-84.

SELECTED BIBLIOGRAPHY

Allison, Graham T. Essence of Decision: Explaining the Cuban Missile Crisis. Boston: Little, Brown, 1971.

Almond, Gabriel. The American People and Foreign Policy. New York: Praeger, 1950.

Ambler, John. The French Army in Politics 1945-1962. Columbus: Ohio State University Press, 1966.

Andrews, William. The Village War. Columbia: University of Missouri Press, 1973.

Armacost, Michael H. The Foreign Relations of the United States. Belmont, Calif.: Dickinson, 1969.

Baldwin, David A., ed. America in an Interdependent World. Hanover, N.H.: University Press of New England, 1976.

Barber, James David. The Presidential Character, 2nd ed. Englewood Cliffs, N.J.: Prentice-Hall, 1977.

Barnett, Vincent M. The Representation of the United States Abroad. New York: Praeger, 1965.

Bartlett, C. J. The Long Retreat. London: Macmillan, 1972.

Baylis, John, ed. British Defence Policy in a Changing World. London: Croom Helm, 1977.

Beaufre, Andre. Introduction to Strategy. London: Faber and Faber, 1965.

Berkowitz, Leonard. Aggression: A Social-Psychological Analysis. New York: McGraw-Hill, 1962.

Beaumont, Roger A. Military Elites. New York: Bobbs-Merrill, 1974.

Bellini, James, and Geoffrey Pattie. A New World Role for the Medium Power. London: Royal United Services Institute, 1977.

Bergsten, C. Fred, ed. The Future of the International Economic Order: An Agenda for Research. Lexington, Mass.: Lexington Books, 1973.

Binken, Martin, and Jeffrey Record. Where Does the Marine Corps Go From Here? Washington, D.C.: The Brookings Institution, 1976.

Blaufarb, Douglas. The Counterinsurgency Era. New York: Free Press, 1977.

Blechman, Barry M., et al. Setting National Priorities: The Next Ten Years. Washington, D.C.: The Brookings Institution, 1976.

Blechman, Barry, et al. The Soviet Military Buildup and U.S. Defense Spending. Washington, D.C.: The Brookings Institution, 1977.

Blechman, Barry M., Stephen S. Kaplan, et al. Force Without War. Washington, D.C.: The Brookings Institution, 1978.

Bliss, Howard, and Glen M. Johnson. Beyond the Water's Edge: America's Foreign Policies. Philadelphia: Lippincott, 1975.

Bloomfield, Lincoln P., and Amelia Leiss. Controlling Small Wars: A Strategy for the 1970s. New York: Knopf, 1976.

Bole, Albert C., and K. Kobata. An Evaluation of the Measurements of the Hamlet Evaluation System. Naval War College for Advanced Research, 1975.

Braestrup, Peter. Big Story: How the American Press and Television Reported and Interpreted the Crisis of Tet-1968 in Vietnam and Washington. Boulder, Colo.: Westview Press, 1977.

Briggs, Ellis. Anatomy of Diplomacy. New York: David McKay, 1968.

Brown, General George S. U.S. Military Posture for FY1979. Statement to the Congress. January 20, 1978.

Brown, Neville. Arms Without Empire. London: Penguin, 1967.

Brown, Seyom. The Faces of Power. New York: Columbia University Press, 1968.

Brown, Seyom. New Forces in World Politics. Washington, D.C.: The Brookings Institution, 1974.

Buchan, Alastair. The End of the Postwar Era. New York: Saturday Review Press, 1974.

Buck, James H., ed. The Modern Japanese Military System. Beverly Hills: Sage, 1975.

Bunzel, John H., ed. Issues of American Public Policy. Englewood Cliffs, N.J.: Prentice-Hall, 1964.

Burns, James MacGregor. Presidential Government. Boston: Houghton Mifflin, 1965.

Butterworth, Robert L. Managing Interstate Conflict 1945-1974. Pittsburgh: UCIS, University of Pittsburgh, 1976.

Buttinger, Joseph. Vietnam: A Political History. New York: Praeger, 1972.

Cable, James F. Gunboat Diplomacy. London: Praeger, 1971.

Cahn, Anne Hessing, et al. Controlling Future Arms Trade. New York: McGraw-Hill, 1977.

Caldwell, Lawrence T. Soviet-American Relations. Atlantic Institute, 1976.

Campbell, Angus, Philip E. Converse, Warren E. Miller, and Donald E. Stokes. The American Voter. New York: Wiley, 1960.

Cannizzo, Cynthia A., ed. Arms Transfers and International Security. New York: Pergamon Press, 1979.

Chinh, Truong. Primer for Revolt. New York: Praeger, 1963.

Churchill, Winston. The Gathering Storm. Boston: Houghton Mifflin, 1948.

Cline, Ray S. World Power Assessment. A Calculus of Strategic Drift. Washington, D.C.: Center for Strategic and International Studies, 1973.

Cochran, Charles L., ed. Civil-Military Relations. New York: Free Press, 1974.

Cohen, Bernard C. The Public's Impact on Foreign Policy. Boston: Little, Brown, 1973.

Cohen, Bernard C. The Press and Foreign Policy. Princeton: Princeton University Press, 1963.

Collins, James L. The Development and Training of the South Vietnamese Army 1960-1972, Vietnam Studies. Washington, D.C.: Department of the Army, 1975.

Collins, John M. Imbalance of Power: Shifting U.S.-Soviet Military Strengths. San Rafael, Calif.: Presidio Press, 1978.

Conley, Michael. The Communist Infrastructure in South Vietnam. Washington, D.C.: Center for Research in Social Systems, 1967.

Cooper, C. L., J. E. Corson, and L. J. Legere. The American Experience with Pacification in Vietnam, Vol. 2. Arlington, Va.: Institute for Defense Analysis, 1972.

Cotright, David. Soldiers in Revolt. Garden City, N.Y.: Anchor Press, 1975.

Cottam, Richard W. Competitive Interference and Twentieth Century Diplomacy. Pittsburgh: University of Pittsburgh Press, 1967.

Crozier, Brian. Masters of Power. London: Eyre and Spottiswoode, 1969.

Dahl, Robert A. Congress and Foreign Policy. New York: Harcourt, Brace and World, 1950.

Dahl, Robert A. Modern Political Analysis. Englewood Cliffs, N.J.: Prentice-Hall, 1970.

Dallin, Alexander, and George Breslauer. Political Terror in Communist Systems. Stanford: Stanford University Press, 1970.

Darby, Philip. British Defense Policy East of Suez 1947-1968. London: Oxford University Press, 1973.

Davison, W. P. Some Observations of Viet Cong Operations in the Villages. Santa Monica, Calif.: Rand, 1968.

Denton, F. H. Volunteers for the Viet Cong. Santa Monica, Calif.: Rand, 1969.

de Tocqueville, Alexis. Democracy in America. J. P. Mayer, ed. Garden City, N.Y.: Doubleday, Anchor Books, 1969.

DiClerico, Robert E. The American President. Englewood Cliffs, N.J.: Prentice-Hall, 1979.

Dinerstein, H. S. War and the Soviet Union. New York: Praeger, 1959.

Dodd, Lawrence C., and Bruce L. Oppenheimer, eds. Congress Reconsidered. New York: Praeger, 1977.

Dollard, John, et al. Frustration and Aggression. New Haven, Conn.: Yale University Press, 1939.

Donnell, J. C., G. P. Pauker, and J. J. Zasloff. Viet Cong Motivation and Morale: A Preliminary Report. Santa Monica, Calif.: Rand, 1965.

Douglass, Joseph D., Jr. The Soviet Theater Nuclear Offensive. U.S. Air Force, 1976.

Elliott, D. W. P., and M. Elliott. Documents of an Elite Viet Cong Delta Unit: The Demolition Platoon of the 154th Battalion—Part One-Five. Santa Monica, Calif.: Rand, 1969.

Ellsberg, Daniel. Papers on the War. New York: Simon and Schuster, 1972.

Enthovan, Alain, and Wayne Smith. How Much Is Enough? New York: Harper and Row, 1971.

Fall, Bernard. Viet-Nam Witness 1953-66. New York: Praeger, 1966.

Fall, Bernard. Street Without Joy. New York: Shocken, 1964.

Fall, Bernard. The Two Vietnams. New York: Praeger, 1967.

Farrar, Lancelot L., Jr. War: A Historical, Political, and Social Study. Santa Barbara, Calif.: ABC-Clio Press, 1979.

Feierabend, Ivo, Rosalind Feierabend, and Ted Robert Gurr, eds. Anger, Violence, and Politics. Englewood Cliffs, N.J.: Prentice-Hall, 1972.

Fitzgerald, Frances. Fire in the Lake. Boston: Little, Brown, 1972.

Frank, Robert S. Message Dimensions of Television News. Lexington, Mass.: D.C. Heath/Lexington Books, 1973.

Frankland, Noble, and Christopher Dowling, eds. Decisive Battles of the Twentieth Century. London: Sedgewick and Jackson, 1976.

Fredman, A. E. The Psychology of Political Control. New York: St. Martin's Press, 1975.

Fulbright, J. William. The Crippled Giant: American Foreign Policy and its Domestic Consequences. New York: Vintage Books, 1972.

Gabriel, Richard A., and Paul L. Savage. Crisis in Command: Mismanagement in the Army. New York: Hill and Wang, 1978.

Galula, David. Counterinsurgency Warfare. New York: Praeger, 1964.

Garthoff, R. L. Soviet Strategy in the Nuclear Age. New York: Praeger, 1958.

George, Alexander L., David K. Hall, and William R. Simons. The Limits of Coercive Diplomacy. Boston: Little, Brown, 1971.

George, Alexander, and Richard Smoke. Deterrence in American Foreign Policy: Theory and Practice. New York: Columbia University Press, 1974.

Giap, General Vo Nguyen. People's War People's Army. New York: Praeger, 1962.

Gillick, Richard O. New Dynamics in National Strategy: The Paradox of Power. New York: Thomas Y. Crowell, 1975.

Gleb, Leslie H., and Richard K. Betts. The Irony of Vietnam: The System Worked. Washington, D.C.: Brookings Institution, 1979.

Glick, Edward. Peaceful Conflict. Harrisburg, Pa.: Stackpole, 1967.

Griffith, Samuel, ed. Mao Tse-tung on Guerrilla Warfare. New York: Praeger, 1961.

Gurr, Ted Robert. Why Men Rebel. Princeton: Princeton University Press, 1970.

Gurr, Ted Robert, and H. Graham, eds. Violence in America. New York: Signet, 1969.

Halperin, Morton H. Bureaucratic Politics and Foreign Policy. Washington, D.C.: Brookings Institution, 1974.

Haselkorn, Avigdor. The Evolution of Soviet Security Strategy, 1965-1975, Strategy Paper. New York: National Strategy Information Center, November, 1977.

Hauser, William L. America's Army in Crisis. Baltimore: Johns Hopkins University Press, 1973.

Heggoy, Andrew. Insurgency and Counterinsurgency in Algeria. Bloomington: Indiana University Press, 1972.

Henkin, Louis. Foreign Affairs and the Constitution. New York: W. W. Norton, 1972.

Hero, Alfred O. Americans in World Affairs. Boston: World Peace Foundation, 1959.

Hero, Alfred O. Mass Media and World Affairs. Boston: World Peace Foundation, 1959.

Hill, Norman L. The New Democracy in Foreign Policy Making. Lincoln: University of Nebraska Press, 1970.

Hilsman, Roger. To Move a Nation. New York: Delta Books, 1964.

Hoeber, Francis P., et al. Arms, Men and Military Budgets: Issues for Fiscal Year 1979. New York: Crane, Russak, 1978.

Hoffman, Stanley. Gulliver's Troubles or the Setting of American Foreign Policy. New York: McGraw-Hill, 1968.

Hoffman, Stanley. Primacy of World Order. New York: McGraw-Hill, 1978.

Hofstetter, C. Richard. Bias in the News: Network Television Coverage of the 1972 Election Campaign. Columbus: Ohio State University Press, 1976.

Holst, Johan, and Uwe Nerlich, eds. Beyond Nuclear Deterrence—New Aims, New Arms. New York: Crane, Russak, 1977.

Horton, Frank B. III, Anthony Rogerson, and Edward L. Warner III, eds. Comparative Defense Policy. Baltimore: Johns Hopkins University Press, 1974.

Hosmer, Stephen. Viet Cong Repression and Its Implications for the Future. Lexington, Mass.: Heath Books, 1970.

Ikle, Fred. Every War Must End. New York: Columbia University Press, 1971.

International Institute for Strategic Studies. East Asia and the World System Part II: The Regional Powers. IISS, Adelphi Paper 92, London, November 1972.

International Institute for Strategic Studies. The Military Balance 1978-1979. London: IISS, 1978.

Japanese Defense Agency. Defense of Japan, 1978. Tokyo, 1978.

Javits, Jacob K., with Don Kellermann. Who Makes War: The President Versus Congress. New York: William Morrow, 1973.

Jenkins, Brian. The Unchangeable War. Santa Monica, Calif.: Rand, 1972.

Joffe, Ellis. Party and Army: Professionalism and Political Control in the Chinese Officer Corps, 1949-1964. East Asian Research Center, Harvard University, 1965.

Johnson, Chalmers. Revolutionary Change. Boston: Little, Brown, 1966.

Johnson, Lady Bird. A White House Diary. New York: Holt, Rinehart and Winston, 1970.

Kahin, George McTurnan, and George Lewis. The United States in Vietnam. New York: Delta, 1967.

Kahn, Herman. On Thermonuclear War. Princeton: Princeton University Press, 1960.

Kahn, Herman. Thinking About the Unthinkable. New York: Horizon Press, 1962.

Keeley, John B., ed. The All-Volunteer Force and American Society. Charlottesville: University Press of Virginia, 1978.

Kelleher, Catherine M. Germany and the Politics of Nuclear Weapons. New York: Columbia University Press, 1975.

Kellen, Konrad. Conversations with Enemy Soldiers in Late 1968/ Early 1969: A Study of Motivation and Morale. Santa Monica, Calif.: Rand, 1970.

Kellen, Konrad. A View of the VC: Elements of Cohesion in the Enemy Camp. Santa Monica, Calif.: Rand, 1969.

Kelman, Herbert C., ed. International Behavior: A Social-Psychological Analysis. New York: Holt, Rinehart and Winston, 1965.

Keohane, Robert, and Joseph Nye. Transnational Relations and World Politics. Cambridge, Mass.: Harvard University Press, 1972.

Keohane, Robert, and Joseph Nye. Power and Interdependence. Boston: Little, Brown, 1977.

Kinnard, Douglas. The War Managers. Hanover, N.H.: University Press of New England, 1977.

Kissinger, Henry. American Foreign Policy: Three Essays. New York: W. W. Norton, 1966.

Kohl, Wilfred I. French Nuclear Diplomacy. Princeton: Princeton University Press, 1971.

Kolkowicz, R. The Soviet Military and the Communist Party. Princeton: Princeton University Press, 1967.

Kolodziej, Edward A. French International Policy Under DeGaulle and Pompidou. Ithaca, N.Y.: Cornell University Press, 1974.

Komer, Robert. Bureaucracy Does Its Thing: Institutional Constraints on U.S.-GVN Performance in Vietnam. Santa Monica, Calif.: Rand, 1972.

Lake, Anthony, ed. The Vietnam Legacy. New York: New York University Press, 1976.

Lansdale, Edward. In the Midst of War. New York: Harper and Row, 1972.

Lefever, Ernest W. TV and National Defense: An Analysis of CBS News, 1972-73. Boston: Institute for American Strategy Press, 1974.

Levering, Ralph B. The Public and American Foreign Policy, 1918-1978. New York: William Morrow, 1978.

McClintock, Robert. The Meaning of Limited War. Boston: Houghton Mifflin, 1967.

McCuen, John. The Art of Counterrevolutionary War. Harrisburg, Pa.: Stackpole, 1966.

McNelly, Theodore. Politics and Government in Japan, 3rd edition. Boston: Houghton Mifflin, 1972.

Margiotta, Franklin D., ed. The Changing World of the American Military. Boulder, Colo.: Westview,Press, 1978.

Marshall, Charles Burton. The Exercise of Sovereignty. Baltimore: Johns Hopkins University Press, 1965.

Miroff, Bruce. Pragmatic Illusions. New York: David McKay, 1976.

Melnik, C. The French Campaign Against the FLN. Santa Monica, Calif.: Rand, 1967.

Morgenthau, Hans J. A New Foreign Policy for the United States. New York: Praeger, 1969.

Morse, Edward L. Foreign Policy and Interdependence in Gaullist France. Princeton: Princeton University Press, 1973.

Moskos, Charles C., Jr., ed. Public Opinion and the Military Establishment. Beverly Hills: Sage, 1971.

Mueller, John E. War, Presidents and Public Opinion. New York: Wiley, 1973.

Murdoka, Kimio. Japanese Security and the United States. International Institute for Strategic Studies (IISS), Adelphia Paper 92, London, February, 1973.

Nathan, James A., and James K. Oliver. United States Foreign Policy and World Order. Boston: Little, Brown, 1976.

Neustadt, Richard E. Presidential Power: The Politics of Leadership. New York: Wiley, 1960.

Nighswonger, William. Rural Pacification in Vietnam. New York: Praeger, 1966.

Nixon, Richard. The Memoirs of Richard Nixon. New York: Grosset and Dunlap, 1978.

Nutting, Antony. No End of a Lesson. London: Constable, 1967.

Office of the Assistant Secretary of Defense (OASD), Special Assistant (SA), SEA Analysis Reports, 162, 313, 316, 613, and 609.

O'Neill, Bard, J. B. Alberts, and Stephen Rossette, eds. Political Violence and Insurgency: A Comparative Approach. Boulder, Colo.: Phoenix Press, 1974.

Osborne, Milton. Strategic Hamlets in South Vietnam. Ithaca, N.Y.: Department of Asian Studies, Cornell University, 1965.

Paret, Peter. French Revolutionary Warfare from Indochina to Algeria. New York: Praeger, 1964.

Paret, Peter, and John Shy. Guerrillas in the 1960's. New York: Praeger, 1964.

Patterson, Thomas E., and Robert D. McClure. The Unseeing Eye: The Myth of Television Power in National Politics. New York: G. P. Putnam's Sons, 1976.

Pauker, Guy. An Essay on Vietnamization. Santa Monica, Calif.: Rand, 1971.

Payne, James L. The American Threat. Chicago: Markham, 1970.

Pierre, Andrew. Nuclear Politics. London: Oxford University Press, 1972.

Pike, Douglas. Vietcong. Cambridge, Mass.: M.I.T. Press, 1967.

Pike, Douglas. The Vietcong Strategy of Terror. Cambridge, Mass.: M.I.T. Press, 1970.

Pious, Richard M. The American Presidency. New York: Basic Books, 1979.

Pohle, Victoria. The Viet Cong in Saigon: Tactics and Objectives During the TET Offensive. Santa Monica, Calif.: Rand, 1969.

Pusey, Merlo J. The Way We Go to War. Boston: Houghton Mifflin, 1969.

Race, Jeffrey. War Comes to Long An. Berkeley: University of California Press, 1972.

Rainey, Gene E. Patterns of American Foreign Policy. Boston: Allyn and Bacon, 1975.

Rapaport, Anatol, ed. Clausewitz on War. Maryland: Penguin Books, 1971.

Rielly, John E., ed. American Public Opinion and U.S. Foreign Policy, 1979. Chicago: The Chicago Council on Foreign Relations, 1979.

Robinson, James A. Congress and Foreign Policy-Making, rev. ed. Homewood, Ill.: Dorsey Press, 1967.

Rosecrance, Richard. Defense of the Realm. New York: Columbia University Press, 1968.

Rosen, Steven, and Walter Jones. The Logic of International Relations. Cambridge, Mass.: Winthrop, 1974.

Rosenau, James. Public Opinion and Foreign Policy. New York: Random House, 1961.

Rosenau, James, ed. Domestic Sources of Foreign Policy. New York: Free Press, 1967.

Rossiter, Clinton, ed. The Federalist Papers. New York: New American Library, 1961.

Sansom, Robert. The Economics of Insurgency. Cambridge, Mass.: M.I.T. Press, 1970.

Sarkesian, Sam C., ed. Revolutionary Guerrilla Warfare. Chicago: Precedent, 1975.

Sarkesian, Sam C., ed. Defense Policy and the Presidency: Carter's First Years. Boulder, Colo.: Westview Press, 1979.

Savkin, V. Ye. The Basic Principles of Operational Art and Tactics. Moscow: Voenizdat, 1972.

Schelling, Thomas C. Arms and Influence. New Haven: Yale University Press, 1966.

Schlesinger, Arthur M., Jr. The Bitter Heritage: Vietnam and American Democracy, 1941-1966. New York: Fawcett World, 1968.

Schlesinger, Arthur M., Jr. The Imperial Presidency. Boston: Houghton Mifflin, 1973.

Scott, Harriet F., and William F. Scott. The Armed Forces of the USSR. Boulder, Colo.: Westview Press, 1979.

Sears, David O. Public Opinion. Englewood Cliffs, N.J.: Prentice-Hall, 1964.

Selected Works of Mao Tse Tung, abridged by Bruno Shaw. New York: Harper and Row, 1970.

Simon, Rita James. Public Opinion in America: 1936-1970. Chicago: Markham, 1974.

Sokolovskii, Marshal V. D. Soviet Military Strategy. Rand Edition.

Spanier, John, and Eric M. Uslaner. How American Foreign Policy Is Made, 2nd ed. New York: HRW/Praeger, 1978.

Steel, Ronald. Pax Americana. New York: Viking Press, 1967.

Stern, Ellen. The Limits of Military Intervention. Beverly Hills, Calif.: Sage, 1977.

Thompson, Kenneth W. The Moral Issue in Statecraft. Baton Rouge: Louisiana State University Press, 1966.

Thompson, Sir Robert. Defeating Communist Insurgency. New York: Praeger, 1966.

Thompson, Sir Robert. No Exit from Vietnam. New York: David McKay, 1968.

Thompson, W. Scott, and Donaldson D. Frizzell, eds. The Lessons of Vietnam. New York: Crane, Russak, 1977.

Thompson, W. Scott. Power Projection: A Net Assessment of U.S. and Soviet Capabilities, Agenda Paper. New York: National Strategy Information Center, April, 1978.

Thompson, W. Scott, ed. The Third World: Premises of U.S. Policy. San Francisco: Institute for Contemporary Studies, 1978.

Tillema, Herbert K. Appeal to Force: American Military Intervention in the Era of Containment. New York: Thomas Y. Crowell, 1973.

Trinquier, Roger. Modern Warfare. New York: Praeger, 1961.

Truman, David B. The Governmental Process. New York: Knopf, 1971.

Tsou, Tang, ed. China's Policies in Asia and America's Alternative. Chicago: University of Chicago Press, 1969.

Tucker, Robert W. Nation or Empire? The Debate Over American Foreign Policy. Baltimore: Johns Hopkins University Press, 1971.

Tucker, Robert W. The Inequality of Nations. New York: Basic Books, 1977.

U.S. Arms Control and Disarmament Agency. World Military Expenditures and Transfers, 1965-1974. Washington, D.C.: Arms Control and Disarmament Agency, 1976.

U.S. Congress, House, Committee on Foreign Affairs. Foreign Assistance Act of 1961. 88th Congress, 2nd Session, 1964.

U.S. Congress, House, Sub-committee on Foreign Operations and Government Information. United States Assistance Programs in Vietnam. 92nd Congress, 1st Session, 1972.

U.S. Congress, House, Committee on Armed Services. United States-Vietnam Relations, 1945-1967. 92nd Congress, 2nd Session, 1973.

U.S. Congress, House, Committee on International Relations. International Security Assistance Act of 1976. 94th Congress, 1st Session, 1976.

U.S. Congress, Senate. U.S. Commitments to Foreign Powers. Hearings, Committee on Foreign Relations, 19th Congress, 1st Session, 1967.

U.S. Congress, Senate, Committee on Armed Services. Achieving America's Goals: National Service or the All-Volunteer Armed Force?

U.S. Department of the Army. Field Manual 31-20, Special Operations—Operations Against Guerrilla Forces. 1961.

U.S. Department of the Army. Field Manual 31-21, Special Forces Operations. June, 1965.

U.S. Department of the Army. Field Manual 31-23, Stability Operations: U.S. Army Doctrine. December, 1967.

U.S. Department of the Army. Field Manual 41-10, Civic Affairs Operations. 1969.

U.S. Department of the Army. Field Manual 31-23, Stability Operations: U.S. Army Doctrine. October, 1972.

U.S. Department of the Army. Field Manual 100-20, Internal Defense and Development: U.S. Army Doctrine.

U.S. Department of Defense. Annual Report, Fiscal Year 1979 and Fiscal Year 1980.

Welch, Claude E., Jr., ed. Civilian Control of the Military. Albany: SUNY Press, 1976.

West, F. J. Area Security: The Need, the Composition, and the Components. Santa Monica, Calif.: Rand, 1968.

Whitson, William W. The Chinese High Command: A History of Communist Politics 1927-71. New York: Praeger, 1973.

Whitson, William W., ed. Foreign Policy and U.S. National Security. New York: Praeger, 1976.

Wilcox, Francis O., and Richard A. Frank, eds. The Constitution and the Conduct of Foreign Policy. New York: Praeger, 1976.

Williams, Geoffrey, and Alan. Crisis in European Defense. London: Charles Knight, 1974.

Wolf, Charles, and Nathan Leites. Rebellion and Authority. Chicago: Markham, 1970.

Yepishev, A. A. Some Aspects of Party-Political Work in the Soviet Armed Forces. Moscow, 1975.

Young, Oran. The Politics of Force. Princeton: Princeton University Press, 1968.

Zasloff, J. J. Political Motivation of the Viet Cong: The Vietminh Regroups. Santa Monica, Calif.: Rand, 1968.

INDEX

Note: This Index is limited to major subject areas and important personalities. There is no attempt to repeat the extensive material presented in the Endnotes for each chapter. Readers are also directed to the detailed Table of Contents and List of Tables and Figures.

Chou En-Lai (PRC), 340
Clifford, Clark, former Secretary of Defense, 152
Cold War, 274
Communist of the Armed Forces, 315
Congress, U. S.: checks on the President, 221; role in foreign affairs, 219-20
Counterinsurgency: American (U. S.) strategy, 138-39; principles, 141-42, 169, 170
Cowboy Strategy, 324
Crisis management, 368-376
Cuba: in Africa, 86, 90, 131, 133
Cuban Missile Crisis, 128, 131
Cultural Revolution, 334

DeGaulle, 130, 257-58
Deterrence: concept, 8-9; American, 375-76; credibility in Europe, 301-302
Disraeli, Prime Minister, 61, 91
Dulles, John Foster, Ambassador, 345

Eastern Europe, 303
Eisenhower, President, 105
Elite public, 224
Europe: strategy, 251; force employment outside Europe, 252; limits of security, 252, 253; war scenario, 62, 73

Force and Obedience Theory: applied to Vietnam, 149-51
France: economic considerations, 260-61; nonnuclear capability, 364; and Third World, 257-58; scope of international involvement, 254, 257-58, 262

Germany: economic infrastructure, 287-88; nonnuclear capability, 278-79; scope of

international involvement, 260, 262
German Federal Government: neutron weapons, 293
Giscard d'Estang, President of France, 262, 264, 265, 269-70
Gorshkov, Admiral (USSR), 315
Green Berets, 128

Half-wars, 236-37; U. S. Defense Department policy, 253-54
Hitler, 137
Hua Huo-feng (PRC), 333

Inoki, Masamichi, former President, National Defense College (Japan), 357
Institute fur Internationale Politik und Sicherheit-Stiftung Wissenschaft und Politik, 290
International Political System, 368-69
Intervention: reasons for, 131-32
Iran, 200 (see also Khomeini)
Izvestiia, 320

Japan: civilian control of the military, 350; Constitution of 1947, 345-46; Democratic Socialist Party, 357; Liberal Democratic Party, 351; National Defense Council, 350; National Defense policy, 346, 354-55; National Police Reserve, 345; Peace Treaty and Security Treaty, 345, 350; Self-Defense Forces, 345-46, 354-55; Soviet threat, 353
Japan Defense Agency, 347, 350, 352-53
Japan-U. S. Security Systems, 356
Japanese defense costs, 347-57
Japanese Diet, 351-52; defense policy, 352
Japanese-Korean relations, 353-54
Johnson, Lyndon, former President

of the United States, 218-19

Kennedy Administration: counterinsurgency, 140-41; Cuban Missile Crisis, 128, 131; defense policy, 128
Kennedy, Senator Edward, 331
Khomeini, Ayotollah, 86, 109,129
Kissinger, Henry, former Secretary of State, 136, 214
Khrushchev (USSR), 311-12
Korean intervention, 337
Kurisu, General (Japan), 357

Law of the Sea, 108
Loi de programmation (1976), 269
Low-intensity conflict: U. S. involvement, 55; definition, 41-42; strategy in Vietnam, 167-68

MacArthur, Douglas, General, 3 345
Mansfield Amendment (1972), 220
Mao Tse-tung, 139-40, 331-32, 334, 340-41
Marshall plan, 113, 129
Marxism-Leninism on War and the Army, 314-15
Max Planck Institute (Federal Republic of Germany), 299
Mayaguez incident, 222
Method in nonnuclear conflicts, 24; direct military intervention, 25-26; indirect intervention, 24-25; multilateral intervention, 26; surrogate forces, 24; UN/Regional Association intervention, 27
Military intervention: U. S. contingency plans, 191; difficulty for the United States, 188-89; force structure, 190, 192-93; political constraints, 235; Presidential authority, 187

Military power: American (U. S.) decline, 48-50, 227; utility, 6-7, 13-14, 29, 43, 110, 114, 210; Vietnam, 169; Western powers, 30
Modell Deutschland, 362
Mood theory, 224-25

National interest, 189, 366-67
National morale, 111; America, 112; Vietnam-GVN, 152; Viet-Cong/North Vietnamese Army, 153
NATO Forces: blitzkrieg assault, 291; use of nuclear weapons, 292
NATO/Warsaw Pact, 324
Nonnuclear and nuclear conflicts: characteristics, 11-13; definition, 5
Nonmilitary instruments of power: U. S. capability, 106, 117; character, 109; definition, 103; economic, 103-104; overlap with military instruments, 105, 107

Pacification Attitude Analysis System, 162
Pentagon (see also U. S. Defense Department), 41
People's Liberation Army (PLA), 331; air and naval forces, 459; categories of military activity, 337; ground strength, 342, 343; interservice issues, 335; leadership groups, 334; modernization, 331-32; regional pressures, 335; theater nuclear forces, 342; veto group, 333
People's Republic of China (PRC): Constitution, 336; relationship with North Vietnam, 337-38, 342
Presidential Review Memorandum, 67-69

Presidential Wars, 211; bureaucracy's role, 214-15; conduct
and termination, 235; constitutional considerations, 213;
elite role, 224; initiation
phase, 226; media and the public, 233-34; media role, 232-
33; presidential character, 215-
16; presidential leadership,
231, 335; public role, 224-26;
three stages, 212; war powers,
213

Rand, 151, 153
Rusk, Dean, Former Secretary of
State, 136

SALT, 45, 200
Schlesinger, James, former
Secretary of Defense, 289
Sekino, Hideo (Japan), 357
Single issue politics, 289
Sino-Indian relations, 338
Sokolovsky (USSR), 322-23
Soviet-American disparity, 226
Soviet Communist Party leadership, 317
Soviet convential theater forces,
311
Soviet strategic policy: alliance
problems, 317; asymmetry
with the United States, 323,
325-26; changes, 314; deterrence, 318, 325
Soviet Union (see also superpowers): conventional capability, 52, 56, 86; European
nonnuclear forces, 302-303;
industrialization, 115; intentions, 64-65; interventionist
policy, 130-31, 133, 135;
vulnerability of forces, 305
Stalin, (USSR), 130, 137; permanent and temporary principles of warfare, 310

Strategic Survey, 86
Strategic theories and doctrines,
323
Strategy, nonnuclear conflict, 16;
influence, 18-19; limited and
major conventional wars, 23;
limited conventional war, 21-
23; quick strike, 21, 53-54;
revolution and counter-revolu-
tion, 16-18; support, 19-20
Strategic security environment, 44;
nuclear balance, 45-46; power
distribution, 44, 63-64, 119;
technology, 47; weapons availability, 47-48; world economy,
45
Suez, 130, 341-42
Superpowers, low-intensity conflict, 132

Taiwan, 135
Ten Hsiao-p'ing (PRC), 333
Third World, 114, 135-142; ener-
gy source, 186; instability, 140;
and France, 257
Tonkin Gulf, 218, 220,
Truman-Acheson policy, 129;
Truman doctrine, 129, 133,
137

United States (see also American
policy): post World War II role
expansion, 126-28; Suez, 129-
30

Vance, Cyrus, Secretary of State,
114
Vietnam: ARVN decline, 164-65,
166-67; Chieu Hoi, 159; CORDS,
155; failure of Diem, 143-44;
force levels, 152-53; Hamlet
evaluation system, 158, 159-
164; pacification, 154-55;
Phung Hoang (Phoenix), 148,
166; post-Diem failure, 146;

ABOUT THE EDITOR AND
CONTRIBUTORS

SAM C. SARKESIAN is Professor and Chairman, Department of
Political Science, Loyola University of Chicago. He has served in a
number of academic positions including service at DePaul University
and in the Department of Social Sciences at the U.S. Military Academy,
West Point, New York. Dr. Sarkesian has published a number of
articles on the military profession and national security issues, and
the African military. These have appeared in the Midwest Journal of
Political Science, Orbis, African Studies Review, Social Science
Quarterly, Military Review, and Armed Forces and Society.
Dr. Sarkesian includes among his publications The Military-Industrial
Complex: A Reassessment (1972); The Professional Army Officer in
a Changing Society (1975); Revolutionary Guerrilla Warfare (1975);
Politics and Power: An Introduction to American Government (1975);
Comparative Politics: An Introduction, with James Buck (1979); and
Defense Policy and the Presidency (1979). He has also contributed
chapters to various books on professionalism and the third world
military. He received his Ph.D. from Columbia University in New
York.

ROGER A. BEAUMONT was formerly Associate Director of the
Center for Advanced Study in Organization Science at the University
of Wisconsin-Milwaukee, and has taught history at the University of
Wisconsin-Milwaukee, UW-Oshkosh, Marquette, Kansas State, and
Texas A&M, as well as at the Industrial College of the Armed Forces,
the U.S. Army Command and General Staff College, and the U.S.D.A.
Graduate School. Author of Military Elites and the forthcoming Sword
of the Raj: The Old Indian Army, and co-editor of War in the Next
Decade, he has had articles published in such journals in the U.S.
and Europe as Horizon, the New York Times, U.S. Naval Institute
Proceedings, Journal of the Royal United Services Institution, and
An Cosantoir. Dr. Beaumont, who served on active duty with the
Army as a Military Police officer, has been a business executive and
publicity writer, as well as teacher. He is currently a trustee of the
American Military Institute, a Fellow of the Inter-University Seminar
on Armed Forces and Society, and a Member of the International
Institute for Strategic Studies, a member of the AMI Editorial Advisory
Board, and an Associate Member of the Science Fiction Writers'
Association.

GEORGE BLUHM was born and raised in Berlin, Germany. He studied Political Science and History at the Free University Berlin and the Albert-Ludwigs University in Freiburg, Federal Republic of Germany, where he received the degree of Doctor Philosophiae in 1962. Dr. Bluhm's dissertation was published under the title: "Die Oder-Neisse Linie in der deutschen Aussenpolitik" (The Oder Neisse Line in German Foreign Policy), Rombach, Freiburg, 1963. During the period 1964-66 he worked on international security problems at the Institute for International Law, University of Kiel. Dr. Bluhm was Senior Research Associate at The Institute for Strategic Studies during 1966-67, where he wrote the Adelphi Paper #40: Detente and Military Relaxation in Europe—A German View. In 1967, Dr. Bluhm came to the United States and is currently Professor of Government at Western Kentucky University.

JAMES H. BUCK is Professor of International Affairs at the Air War College, on leave (1978-80) from the Office of the Vice President for Academic Affairs, University of Georgia. He is editor of The Modern Japanese Military System (1975), a contributor to Claude E. Welch (ed.), Civilian Control of the Military and Wm. W. Whitson (ed.), Foreign Policy and U.S. National Security (1976), and co-author with Sam C. Sarkesian of Comparative Politics: An Introduction (1979). He received his Ph.D. from American University.

EDWIN H. FEDDER is currently Professor of Political Science and Director of the Center for International Studies at the University of Missouri-St. Louis. He is the author of NATO: The Dynamics of Alliance in the Postwar World, and editor of NATO in the Seventies. Dr. Fedder has written numerous articles and papers on NATO, alliance theory, international politics, and foreign policy. He is also serving as the Chairman for North America of the Committee for Atlantic Studies.

LAWRENCE E. GRINTER is Professor of International Affairs, Department of National Security Affairs, Air War College. He has served in a variety of positions, including Peace Corps Volunteer Teacher in Sierre Leone and Field Researcher in Vietnam. Dr. Grinter was a postdoctoral fellow at the Foreign Policy Research Institute, 1972-74, and served in academic posts at Haverford College, the National War College, and Georgetown University. He has written numerous articles on national security matters with particular focus on Southeast Asia, and the following monographs (published by the National Defense University, 1978): The Philippine Bases: Continuing Utility in a Changing Strategic Context; Peace in Korea: Managing the

Risks; <u>Third World Conflicts and United States Policy</u>. He received his Ph. D. from the University of North Carolina.

CATHERINE McCARDLE KELLEHER is currently Associate Professor at the Graduate School of International Studies at the University of Denver and Faculty Associate at the Center for Political Studies of the Institute for Social Research of the University of Michigan. A graduate of Mount Holyoke College, she received her doctorate in Political Science from the Massachusetts Institute of Technology and has taught at Barnard College, Columbia University, the University of Illinois at Chicago Circle, and the University of Michigan. Dr. Kelleher is the author of a number of books and articles on European and American security issues, and serves as a consultant to several governmental and research agencies. She has received awards from the Fulbright Program, the Council on Foreign Relations, and the Social Science Research Council.

ROMAN KOLKOWICZ is Professor of Political Science and Director, Center for International and Strategic Affairs, University of California, Los Angeles. He has served on the staff of the Institute for Defense Analysis and the Rand Corporation. Dr. Kolkowicz has also served in academic positions at George Washington University, University of Virginia, and the City University of New York. A specialist in arms control and international security problems, he has published a number of monographs and has had articles published in such periodicals as <u>World Politics</u>, <u>Comparative Politics</u>, <u>Military Review</u>, <u>Osteuropa</u>, <u>Slavic Review</u>, and <u>American Political Science Review</u>. Dr. Kolkowicz has published <u>The Soviet Military and the Communist Party</u> (1967), <u>The Soviet Union and Arms Control</u> (1970), and has contributed chapters to such books as <u>Interest Groups in Soviet Politics</u> (1970), <u>Communist Systems in Comparative Perspective</u> (1974), and <u>The Twenty-Fifth Congress of the CPSU</u> (1977). Among current research, Dr. Kolkowicz includes "Soviet Strategic Doctrine and Policy Under Brezhnev," "The Grand Illusion: The Kissinger Detente and the Soviet Union," and "Balance of Terror and Balance of Power." He received his Ph. D. from the University of Chicago.

ALAN NED SABROSKY is Associate Professor of Politics at Catholic University and Co-Editor of the <u>International Security Review</u>. He has been affiliated with Middlebury College, the Foreign Policy Research Institute, and the United States Military Academy, and is a Fellow of the Inter-University Seminar on Armed Forces and Society. Dr. Sabrosky's publications include <u>Blue-Collar Soldiers?</u>

Unionization and the U.S. Military (1977), Defense Manpower Policy: A Critical Reappraisal (1978), A Power in the World: Readings in American Foreign Policy (1979), The Eagle's Brood: American Civil-Military Relations in the 1980s (forthcoming), The Structure of International Conflict: Power, Pacts, and War (forthcoming), and over forty articles and book reviews in numerous anthologies and professional journals. He received his Ph.D. from the University of Michigan.

RICHARD SHULTZ is an Assistant Professor of Political Science at Northern Illinois University, where he teaches International Relations and National Security Policy. His major research interests include counterinsurgency, insurgency, and terrorism. Dr. Shultz has published articles in Polity, Western Political Quarterly, Journal of Peace Research, Journal of Politics, Journal of International Affairs, and other journals. He is also co-editor and contributor to Responding to the Terrorist Threat: Security and Crisis Management (forthcoming, September 1980). He received his Ph.D. from Miami University.

WILLIAM P. SNYDER is Visiting Professor of Political Science at the U.S. Army War College. A 1952 graduate of the Military Academy, he was a member of the Social Sciences Department faculty at West Point from 1962 to 1966. Dr. Snyder retired from the Army in 1975 after serving as Director of the Army ROTC Program at Princeton University, and is now a member of the Political Science faculty at Texas A&M University and a Fellow of the Inter-University Seminar on Armed Forces and Society. He is the author of The Politics of British Defense Policy, 1945-62 and of Case Studies in Military Systems Analysis. Dr. Snyder received his Ph.D. from Ohio State University.

LEWIS SORLEY is with the Office of the Inspector General of the Central Intelligence Agency. A former soldier, he is a graduate of West Point and holds Master's degrees in English and public affairs from the University of Pennsylvania and Pennsylvania State, respectively, and a doctorate in foreign policy from Johns Hopkins. Dr. Sorley's military service included duty as a policy analyst in the Office of the Secretary of Defense and in the Office of the Chief of Staff of the Army, faculty assignments at the Army War College and at West Point, and command and staff assignments with tank and armored cavalry units in Europe, Vietnam, and the United States. He is a member of the International Institute for Strategic Studies and a Fellow of the Inter-University Seminar on Armed Forces and

Society. He has lectured and written extensively on institutional ethics and policy formulation.

DAVID TARR received his undergraduate education at the University of Massachusetts and his Master's and Ph.D. at the University of Chicago. After a brief teaching stint at Amherst College and Mount Holyoke, he served as a National Defense Analyst in the Legislative Reference Service of the Library of Congress. In 1963 he joined the staff of the Political Science Department at the University of Wisconsin, serving recently (1972-75) as its Chairman. In 1977 Dr. Tarr was Research Associate at the Program for Science and International Affairs at Harvard University. He is author of American Strategy in the Nuclear Age (1968) and co-editor of Modules in Security Studies (1974). Dr. Tarr has published numerous articles in professional journals.

WILLIAM WHITSON is Chief, Foreign Affairs and National Defense Division, Congressional Research Service, Library of Congress, a position he has held since 1976. Other previous positions include Director of Policy Research at the BDM Corporation; Senior Social Scientist (China) at the Rand Corporation; Policy Planning Staff, Office of the Secretary of Defense; Political Analyst, American Embassy, Taiwan; and Instructor in Economics and International Relations, West Point. The author of numerous articles in Asian Survey and China Quarterly, Dr. Whitson gained extensive writing experience in the Department of Defense (political, economic, and elite analysis). He is the author of The Chinese High Command: A History of Communist Military Politics, 1927-71, published by Praeger in 1973. In addition, he is the editor of several other books, all dealing with China or national security issues. A graduate of the U.S. Military Academy, Dr. Whitson received his M.A. and Ph.D. from Fletcher School of Law and Diplomacy. He studied graduate economics at the Ateneo of Manila, the Littauer School of Public Administration, and Harvard University.